COMMUNICATING IN BUSINESS ANI

"Success is a journey, not a destination." —BEN SWEETLAND

Communicating in Business and the Professions

The Inside Word

Constance Courtney Staley
[UNIVERSITY OF COLORADO AT COLORADO SPRINGS]

Robert Stephens Staley II
[UNIVERSITY OF COLORADO AT COLORADO SPRINGS]

Wadsworth Publishing Company • Belmont, California • A Division of Wadsworth, Inc.

To our parents, siblings, and children — our family,
the greatest organization of them all

Communications Editor: Holly Allen
Editorial Assistant: Katherine Hartlove
Production Editor: Gary Mcdonald
Managing Designer: Andrew H. Ogus
Print Buyer: Karen Hunt
Art Editor: Donna Kalal
Permissions Editor: Jeanne Bosschart
Designer: Seventeenth Street Studios
Copy Editor: Steve Bailey
Photo Researcher: Judy Mason/Seventeenth Street Studios
Technical Illustrator: Precision Graphics
Cover: Seventeenth Street Studios
Compositor: TypeLink
Printer: Arcata Graphics/Fairfield
Cover and part opener photos © Bettmann Archive.

This book is printed on acid-free paper that meets
Environmental Protection Agency standards for recycled paper.

3 4 5 6 7 8 9 10 — 96 95 94

Library of Congress Cataloging-in-Publication Data

Staley, Constance Courtney.
    Communicating in business and the professions : the inside word /
Constance Courtney Staley, Robert Stephens Staley II.
      p.   cm.
    Includes bibliographical references and index.
    ISBN 0-534-15012-8 (alk. paper)
    1. Business communication.   2. Communication in organizations.
I. Staley, Robert Stephens II.   II. Title.
HF5718.S685   1992
650.1'3 — dc20   91-32017

⌧ Contents

PART II: THE WRITTEN WORD

Chapter 2: Writing Effectively in Organizations   40

PART III: THE SPOKEN WORD

Chapter 9: Communicating and Leading in Small Groups

PART V: THE ELECTRONIC WORD

Chapter 12: Communicating Technologically in Organizations   440

⊠ Preface

According to scholars, visionaries, and popular writers, organizational communication may be the key to the United States' future economic success. We are largely an information society rather than an industrial society. Our organizations are streamlining; our values are shifting.

The new watchword in today's organizations is *quality* — doing the job right, making the customer happy, striving for "zero defects" — all to meet the challenges of global competition. At the same time, however, corporations find themselves downsizing or, more euphemistically, "rightsizing" to cope with national and worldwide economic change. Simply put, doing more with less requires a broader base of well-cultivated communication skills, as the following items will demonstrate:

- A study by the University of Michigan's Graduate School of Business asked 1,158 newly promoted chairmen, presidents, and vice-presidents in a variety of businesses, "Which courses best prepare one for business leadership?" Business communication courses were most often named even over courses in finance, accounting, business, and marketing (*Nation's Business*, April 1982).
- In 1979, *Fortune* magazine talked to many successful corporate executives about what business schools should teach. Interviewers asked: "What kind of academic program best prepares students to succeed in their careers?" Pretty much ignoring the question, executive after executive said in frustration, "Teach them to write better." This "simple wish," as *Fortune* called it, was anything but a call for fancy writing: It was a plea to teach

a fundamental skill that few people develop these days—writing with clarity, precision, brevity and the force of logic (*Writing That Works*, Roman and Raphaelson, 1981).

- Staley and Shockley-Zalabak (*Communication Education*, April 1985) surveyed seventy-nine managers in fifty-two organizations and found that developing skill in business writing was one of a dozen curriculum areas given top priority by prospective employers. Another study indicates that "according to surveys of top officials in major American corporations, the greatest need among managers at all levels is to become more effective speakers and writers. . . . The time and money wasted—not to mention the clients lost—by poor writing are staggering in scope" (*Supervisory Management*, April 1977).

- A survey of Fortune 500 vice-presidents, which appeared in the *Journal of Business Communication*, indicated that 98 percent of respondents give oral presentations, 98 percent write memos, 91 percent write informational reports, 100 percent write letters, and 91 percent write analytical reports (Spring 1986).

- An executive interview produced the following realistic, if not pessimistic, commentary on the value of communication skills: "If there is one other thing I wish I had learned at the Harvard Business School, it is how to communicate. I learned a lot of the most useful things I know about the work world and organizations there, but I didn't learn how to communicate; perhaps this is something you have to learn by experience, you have to learn it in life—maybe it can't be taught" (*101 Ways to Protect Your Job*, George deMare, 1984).

We believe communication skills *can* be taught through an engaging and practical approach that focuses on the four fundamental communication skills—speaking, listening, writing, and reading—and their combined application in business and professional settings.

In recent years, we have seen a proliferation of organizational communication skills courses, both as offerings at the college and university level and as in-house on-the-job training programs within corporations. In fact, organizations now vie with colleges and universities for the top dollars spent on training and education. According to the American Society for Training and Development, U.S. employers currently spend $30 billion per year on formal training and another $90 billion to $180 billion on informal training. The Society projects that within the next three years, 93 percent of the nation's largest firms will be providing employees with training in basic skills.

Why We Wrote This Text

Thirty years of combined experience in business, the professions, and academia have taught us a great deal about the practical aspects of communicating in organizations.

Constance Staley is an associate professor of communication at the University of Colorado at Colorado Springs (UCCS) in a department that offers a strong program in organizational communication. While completing this book, she joined the human resources department of a Fortune 100 company, where she designed, administered, and taught management and communication skills programs for two years.

Steve Staley taught speech, composition, organizational communication, business writing, and technical writing until recently at the United States Air Force Academy in Colorado Springs. He now is professor of strategy and policy at the Naval War College, Newport, Rhode Island, where he also teaches organizational communication and effective writing. His experience includes more than a decade with the Air Force Executive Writing Course, teaching government and business executives around the country how to communicate more effectively. The course stresses clarity, organization, and conciseness through linking the written and spoken word.

This text was developed for "Business and Professional Communication," a one-semester course at UCCS required for organizational communication majors and taken as an elective by students from other disciplines within the university. The focus is on performance rather than theory; *skill building* is the instructor's primary goal. Although they certainly offer valuable information, theory courses in organizational communication do not arm students with the real-life, day-to-day, practical communication skills they will be required to use with or without adequate preparation. In the *Harvard Business Review*, Henry Mintzberg reports that we will begin the serious training of managers

> when skill training takes a serious place next to cognitive learning. Cognitive learning is detached and informational, like reading a book or listening to a lecture. No doubt much important cognitive material must be assimilated by the manager-to-be. But cognitive learning no more makes a manager than it does a swimmer. The latter will drown the first time she jumps into the water if her coach never takes her out of the lecture hall, gets her wet, and gives her feedback on her performance (March–April 1990, 163–176).

Because of the natural interrelationship between productive and receptive skills, the course and this text use a holistic approach to business and professional communication as set forth in four parts: *The Written Word*, *The Spoken Word*, *The Unspoken Word*, and *The Electronic Word*.

Using research studies of Fortune 500 executives (Beam, 1981), research done by communication scholars (DiSalvo, 1980), and our own research (Staley and Shockley-Zalabak, 1985), our course begins with a discussion of writing in organizations. We believe that the teaching of writing is central to any comprehensive business and professional communications course. Why? Because, as John Naisbitt and Patricia Aburdene report in *Re-Inventing the Corporation*, a national study showed, "appallingly, [that] only 3 percent of classroom time and 3 percent of homework in high school require writing so much as a paragraph" (130). No wonder then that writing skills in today's corporations are critically lacking. The number of contracts, sales, and proposals lost—because potential clients were confused by indecipherable prose—is staggering. To rectify this alarming situation, many colleges and universities have joined the national "Writing Across the Curriculum" movement. Even so, many teachers assume incorrectly that some other course will handle the writing component in a student's repertoire of communication skills.

Even if students write extensively in high school, they often assume that a business letter or memo should read like a college paper. They don't understand that business writing should be direct and simple, and that "simple writing is *not* simple-minded." But thanks to a national "plain English Revolution," business writing now focuses on the intended reader and *talks* to him or her on paper. And, fortunately, the old "pursuant to" and "heretofore" style is dying out on company letterheads across the country.

The framework of our business and professional communication course is novel, and it has been overwhelmingly successful. To facilitate learning and practice, the course simulates a corporate environment. Class members and the instructor work for a hypothetical corporation; each class member assumes the role of director of training and development, and the instructor assumes the role of vice-president of human resources. Assignments such as memos, letter drafts, and reports are written on company letterhead as dialog between class members and the instructor. Students are encouraged to be creative in developing a corporate context and a professional relationship with a "supervisor" through these writing exercises.

From each assignment, the instructor makes transparencies of student writing (with names removed), and the class engages in group editing. Instructors who wish to use this simulation will find more detailed instructions as well as transparency masters in the Instructor's Manual; these will simplify teaching this portion of the course. Beginning with Chapter 2, optional Decco Exercises are provided at the end of each chapter to continue the simulation throughout the semester. Even without business or consulting experience, instructors will find this approach workable and rewarding.

In our classes, each student also prepares a report for the vice-president on some aspect of organizational communication that needs to be developed in the class corporation. This assignment requires both research and creativity in recommending changes in the corporation. From the written report, students then develop audiovisual presentations (see Part III, The Spoken Word) for classmates playing corporate management roles. Our students have completed projects on everything from *initiating flextime* to *adopting a new performance-appraisal system* to *building an on-site day-care facility* to *designing a company fitness center*. We have found that this framework integrates disparate course material, provides a rationale for assignments, and brings students and the instructor together as teammates. And for both instructor and class, the approach is as enjoyable as it is useful.

....

Unique Features of This Text

Our text is "reader friendly." We *talk* with readers honestly, sensibly, and enthusiastically. And because our approach is oriented toward skills rather than theory, the instruction we provide is pragmatic and real. You'll notice examples and introductions designed to "pull" readers in and arouse interest in the topic.

Chapter 2 presents an organized set of techniques for writing clearly, completely, correctly, concisely, compellingly, credibly, and courteously. We see this chapter as one of the text's significant strengths.

Chapter 3 is a *self-teaching exercise* that develops the skill of business reading. Here readers have the opportunity to read six lively articles from *Business Week Careers*, time their reading, test their comprehension, and learn to recognize the most common organizational formats used in business articles and reports. Because reading for pleasure has considerable competition from movies, MTV, sports, and a host of other attractions, this chapter is an important one.

Readers also will find that this text deals with subtle *gender issues* in an evenhanded way. Bosses in our examples often are female, and pronoun gender alternates from one example to the next. We also include instruction on how to avoid sexist language in organizational writing. And as Chapter 1 demonstrates, more and more women are entering the work force; the likelihood of working for women thus should become a matter of course. The same is true of the increased cultural diversity that we can expect to see in the work force of the 1990s and beyond.

Our text focuses not only on communication knowledge and skills but also on *communication sensitivities* and *communication values*, with discussions on such topics as Machiavellianism, ethics, discipline, listening in stressful situations, and romantic relationships on the job. Through our research on major U.S. corporations, we've learned from corporate leaders that developing communication sensitivities is at least as important as developing concrete knowledge and practical skills.

Our text also provides instructors with a *broad range of options;* they may use the text in its entirety or selectively. Some teachers may wish to focus on their own strengths and deemphasize areas they deem less important. Some may choose to vary the course from one semester to the next by selecting different focus areas. Such "cafeteria" approaches have been successful in interpersonal communication courses, and business and professional communication instructors deserve the same opportunities.

We close the text with Part V, the Electronic Word, and Chapter 12, "Communicating Technologically in Organizations." The dramatic changes in office automation, electronic mail, computer data-base systems, and media graphics warrant treatment of this topic in any comprehensive business and professional communication text. New entrants to the work force must be aware of new and developing communication technologies not only for success but also for survival.

Our ultimate goal has been to make this text realistic, accessible, lively, and enjoyable for readers preparing to launch careers in business and the professions. Simply put, we believe in the *holistic* and *integrated* approach that we use in *Communicating in Business and the Professions*. It works. And while we don't wish to suggest that success will come to everyone automatically, our focus is on confidence and success through planning, preparing, developing strategies, and communicating at our best.

ACKNOWLEDGMENTS

We would like to thank all the people who reviewed this book: Thompson Biggers, University of Miami; Thomas Birk, University of Arizona; Georgia Anne Bomar, East Texas State University; Martin H.

Brodey, Montgomery College; Anne Cunningham, Bergen Community College; Sue DeWine, Ohio University; Lois Einhorn, SUNY at Binghamton; James V. Fee, University of Akron; Thomas E. Harris, University of Alabama, Tuscaloosa; Janet J. Harszlak, SUNY at Buffalo; James Helmer, Syracuse University; Bill Henderson, University of Northern Iowa; William E. Jurma, Texas Christian University; Harold J. Kinzer, Utah State University; Joseph Martinez, El Paso Community College; Elizabeth Mechling, California State University, Fullerton; Don Ochs, University of Iowa; Paul E. Scovell, Salisbury State University; Ronald H. Subeck, Wright College; George E. Tuttle, Illinois State University; Doris Werkman, Portland State University; Frazer D. White, University of Miami; Larry N. Wilder, UNC at Chapel Hill; Tom E. Wirkus, University of Wisconsin, La Crosse. Input from so many experts in the field has greatly enriched this text.

We'd also like to thank the many people who helped our efforts in numerous ways: the staff at Wadsworth, especially Holly Allen, Peggy Randall, Kris Clerkin, Gary Mcdonald, Andrew Ogus, and Jeanne Bosschart, for their persistence and hard work; Connie's colleagues at UCCS for their inspiration and resourcefulness and her "home away from home" colleagues at the University of Rhode Island; Steve's colleagues at the Air Force Academy and the Naval War College for their support, intellectual stimulation, and friendship; our student assistants, Meredith Davis and Summer Kircher, for helping us research the second half of the text; our many students over the years who taught us far more than we taught them.

We'd also like to extend our thanks to the numerous fine people in the business world with whom we've consulted and from whom we've learned so much: J. Robert Connor, Editor-in-Chief of the superb (but unfortunately discontinued) student magazine, *Business Week's Guide to Careers* (later renamed *Business Week Careers*), for helping us locate the authors of the articles included in Chapter 3; colleagues who contributed the testimonials in Chapter 1 on the importance of communication skills; Connie's corporate co-workers on the East Coast; our many teachers, mentors, and friends, including Terry Bangs of Hewitt Associates; professionals in the international community whose communication skills stand as examples to us, especially Esko Illi of Finland, Chia-Cheng Gong of Taiwan, Atilla Alp of Turkey, and Sasha Garin of Russia by way of Germany.

Finally, our thanks to our parents, Sam and Evelyn Courtney and Bob and Liz Staley, for their confidence and encouragement; to our daughters, Shannon and Stephanie, who generously shared their parents with the PC in the study; and to each other for being there when the deadlines were tight, hours long, fuses short, and eyelids heavy.

✉ **Prologue**
In the Beginning Was the Word

Dear Reader:

This textbook is the result of many years of teaching in colleges, consulting and training in organizations around the country, and working in both big business and big government. One of us is an associate professor of communication who, while completing this book, worked as a human resources professional for a Fortune 100 company; the other is a professor of strategy and policy and a U.S. Air Force pilot. Our combined vantage points will expose you to a broad spectrum of organizational experience.

If you're like most of the students we've come across in our thirty combined years of teaching, you're interested in *success*. You'd like to reach the goals you've set for yourself — becoming a surgeon, teacher, attorney, counselor, businessperson, or whatever career you have chosen. And beyond these tangible goals are some very important yet intangible ones: doing stimulating and rewarding work, stretching yourself to continually learn and grow, and feeling good about who you are and what you contribute.

The quotation at the beginning of this book makes an important point: "Success is a journey, not a destination." In other words, success isn't a distant image on the horizon of your future. Success is something you begin today. Success — *your* success, specifically — is what this textbook is all about.

We don't mean to imply that simply reading this book will transform you into a John D. Rockefeller or a Lee Iacocca. What we do mean is that working through this text will help you develop confidence and competence in your ability to use the written word, the spoken word, the unspoken word, and the electronic word. You'll find that we'll *talk* with you—just as we're doing now—honestly, openly, and sensibly. Many of our colleagues and students have described *Communicating in Business and the Professions* as "reader friendly." Our approach is designed to be practical in helping you cultivate the many communication skills you'll need on the job.

Beyond *skills*, however, we hope you'll also develop the *knowledge*, *sensitivities*, and *values* to accompany them. Our research tells us that today's employers look for all four aspects of communication competence. Throughout this text, you'll find information about ethics, advice on romantic relationships on the job, counsel on disciplining employees, recommendations for dealing with stress and burnout, and suggestions on a host of other real-life situations that you're likely to face.

So there you have it. Go ahead and begin the journey with *Communicating in Business and the Professions: The Inside Word* in hand. If you read, listen, think, prepare, and practice with "communicating at your best" as your ultimate goal, you're well on your way. Much of the content of this book is what we wish we had known when we stood where you stand now. This text and this course *can* make a difference!

All the best,

Constance Courtney Staley

Robert Stephens Staley II

COMMUNICATING IN BUSINESS AND THE PROFESSIONS

Part I  **The Word**

Chapter 1 ✏️ Communicating in Organizations

✏️ *Success is simply a matter of luck. Ask any failure.* —Earl Wilson

✏️ **G**raduation day at last—what excitement! You're surrounded by cheers, pats on the back, spouting champagne bottles, your beaming family, and all the friends you've made during your college career. Deep down, you feel a keen sense of accomplishment. But after it's all over and you step out of your cap and gown, reality hits home. Soon, degree in hand, you will enter your chosen profession. As you anticipate what is ahead, you wonder, "Am I ready? Will I achieve my potential? How can I be successful?"

In the epigram above, Earl Wilson implies that only someone who is a failure would attribute your future success to mere luck. Those of us with more savvy know that success is a matter of preparation, determination, and hard work. The determination and hard work are up to you, but this text will provide the preparation.

THE CHANGING NATURE OF ORGANIZATIONS

Success in today's organizations requires many skills. In the past— when your grandparents began their careers, for example—speaking and writing well were the primary communication skills required for success. Yet even though today's jobs still require the ability to speak and write well, developing a broader repertoire of skills is essential not only for success but also for survival.

According to former U.S. Secretary of Labor Elizabeth Dole, "Across the board, jobs are demanding better reading, writing, and reasoning skills. The fastest-growing jobs demand much higher math, language, and reasoning competencies than today's jobs. New production methods require a broadened set of workplace basics, including problem solving, teamwork, and leadership skills. This trend will continue in the years to come."[1] One group of experts sums things up this way: "Technological change, innovation, and heightened competition drive the *upskilling* of work in America."[2]

The bottom line is that times have changed. In his influential book *Re-Inventing the Corporation*, futurist John Naisbitt predicts that most jobs "will require sophisticated high-tech tools and the advanced skills to operate them."[3] In one study, three-fourths of workers interviewed said that technology made their jobs "freer and more interesting, rather than more routine, and that the subsequent challenges motivated them to perform better."[4] Communicating technologically in the organization— a topic we explore in detail in the final chapter—will provide exciting new options *and* requirements for a host of new skills. However, despite the efficiency of allowing machines to do some of our work for us, we still need human contact through meetings, conferences, and telephone calls. Interestingly enough, the more technology we introduce into our organizations, the more we compensate by increasing our interpersonal contact. In some ways, as the old saying goes, "the more things change, the more they stay the same."

Experts tell us that our organizations are changing so rapidly that most of us no longer can expect to remain in the same profession for life. Instead, job retraining will be the norm: "We are moving from the specialist who is soon obsolete to the generalist who can adapt."[5]

What is the impetus for all of this sweeping change? As Naisbitt observed in his 1982 best seller *Megatrends*, we are no longer an industrial society, but are instead an information society: "We now mass-produce information the way we used to mass-produce cars. . . . and this [mass-produced] knowledge is the driving force of our economy."[6] Only 13 percent of today's work force is engaged in manufacturing. More than 60 percent of those in the work force now produce, dispense, and transfer information — including teachers, programmers, stock brokers, accountants, lawyers, and bankers.[7] As Naisbitt proclaims, "The life channel of the information age is communication."[8] In today's information age, he writes, "'Work' is what goes on inside people's heads at desks, on airplanes, in meetings, at lunch. It is how they communicate with clients, what they write in memos, what they say at meetings."[9]

Let's look at the transition in U.S. organizations from another angle. Now nearly two-thirds of the country's gross national product comes from service industries such as transportation, health care, financial services, telecommunications, and fast food; and 75 percent of us are employed in the service sector.[10] Service industries "are people selling their ideas and abilities to other people . . . [without] the luxury of having tangible products to act as buffers between the company and the customer. The company — in essence, the bank teller, the flight attendant, the respiratory therapist — is the product."[11] But just what is that product? We aren't buying a bank teller or a respiratory therapist, we're buying their *information* and their *ability to communicate* that information. Now more than ever before, communication skills pay off.

Not only is the organization changing, but so is the U.S. worker. For example, the Bureau of Labor Statistics estimates that 60 percent of all women will be working by 1995. Even today, as many women as men in their twenties and thirties work, and women with children under six years of age now make up the fastest-growing segment of the work force.[12] Women currently hold the majority of professional — versus clerical, technical, and laborer — jobs in the United States.[13]

Cultural diversity also will be increasingly important in the work force of the future.[14] By the year 2000, nonwhites will make up 29 percent of all newcomers to the work force — twice their current representation — and the United States will have experienced the largest influx of immigrants into the work force since World War I.

••••••••••••••••••••
Ann Gorton Hair, G.R.I., C.R.S., Realtor, McGinnis and DeLay Realtors

"The ability to communicate is vital to realtors. Using conversational and listening skills, we must help clients and customers clarify their thinking, evaluate differences, explore possibilities, and make decisions. We must state facts accurately and write contracts clearly so that there are no misinterpretations. Realtors communicate daily with lenders, appraisers, attorneys, and closers, each speaking a slightly different language. Without effective communication, realtors cannot properly serve their clientele."
••••••••••••••••••••

With all of this change under way, you must begin your first position with your communication skills already well developed. Waiting for on-the-job training, expecting your communication skills to improve naturally as you "learn the ropes," or assuming other college or university courses will give you enough basics to help you get by—these are not the best strategies. Instead, we'd like to help you strengthen your communication skills now.

THE IMPORTANCE OF COMMUNICATION SKILLS IN ORGANIZATIONS

If communication truly plays such a major role in the organization, then what do people in organizations have to say about which communication skills are *most important*, *most used*, and *most in need of enhancement*? Many studies have sought to answer these questions, and the results are consistent and persuasive. Read on—the research speaks for itself.

First, if you are like many college graduates, a few years in the work force will convince you that your communication skills may be your greatest asset. In one recent study, regardless of their career fields, graduates proclaimed the importance of effective communication, many valuing communication skills over the knowledge gained in pursuit of their college majors.[15] When 1,158 newly promoted chairmen, presidents, and vice-presidents from a variety of businesses were asked to name the courses that best prepare students for business leadership, they more frequently named courses in communication than courses in finance, accounting, business planning, and marketing.[16]

Second, communication, particularly the *quality* of communication between you and your immediate supervisor, will be related directly to your job performance and your job satisfaction.[17] Or consider this piece of negative motivation: Of all employees fired, 85 percent do not lose their jobs because they lack technical competence; they are fired because they lack human relations or interpersonal communication skills.[18] Communication skills thus have been identified as *the* most important prerequisite for management success today.[19]

Which Communication Skills Are Most Important?

Let's address a more specific question: *Which* skills are most important? A recent study conducted at the University of Colorado surveyed seventy-nine managers in fifty-two organizations to find out what types of communication knowledge, sensitivities, *skills*, and values were most important in their organizations. These managers identified *business writing, listening, interviewing*, and *telephone communication* as most important.[20] In a similar study, college graduates ranked the communication skills that were most important to their job success as *listening, persuading, advising, instructing*, and *small-group problem solving*.[21] Among Fortune 500 vice-presidents who were surveyed, 85 percent named interpersonal communication skills as mandatory, 83 percent cited written communication skills, and 74 percent cited oral communication skills as mandatory; and all others rated these three skills as important.[22]

A similar survey of 428 personnel administrators found that *oral* and *written communication skills* were the most important factors in getting a job, while *interpersonal, oral,* and *written skills* ranked highest for successful job performance. Of the college courses identified as most important for entry-level management success, *written communication, interpersonal communication*, and *public speaking* ranked first, second, and fourth, respectively.[23]

To some extent, the need for particular skills depends on the type of career you enter and the type of organization you join. However, when DiSalvo and Larsen surveyed professionals in finance, management, engineering, and law to determine their communication activities and problems, they found a core of five important communication skills: *building relationships, listening, giving feedback, exchanging routine information*, and *soliciting feedback*.[24] When asked which communication activities were important for job success, these professionals also cited *advising* and *persuading*. Regardless of the demands of particular career fields, employees value the same broad repertoire of communication skills.

Which Communication Skills Are Most Used?

Note these findings: Of Fortune 500 vice-presidents who were asked to describe their own communication, 100 percent said they write letters, 98 percent give oral presentations, 98 percent write memos, 91 percent write informational reports (information only), and 91 percent write analytical reports (information, recommendations, and conclusions).[25] It stands to reason that the skills identified as most important are also the skills most often used. On the other hand, although some skills may be used infrequently, they are highly visible *when* used. You may address the board of directors only once a year, but it may be your single most important communication event from one year to the next. Frequency, as it turns out, is not the only measure of importance.

Which Communication Skills Most Need to Be Enhanced?

When people in organizations are asked, "Which skills most need to be enhanced?" they often voice strong opinions. Several years ago, *Fortune* magazine surveyed many successful corporate executives to determine what subjects business schools should teach. The answer hits home: "Teach them to write better," said executive after executive.[26] Another report indicates that "according to surveys of top officials in major American corporations, the greatest need among managers at all levels is to become more effective speakers and writers. . . . The time and money wasted — not to mention the clients lost — by poor writing are staggering in scope."[27] Coopers & Lybrand, a prestigious accounting firm, is in such desperate need of good proposal writers that it has considered hiring English majors and providing them with on-the-job training in accounting.[28]

Developing strong interpersonal skills also has been identified as a critical area needing improvement.[29] At least one study targeted listening and motivating people as skills needing enhancement.[30] Some experts, on the other hand, underscore the importance of a broad range of skills. In a recent survey, personnel directors indicated that they prefer to hire graduates who have strong oral and written communication skills *and* a foundation of knowledge about business in our society. Based on this finding, the researchers urge that communication and business departments teach the skills most essential to career success.[31] In fact, some experts in the field are calling for development of "total communication skills" — that is, writing, speaking, listening, and reading.[32]

WHAT CAN EFFECTIVE COMMUNICATION SKILLS DO FOR YOU?

Now that we have identified what people in organizations think about the importance of organizational communication skills, let's personalize the discussion. What can effective communication skills do for *you?* They can enhance your "hirability," your work effectiveness, your reputation, and your promotability.

Enhance Your "Hirability"

What do managers look for in hiring new employees? According to a recent survey conducted by the Association for Management Success, *experience* is the best qualification you can bring to a job. But the qualifications ranked second and third by managers are *communication skills* and *enthusiasm/motivation*.[33] (Large corporations of 10,000 or more employees, by the way, seem to value enthusiasm and motivation over experience.) Because a long history of work experience isn't likely to be your strong suit as a new college graduate, *communicating effectively* and *communicating enthusiastically* become key assets. When asked to name the most common deficiency of job applicants, managers identified a lack of communication skills, or *applicants' inability to express themselves clearly*. Therefore, if your communication abilities stand out, then so will you as an applicant. In another recent study in which three hundred company presidents were asked what skills they expect college graduates to have, communication — both written and oral — was at the top of the list; interpersonal communication skills ranked second.[34]

Enhance Your Work Effectiveness

If you can write a report without struggling, you will outshine your colleague who wastes valuable time and energy wrestling with the same task. If you double your reading speed without losing comprehension — 500 words per minute instead of the usual 250 — then you may save yourself and your organization hundreds of hours per year. If your listening efficiency is better than the average of 25 percent, then you may save your company from costly errors and yourself from embarrassing mistakes, and you will most likely become a better decision maker and a valued supervisor.

Enhance Your Reputation

If you are known for your crisp presentations, your clear memos, or your sympathetic ear, your reputation as a skilled communicator will be enhanced. In fact, if you work for a large corporation, for example, many people may "know" you only through your letters and memos. One of us once wrote a memo to a university administrator who later telephoned to praise its clarity and completeness. Because the memo outlined key points clearly, the administrator then asked for permission to reproduce the memo and use it as an agenda for top administrators on campus who were meeting the next day to discuss related issues. For a young faculty member new to the university, the memo was a "proxy" introduction to others in powerful positions.

Enhance Your Promotability

Obviously, if your communication skills help you to get hired, work more effectively, and establish a reputation for competence within the organization, then they also will help you to ascend the organizational ladder. In one study, *Harvard Business Review*'s subscribers rated communication skills as the most important characteristic of promotable executives — more important than ambition, education, or a capacity for hard work.[35] In another survey, 97.7 percent of Fortune 500 vice-presidents believed that effective communication skills helped them to reach top executive positions; 93.5 percent believed that such skills would have a major effect on the upward mobility of executives in the future.[36] Lee Iacocca puts it this way: "You can have brilliant ideas, but if you can't get them across, your brains won't get you anywhere."

DEFINING TERMS

Organization

Up to this point, we've been using key terms such as *organization* and *communication* somewhat loosely. You know generally what these terms mean, but now we offer more specific definitions.

Dozens of *organizations* influence your life from day to day: your college or university, your doctor's office, your favorite restaurant, the stores where you buy your clothes, the businesses you frequent, the government agencies you visit, telephone, or write. But as we begin our discussion, we will define the term *organization* more formally. What goes on behind the scenes is really the essence of an organization.

Generally speaking, an organization is formed "any time two or more people are required to share time or space, goods or services."[37] Under this broad definition, General Motors obviously is an organization; but then so is the family in which you grew up.

Let's tighten our definition so that it describes the kind of business or professional organization you'll join. We can define that kind of organization as a "system of individuals who work together to achieve, through

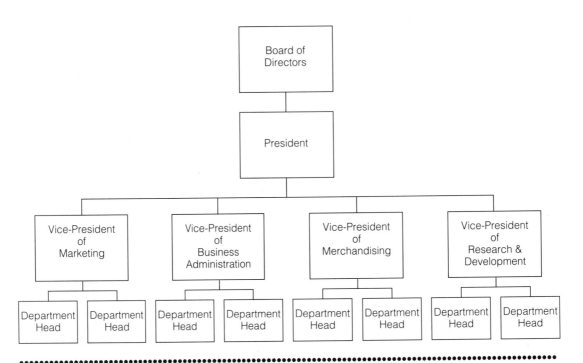

Figure 1.1 *Traditional Organizational Chart*

a hierarchy of ranks and divisions of labor, common goals."[38] This definition helps us focus on three critical characteristics: *goals, hierarchy,* and *division of labor.* Let's examine these three characteristics more closely, contrasting the traditional meaning of each term with its meaning in today's best-run organizations.[39]

Goals. What kinds of goals do organizations have? If the organization is McDonald's, its goal is to sell as many hamburgers as possible. If the organization is American Airlines, its goal is to fly as many passengers as possible. Organizational goals usually relate to the production of quality goods and services at competitive prices. Whatever the goal, ideally everyone in the organization knows what it is and will work to achieve it. According to *In Search of Excellence*, Peters and Waterman's analysis of America's top companies, employees in these organizations usually share the company's values and see themselves as part of an extended family. It's probably safe to say that those factors have traditionally characterized well-run organizations and continue to do so.

Hierarchy. Most organizations operate through a vertical chain of command with, for example, a board of directors at the top, a president or chief executive officer on the next rung down, vice-presidents who oversee division heads below them, and so forth (Figure 1.1). Tradi-

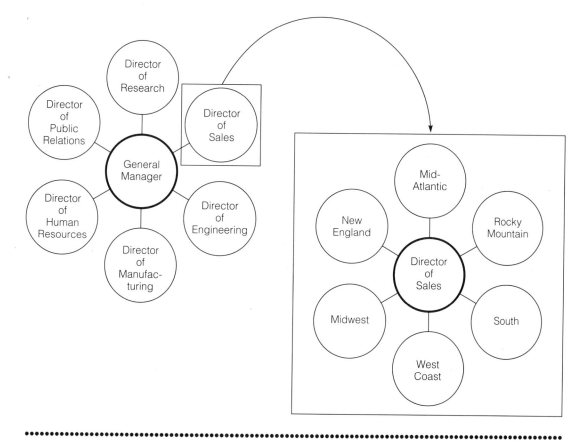

Figure 1.2 *Nontraditional Organizational Chart*

tionally, lines of authority and channels of communication have been based on this clearly defined vertical structure; in many organizations, they still are.

However, hierarchical organization often is deemphasized today among more progressive companies. Instead, these companies are characterized by fluidity and informality. Structure is more an "on-paper" concept than a day-to-day reality. Figure 1.2 shows an organizational chart that attempts to minimize hierarchical rigidity. In the companies that Peters and Waterman describe, it is not uncommon to see executives' desks in cubicles next to those of lower-level employees. Supervisors manage by "walking around," and decision making is a more horizontal, cooperative effort in which everyone has a voice. The authors summarize:

> The major complaint about organizations is that they have become more complex than is necessary. Refreshingly, the excellent companies are responding by saying: If you've got a major prob-

lem, bring the right people together and expect them to solve it. The "right people" very often means senior people who "don't have the time." But they do, somehow, have the time at Digital, TI, HP, 3M, IBM, Dana, Fluor, Emerson, Bechtel, McDonald's, Citibank, Boeing, Delta, et al. They have the time in those institutions because those companies aren't transfixed with organization charts or job descriptions. . . . Learn from your tries. That's enough.[40]

Excellent companies, according to Peters and Waterman, have a bias for action, a preference for doing something — *anything* — rather than bogging down in rigid lines of authority, "correct procedures," and "analysis paralysis," as it has been called.[41] (If you've ever shuffled endlessly from office to office trying to enroll for courses or pay a fine, you know what the authors are talking about.) In our best-run companies, the emphasis is on productivity through people; everyone's best effort is essential, and when the company succeeds, so do the individuals who make up the company.

Division of Labor. Obviously, the best way to get work done is for individuals or groups to divide the workload. Through cooperative effort, more can be accomplished — the assembly-line principle generalized throughout the organization. In excellent companies, the small group often functions as the organization's primary building block instead of divisions or departments. Small groups serve as "chunking devices" or means of dividing up work; teams, task forces, project centers, quality circles (problem-solving groups), and ad hoc committees are formed and disbanded from project to project. In today's most progressive companies, work is divided by combining the right people to do the job no matter where they work in the organization or at what level. The resulting atmosphere is one of dynamism, creativity, and action.[42]

Communication

Just exactly how does all this take place? What makes the organization work? The answer obviously is *communication*, which functions as both the lubricant to allow the free flow of ideas and the cement to solidify working relationships.

Communication in organizations takes place in a variety of contexts: while reading, writing, speaking, or listening during presentations, meetings, interviews, one-on-one conversations, and so forth. The process is a complex one; typically, the larger the organization, the more potentially complex the communication. From a purely mathematical point of view, if 50 people work for a small company, then there are 1,225 possible combinations for two-person communication. But if 5,000 people work for a large corporation, then 12,497,500 such possibilities exist![43] And if we expanded our projections to include small groups, sections, and departments, then the figure would be mind-boggling.

How does the communication process work in organizations? Consider the following definition, paying particular attention to the words in bold:

> Communication is a **dynamic transaction**
> of **simultaneously exchanged**
> **verbal** and **nonverbal messages**
> resulting in shared meaning between two or more people.
> Messages occur through **formal** or **informal channels**
> in **upward, downward,** or **horizontal directions.**
> Communication helps form the basis for an
> organization's **climate** and contributes to an
> organization's **culture.**

Now let's dissect our definition and examine its components.

Dynamic Transaction. Communication is a *dynamic transaction.* Even though our communication appears to stop and start—I talk to you and you talk back—communication is more like watching a movie than looking at a series of snapshots. Actually, we simultaneously communicate with each other nonverbally through our eye contact, posture, gestures, and facial expressions. We can't really talk about a message *sender* and a message *receiver* because messages flow in both directions at once. Even as a listener, you are sending the speaker continuous *feedback* about how you're interpreting the message. And think of all the various factors that influence you as you communicate: room decor, time of day, your partner's reaction, and your physical and emotional states—not to mention the collection of previous communication experiences you bring with you. If you stop in the hallway to "touch base" with a co-worker, your communication may be affected initially by the construction team's blasting machinery, by your hunger pangs, by his fleeting scowl, and by the grueling meeting you just left, all of which are examples of either internal or external *noise.* But during the conversation, your frame of mind, and hence your communication, may change when the construction team stops for a break, when you remember the excellent performance review your boss gave you this morning, when you think back over the deal you closed over lunch, or when you hear the news that your best friend has been promoted. In short, communication changes as the context in which it occurs changes, and participating in a communication event changes both you and your partner.

Verbal and Nonverbal Messages. Communication includes *verbal* and *nonverbal* messages. If your boss calls you into her office and closes the door behind you, not only will you listen intently to the first words she utters, but you also will scan her face, inch by inch, for clues about what is to come. Although we may not realize it, we often extract more meaning from nonverbal cues than we do from words themselves. The changing cues sent through our eyes, voices, facial expressions, touches, gestures, and movements are all part of the messages we send. The words you speak constitute the *content* of the message, but your nonverbal messages communicate your feelings about your *relationship* with your conversational partner. Each time you communicate, your messages contain these two dimensions—content and relationship—or "what you say" and "how you say it." As you write and speak in the organization, you'll want to consider content and relationship. Throughout our discussions, we'll deal with issues sensitive to both dimensions.

Formal Versus Informal Channels. Messages are exchanged through both established *formal* means of contact and *informal* networks of interaction. *Formal* communication channels in organizations include memoranda, employee handbooks, policy and procedure manuals, bulletin boards, on-the-job training, interviews, annual reports, committee meetings, quality circles, suggestion programs, and now in some companies, video magazines. Formal channels usually are management's vehicles for distributing messages throughout the organization. Policies and procedures help to ensure that everyone is treated the same way, and annual reports keep employees informed about the current business picture. However, formal channels are not always highly effective means of communication.

Informal channels, on the other hand, exist because people in organizations need them. The informal network, or "grapevine," typically is a faster and often more reliable conduit of information than are formal channels (see Figure 1.3). Rather than search through the employee handbook to find out the new company policy on requesting preferred vacation dates, most of us probably would ask a colleague for the information during a coffee break. When you need information, you probably will turn to someone in an adjacent office, someone whose common interests have developed into a friendship, or someone who shares your attitudes toward the organization.

•••••••••••••••••••
Michael Beatty, General Counsel and Executive Vice-President, Coastal Corporation

" 'Lawyering' does not exist except as a form of communication. Arguments to judges and juries, advice to clients, and the codification of laws themselves embody the merger of inchoate thought with our ability to communicate. Just as expression without substance is thoughtless babble, so also thought without effective expression is lost forever."
•••••••••••••••••••

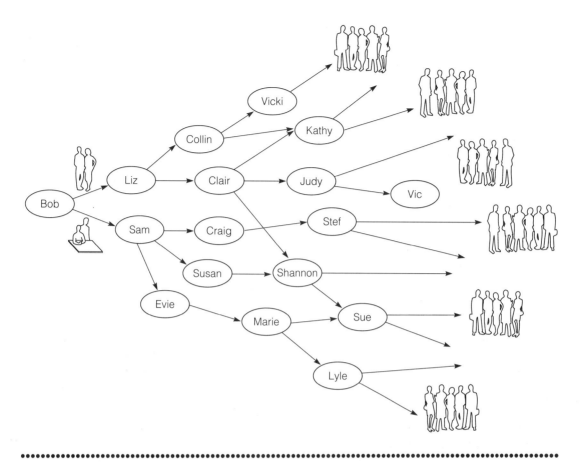

Figure 1.3 *The Organizational Grapevine*

Here's an example of the informal channel in operation. Not long ago, one of us was selected for an Air Force promotion. The list of promotees for the entire Air Force was to be made public on Thursday at 8 A.M. Three days before, on Monday, the congratulatory phone calls and pats on the back began. As is typical with promotion lists, word had leaked out and provided the necessary current to spark not only the local informal network but also the nationwide network of Air Force officers.

The informal network was faster and more effective than the formal publication, which came through established channels. According to some experts, approximately 90 percent of what transpires in organizations has little to do with formal channels, and studies have demonstrated that the grapevine is 80–90 percent accurate.[44] As we've suggested, informal communication is the lifeblood of today's best organizations, where it is continuous, intense, and ubiquitous. Regardless of the type of career you select, tapping into your organization's informal network and cultivating a wide array of informal contacts will be key to your organizational success. We've seen promising careers miss their mark because of inabilities to work the informal network.

Direction: Downward, Upward, and Horizontal. Communication occurs in a variety of directions: *downward* from superiors to subordinates; *upward* from subordinates to superiors; and *horizontally* between peers. *Downward* messages — from your boss or those in leadership positions within the company — include instructions, policies, rationales, and other types of information typically sent through formal channels. And even though top-down messages are necessary, employers at times are slightly "out of touch" with what is happening in the lower ranks, which leads them to send outdated or irrelevant messages. Employees also sometimes complain that they are deluged with top-down messages — long, complex memos that continue to pile up day after day. They have difficulty in keeping up with continuous streams of downward communication. In these cases, more is not better.

Downward communication can be particularly problematic when *serial* message transmission is involved: Corporate Officer A communicating with Division Chief B communicating with Manager C communicating with Supervisor D communicating with Employee E and so on down the ranks. From playing the game of "gossip" or "telephone" as a child, you know that addition, subtraction, and distortion often keep the original message from arriving intact at its final destination. The same principle applies in organizations. Serial messages reach different "rungs" of the corporate ladder at different times. A message from corporate officers about tightened budgets may originate on Monday, reach senior managers on Tuesday, middle managers on Wednesday, first-line supervisors on Thursday, and the rank and file on Friday. In the meantime, the grapevine may be overloaded with speculation about what really is going on and productivity may suffer. One obvious solution is to send a written message *simultaneously* to everyone. However, this strategy may not always be appropriate. In our example, managers may need time to make specific decisions about what programs to cut before the budget news becomes general knowledge. Thus, serial versus simultaneous message transmission is an important consideration for organizational communicators.

Upward communication, on the other hand, takes place when you initiate communication with your superiors to communicate your progress on a project, the problems you are encountering with co-workers, or your ideas on how to improve a situation. In sending upward-bound messages, you accomplish two important tasks. First, you provide your superiors with the feedback they need; second, you play a role in decision making and change. Although upward communication is important

H. Dalton Conner, D.D.S., M.S.D., Periodontist

"Communication is the common denominator for achieving success in the profession of dentistry. Dentistry has so much to offer patients in terms of better health, comfort, speech and appearance, but dentists must overcome the public's fear of pain and worry over expense. The ability of doctors and their staff members to reduce anxiety and convey helpful information is of paramount importance for successful practice in today's professional market."

and often productive, it sometimes takes courage, particularly if your message is a negative one. You may not want to admit that your project is three weeks behind schedule or that you and a colleague aren't getting along. In so doing, you risk having your negative message misinterpreted as a lack of ability or having it generalized to your performance in other areas. For this reason, most of us are more likely to send positive messages upward, perhaps presenting superiors with a somewhat inaccurate picture.[45]

Horizontal communication occurs when you ask a colleague to attend a meeting on next month's sales projections, when you report to another division head that an influx of orders is expected from a planned promotional campaign, when you compliment an office mate on a superb presentation, or when you call your least favorite department mate to propose a problem-solving session. Horizontal communication, which is typically the most frequent type in which you'll engage, takes place with people whose power and status are equivalent to yours. By communicating horizontally, you find the support, cooperation, information, and coordination you need in the day-to-day performance of your job.

Organizational Climate. Communication forms the basis for an organization's *climate*. Whether horizontal, upward, downward, formal, or informal, all of the communication that takes place in an organization will contribute to its climate or prevailing "mood." You can think of climate as a barometer that measures the quality of all the relationships that exist among an organization's members. Like geographical or meteorological climates, organizational climates can be "cool" or "warm," "comfortable" or "uncomfortable." They can be characterized by "shifting winds" or "turbulent times." Of course, the surroundings in which employees work and the salaries they receive also play a role in determining overall climate. But the quality of communication and people's reactions to that communication do more than anything else to create organizational climate — and determine whether it is positive or negative.

If members of an organization send an abundance of impersonal, tangential, irrelevant, ambiguous, or incongruous messages that devalue or disconfirm other members, for example, then the climate created will make it difficult to retain quality employees. A boss who says, "Come to me anytime with a problem" but then acts annoyed when employees do so is likely to damage her relationship with her staff and worsen the organization's overall climate. If formal, downward messages make employees feel like little more than social security numbers or personnel files, then the organization's climate probably is negative.

••••••••••••••••••••
**Joanne Hendrick,
O.D., Optometrist**

"As in any health profession, communication with patients is essential. Without adequate skills we would be unable to deal with our patients' basic questions as well as their fears. In order to get patients to comply with recommended therapy, doctors must help people understand why the therapy is important and what the consequences are of not following their doctor's advice. Furthermore, with the very real prevalence of lawsuits ever on the rise, communicating effectively with our patients becomes our best protection."
••••••••••••••••••••

Positive climates, on the other hand, result from communication patterns in which people are honest, tactful, supportive, open-minded, and oriented toward problem solving rather than blaming or controlling one another.[46] Climate has a great deal to do with whether employees believe they are valued by the organization. Take the case of the manager who says, "We have a problem here, Fred. What productive steps can we take to solve it?" Contrast that approach with this one: "Fred, you blew it with a capital B! Now figure out how to save your hind side!" Over time, the first manager will contribute significantly to a positive climate in his organization. Climate is produced — and sustained — by the quality of the organization's communication.

Organizational Culture. Communication contributes to an organization's *culture*. If climate is defined as the prevailing mood of an organization, then culture can be defined as an organization's personality. Organizations have personalities just as do people. Some are slow and considered, some are sophisticated and serious, some are frenetic and crazy. Even as a consumer, you can sometimes "see" and "feel" an organization's personality. One store or restaurant, for example, has a very different feel from another. In some establishments you may feel relaxed and comfortable; in others, you may rush to escape as soon as possible. If you entered a sophisticated gourmet restaurant in a faded T-shirt and torn sneakers, stood up and screamed across the room at the top of your lungs to get your waiter's attention, and then ordered a hot dog and soft drink, you'd be guilty of (among other things) ignoring the restaurant's "personality."

More specifically, culture is defined as an insider's view of the "system of shared *values* (what is important) and *beliefs* (how things work) that interacts with a company's people, organizational structures, and control systems to produce behavioral *norms* (the way we do things around here)."[47] In other words, organizational culture revolves around *values*, *beliefs*, and *norms*.

Values relate to what the organization and its employees consider to be important. *In Search of Excellence* authors Peters and Waterman have identified the following shared values of the best U.S. corporations.[48]

1. *Bias for action*: doing something — anything — rather than killing ideas through endless analysis.
2. *Staying close to the customer*: knowing the customer's preferences and catering to them.
3. *Autonomy and entrepreneurship*: breaking the company into smaller units and encouraging each to think independently and competitively.

••••••••••••••••••••

Susan Watkins, Director of Public Relations, City of Colorado Springs

"In a large organization, it's a professional public relations person's job to promote the benefits of internal and external communication. Those who lack their own personal communication skills will obviously face an uphill and probably losing battle."

••••••••••••••••••••

••••••••••••••••••••
Arthur G. Elser, Ph.D., Technical Writer and Consultant, Meadowlark Associates

"Because I'm a technical communicator, it would seem obvious that communication skills are very important to my success. How else can I write and illustrate technical books that work? But that's only the surface. Every day I must convince engineers that I can communicate with them on very technical subjects. I must convince executives and managers to spend money on better paper and bindings for their documentation so they will communicate 'quality' to customers. To sell my ideas, I must have good communication skills. A very bright friend of mine, a Ph.D. electrical engineer, is fond of saying 'intellectual capital is today replacing financial capital as the most important currency of exchange.' And, of course, he is right. We can invest our intellectual capital only through successful communication. Our ideas become capital only when we communicate them to others who can add the physical resources to make them concrete. This is why we must learn to communicate effectively."
••••••••••••••••••••

4. *Productivity through people*: creating an awareness that the best efforts of all employees are essential and that the company's success will mean success for everyone.

5. *Hands-on, value-driven*: requiring that executives stay in touch with the organization's essential business and play a role in encouraging a strong corporate culture.

6. *Stick to the knitting*: staying with those businesses that the company knows best.

7. *Simple form, lean staff*: having few administrative layers with few people at the top.

8. *Simultaneous loose–tight properties*: promoting dedication to the company's central values but also allowing individuals some degree of autonomy.[49]

Although related to values, *beliefs* also pertain to such factors as authority and power, the use of formal groups, and the organization's standard operating procedures — the ways in which it gets things done. The *norms* that result are established rules of conduct or patterns of behavior. In many organizations, a broken norm is readily recognized and brought to the perpetrator's immediate attention. Wearing the wrong company "uniform," sending an unsuitable message as a newcomer, or violating a long-standing tradition probably will be pointed out by company "old timers": "These are the sorts of things we just don't do around here." When you join your first organization, you'll learn the corporate culture just as you learn the demands and requirements of your particular job.

In *Organizational Culture and Leadership*, Edgar Schein, a well-known expert in organizational behavior, provides two examples of the importance of organizational culture.[50] Several years ago, Schein was hired as a consultant for two quite different organizations — Company A ("Action Company") and Company B ("Multi Company"); both are pseudonyms. He was asked to help improve group communication within Action Company and to stimulate innovation within Multi Company.

The difference between the two corporate cultures was startling. Action Company was a young, dynamic, rapidly-paced organization that valued creativity, spontaneity, individual responsibility, and group consensus. The physical setting emphasized an open floor plan, casual dress, and a noticeable lack of status symbols for upper-level executives. Meetings were frequent and lively debates in which Schein often had to fight for "air time." The organization was characterized by a strong and loyal "family" spirit. Employees were encouraged to think for themselves, to go against previous decisions if necessary, and to disagree with the boss if the outcome would improve the organization. At Action Company, truth was seen to emerge from conflict.

•••••••••••••••••••
Mark H. Miller, D.Min., Pastor, St. Peter's United Church of Christ, Elmhurst, Illinois

"A friend once suggested every minister would do well to remember that God gave us two ears and one mouth. In ministry the gift of listening cannot be over-rated. No matter the conversation, a message is being conveyed, for in a dialogue there is the business of what is said and the power of what is meant. Communication in ministry requires a movement from statement to meaning, from objective datum to subjective feelings. When that happens, real communication, and at times healing, takes place."
•••••••••••••••••••

Multi Company, on the other hand, provided a sharp contrast. More than one hundred years old and headquartered in Europe with primarily European managers, the company was housed in a large building with formal offices, quiet hallways, and many status symbols for the upper echelons. Employees used formal titles ("Doctor") to address one another, and seniority and status were valued by all organization members. Conflict was avoided, careful planning was essential, and the pace was slow and considered. At Multi Company, truth was perceived to emerge from the contributions of individual researchers.

In each case, understanding the organization's culture was Schein's key to success as a consultant. At Action Company, Schein's early suggestions for improving group communication were ignored. Among other things, he suggested that group members interrupt each other less and become less confrontational — admonitions that were in direct conflict with cultural values. When he began to understand the problem and focus his suggestions on group *decision making* rather than on group *communication*, employees paid attention. His suggestions on time management, agenda setting, summarizing, and other task-related group behaviors were put into practice.

At Multi Company, on the other hand, where knowledge was held in high esteem, Schein was seen as an academic expert and his ideas were accepted readily. However, Multi's rigid structure and reverence for seniority meant that newcomers' suggestions were not welcome. New employees, who brought objective viewpoints and fresh ideas, were seen as too inexperienced to make suggestions about better ways of doing things. The culture itself was an obstacle to Schein's assigned task of increasing innovation.

Understanding a particular culture is crucial to "working" the organization either as an outside expert, as did Schein, or as an inside player. Organizational values, beliefs, and norms form a powerful basis for individual and group behavior. If you find resistance to the methods or ideas you propose as a new employee, then you may be challenging deep and sometimes immovable cultural truths.

According to Deal and Kennedy, authors of *Corporate Cultures*, organizations take on one of four basic personality types. Within each cultural archetype, one finds varying business environments, values, rituals, and communication patterns.[51]

1. In "tough-guy, macho" cultures, entrepreneurship and risk-taking are valued, and feedback is immediate on whether actions are right or wrong. Police departments, construction companies, cosmetics companies, venture-capital enterprises,

and the entertainment industry are typical examples. Capital outlays are large, and companies know within a short time whether such investments will pay off. Universal Studios knows whether its latest motion-picture gamble will be a success almost immediately after initial box-office tallies.

2. In "work hard/play hard" cultures, activity is frenetic but the stakes are relatively low. Real-estate companies, door-to-door sales, and retail stores are examples of this type of organizational culture. No single sale will make or break a salesperson, but the constant routine of "one more phone call" must go on. Values within this organizational culture center on customers and their needs. Tupperware is a good example of a work hard/ play hard organizational culture. Managers spend a full month each year attending rallies and award ceremonies to reward their salespeople.[52]

3. In "bet-your-company" cultures, high-stakes investments are routine, but feedback is slow in coming. Capital-goods companies, mining and smelting companies, the oil industry, and the military (whose planners spend millions of defense dollars preparing for wars they hope they never fight) are examples. The future — and investments in it — are primary organizational values.

4. In "process" cultures, considerable emphasis is placed on the "how" rather than the "what" of work. The risk factor is low, and feedback is almost nonexistent. For these reasons, workers begin to concentrate on process, sometimes "inventing" paperwork and developing perfectionist values. Banks, insurance companies, government agencies, and utility companies are examples of process cultures.

Often one of the best ways to unlock the secrets of an organization's culture is to look at its history. For example, consider Foxboro, a high-technology company that desperately wanted to solve a particular design problem in order to stay abreast of the competition in its early days. Late one evening, a scientist rushed into the president's office with a simple but effective solution. Awestruck and delighted, the president rummaged through his desk for a token of his appreciation. All he could find was a banana, which he handed the successful scientist with great drama. To this day, the company's "gold banana" pin is the highest recognition a company scientist can receive.[53]

Communication in the organization shapes both its culture (or personality) and its climate (or prevailing mood). And even though organizational culture and climate are complex phenomena involving communication, values, beliefs, and norms, you'll be most productive and most satisfied with your work if you do two things.

First, try to find a match between your personal style and the culture of the organization you join. No doubt some of you would be more comfortable jumping right into the "chaos" at Action Company, while others would prefer the formal structure of Multi. A "cultural mismatch" is one of the main reasons why people leave organizations. If you value creativity and spontaneity but find yourself working in a company that takes six weeks to route a purchase order and six months to reach a decision on a new proposal, then your frustration and stress levels eventually may skyrocket. On the other hand, if you want time to do conclusive research, but your boss keeps pushing you toward immediate action, then you may feel the same effects. Because you will spend almost as much time with the organization as with your spouse, consider your decision carefully!

Second, do your best, through your own communication choices, to create a positive organizational climate. Whatever your role in the organization, you will be a factor in its overall climate.

A BRIEF HISTORY OF ORGANIZATION THEORY

Although the major focus of *Communicating in Business and the Professions* is on *skills* rather than on *theory*, we close this chapter with a brief overview of major theories as they relate to organizations.[54] (See Table 1.1.) Today's thoughts about organizational communication, management, structure, satisfaction — many of the topics we'll discuss throughout this text — have an instructive history, and we'd like to provide a historical backdrop for our treatment of these topics later on.

....

The Classical School

We begin in the late nineteenth and early twentieth centuries with what we now call the *Classical School* of organization theory. During that time, owners and managers ran their own businesses, usually through intimidation and fear, and workers were plentiful, unsophisticated, and motivated by the most basic human needs — providing minimal food and shelter for their families, for example.

Three prominent theorists are associated with the Classical School: Frederick Taylor, Henri Fayol, and Max Weber.[55] Now known as a *scientific theorist*, Taylor was intent on increasing productivity by improving workers' techniques and methods. He is best known for his time and motion studies, which provided minute-by-minute analyses of individual jobs and broke them down into their basic parts to improve productivity. He advocated designing jobs scientifically to find the most efficient ways of doing things, selecting workers by their ability to complete specific tasks, and training and rewarding employees for productivity with monetary incentives. Unfortunately, although Taylor's motives were admirable, his techniques often were used by inhumane managers intent on squeezing every drop of productivity from employees. The needs of the organization were deemed more important than the needs of the individual, and workers were treated as if they were little more than machines.

Henri Fayol of France and Max Weber of Germany, both contemporaries of Taylor and also considered members of the Classical School, often are labeled *bureaucratic theorists*. They focused on management efficiency, rather than worker efficiency, through structure, division of labor, and chain of command — aspects of organizations we discussed earlier in this chapter. With their emphasis on rules, rationality, and predictability, bureaucratic organizations were seen as the ideal. To the bureaucratic theorists, communication was used by managers to command and control through vertical channels. Organizations were characterized by formal and impersonal downward communication and little upward communication. Employees' viewpoints were considered irrelevant, and those who expressed dissatisfaction were ushered out the door. A rigid, militaristic style prevailed; business was conducted through the chain of command.

Both the scientific and bureaucratic theorists of the Classical School were concerned about productivity in organizations. The primary difference between the two was one of approach. Scientific theorists were intent on improving organizations from the bottom up through worker efficiency. Bureaucratic theorists emphasized a top-down effort to increase productivity through organizational structure and management control.

Although the Classical School placed too much emphasis on task over people, it made a lasting impact on the field. Today's focus on organizational productivity, structure, division of labor, and chain of command demonstrates the contributions of the Classical theorists.

Table 1.1

SCHOOL OF THOUGHT		PRIMARY PRINCIPLES	CHARACTERISTICS OF COMMUNICATION
Classical School Scientific Theorists	**Taylor**	Productivity through worker efficiency	One-way, top-down, impersonal
Bureaucratic Theorists	**Fayol and Weber**	Productivity through management control	One-way, top-down, impersonal
Human Relations School	**Mayo, Lewin, Lippitt and White, Coch and French**	Productivity through employee satisfaction	Open, friendly, employee-centered up, down, and across the organization
		Motivational value of informal work groups	Informal, horizontal
		Participative decision making related to motivation and satisfaction	Informal, horizontal
Human Resources School	**McGregor**	Theory Y	Used to motivate and encourage employees
		Theory X	Used to control and intimidate employees
	Likert	Four management styles (Systems 1–4)	Continuum from controlling and downward to open, supportive, and multidirectional
	Blake and Mouton	Managerial Grid (Later renamed Leadership Grid)	Task-related versus people-related

Table 1.1 *(continued)*

SCHOOL OF THOUGHT		PRIMARY PRINCIPLES	CHARACTERISTICS OF COMMUNICATION
Modern Schools of Thought			
Systems Theory	**Katz and Kahn**	Interdependence, subsystems, open versus closed	Central, internal versus external, dynamic
Contingency Theory	**Fiedler**	No one method best	Variable by situation
Japanese School	**Ouchi**	Value of communication, cooperation, culture	Strong interpersonal skills

The Human Relations School

World War II and the economic prosperity that followed brought changes in the way industry viewed employees. Before this time, individuals rose to the top in organizations through hard work or nepotism — by working their way up the ranks or by capitalizing on family connections. After the war, colleges and universities began turning out large numbers of well-educated, valuable professionals. Organizations were forced to reevaluate their views and focus more attention on the satisfaction and needs of white-collar workers.

The catalyst for what we now call the Human Relations School was a series of experiments conducted at the Western Electric Hawthorne plant in Cicero, Illinois, from the mid-1920s to the early 1930s. A study by the National Academy of Sciences to determine the level of light most conducive to employee productivity brought unusual results: There appeared to be no relationship between the intensity of light and workers' productivity. Productivity improved no matter what researchers did; whether lighting increased, decreased, or remained constant, productivity improved.

Perplexed by these study results, plant executives invited Elton Mayo and his associates from the Harvard University Graduate School of Business to investigate the situation. The Harvard team conducted studies over several years and found that even when researchers provided poor lighting, allowed fewer rest periods, and required longer workdays, workers' productivity steadily improved.

In the final analysis, Mayo found that the results of the Hawthorne studies had nothing to do with the actual changes that researchers made to work conditions. What was important, he concluded, was the special *attention* given to workers. Interviews with senior managers, monthly check-ups by company physicians, and the constant presence of the Harvard team convinced employees that something important was taking place and that their participation was central to its success. As a result, Mayo and his contemporaries concluded that motivation and productivity are related directly to how employees are treated. He and other researchers from the Human Relations School (for example, Lewin; Lippitt and White; and Coch and French) also found that informal work groups motivate workers to produce (through peer pressure) and that a democratic approach that allows workers to participate in decision making improves productivity and satisfaction.[56]

Although the Classical School was criticized for overemphasizing the importance of the task, the Human Relations School was criticized for overemphasizing people-oriented concerns. Supportive top-down communication was encouraged, and informal, horizontal communication in work groups was acknowledged. Unfortunately, the principles of Human Relations often were used not because managers believed in them, but to manipulate employees. Critics of the approach also contested the notion that friendly, open climates always improve productivity.[57] Nevertheless, the Human Relations emphasis on employee satisfaction has made important contributions to our understanding of today's organization.

The Human Resources School

By the 1960s, the Human Resources School of thought gradually replaced the Human Relations School. A new breed of researcher began to emphasize the value of productive relationships in organizations.[58] Each employee was believed to be capable of contributing to the organization; each worker was seen as an untapped source of creative ideas. One researcher, in particular, drew a powerful comparison between newer ideas about management and the philosophy popularized by Classical School theorists.

•••••••••••••••••••
Michael B. Guthrie, M.D., M.B.A., Chief Operating Officer, Penrose–St. Francis Healthcare System

"To a hospital administrator, communication skills are important in several specific functions of management: leadership, strategic planning, and control. To lead, you must be able to inspire employees and co-workers through an enthusiastic description of a vision of the future. To plan strategically, you must be able to clearly articulate goals, targets, and tactics. To control the functioning of the organization and your employees, you must be able consistently to report evaluations of performance and to describe achievements. All of these require the ability to speak, write, and, of course, listen effectively."

•••••••••••••••••••

Douglas McGregor wrote about the difference between two opposite sets of managerial beliefs: Theory X and Theory Y. According to McGregor, Theory X managers (those who adhere to the Classical School of thought) believe that most people dislike work, avoid responsibility when possible, have little ambition, want to be told what to do, value security above all else, and will not work toward organizational objectives. Theory Y managers (who believe in the Human Relations model), on the other hand, believe that people can commit to organizational goals, can become self-directed and self-controlled when committed, want and seek responsibility, are basically ingenious and creative, and often are intellectually underutilized. Theory Y managers believe that work is as natural as play if managers believe in their workers and demonstrate those beliefs.

McGregor believed that although Theory X management is required in certain situations, Theory Y beliefs produce the best managers and the most satisfied employees. Theory X managers make decisions autocratically, issue commands and orders through formal channels, show little interest in eliciting employee input, and often create climates of fear and distrust. Theory Y managers, by contrast, encourage messages in all directions, desire employee feedback, and create an environment of openness and trust. Although his profiles were powerful, McGregor's critics objected to the extreme pictures he painted, noting that overlapping styles of management or a middle ground between the two are possible.

Rensis Likert provided a compatible view of management styles with his continuum of Systems 1, 2, 3, and 4.[59] According to Likert, System 1 managers (exploitive/authoritarian) are much like Theory X managers and emphasize downward communication, make decisions autocratically, and engender climates of fear and distrust. At the other end of the continuum are System 4 managers (participative), who act much like Theory Y managers and focus on communicating up the chain of command, create trust between themselves and their employees, share participation in decision making, and encourage unrestricted communication.

Between these two extremes fall Systems 2 and 3. In System 2 organizations, benevolent/authoritarian managers demonstrate a condescending trust in subordinates, and most emphasis remains on task rather than people. Important decisions still are made at the top. System 3 (consultative) managers create a more trusting climate and increased participation in decision making. Broad policy decisions may be made at the top, but situation-specific decisions are made at lower levels. According to Likert, System 1 organizations typically are least productive and System 4 organizations are most productive; however, far too many organizations, Likert contended, adhere to a System 1 (Classical) approach.

Two other names — Robert Blake and Jane Mouton — also stand out as major contributors from the Human Resources School. Their Managerial Grid characterizes five archetypal management styles based on two major variables: concern for *task* (the Classical School) and concern for *people* (the Human Relations School). The ideal organization is one in which managers demonstrate a high level of commitment to both task and people. Chapter 9 of our text describes Blake and Mouton's theory in more detail.

Of all the schools of thought we've discussed thus far, the Human Resources School was the first to stress the importance of upward communication. In organizations that subscribe to this approach, employees' contributions are valued, encouraged, and rewarded. Downward communication is not used simply to command and control employees. Instead its mission is to relay information, provide feedback on current projects, and stimulate messages upward.

Modern Schools of Thought

Although elements of all the organization theories highlighted thus far still can be found in today's literature (and organizations, for that matter), several recent approaches have made far-reaching contributions. The Systems School, Contingency School, and Japanese School have made dramatic impacts on the way we view organizations and, more specifically, communication within organizations.

Systems Theory. Systems Theory, which originated from the field of biology, looks at organizations as living organisms in which the whole is greater than the sum of its parts.[60] Within each organization are several subsystems — divisions, functions, departments — that are interdependent. What happens in one part of the organization affects other parts. A budget cutback that hits the training department will be felt in the rest of the organization when fewer programs are offered. A layoff in the manufacturing division may be needed so that more design engineers may be hired for a particular contract. Communication, from a systems perspective, is the "glue" that holds an organization together. Classical factors that relate to structure and division of labor and Human Relations factors that relate to morale, informal work groups, and communication are both important in a Systems approach.

Communication is particularly important in the way that organizations interact with their environments. According to the Systems School, organizations are *open* systems that allow communication to flow in and out rather than being *closed* systems that exist as static, unchanging entities. Contact with the outside world takes place through public relations

•••••••••••••••••••
William M. Stone, Ph.D., Vice-President for Marketing and Business Development, Colorado National Bank

"As a banker, I find communication skills are every bit as important as an understanding of business. In order to market financial services and products, you must be able to communicate successfully with the public — and that's not always an easy task. If you can't communicate with your employees, your customers, and your prospective customers, you'll join the list of failed institutions. There's a considerable amount of technical information in the financial services industry, and it's not enough to know it well. You must also be able to translate it into understandable issues and ideas for your less-sophisticated customers. And as the number and sophistication of both products and services increase, so does the need to communicate, both verbally and nonverbally, with a broader cross-section of prospective clients. Number-crunching is the easy part — communicating the results is much more difficult."
•••••••••••••••••••

departments; communication with subcontractors, subsidiaries, or competitors; and participation in local events (the United Way fund drive, for example). Some theorists would say that staying in touch with changes in the environment is key to long-term organizational survival in today's highly competitive, global marketplace. Open systems are dynamic, flexible, and responsive to changes in the environment around them; thus, organizations must be dynamic, flexible, and responsive to changes in the marketplace.

The interdependence between the parts of the organization, the centrality of communication, and the melding of both Classical and Human Relations schools of thought have been the most important contributions made by Systems Theory to the study of organizations.

Contingency Theories. Contingency Theories, which are relative newcomers to the study of organizations, stress that no one leadership style and no one organizational structure is best in all situations. Fred Fiedler, originator of one of the most widely known contingency theories, found that three variables are important in selecting the best leadership style in any given case: how well the leader is liked, how much power the leader has, and how well defined the task is.[61] If a manager is well liked and has a great deal of power, and the task is well defined, she may effectively use a task-oriented approach. Ironically, the same is true under the opposite conditions. If the manager is disliked, has little power, and the task is unclear, a task-oriented approach is essential to getting the job done. A people-oriented approach works best in situations that fall between the two extremes: the manager is liked to some degree, has some power, and is given a moderately defined task. The challenge for managers is to know the critical contingent variables and to recognize when to modify their leadership styles.

Both Systems Theory and Contingency Theories stress the dynamic nature of complex organizations and the importance of communication in the productivity and satisfaction of employees. Both have contributed a great deal to modern organization theory.

The Japanese School. The Japanese School is perhaps best described as the importation of Japanese management principles into U.S. organizations. According to William Ouchi, author of *Theory Z: How American Business Can Meet the Japanese Challenge*, employees in the United States in the past have valued individual decision making, specialization of capabilities, rapid promotions, and distinct and separate business and social lives. In today's world, time and geography have reduced our ability to develop relationships outside the workplace. We no longer have local family ties where we live or close friends in our neighborhoods. The typical U.S. "Type A" (Theory X) organization no longer meets our social needs. Theory Z organizations combine the positive aspects of the Type A organization with the highly successful Japanese approach:

> A Theory Z culture assumes that any worker's life is a whole, not a Jekyll-Hyde personality, half machine from nine to five and half human in the hours preceding and following. Theory Z suggests that humanized working conditions not only increase productivity and profits to the company but also the self-esteem for employees. An increased sense of ease makes everyone function better as people. Up to now American managers have assumed that technology makes for increased productivity. What Theory Z calls for instead is a redirection of attention to *human* relations in the corporate world.[62]

In Ouchi's view, Theory Z organizations stress the following elements:

- *Cooperation and collaboration:* "While Americans still busily protect our rather extreme form of individualism, the Japanese hold their individualism in check and emphasize cooperation" (p. 66).
- *Shared decision making:* "When an important decision needs to be made in a Japanese organization, everyone who will feel its impact is involved in making it" (p. 44).
- *Interpersonal communication skills:* "Skills that involve dealing with clients, customers, even family, are the kinds of skills that people must learn to adapt to colleagues and co-workers. Interpersonal skills are central to the Z way of doing business, because working cooperatively and considerately is not just a means for soothing egos or getting your way. The stakes are much larger" (p. 106).
- *Trust:* "Intimacy and trust are cornerstones of the culture both in and out of the business setting" (p. 204).
- *Close personal relationships on the job:* "When economic and social life are integrated into a single whole, then relationships between individuals become intimate" (p. 54).
- *Long-term employment:* "In the United States we conduct our careers between organizations but within a single specialty. In Japan people conduct careers between specialties but within a single organization" (p. 33).
- *Worth of each contributor:* "Egalitarianism is a central feature of Type Z organizations" (p. 81).

••••••••••••••••••••
David Evans, Ph.D., Program Manager, Aerospace Corporation

"Like every other type of business, the aerospace industry depends on communication for its survival. On a daily basis, I am inundated with technical jargon covering every possible subject: advanced algorithms for signal processing, satellite line-of-sight stabilization, focal plane readouts — you get the idea. I have found that the people who are in the key decision-making roles are the individuals who can speak and write clearly and effectively to share their knowledge with others. They also think very clearly. This suggests that they listen well, grasping the essence of what is presented to them. In short, these are the people who can act on ideas because they know how to communicate them to others."

••••••••••••••••••••••

• *Community ("family") spirit at work:* "Organizational life is a life of interdependence, of relying upon others" (p. 76).

In the last decade, Americans have become fascinated with importing Japan's highly successful management practices along with its high-quality automobiles, videocassette recorders, and compact-disc players. Although the principles of Japanese management may not be transferable point by point to U.S. corporations, we cannot argue with the immeasurable benefits of communication and collaboration in today's highly competitive organizations.

A FINAL NOTE

Throughout this chapter, our goal has been to convince you that the information in *Communicating in Business and the Professions* is important in preparing you for your first position, in establishing a reputation as a competent communicator, in climbing the organizational ladder, and in cultivating a personal sense of proficiency, achievement, and confidence. Our message grows directly out of our own organizational experience in government, private industry, and academia, as well as from our work as consultants with professionals around the country. We believe strongly in what we've learned. But you don't simply have to take our word for it. We've also asked some of our associates to speak for themselves.

Scattered throughout this chapter you have read the words of successful communicators in many different fields. They have cultivated their reading, writing, speaking, and listening skills. Every day they communicate in meetings, interviews, and one-on-one relationships on the job. They recognize the role of communication in achieving success in today's organization. Regardless of what they do, communication is how they do it.

To us the word *success* means not only achieving power and prestige but also eliciting cooperation, achieving results, making things happen — the results of communication skills that work for you and help you to build a reputation of competence within the organization. We cannot overemphasize the importance of cultivating *now* the organizational communication skills that will become so important to you later. You will see that our goal in *Communicating in Business and the Professions* is to help you make that happen.

CHAPTER SUMMARY

In this first chapter we described some of the changes occurring in today's organizations: recent advances in technology, the shift from an industrial society to an information society, and the changing nature of the work force. Now more than ever, multifaceted communication skills are a prerequisite to success.

We then discussed more specifically *the importance of communication skills in organizations*. In particular, we concentrated on research that identifies which skills are *most important, most used*, and *most in need of enhancement*. We personalized the discussion by asking, "What can effective communication skills do for you?" And we pointed out four benefits of enhancing your skills: improved hirability, better work effectiveness, an image of competence within the organization, and increased opportunity for success. Throughout the chapter, you also read testimonials from businesspeople and professionals, all of whom attested to the value of effective organizational communication.

Defining terms such as *organization* and *communication* were the final order of business. And throughout our discussion, we contrasted traditional aspects of these definitions with the way they are described in the best-run companies today. We offered a definition of communication as "a *dynamic transaction* in which *verbal and nonverbal messages* are simultaneously exchanged resulting in shared meaning between two or more people. Messages occur through *formal or informal channels* in *upward, downward, or horizontal directions*. Communication forms the basis for an organization's *climate* and contributes to an organization's *culture*." We concluded the chapter with a brief history of organization theory.

In Chapter 2, we begin the process of enhancing specific communication skills for organizational success. Our first subject will be Writing Effectively in Organizations. We'll cover several principles that work equally well for spoken or written language, and our examples will show *how* to become a more effective organizational writer.

MEASURING SUCCESS

1. In this first chapter of *Communicating in Business and the Professions*, we've been considering the nature of organizational communication. Focus on two dimensions of our discussion: *message direction*

(downward, upward, or horizontal) and *message channel* (formal versus informal). Provide several examples of the kinds of messages sent in terms of both direction and channel for each of the following organizations:

   a. your college or university
   b. your family
   c. your sorority, fraternity, or a club of your choice

2. Interview a business or professional person to determine his or her opinions on the three research issues presented in this chapter:

   a. Which communication skills are *most important* in his or her organization?
   b. Which communication skills are *most often used* in his or her organization?
   c. Which communication skills are *most in need of enhancement* in his or her organization?

Provide your interviewee with the following list of communication skills to consider:

   1. interviewing
   2. listening
   3. giving oral presentations
   4. using communications technology
   5. leading/managing techniques
   6. managing conflict
   7. diagnosing organizational problems
   8. handling grievances
   9. motivating people
   10. delegating authority
   11. group problem solving
   12. giving directions
   13. building interpersonal relationships
   14. writing letters, memos, and reports
   15. negotiating

Prepare a brief report that summarizes the results of your interview.

3. Without referring back to the chapter, write a radio advertisement for your business and professional communication course. Assume the students at your college or university will be the listening audience; stress the benefits of enhancing communication skills and whatever other pertinent information you choose.

4. Assume that you are a department store supervisor who has just been given the news that you must inform five of twenty people in your department that they have been laid off indefinitely. How would you approach this task, considering the following?

a. formal versus informal channels
b. downward, upward, and horizontal communication
c. verbal and nonverbal messages
d. the organizational climate
e. the organizational culture

5. Assume that you work in an organization with an increasingly negative climate. Because of three uncertainties—future business prospects, a new incoming (and unknown) general manager, and the abolition of a large division—low morale, poor motivation, and general griping are becoming the norm. If you were the assistant general manager and wanted to improve the organizational climate, how would you go about it? Discuss specific steps that you would take to begin the process, viewing the situation from each of the schools of thought discussed in this chapter.

Notes

1. Catherine M. Petrini, "'Ready, Set, Work,' Says Labor Secretary," *Training & Development Journal* 44 (May 1990): 18.

2. Anthony P. Carnevale, Leila J. Gainer, Ann S. Meltzer, and Shari L. Holland, "Workplace Basics: The Skills Employers Want," *Training & Development Journal* 42 (October 1988): 23.

3. John Naisbitt and Patricia Aburdene, *Re-Inventing the Corporation: Transforming Your Job and Your Company for the New Information Society* (New York: Warner, 1985), 120.

4. Naisbitt and Aburdene, *Re-Inventing*, 119.

5. John Naisbitt, *Megatrends: Ten New Directions Transforming Our Lives* (New York: Warner, 1982), 37.

6. Naisbitt, *Megatrends*, 16.

7. Naisbitt, *Megatrends*, 14.

8. Naisbitt, *Megatrends*, 22.

9. John Naisbitt and Patricia Aburdene, *Megatrends 2000: Ten New*

Directions for the 1990's (New York: William Morrow & Co., 1990), 220.

10. Tom Peters, *Thriving on Chaos: Handbook for a Management Revolution* (New York: Alfred A. Knopf, 1987), 6.

11. Laurence D. Ackerman, "What Makes Successful Service Companies Distinctive?" *IABC Communication World* 3 (October 1986): 17.

12. Naisbitt and Aburdene, *Re-Inventing*, 208; E. Ehrlich and S. B. Garland, "For American Business, a New World of Workers," *Business Week*, 19 September 1988, 112.

13. Naisbitt and Aburdene, *Megatrends 2000*, 220; William R. Greer, "In Professions, Women Now the Majority," *New York Times*, 19 March 1986, p. C1, C10.

14. William B. Johnston and Ronald E. Packer, *Workforce 2000* (Washington, DC: U.S. Government Printing Office, 1989), xx.

15. Gerald Goldhaber, *Organizational Communication*, 2nd ed. (Dubuque, IA: Wm. C. Brown, 1979), 143.

16. *Nation's Business*, April 1982, 17.

17. J. David Pincus, "Study Links Communication and Job Performance," *IABC Communication World* 1 (November 1984): 27–30.

18. Kathryn Martin, "Video Teaches Personal Skills to Students," *Colorado Springs Gazette Telegraph*, 8 September 1987, p. B1.

19. Yvone Bogorya, "Innovative Approaches to Management Education: Prepare for the Challenges of the 80's," *Canadian Manager* 1 (Summer 1986): 21–22.

20. Constance C. Staley and Pamela Shockley-Zalabak, "Identifying Communication Competencies for the Undergraduate Organizational Communication Series," *Communication Education* 34 (April 1985): 156–161.

21. Vincent DiSalvo, David Larsen, and William Seiler, "Communication Skills Needed by Persons in Business Organizations," *Communication Education* 25 (1976): 269–275.

22. James C. Bennett and Robert J. Olney, "Executive Priorities for Effective Communication in an Information Society," *Journal of Business Communication* 23 (Spring 1986): 13–22.

23. Dan B. Curtis, Jerry L. Winsor, and Ronald D. Stephens, "National Preferences in Business and Communication Education," *Communication Education* 38 (1989): 6–14.

24. Vincent S. DiSalvo and Janet K. Larsen, "A Contingency Approach to Communication Skill Importance: The Impact of Occupation, Direction, and Position," *Journal of Business Communication* 24 (Summer 1987): 3–22.

25. Bennett and Olney, "Executive Priorities," 16.

26. Kenneth Roman and Joel Raphaelson, *Writing That Works* (New York: Harper & Row, 1981), 1.

27. Robert R. Max, "What's Your Communications 'IQ'?" *Supervisory Management* 22 (1977): 12–15.

28. Jack B. Rochester and John L. DiGaetani, "Managerial Communication: Total Business Communication for the 1980s," *ABCA Bulletin* 44 (September 1981): 9–10.

29. Curtis, Winsor, and Stephens, "National Preferences," 13.

30. Thomas E. Harris and T. Dean Thomlison, "Career-Bound Communication Education: A Needs Analysis," *Central States Speech Journal* 34 (Winter 1983): 260–267.

31. Curtis, Winsor, and Stephens, "National Preferences," 13.

32. Rochester and DiGaetani, "Managerial Communication," 9.

33. Association for Management Success, "1986–87 Association for Management Success Career Strategies Survey" (Willow Grove, PA: Association for Management Success, 1987).

34. H. Zollitsch and R. Krusing, "Business Executives' Expectations of Business Administration Graduates: A Marquette Survey," *Marquette Business Review* 14 (1970): 4.

35. G. W. Bowman, "What Helps or Harms Promotability?" *Harvard Business Review* 42 (January–February 1964): 14.

36. Bennett and Olney, "Executive Priorities," 15.

37. Gerald M. Phillips, *Communicating in Organizations* (New York: Macmillan, 1982), 5.

38. Everett Rogers and Rehka Agarwala-Rogers, *Communication in Organizations* (New York: Free Press, 1976), 6.

39. Thomas J. Peters and Robert H. Waterman, Jr., *In Search of Excellence: Lessons from America's Best-Run Companies* (New York: Harper & Row, 1982).

40. Peters and Waterman, *In Search*, 155.

41. "Who's Excellent Now?" *Business Week*, 5 November 1984, 77.

42. Peters and Waterman, *In Search*, 125–134.

43. Ronald B. Adler, *Communicating at Work*, 2nd ed. (New York: Random House, 1986), 24.

44. Terrence E. Deal and Allen A. Kennedy, *Corporate Cultures: The Rites and Rituals of Corporate Life* (Reading, MA: Addison-Wesley, 1982), 86; Gerald Goldhaber, *Organizational Communication*, 4th ed. (Dubuque, IA: Wm. C. Brown, 1986), 175–176.

45. Lawrence Berkowitz and Warren Bennis, "Interaction Patterns in Formal Service-Oriented Organizations," *Administrative Science Quarterly* 5 (1961): 210–222.

46. E. Sieburg, "Confirming and Disconfirming Communication in an Organizational Setting." In J. Owen, P. Page, and G. Zimmerman, Eds., *Communication in Organizations* (St. Paul, MN: West, 1976), 129–149; Adler, *Communicating*, 41–42, 103–110.

47. Bro Uttal, "The Corporate Culture Vultures," *Fortune*, 17 October 1983, 66.

48. Peters and Waterman, *In Search*, 13–15; "Who's Excellent Now?", 77.

49. It is an interesting and salient fact that two years after the publication of *In Search of Excellence*, fourteen of the book's original forty-three excellent companies had "lost their luster." By 1990, only fourteen of the original companies still deserved the label. Declines in earnings, business problems, and management problems have been the cause. Companies either broke one or more of the book's "eight commandments" or failed to respond to rapidly changing business environments. For further reading, see the *Business Week* article, "Who's Excellent Now?" (cited above) or Richard Tanner Pascale, *Managing on the Edge: Companies That Use Conflict to Stay Ahead* (New York: Simon & Schuster, 1990).

50. Edgar H. Schein, *Organizational Culture and Leadership* (San Francisco: Jossey-Bass, 1985).

51. Deal and Kennedy, *Corporate Cultures*, 107–127.

52. Peters and Waterman, *In Search*, 124.

53. Peters and Waterman, *In Search*, 70–71.

54. Portions of the following discussion are adapted from Patricia H. Andrews and John E. Baird, Jr., *Communication for Business and the Professions*, 4th ed. (Dubuque, IA: Wm. C. Brown, 1989), and Cheryl Hamilton and Cordell Parker, *Communicating for Results*, 3rd ed. (Belmont, CA: Wadsworth, 1990).

55. Frederick Taylor, *Scientific Management* (New York: Harper & Row, 1911); Henri Fayol, *General and Industrial Management* (London: Sir Isaac Pitman and Sons, 1949); Max Weber, *The Theory of Social and Economic Organization* (New York: Oxford University Press, 1947).

56. Fritz J. Roethlisberger and William J. Dickson, *Management and the Worker* (Cambridge, MA: Harvard University Press, 1939); Kurt Lewin, "Group Decision and Social Change," in *Readings in Social Psychology*, G. E. Swanson et al., Eds. (New York: Holt, Rinehart & Winston, 1952), 459–473; Ronald L. Lippitt and Ralph K. White, "An Experimental Study of Leadership and Group Life," in *Readings in Social Psychology*, 340–355; Lester Coch and John R. P. French, "Overcoming Resistance to Change," *Human Relations* 1 (1948): 512–532.

57. Nancy A. Euske and Karlene H. Roberts, "Evolving Perspectives in Organization Theory: Communication Implications," in *Handbook of Organizational Communication*, Fredric M. Jablin, Linda Putnam, Karlene H. Roberts, and Lyman W. Porter, Eds. (Newbury Park, CA: Sage, 1987), 45.

58. Douglas McGregor, *Human Side of Enterprise* (New York: McGraw-Hill, 1960); Rensis Likert, *The Human Organization* (New York: McGraw-Hill, 1967); Robert Blake and Jane Mouton, *The Managerial Grid* (Houston, TX: Gulf, 1964).

59. Rensis Likert, *New Patterns of Management* (New York: McGraw-Hill, 1961); *The Human Organization* (New York: McGraw-Hill, 1967).

60. Ludwig von Bertalanfy, *General Systems Theory* (New York: Braziller, 1968); Daniel Katz and Robert L. Kahn, *The Social Psychology of Organizations* (New York: John Wiley, 1966).

61. Fred Fiedler, *A Theory of Leadership Effectiveness* (New York: McGraw-Hill, 1967); Fred Fiedler, M. Chemers, and L. Mahar, *Improving Leadership Effectiveness* (New York: John Wiley, 1976).

62. William G. Ouchi, *Theory Z: How American Business Can Meet the Japanese Challenge* (Reading, MA: Addison-Wesley, 1981), 195–196.

Part II ✐ The Written Word

Chapter 2 ✎ **Writing Effectively in Organizations**

The finest eloquence is that which gets things done. — David Lloyd George

Those who write clearly have readers; those who write obscurely have commentators. — Albert Camus

No one disputes the importance of language skills — of writing and speaking effectively — in organizations. But although we admit its importance, skill in using the English language is not as widespread as you'd think in many organizations. Why not? Because while we agree we should be better writers and speakers, often we don't know how — or, even worse, the "how" we know just doesn't work.

Many high school and college courses teach "scholarly" writing techniques that are crucial in completing a history or political science assignment. But while useful in your education, these are not the practical skills you'll use in organizations throughout your life. Letters, memos, reports, instructions, sales presentations, interviews, and contracts — *these* are the means by which we exchange and record ideas, plans, needs, and disagreements — in short, the information that keeps the organization alive. And often these are the tools of growth, the means we use to come up with new ideas and more effective methods of doing business. These are the new "assignments" you'll encounter on the job.

This chapter will concentrate on your language skills — the basis of your writing and speaking abilities — within the organization. Throughout much of this text we'll deal extensively with the spoken word, because, like most organizational communicators, you'll spend more time speaking and listening than you will writing. However, in this chapter we'll focus many of our explanations of language skills on *effective writing techniques*. Why? For three reasons:

1. Because writing is a form of communication in which you have more time to make choices.
2. Because writing is more overt, concrete, and permanent than speaking.
3. Because the principles of effective writing also apply to effective speaking habits.

Your writing skills are crucial to your success within an organization — and these are skills that may well need strengthening.

WHY YOUR LANGUAGE ABILITIES COUNT

Chief executives and personnel officers across the country agree: Those who write and speak well are valuable to the organization.[1] Those who don't, aren't. If these leaders had their way, college graduates would learn to write and speak more effectively than most do.[2] From these experts' comments, you might fairly draw this conclusion: If you learn to write and speak well, you'll stand out in a field of inept (or at best mediocre) communicators.[3]

Who'll read your writing? Much of the writing generated within an organization stays there, and most of your conversations may be "local." On any given day, you'll write a memo to your peers, talk over a project with a coworker, prepare a report for your supervisor, send a letter to your subordinates, and perhaps even take notes or prepare documents for your own future use. Such *internal writing and speaking* is absolutely necessary in any organization with more than a few people.

You'll also aim a good deal of your communication outside the organization. Letters to customers, associates, competitors, suppliers, lawyers, and even government agencies all produce far-reaching results that affect your organization — for good and for ill. Your *external writing* not only affects your organization's public image but also its competitive success.

Why do we say *your* writing? Because your language skills are peculiar to *you*, not the organization. Corporations don't communicate — *you* do. Your words not only contribute to the organization's success but also help you succeed within the organization.

But this is not to say that individuals in organizations write in isolation. Far from it. Organizational writing often is a team effort. Colleagues collaborate on projects, contribute sections to a report, edit one another's work, and even check one another's spelling. To be an effective part of that collaborative undertaking, your own skills must be sharp.

Clear, concise writing also is important to the organization's "bottom line." From annual surveys conducted by the Dartnell Institute of Business Research, we estimate that in the next few years the average cost of producing one business letter — writing, dictating, revising, typing, processing, mailing, filing, and ultimately reading — will climb to more than $11.[4] Altogether, letters alone cost U.S. companies more than $100 billion each year.

We agree, then, that language skills are important in the organization, and that you want to be an effective writer. The next question we must answer is "How?" How do *you* become more effective in using the English language?

THE WRITING PROCESS

Writing doesn't just happen — at least not often. More often than not, the writer works through a three-stage process of prewriting, writing, and rewriting.[5]

Prewriting

Even on a particular project, the process of writing starts well before pen touches page or fingers hit keys. Writing begins in thought, in observation, in searching, and perhaps even in worrying. You usually have some idea of what you want to say before you begin to speak, even though you may not be sure exactly what words will surface in the act of speaking. And the same thing happens in writing. So realize that even though you've nothing on paper yet, some of the work, some of the writing process — what we call *prewriting* — already has been accomplished.

To begin, think about your task. Ask questions about your audience and your purpose: "Who am I writing to, and what do I want them to know or do?" You also may ask what facts and opinions you'll need, and where you'll find them. To find them, you may read, interview, discuss, observe, brainstorm, and reflect. Unless you have a perfect memory or a very simple writing task, you'll probably also take notes. And as your research progresses, you'll find yourself forming an opinion, favoring a particular point of view or a certain way of seeing your task. You also may discover a useful way to organize what you find.

Notice that you're probably already doing some writing in this prewriting stage. If you've taken notes or written questions, opinions, or phrasings, you're helping yourself begin the writing process. These notes do *not* have to be grammatically correct or in any sense final or finished. Rather they're only pieces of your work in progress. They're raw material for later use. And that attitude, that realization, is liberating. Hold onto it even into the writing stage. Nothing has to be perfect, nothing is permanent, as you put together your thoughts. That's for later.

Writing

Have you ever had the frustrating experience of sitting down to write a paper and finding that you just didn't know how to start? This common problem sometimes is called "writer's block" or "the tyranny of the blank page." But whatever you call it, you'll be relieved to know there are ways around it.

Some professional writers resort to strange, almost ritualistic strategies to get going. Victor Hugo supposedly wrote at the same time every day in his study — without clothes on! His valet was ordered to lock away all Hugo's clothes until each day's writing was done.[6] Apparently, the method worked — witness *Les Miserables*. But we're sure this technique would not be received well in most organizations.

A simpler way of starting is simply to start. Just write freely on whatever comes into your head, whether it gets right to the point or not. For example, imagine that your boss wants a report by tomorrow morning on your division's morale. You've already prewritten this report: You've asked her what specifically she is looking for, you've interviewed some of your co-workers, and you've done some reading and taken some notes on previous morale problems (and their solutions) in your organization. Having done this much, you might begin by writing what's on your mind:

> I'm having trouble starting this report because there's a lot at stake. Our morale problems seem to result from an overactive rumor mill — overactive because we don't get enough accurate information quickly enough from the top. . . .

Now stop and look at what you've written. If you take away the first sentence and the doubtful "seem to," you'll discover a useful beginning for a first draft:

> Our morale problems result from an overactive rumor mill — overactive because we don't get enough accurate information quickly enough from the top.

Another starting technique is to begin with the words, "The purpose of this letter [or "report" or "briefing" or "study"] is. . . ." As in the preceding example, you'll find yourself with plenty to say if you've already done your prewriting. And because you know you can get rid of these starter words later *and* change what follows, you're on your way to a useful first draft.

Another technique is to work step by step from an outline toward a finished product. Take the facts and ideas you collected during the prewriting stage and organize them in whatever way makes sense for now. It doesn't have to be perfect; in fact, you'll be better off if you *expect* your outline to change as you proceed. Once you have an outline, write a provisional statement that expresses your opinion, your argument, or in some way summarizes what all this prewriting boils down to. Place that *thesis statement* at the top of the outline. Then write a sentence (or several) to summarize each major section of your outline. Follow each statement with the items of support or information you've found, and build each into a paragraph one by one. You'll end up with a collection of paragraphs that, when tied together with transitions, will prove a serviceable rough draft.[7]

....

Rewriting

This last stage is concerned with both form and content. Here you'll make the wording changes that provide your reader with the clearest, most powerful product possible. Here you'll ensure that grammar, punctuation, and spelling are correct and that your document looks good. But beyond such necessary technical considerations, you'll also take a fresh look at what you've said.

Rewriting often is called *revision*, and we think the term is a powerful one. It can mean not merely changing, but literally reseeing or *reenvisioning* your work. To help you see your work as others will see it, set it aside for a time before rewriting. "How long is 'a time'?" you ask. We can only answer, "As long as you can comfortably afford." The Roman writer Horace advised his students to put their work aside for seven years before revising. In most modern organizations, seven *hours* may be too long! But if you can plan ahead and give yourself an hour, a day, or a week before revising, you will have distanced yourself from your work enough to see its true weaknesses and to correct them.

As you reexamine your writing, ask whether it makes sense. Is it clear? Could it be better expressed in any part? Is the organization easy to follow? Does it accomplish what you set out to accomplish?

One effective way to discover how your writing will affect others is by simply asking them. Show someone your draft or revision. Ask someone whose judgment you trust to give you feedback on your work, in part or in whole. As we stated earlier, much of the writing in organizations results from collaboration between colleagues. So share your writing *before* it becomes final.

One more tip. Throughout these three stages be prepared to move fluidly from one to the other at the slightest provocation. In the middle of your *rewriting*, if you come across some *prewriting* information — new information that would prove useful — copy it down and fit it in. In the *prewriting* stage, if you think of *writing* a good argument or a phrase that strikes you as powerful, then write it down.

Finally, realize the importance of polishing, proofing, and presenting the final document in perfect form. Be positive you've no spelling errors and be proud of the document's final appearance — paper clean, type dark and crisp, margins consistent, headings useful, names and addresses correct. If everything else is done perfectly, but you misspell your reader's name, then you lose.

In the pages that follow, we'll demonstrate principles that will be eminently useful in your writing, especially in the rewriting stage.

THE URBAN RENEWAL STRATEGY: WRITING THAT WORKS

In many ways, writing is like building. But instead of using nails, planks, and plasterboard to construct our communications, we use words, sentences, and paragraphs. To ensure that our constructions work the way we want them to—in our letters, memos, instructions, briefings, and reports—we recommend that you use our URBAN renewal strategy. This simple memory device will help you to select and order not only the information you include, but the words and sentences you use. If you become a successful URBAN writer, then you'll communicate so that your *readers* will:

Understand
Remember
Believe
Act—and *you* as *writer* will:
Note results.

No one item in this simple mnemonic list is effective by itself. Instead, all five work together to produce effective organizational language skills. To see how and why each item is important, let's examine each in order.

Understand. Before you can influence someone, your writing must be *clear, complete*, and *correct*. Each principle contributes to understanding, and without all of them you run the risk of writing gobbledygook.

Remember. Your writing also must have impact. Your reader must remember *what* you've said for more than just a few seconds. So in addition to the principles that lead to understanding, strive for writing that is *concise* and *compelling*. You will see that compelling writing is *precise, vivid, positive, active*, and *personal*. And don't be afraid to let your own personality shine through your writing.

Believe. If your reader understands and remembers what you've said but isn't convinced that you're right or simply doesn't believe you, then you've lost the battle. Both *you* and *your presentation* must be *credible*.

Act. Often you'll want your reader to do something specific. At this stage, you must convince your reader not only that you're right but also that your ideas are important enough to act upon.

This is where understanding, remembering, and believing are doubly important. And this is where *courtesy* counts.

Note results. If your reader understands, remembers, believes, and acts as you want, then you'll be ready to note the results — results that may even surpass your expectations. You'll want to follow up your original writing through observation, a phone call, or even more writing. And when you find you've had the effect you wanted, you'll continue with positive reinforcement — a note, a letter of appreciation to your reader's boss, even a personal word of thanks. At your best as an URBAN writer, you'll recruit people to support your ideas by writing or calling you with comments, suggestions, and support. In short, you'll build a network of allies as one result of such powerful writing.

We've made preliminary remarks on the writing principles necessary in each stage of the URBAN process. But we're sure that you've noticed that these principles aren't truly separate. In fact, we view the URBAN process as a continuum, and the principles we examine next fall along that continuum merely in terms of emphasis as in Table 2.1.

PRINCIPLES OF URBAN WRITING

Be Clear

During the Mad Hatter's tea party in Lewis Carroll's *Alice's Adventures in Wonderland*, the March Hare tells Alice that it is never enough just to mean what you say; you also must "say what you mean." That is, the words you choose must express your ideas and feelings clearly to your

Table 2.1 *The URBAN Renewal Continuum*

If your reader	**Understands → Remembers → Believes → Acts**
	Clear ——→ Concise ——→ Credible → Courteous Complete —/ Compelling —/ Correct —/
Then you	**Note Results**

reader. Not bad advice from an insane rabbit. And while this advice applies quite obviously to speaking, it's also true of writing. Unfortunately, the English language gives you many opportunities to confound your reader or to write something quite different from what you mean. The great storyteller and essayist E.B. White once gave this advice to writers: "When you say something, make sure you have said it. The chances of your having said it are only fair."[8]

Read the following memo quickly. Then ask yourself, "Was it clear? Am I confident I know what it said?"

> It will be appreciated by all personnel that company expenditures over the period of the last fiscal year have disproportionately propagated and accrued. Maximization of personal recompense will of necessity be prorogued. In future periods it is hoped that utilization of said personnel will be equitably met with adequate remuneration. The heretofore mentioned policy will be immediately promulgated to all concerned.

Yes, many of us will be able to figure it out, although we may need to check the dictionary or ask someone at the next desk what *prorogued* means. And even then we may be left with more questions than answers. Who are "all concerned"? Does "future periods" mean next week or the next decade? That's not the effect you want from your writing, and that's not the kind of writing you'd like on your desk when you get to work in the morning. The memo is not clear and as a result it's wasteful and frustrating.

Why would anyone write this way? Some organizational writers overuse difficult and abstruse words because they want to sound formal and important. That's a mistake. First, your task is to *express* an idea clearly rather than *impress* your reader with your importance. And second, you may end up sounding pompous or even ridiculous, as did the memo writer above.

Simple Words. To begin, we make our writing most clear by choosing words that are easy to understand. These are words we're used to hearing, and so we understand them quickly and effortlessly.[9] In the example above, *promulgate* is a valid word: it's in the dictionary, it has an honorable history, and many people know approximately what it means. But *make known* or *publish* also are valid choices, and in most organizational contexts they mean the same as *promulgate*. Most readers will more easily, more quickly, and more correctly interpret *publish* than *promulgate*. That adds to clarity not only for the particular idea behind the word but also for the total message you're sending. The greater the

Table 2.2 *Simple Words*

WHY *UTILIZE* . . .	WHEN YOU CAN *USE* . . .
acquiesce	agree
approximately	about
ambiguous	not clear
augmentation	increase, addition
cessation	stop, end, pause
cognizant of	know, aware of, recognize
comprehend	see, understand
comprised	made up of
conjecture	think, believe
consummate	perfect, finish
corroborate	confirm
currently	now
deliberate upon	think about
disburse	pay, give
eliminate	cut
expedite	speed up
fallacious	false, wrong
finalize	finish
incorporate	include
increment	increase, raise
indicate	show, tell
initial	first
initiate	start
interrogate	ask, question
maximal, maximum	best, most
originate	begin, start
position	place
predicated	based
presently	now
promulgate	publish, make known
peruse	read, look over
rationale	reason
remunerate	pay
scrutinize	inspect
transpire	happen
ultimate	final
utilize	use

mass of unusual or difficult words you use, the less clear your writing — or your speaking.

We're not against difficult or unusual words. They have their place, but organizational writing isn't it. When your reader is busy, when time is money, then appropriateness and simplicity count. Mark Twain believed and practiced this principle: "I never write *metropolis* for seven cents," he once said, "because I can get the same price for *city*."

But can't you use a difficult word once in awhile? Yes, the occasional unusual word will catch your reader's attention and emphasize a point. But if you're in the *habit* of reaching down deep for a superimpressive word, instead of a simply expressive word, then try using the list in Table 2.2 on p. 49 to break that habit.

One final warning: Don't sacrifice accuracy for simplicity. If you mean *ultimate*, then use it instead of *final*. But the simpler, more familiar word is most often the best one for effective organizational writing.

Transitions. Clarity is a function not only of word choice, but also of how words and sentences are assembled. If you attempt to move your reader from one idea to the next, but your words don't provide a clear *transition*, then your reader may miss the connection. As a result, your writing will be unclear — even though *you* knew exactly what you meant, where you were going, and how you were getting there. Transitions help your reader make connections and understand the relationships between ideas as he moves from beginning to end: This *causes* that, these *follow* those, her qualities *differ from* his.

How easy is it to understand the connection between the two major ideas in this sentence?

> Because the Decco Corporation's offer is the highest we've received, it appears we'd better accept. We still have two weeks.

Does the second sentence support the first, or does it make a new point? Without a transitional marker, your reader probably will worry about the ambiguity — and that's not what you want. Clarity increases markedly when you add one little word to show a contrast between the first claim ("Let's act now") and the second ("Let's wait").

> Because the Decco Corporation's offer is the highest we've received, it appears we'd better accept. **However**, we still have two weeks.

The word *however*, of course, shows your reader that a contrast exists between the claim of the first sentence and the implication of the second.

Table 2.3 *Useful Transitions*

To add one thought to another	and, in addition, moreover, besides, further, furthermore, likewise, nor, too, next, first, second, in the first place, in the second place, last, finally
To compare	likewise, in like manner, similarly, in the same way
To contrast	but, yet, however, still, on the contrary, on the other hand, nevertheless, nonetheless, even so, although
To show place	here, there, beyond, nearby, opposite to, next to, adjacent to
To show time	meanwhile, now, soon, then, afterward, before, later, once, in the past, in the meantime, while, when, eventually
To show a result	hence, thus, then, therefore, accordingly, consequently, as a result
To summarize	in sum, in brief, in a word, in short, in other words, so, thus, then, in conclusion

You could have used any of several contrast markers, such as *on the other hand* or *yet*, but such a transition clearly helps your reader make sense of the shift.

Use the transitions in Table 2.3 to help your reader move with understanding from point to point.

Be Complete

"What does my reader need to know?" When you empathize with your reader, when you put yourself in his shoes, you'll find you sometimes take details for granted that you can't expect him to know.

If you announce a meeting, for example, you must be explicit in answering *each* of the standard questions asked by any good reporter: who, what, where, when, why, and how? If you fail to answer even one of these questions, your readers may fail to show up—or at best you'll receive calls asking "where?" or "when?" And meetings aren't the only subjects that demand such complete coverage. Everything you write needs the conscientious scrutiny that puts you, the writer, in the place of your reader who asks, "What's missing? What must I find here to understand the complete message?"

One final hint: Sometimes you're too close to your subject to notice what's missing in your writing. Because it *is* difficult to put yourself in your reader's place, we suggest you have someone else read your writing for completeness. Often she will notice a gap in your information: "You left out the meeting place" or "How much will it cost?" It pays to double-check completeness with someone who is removed from your subject.

Be Correct

Letter and Memo Formats. Even a first glance at your writing communicates volumes to the reader. Neatness and format produce a halo effect that you can't afford to ignore. Use a consistent, generally accepted format for your letters and memos. Unless your organization dictates a given format, use one of those shown in Figures 2.1, 2.2, or 2.3.

Heading: Headings are unnecessary if you use letterhead stationery, but you still must add a dateline. Use no abbreviations except the post office's official state abbreviations. You may write the date as in the sample, 1 April 1993, or as April 1, 1993.

Inside address: Include the reader's title whenever possible. When writing to several specific readers, include these names on separate lines. Unless you have more precise information, use Mr. for a man and Ms. for a woman. If you have no name for your reader, simply use a generic title such as Claims Adjuster or Sales Manager.

Subject line: Although not always necessary, a subject line often aids the recipient in filing and retrieving your letter. Keep the subject line short.

Salutation (or greeting): Use colons following the salutation for formal letters, commas for more personal letters. Avoid To Whom It May Concern (stuffy) or Gentlemen (sexist) when you don't know who will read your letter. Better to call the company and ask for a name. If that doesn't work, use a generic title such

1-in. margin

[2–6 lines, or to center]

```
1946 Uintah Avenue                              Heading
Watford City, CO 80903-7532
1 April 1993                                   Date Line
```
[2 lines]
```
Mr. J. Wilson Freeman, Director            Inside Address
Freeman Associates
1002 Madison Avenue
New York, NY 10017-5643
```
[2 lines]
```
Subject: Block Format Example               Subject Line
```
[2 lines]
```
Dear Mr. Freeman:                           Salutation
```
[2 lines]
```
This is a sample letter that demonstrates the full-
block format. Notice that every item begins at the
left margin, and paragraphs are not indented.
```
[2 lines]
```
Even the signature block will be found at the left
margin in the full-block style.
```
[2 lines]
```
Notice as well that even though you use one space
between lines inside a paragraph, you should use two
lines between paragraphs.
```
[2 lines]
```
Sincerely,                             Complimentary Close
```

[4 lines]

```
Ralph B. Crampton                         Signature Block
Letter Format Specialist
```
[2 lines]
```
RC/ss                                    Identification Line
```
[2 lines]
```
Enclosure: Sample                          Enclosure Line
```
[2 lines]
```
Copy: Mr. Jack B. Quikk, Writer          Distribution Line
```

Figure 2.1 *Full-Block Format*

1½-in. margin

1-in. margin

[2–6 lines, or to center]

1946 Uintah Avenue — *Heading*
Watford City, CO 80903-7532
1 April 1993 — *Date Line*

[2 lines]

Mr. J. Wilson Freeman, Director — *Inside Address*
Freeman Associates
1002 Madison Avenue
New York, NY 10017-5643

[2 lines]

Subject: Block Format Example — *Subject Line*

[2 lines]

Dear Mr. Freeman: — *Salutation*

[2 lines]

This sample letter demonstrates the modified block format. Here the heading, complimentary close, and signature block are indented to leave a one-inch margin on the right side of the page.

[2 lines]

This older style still is used in many organizations.

[2 lines]

Notice that all other format requirements are unchanged.

[2 lines]

Sincerely, — *Complimentary Close*

[4 lines]

Ralph B. Crampton — *Signature Block*
Letter Format Specialist

[2 lines]

RC/ss — *Identification Line*

[2 lines]

Enclosure: Sample — *Enclosure Line*

[2 lines]

Copy: Mr. Jack B. Quikk, Writer — *Distribution Line*

***Figure 2.2** Modified Block Format*

```
MEMORANDUM
[2 lines]
TO:        A. Lincoln, President
[2 lines]
FROM:      U. Grant, General Manager [initials]
[2 lines]
SUBJECT:  Union Activities
[2 lines]
DATE:      1 April 1993
[2 lines]
Often called memos, these internal
documents are less formal than letters.
Organizations often use their own
specific formats, but this sample is
useful.
[2 lines]
Rather than sign memos, writer and
readers often simply initial their
names at the top.
```

Figure 2.3 Memorandum Format

as Dear Sales Manager. Or when you're completely stumped, simply skip the greeting.

Text: Keep your paragraphs short. Single-space inside, double-space between.

Complimentary close: Use a common formal ending, such as Sincerely, Sincerely yours, or Cordially.

Signature block: Leave four lines for your signature above your name and title.

Identification line: Put your initials in caps, followed by a slash and your typist's lowercase initials. If you typed it yourself, omit this line.

Enclosure line: You may mention several enclosures, but put the number in parentheses; for example, Enclosures: (2)

Distribution line: Here you let the reader know who else is receiving the letter. You may use Copy: (or Copies:) or the older cc: with names and titles.

Punctuation, Grammar, and Spelling. Imagine receiving this letter from a corporation that you thought might handle some of your accounts:

```
Dear Sir or Madame

Thank you for you're letter of Septenber 14th. We are
quite interested in lying to rest any fears you might
have about our competence we are quite competent,
many of our customers have told us so. Such as those
on the accompanying list. We have also sent you a
braschure with vital fats about our recent reorgan-
ization which you should look at. We are quite proud,
of it, and, we feel, you will be, to.

Hopping to hear form you soon.

Mr. Bill Buffoon
```

Although none of us is perfect, few of us are consistently as bad as this writer. But the problem with committing even one of these writing errors is that people tend to generalize about the writer: "If he's that sloppy writing a letter, how careless is he with numbers? Attention to detail is important in our line of work, and this letter shows a frightening lack of attention to detail! We'd better find another company to deal with."

If grammar, punctuation, and usage aren't your strong points, then use one of the many grammar handbooks on the market. And as with completeness, so with correctness: Share your drafts with readers whose judgment you trust, and ask for their suggestions.

How to punctuate

....

Russell Baker

International Paper asked Russell Baker, winner of the Pulitzer Prize for his book *Growing Up* and for his essays in *The New York Times*, to help you make better use of punctuation, one of the printed word's most valuable tools.

When you write, you make a sound in the reader's head. It can be a dull mumble — that's why so much government prose makes you sleepy — or it can be a joyful noise, a sly whisper, a throb of passion.

Listen to a voice trembling in a haunted room:

"And the silken, sad, uncertain rustling of each purple curtain thrilled me — filled me with fantastic terrors never felt before . . ."

That's Edgar Allan Poe, a master. Few of us can make paper speak as vividly as Poe could, but even beginners will write better once they start listening to the sound their writing makes.

One of the most important tools for making paper speak in your own voice is punctuation.

When speaking aloud, you punctuate constantly — with body language. Your listener hears commas, dashes, question marks, exclamation points, quotation marks as you shout, whisper, pause, wave your arms, roll your eyes, wrinkle your brow.

In writing, punctuation plays the role of body language. It helps readers hear you the way you want to be heard.

"Gee, Dad, have I got to learn all them rules?"

Don't let the rules scare you. For they aren't hard and fast. Think of them as guidelines.

Am I saying, "Go ahead and punctuate as you please"? Absolutely not. Use your own common sense, remembering that you can't expect readers to work to decipher what you're trying to say.

There are two basic systems of punctuation:

1. The loose or open system, which tries to capture the way body language punctuates talk.

2. The tight, closed structural system, which hews closely to the sentence's grammatical structure.

Most writers use a little of both. In any case, we use much less punctuation than they used 200 or even 50 years ago. (Glance into Edward Gibbon's *Decline and Fall of the Roman Empire*, first published in 1776, for an example of the tight structural system at its most elegant.)

No matter which system you prefer, be warned: punctuation marks cannot save a sentence that is badly put together. If you have to struggle over commas, *(continued)* semicolons and dashes, you've probably built a sentence that's never going to fly, no matter how you tinker with it. Throw it away and build a new one to a simpler design. The better your sentence, the easier it is to punctuate.

Choosing the right tool

There are 30 main punctuation marks, but you'll need fewer than a dozen for most writing.

> **"My tools of the trade should be your tools, too. Good use of punctuation can help you build a more solid, more readable sentence."**

I can't show you in this small space how they all work, so I'll stick to the ten most important—and even then can only hit highlights. For more details, check your dictionary or a good grammar.

Comma [,]

This is the most widely used mark of all. It's also the toughest and most controversial. I've seen aging editors almost come to blows over the comma. If you can handle it without sweating, the others will be easy. Here's my policy:

1. Use a comma after a long introductory phrase or clause: *After stealing the crown jewels from the Tower of London, I went home for tea.*

2. If the introductory material is short, forget the comma: *After the theft I went home for tea.*

3. But use it if the sentence would be confusing without it, like this: *The day before I'd robbed the Bank of England.*

4. Use a comma to separate elements in a series: *I robbed the Dover Mint, the Bank of England, the Tower of London and my piggy bank.*

Notice there is no comma before *and* in the series. This is common style nowadays, but some publishers use a comma there, too.

5. Use a comma to separate independent clauses that are joined by a conjunction like <u>and, but, for, or, nor, because</u> or <u>so</u>: *I shall return the crown jewels, for they are too heavy to wear.*

6. Use a comma to set off a mildly parenthetical word grouping that isn't essential to the sentence: *Girls, who have always interested me, usually differ from boys.*

Do not use commas if the word grouping *is* essential to the sentence's meaning: *Girls who interest me know how to tango.*

7. Use a comma in direct address: *Your majesty, please hand over the crown.*

8. And between proper names and titles: *Montague Sneed, Director of Scotland Yard, was assigned the case.*

9. And to separate elements of geographical address: *Director Sneed comes from Chicago, Illinois, and now lives in London, England.*

Generally speaking, use a comma where you'd pause briefly in speech. For a long pause or completion of thought, use a period.

If you confuse the comma with the period, you'll get a run-on sentence: *The Bank of England is located in London, I rushed right over to rob it.*

Semicolon [;]

A more sophisticated mark than the comma, the semicolon separates two main clauses, but it keeps those two thoughts more tightly linked than a period can: *I steal crown jewels; she steals hearts.*

Dash [—] and Parentheses [( )]

Warning! Use sparingly. The dash SHOUTS. Parentheses whisper. Shout too often, people stop listening; whisper too much, people become suspicious of you. The dash creates a dramatic pause to prepare for an expression needing strong emphasis: *I'll marry you—if you'll rob Topkapi with me.*

Parentheses help you pause quietly to drop in some chatty information not vital to your story: *Despite Betty's daring spirit ("I love robbing your piggy bank," she often said), she was a terrible dancer.*

Quotation marks [" "]

These tell the reader you're reciting the exact words someone said or wrote: *Betty said, "I can't tango."* Or: *"I can't tango," Betty said.*

Notice the comma comes before the quote marks in the first example, but comes inside them in the second. Not logical? Never mind. Do it that way anyhow.

Colon [:]

A colon is a tip-off to get ready for what's next: a list, a long quotation or an explanation. This article is riddled with colons. Too many, maybe, but the message is: "Stay on your toes; it's coming at you."

Apostrophe [']

. The big headache is with possessive nouns. If the noun is singular, add *'s: I hated Betty's tango.*

If the noun is plural, simply add an apostrophe after the *s: Those are the girls' coats.*

Punctuation puts body language on the printed page. Show bewilderment with a question mark, a whisper with parentheses, emphasis with an exclamation point.

The same applies for singular nouns ending in *s*, like Dickens: *This is Dickens's best book.*

And in plural: *This is the Dickenses' cottage.*

The possessive pronouns *hers* and *its* have no apostrophe.

If you write *it's*, you are saying *it is.*

Keep cool

You know about ending a sentence with a period (.) or a question mark (?). Do it. Sure, you can also end with an exclamation point (!), but must you? Usually it just makes you sound breathless and silly. Make your writing generate its own excitement. Filling the paper with !!!! won't make up for what your writing has failed to do.

Too many exclamation points make me think the writer is talking about the panic in his own head.

Don't sound panicky. End with a period. I am serious. A period. Understand?

Well . . . sometimes a question mark is okay.

Sexist Language. Here's a subpoint under the heading of "correct writing": You should *avoid sexist language.* Once upon a time, certain occupations were reserved for men alone, and others were reserved for women. More recently, however, we have been able to cross those lines. Now women can be physicians, and men can be nurses. And even more to the point, a woman can be a businessman — or, rather, a businessperson. In fact, if you rely on exclusively male pronouns and nouns in your writing, you risk offending half of your audience.

So what can you do with a language that seems too comfortable with the masculine generic — where *man* pretends to mean the *whole human race*, and *he* claims to include *she*? We suggest you be alert to the following possibilities.

1. Substitute *you* and *they* for *he, his,* and *him* when writing to a mixed-gender audience.

INSTEAD OF: The office worker must know *his* job.

TRY: Office workers must know *their* jobs.

OR: As an office worker, *you* must know *your* job.

2. Substitute nouns for *he, his,* and *him.*

INSTEAD OF: Consider your audience; know *his* background.

TRY: Consider your audience; know the *reader's* background.

3. When you've a mixed audience or subject, mix your pronouns.

INSTEAD OF: The typical student has many options. *He* might, for example, pursue a medical degree. Or *he* could investigate a career in business.

TRY: . . . *She* might, for example, pursue a medical degree. Or *he* could. . . .

4. Simply get rid of *he, his,* and *him* by rephrasing.

INSTEAD OF: The successful CEO makes up *his* mind quickly.

TRY: The successful CEO decides quickly.

Be Concise

Thomas Jefferson once said, "The most valuable of all talents is that of never using two words when one will do." As we said earlier, say what you mean — but say it in as few words as possible. Why? This principle is closely related to both clarity and efficiency.

Remember high school physics? There we learned that a force applied over a large area produces relatively little impact. But the same force applied to a small area penetrates deeply. Snowshoes, for example, distribute your weight so effectively that you remain on top of the deepest snowdrift. Yet visualize the effect of stiletto high heels on a soft pine floor. The physics equation might look like this:

$$\frac{\text{Force}}{\text{Area}} = \text{Impact}$$

We see a similar relationship between ideas and words. In this analogy, our new writing equation looks like this:

$$\frac{\text{Ideas}}{\text{Words}} = \text{Impact}$$

A given idea expressed in many words has relatively little impact. But that same idea expressed in a few well-chosen and well-combined words is penetrating indeed. Of course, you don't want to punch holes in your reader. But in terms of ideas, you want to do something similar. You want your ideas to punch holes in your reader's preconceptions. You want your writing to have an effect, to have impact. You could say:

Whether or not a penny, or any amount of money, is earned or saved, it has the same or at least a similar value, fiscally speaking, in the long run.

But compare that weak and wordy blather with this concise expression:

A penny saved is a penny earned.

Poor Richard had the right idea.[10]

Not only will your ideas have more impact, but you'll save your reader time (and we hope pennies) if you write concisely. In one recent study comparing high-impact writing with bureaucratic writing in a profes-

Drawing by D. Reilly; © 1987 The New Yorker Magazine, Inc.

sional setting, readers took as much as 23 percent less time to read and understand high-impact writing. Twice as many who read the bureaucratic writing felt the need to reread it to understand its meaning.[11]

Try rewriting for impact. Turn the *Chicago Tribune*'s list of "techno-speak" statements in Table 2.4 into their powerful and concise proverbs.

Cut Needless Ideas. One simple rule is this: If your reader doesn't need it, don't say it. In the following example, ask yourself what a busy executive would need to know:

> We feel strongly that Ephemeral Technologies should support existing research programs. Of course, some may disagree, and others may not have strong opinions either way. And whether or not unanimous agreement now exists, we would experience difficulties in maintaining such unanimity. In fact, there is some question as to whether or not we could ever totally agree. . . .

Only the first sentence is meaningful to the person who needs this recommendation—and it should be followed by specific reasons why the writer takes that position. But the fill that follows in the example is wordy, wasteful, and confusing.

Table 2.4 *Revise The Following "Technospeak" Proverbs*

1. Avian species of identical plumage congregate.
2. Freedom from incrustations of noxious substances is contiguous with conformity to divine prescription.
3. Pulchritude possesses solely cutaneous profundity.
4. A superannuated canine is immune to indoctrination in innovative maneuvers.
5. Ululate not over precipitated lacteal secretion.
6. All that coruscates with resplendence will not assay auriferous.
7. The existence of visible vapors from ignited carbonaceous materials confirms conflagration.
8. Mendicants are interdicted from elective recipiency.
9. Probity gratifies reflexively.
10. Male cadavers are unyielding of testimony.
11. Inhabitants of vitreous edifices ill-advisedly catapult petrous projectiles.

Answers: 1. Birds of a feather flock together; 2. Cleanliness is next to godliness; 3. Beauty is only skin deep; 4. You can't teach an old dog new tricks; 5. Don't cry over spilled milk; 6. All that glitters is not gold; 7. Where there's smoke there's fire; 8. Beggars can't be choosers; 9. Virtue is its own reward; 10. Dead men tell no tales; 11. People who live in glass houses shouldn't throw stones.

From "Midterm exam in in technospeak" by Clarence Petersen. Copyright 1987, Chicago Tribune Company. Reprinted with permission.

Cut Wordy Expressions. Another way to be concise is by cutting wordy expressions. Cut them down and, when you can, cut them out. As Mark Twain advised, cut every third word just as a matter of principle: "You have no idea what vigor it adds to style." To learn what we mean, study the list of wordy phrases and concise substitutes in Table 2.5.

Cut "It Is." You also should cut unnecessary "There are" and "It is" openers. You'll find that you not only eliminate two useless delayers, but also often cut additional verbiage.

WORDY: *There are* three conditions limiting the contract.

CONCISE: Three conditions limit the contract.

WORDY: *It is* not possible to get there from here.

CONCISE: You can't get there from here.

Table 2.5

WORDY PHRASES	CONCISE SUBSTITUTES
afford an opportunity	let, allow
along the lines of	like, as
at all times	always
at the present time	now
at this time	now
attached herewith is	here is
consensus of opinion	consensus
costs the sum of	costs
date of the policy	policy date
due to the fact that	because
during the time that	while
during the year of	during, in
enclosed please find	here is
few and far between	seldom, scarce
for a price of	for
for the purpose of	for
for the reason that	because
from the point of view of	as
have a capability	can
have a need for	need
in accordance with your request	as you asked
in connection with	by, for, in
in the amount of	for
in the event that	if
in the neighborhood of	about
in view of the fact that	because, since
is cognizant of	knows
please don't hesitate to write	write
provides guidance for	guides
subsequent to	after
we would ask that	please
with reference (or regard) to	about

Cut "Which" and "That." Another instance of wordiness is the phrase beginning with an unnecessary "which" or "that." When you find either of these words and decide it's not needed for clarity, cut it. And once you cut it, you may find additional cutting is in order.

WORDY:	The shipment *which is* coming in today is late.
CONCISE:	The shipment coming in today is late.
BETTER YET:	Today's shipment is late.
WORDY:	The charges *that* we forwarded were incorrect.
CONCISE:	The charges we forwarded were incorrect.
BETTER YET:	We sent incorrect charges.

Revive Verbs. Of the many paths to wordiness, turning lively verbs into dead noun phrases is one of the worst. Verbs not only do the work in your writing but also do it best when they're unencumbered. Weak, cluttered writing overuses wordy noun phrases where a specific single verb would do. Note the differences.

WORDY:	The board *held a meeting.*
CONCISE:	The board *met.*

WORDY:	The boss will *conduct an investigation.*
CONCISE:	The boss will *investigate.*

WORDY:	You should *be in compliance* with this directive.
CONCISE:	You should *comply* with this directive.

WORDY:	I've *made a decision.*
CONCISE:	I've *decided.*

Now that you've seen these common examples, notice in your own writing how often you kill a perfectly useful verb such as *decide* by turning it into the noun *decision*, which in turn requires the general helper verb *make* — and so you *make a decision.* Sensitize yourself to these murdered verbs and bring them back to life by cutting off the noun endings and the general verb helpers. You'll make your writing not only more concise, but also more lively and precise.

Cut Doubles. One final category of wordiness is *doubling*: using two words that mean approximately the same thing. How often have you written "You have our thanks and appreciation," when either "thanks" or "appreciation" would have done nicely by itself? Look for such doublings and cut one of the two redundant ~~and repetitive~~ (oops!) words. But cut *only* if you can do so without losing precision.

WORDY: Collect and compile important documents.

CONCISE: Compile important documents.

WORDY: The letter is valid and authentic.

CONCISE: The letter is valid.

WORDY: Our program is effective and efficient.

CONCISE: Our program is effective.

(Note: Sometimes you will mean *both* "effective" and "efficient"; in those cases you generally can rely on your reader to know the precise difference between the two. But often we use this trusty twosome to mean merely that "things are going pretty well." *Effective* means just that—without needing any help from *efficient*.)

Be Compelling

Precise, vivid, visual, positive, active, and personal writing: This is what compels your reader to remember your message—and you. And this is the style that prompts your reader to act and even go beyond your immediate purpose.[12] But just what are these six principles, and how might we better use them in our organizational writing?

Be Precise. Over the years, writers in large and impersonal organizations have tended toward large and impersonal writing. We tend to say in vacuous abstractions what might better be said in precise and compelling details. Thus a writer might say, "The new facility is enormous" when she really means, "The new building has 80 percent more working floor space than the old one." Or you might read "The Fribus costs somewhat less than the Fractus" when you'd learn more from "The Fribus costs $210 less than the Fractus."

Of course, you must determine the times when approximations and generalities are appropriate. But when you can't think of a reason for broad generalities, precision helps a reader become more strongly involved in your subject—and thus more strongly moved to believe and act as you desire.

Be Vivid. Another way to write compelling prose is by avoiding dull, overused words that mean so many things that they finally mean—well, *zip!* How many times have you read something like this: "Following the financial report, Ralph gave a *nice* presentation on. . . ."? About all you can imagine is that the writer doesn't want to say anything distasteful about Ralph's presentation. Quite possibly the writer felt differently, and yet she failed to say precisely *how* she viewed Ralph's speech. Instead of *nice*, perhaps she meant *useful, glowing, dynamic, challenging, lively, blistering,* or *factual* — or any *one* of a hundred specific words that could communicate more vividly what she meant and more readily fire her reader's imagination.

You can go even further. You can compare an unknown to a vivid known quantity to help your reader visualize or feel by analogy. "Their contractor was difficult to deal with" becomes "Their contractor was tighter than Ebeneezer Scrooge," a point more effectively portrayed with a precise, imaginative comparison than with a general word such as *difficult.*

Must you be careful not to overstate, to be too vivid, too imaginative? Of course. Any strength taken to excess is destructive. But used wisely, vivid writing helps your reader understand, remember, and act more effectively than does flat, abstract, unimaginative plodding.

Be Visual. Use visual, nonverbal techniques on the page to compel your reader. Try using the following.

- Serial markers such as 1, 2, 3 (or I, II, III; or A, B, C)
- Lists of items in columns, each item beginning with
  1. numbers
  B. letters
  * asterisks
  - hyphens
  • bullets
- CAPITALIZED WORDS for emphasis
- <u>Underlining</u> (or even <u>double underlining</u>)
- Borders
- *Various* **styles** of typeface
- Different print sizes
- Graphics
- Highlighting with color
- Various margins and w h i t e space[13]

Be Positive. Readers react positively to positive writing. Unfortunately, the opposite is also true: Readers react negatively to negative writing. How do you respond to this appeal for your cooperation?

The Nidwit Corporation does not hesitate to discourage its employees from withholding their support for the annual "Don't Say No" anticancer drive.

How much more enthusiastically might you react if you read:

The Smart Corporation encourages its employees to support the annual "Say Yes" drive. Together, we'll help find a cure for cancer.

Yes, each paragraph says the same thing. But the second says it positively—and thus more powerfully.

Be Active. We've already seen one way to write more actively: Bring back to life the vigorous verb buried in a deadened noun phrase. Another way to ensure active writing is by *avoiding the passive voice*. Just what is the difference between the active voice and the passive voice? See if you can sense the difference in this exchange:

BOSS: Why do you insist on overusing the passive voice in your writing, Frisney?

FRISNEY: It is not agreed to by me that the passive voice is overused in my writing, Boss. Various jobs have been done in this manner by me in other corporations, and no complaints were leveled.

BOSS: Perhaps they don't realize, Frisney, that most speaking uses active verbs—and most effective writing does, too.

FRISNEY: Perhaps. But an awful lot of the official writing observed by me has been enscribed in the passive voice. It was thought by me that it was the thing to be done. Besides, what problems have been caused?

We're sure you noticed how unnatural, how inhuman, Frisney's verbs appear. That sort of tortured, passive language produces several unwanted results: It's unnecessarily wordy, it makes the writer appear officious, and it is imprecise because we're not sure who is doing the acting. As a result, passive writing just isn't compelling. You should avoid it when you can, and edit it out of others' writing when you have the chance. (Frisney, by the way, was fired minutes after this exchange, and he hasn't been able to find work since.)

But how can you tell the difference between passive and active verb forms? Simple. First, look for a verb ending with an *-ed* or *-en* (or the simple *-d* and *-n* variants), and following some form of the verb *to be*, such as *is, are, was, has been, will be,* and *should be.* These passive verbs will take this form:

is lik*ed*	*are* driven
was accomplish*ed*	*has been* fir*ed*
will be foun*d*	*should be* rehir*ed*

A second way to identify passive formats is by looking for a reversal of the action in the sentence. Normal active sentences put the *actor* first, the *action* second, and the *acted upon* last. Thus, the active sentence:

The president	signed	the bill.
(actor)	(action)	(acted upon)

But in the passive voice, we reverse the natural order of things, and put the *acted upon* first, the *action* second, and the *actor* third — if we include it at all. And the actor now follows an *added preposition* such as *by* or *through.* Transformed to the passive form, the sentence above becomes:

The bill	*was* sign*ed*	by	the president.
(*acted upon*)	(*action*)	(*added*)	(*actor*)

We have not only twisted things around but also added two more words: *was* and *by.* Two words by themselves aren't much, we admit, but that's a 40-percent increase in wordiness, and wordiness is an enemy of compelling writing. So when you can, stick with the active voice.

Sometimes organizational writers such as Frisney use the passive voice to avoid responsibility, and that's when they drop the "by me" or "by us." They think their readers will assume that things just happen. "The ball was dropped." By whom? "The program was mismanaged." Whodunit?

We read recently about a grotesque mistake committed by members of a hospital operating team: They performed a painful ear operation on a little boy who only needed his tonsils removed. Why? Because they didn't read the identification band on his wrist. And what did the hospital's press release say? "A mistake was made. We are sorry." The hospital administrators regretted the mistake, but they were too self-protective to admit *they* might have made that mistake. And the passive voice is just what they needed to avoid the admission.

Lee Iacocca, on the other hand, realizes that the public is not easily duped by such passive buck-passing. When Chrysler Corporation was caught test-driving new cars with their odometers disconnected, Iacocca went public in the active voice: "Did we screw up? You bet we did."

For those who still believe that "honesty is the best policy," for those who still believe that, in the long run, accountability and accuracy pay off for the organization — for these writers, the active voice is a powerful tool.

Be Personal. Impersonality is another bad habit that seems to permeate the worst organizational writing. We drop the normal, spoken markers of human communication and become "ghost writers" — writers who don't really exist. Thus, we often write "It would be appreciated" instead of the much more human "I would appreciate" or "We would like." Or we write "This office has examined said record" instead of "We've looked over your record."

How can we recover from the habit of impersonal writing? First, as you write, imagine that you're conversing with your reader over a cup of coffee. Remember, one of the important reasons we write in the first place is because we can't be there with the reader; in that case, writing merely takes the place of speaking. Imagine what you'd say if your reader were listening intently not more than five feet away — and then use those words. What specific suggestions might you come up with this way? Try the following:

- use *personal pronouns*, especially *you*
- use your *reader's name* from time to time
- use *contractions* when they sound natural
- ask *questions* when you need information
- write to an *individual reader* rather than all readers

Your reader will sense the sincerity of a personal letter and respond more warmly, more positively, even more voluntarily if you treat her as an individual rather than as a faceless abstraction. And if you can re-create for your reader the illusion that the two of you are sitting together in the same room, talking over a subject of mutual benefit, rather than sitting half a continent apart on different days, then you're much more likely to create a shared concern — and action. That illusion comes more easily when you write in spoken language. Which is the more spoken style?

THIS?	It is desired that the meeting time be forwarded to this office posthaste.
OR THIS?	What time will you begin the meeting?
THIS?	Do not worry. We will take care of the problem right away.
OR THIS?	Don't worry. We'll take care of the problem right away.
THIS?	All taxpayers should remit overdue taxes.
OR THIS?	You should send in your overdue taxes.

In each case, the answer is pretty obvious, but many of us must get used to such direct and personal writing.

A final hint on writing personally: From time to time you may want to handwrite a note at the top or bottom of your correspondence, addressing your reader personally, perhaps referring to something important in her life. "Great presentation yesterday, Doris. Keep up the good work!" A short note like this scrawled at the bottom of a business letter can work wonders for the reader — and thus for the writer.

Be Careful. Avoid unintended secondary meanings. When you write to a colleague with suggestions for improving one of his projects, you may seek to be helpful in saying:

> If you need help with the Crankcase project, don't hesitate to give me a call. I've directed many such projects in the past, with excellent results. . . .

Unfortunately, the reader may infer an unintended message:

> I'm not sure you can handle this project. You are doing a lousy job at the moment. I can move in and show you how to do things and you'll be better off. . . ."

In such sensitive circumstances, a conversation might be more effective at avoiding unintended messages. But when you must put it in writing, read for secondary meanings before sending it off.

How to write a business letter

Some thoughts from Malcolm Forbes

President and Editor-in-Chief of Forbes Magazine

A good business letter can get you a job interview.

Get you off the hook.

Or get you money.

It's totally asinine to blow your chances of getting *whatever* you want—with a business letter that turns people off instead of turning them on.

The best place to learn to write is in school. If you're still there, pick your teachers' brains.

If not, big deal. I learned to ride a motorcycle at 50 and fly balloons at 52. It's never too late to learn.

Over 10,000 business letters come across my desk every year. They seem to fall into three categories: stultifying if not stupid, mundane (most of them), and first rate (rare). Here's the approach I've found that separates the winners from the losers (most of it's just good common sense)—it starts *before* you write your letter:

Know what you want

If you don't, write it down—in one sentence. "I want to get an interview within the next two weeks." That simple. List the major points you want to get across—it'll keep you on course.

If you're *answering* a letter, check the points that need answering and keep the letter in front of you while you write. This way you won't forget anything—*that* would cause another round of letters.

And for goodness' sake, answer promptly if you're going to answer at all. Don't sit on a letter—*that* invites the person on the other end to sit on whatever you want from *him*.

Plunge right in

Call him by name—not "Dear Sir, Madam, or Ms." "Dear Mr. Chrisanthopoulos"—and be sure to spell it right. That'll get him (thus, you) off to a good start.

(Usually, you can get his name just by phoning his company—or from a business directory in your nearest library.)

International Paper asked Malcolm Forbes to share some things he'd learned about writing a good business letter. One rule: Be crystal clear.

Tell what your letter is about in the first paragraph. One or two sentences.

Don't keep your reader guessing or he might file your letter away—even before he finishes it.

In the round file.

If you're answering a letter, refer to the date it was written. So the reader won't waste time hunting for it.

"Be natural. Imagine him sitting in front of you—what would you say to him?"

People who read business letters are as human as thee and me. Reading a letter shouldn't be a chore—*reward* the reader for the time he gives you.

Write so he'll enjoy it

Write the entire letter from his point of view—what's in it for *him*? Beat him to the draw—surprise him by answering the questions and objections he might have.

Be positive—he'll be more receptive to what you have to say.

Be nice. Contrary to the cliché, genuinely nice guys most often finish first or very near it. I admit it's not easy when you've got a gripe. To be agreeable while disagreeing—that's an art.

Be natural—write the way you talk. Imagine him sitting in front of you— what would you *say* to him?

Business jargon too often is cold, stiff, unnatural.

Suppose I came up to you and said, "I acknowledge receipt of your letter and I beg to thank you." You'd think, "Huh? You're putting me on."

The acid test—read your letter *out loud* when you're done. You might get a shock—but you'll know for sure if it sounds natural.

Don't be cute or flippant. The reader won't take you seriously. This doesn't mean you've got to be dull. You prefer your letter to knock 'em dead rather than bore 'em to death.

Three points to remember:

Have a sense of humor. That's refreshing *anywhere*—a nice surprise in a business letter.

Be specific. If I tell you there's a new fuel that could save gasoline, you might not believe me. But suppose I tell you this:

"Gasohol"—10% alcohol, 90% gasoline—works as well as straight gasoline. Since you can make alcohol from grain or corn stalks, wood or wood waste, coal—even garbage, it's worth some real follow-through.

Now you've got something to sink your teeth into.

Lean heavier on nouns and verbs, lighter on adjectives. Use the active voice instead of the passive. Your writing will have more guts.

"I learned to ride a motorcycle at 50 and fly balloons at 52. It's never too late to learn."

Which of these is stronger? Active voice: "I kicked out my money manager." Or, passive voice: "My money manager was kicked out by me." (By the way, neither is true. My son, Malcolm

(continued)

Jr., manages most Forbes money — he's a brilliant moneyman.)

Give it the best you've got

When you don't want something enough to make *the* effort, making *an* effort is a waste.

Make your letter look appetizing — or you'll strike out before you even get to bat. Type it — on good-quality 8½″ × 11″ stationery. Keep it neat. And use paragraphing that makes it easier to read.

Keep your letter short — to one page if possible. Keep your paragraphs short. After all, who's going to benefit if your letter is quick and easy to read?

You.

For emphasis, underline important words. And sometimes indent sentences as well as paragraphs.

Like this. See how well it works? (But save it for something special.)

Make it perfect. No typos, no misspellings, no factual errors. If you're sloppy and let mistakes slip by, the person reading your letter will think you don't know better or don't care. Do you?

Be crystal clear. You won't get what you're after if your reader doesn't get the message.

Use good English. If you're still in school, take all the English and writing courses you can. The way you write and speak can really help — or *hurt*.

If you're not in school (even if you are), get the little 71-page gem by Strunk & White, *Elements of Style*. It's in paperback. It's fun to read and loaded with tips on good English and good writing.

Don't put on airs. Pretense invariably impresses only the pretender.

Don't exaggerate. Even once. Your reader will suspect everything else you write.

Distinguish opinions from facts. Your opinions may be the best in the world. But they're not gospel. You owe it to your reader to let him know which is which. He'll appreciate it and he'll admire you. The dumbest people I know are those who Know It All.

"Don't exaggerate. Even once. Your reader will suspect everything else you write."

Be honest. It'll get you further in the long run. If you're not, you won't rest easy until you're found out. (The latter, not speaking from experience.)

Edit ruthlessly. Somebody ~~has~~ said that words are ~~a lot~~ like inflated money — the more ~~of them that~~ you use, the less each one ~~of them~~ is worth. ~~Right on.~~ Go through your entire letter ~~just~~ as many times as it takes. ~~Search out and~~ Annihilate all unnecessary words~~,~~ ~~and~~ sentences — even ~~entire~~ *paragraphs*.

Sum it up and get out

The last paragraph should tell the reader exactly what you want *him* to do or what *you're* going to do. Short and sweet. "May I have an appointment? Next Monday, the 16th, I'll call your secretary to see when it'll be most convenient for you."

Close with something simple like, "Sincerely." And for heaven's sake sign legibly. The biggest ego trip I know is a completely illegible signature.

Good luck.

I hope you get what you're after.

Sincerely,

Malcolm S Forbes

Be Credible

If your reader is to believe your writing, you must inspire confidence both in you as a writer and in what you say. Your position, your title, your reputation—all of these help your reader decide whether to trust you as a writer; but when your reader doesn't know you, you must establish your credibility even more firmly through what you say and how you say it.

We mentioned earlier that simple mistakes in spelling, grammar, and word usage can hurt your credibility through an undesirable halo effect. But overt bias, sarcasm, exaggeration, and unsupported claims can harm your credibility even more.

Avoid Overt Bias and Sarcasm. A certain amount of bias is inescapable in our lives. But effective organizational writers know how to avoid stepping over the line of acceptable opinion and into a mode of writing that destroys their credibility. Imagine, for example, that you received an interoffice memo containing the following paragraph:

> I recommend, therefore, that you look with some suspicion on the ridiculous claims of the so-called experts down the hall, whose rather spurious efforts at what appears to be objectivity are in fact thinly disguised attempts at achieving a much-broadened power base in support of certain vested interests, which I shall not dignify by responding to. . . .

This sort of biased and sarcastic writing relies upon name-calling and innuendo rather than an examination of the issues at hand. It reveals a level of arrogance and immaturity in the writer that tells the reader, "Don't trust this writer's judgment."

Avoid Exaggeration. If a poll revealed that 51.6 percent of your co-workers favor your plan for a new flextime proposal, avoid the temptation to claim the support of "well over half" or "a solid majority." If you exaggerate in those terms, a cursory glance at the poll itself will destroy your credibility. Instead, refer directly to 51.6 percent, round off to 52 percent, or claim "slightly more than half." Also avoid another form of exaggeration that surrounds accurate numbers with inaccurate implications, intensities, or feelings. One writer might report:

> While only 58 percent of those polled would accept the new parking policy, fully one-third refuse to accept such a difficult change.

But imagine reading the same poll interpreted differently:

> Almost two-thirds of our employees back the new parking proposal, doubling the number still hanging on to the old system.

Support Your Claims. You'll inspire confidence in what you say if you support your views with solid evidence and credible testimonials. If you can give specific examples to illustrate your point — anecdotes, experience, analogies, facts, statistics — then your reader will more readily believe that you know what you're talking about. And be clear about where you found your supporting evidence.

Facts and statistics, however, aren't the only forms of support you should use to make your claims credible. Another effective technique is to refer to the testimony of experts in the area in which you're working. If an expert on morale in large organizations feels your plan for flextime will improve worker satisfaction and productivity, use her testimony. And if Aristotle stated that credibility is a crucial part of one's communication effectiveness (and he did), refer to his opinion in your book on communication skills (and we did).

....

Be Courteous

Because you'll want your reader not only to *believe* you but also to *act* so that you *notice results*, you must treat your reader courteously. Don't demand results or order people around — especially when they can ignore you or take their business elsewhere.

Which works best?

THIS? Any and all bids must be in receipt of this office not later than close of business, March 4th.

OR THIS? Please send us your bid by March 4. Thank you.

Please, thanks, you're welcome, sorry, we'll try, you're right: These are the markers of courteous and effective writing. Why? Because as they honor the reader, they make the reader feel important. Someone who senses you're on her side is likely to be on *your* side — and act on your behalf.

What do you *and* your organization gain from such courteous and compelling writing? You gain the goodwill and support of your readers, a prize worth many times more than the small amount of energy you spend.

Be Consistent. Sometimes you'll run across laughable letters, such as this one from a federal bureaucrat:

```
Dear Sir

Unless payment on your delinquent account is received
in full by close of business, Friday, 21 March, all
accounts and goods under your control will be
confiscated and held until proper disposition can be
made by the courts.

Have a good day.
```

Our point? If you must be "businesslike," don't suddenly veer off into an absurd friendliness. Keep your tone consistent throughout.

These are the principles that will help you use language effectively in organizations — certainly as you speak, but especially as you write. The URBAN process can focus your writing as you begin a task and can be especially valuable as you review your drafts of a project — a letter as well as an oral presentation. As you read your work, ask whether it communicates as you want. Will those who read or listen to you *understand* what you mean, *remember* it, *believe* that it's true and important, and *act* as you want? Finally, will you *note* the results by following up? Has your communication been clear, complete, correct, concise, compelling, credible, and courteous?

Use these principles throughout your career, and you'll find you've earned a reputation as a skillful and effective organizational communicator.

CHAPTER SUMMARY

We began by describing the role that language usage, in both oral and written communication, plays in successful organizations: It keeps the organization alive and helps it to grow. Your writing will be either internal or external to the organization, but ultimately it's *your* writing; corporations don't write — *you* do. And studies prove that if you can write and speak effectively, you will stand out in a field of mediocre communicators.

Writing is a process composed of three stages: prewriting, writing, and rewriting. Prewriting involves research, recording, and thought. Working through "writer's block" involves techniques that produce raw material to be perfected later. And rewriting involves a combination of revision and proofreading.

Use our URBAN project to ensure that your *reader* will:

Understand
Remember
Believe
Act—and *you* as *writer* will:
Note results.

The principles of URBAN writing are these: Be clear, complete, correct, concise, compelling, credible, and courteous.

Keep these principles of effective language use in mind as you learn the techniques of preparing successful presentations in the next chapter.

MEASURING SUCCESS

1. Assume you have just landed a job in a large corporation's training and education division. Knowing that you took this communication course, your boss asks you to draft a brief memo that describes both the *importance* of clear writing and several *techniques* to help the company's employees write more clearly. As you write, use the very techniques you describe.

2. Rewrite one of the following paragraphs so that it's clear to the average reader in your class.

   a. It would be appreciated if the task of compiling and amassing corporate records were to be simplified by the incremental removal of any and all files, dockets, and/or catalogues referring to business undertakings accomplished prior to the advent of the last decade.
   b. As all employees are cognizant of, vehicles belonging to and exclusively the property of Hubbahubba Industries are not to be utilized in any wanton manner, or in any manner which recklessly endangers either the vehicle, other property, or Hubbahubba employees.
   c. In the event of unforeseen incendiary accidents, all personnel, whether engaged in productive endeavors within the confines

of the plant or recreating in more personal environs, are hereby and forthwith reminded to be at all times within effective and efficient reach of fire-retardant mechanisms.

3. Revise these sentences so that they contain strong, active verbs:

a. Work should be initiated by 7:30 in the morning.
b. Our club has been joined by the Dullards.
c. The call was made by the official.
d. Far too much money was expended on this project.
e. The computer has not yet been received.
f. The appendix is forwarded for your review.
g. It is estimated by the doctor that the operation will be survived by the patient.
h. The tire should be kicked and the fire should be lit.
i. All personnel are reminded that records are not to be falsified.

4. One of your peers is writing a memo and asks you to revise it as you see fit. You know the memo will address an audience that is almost equally men and women. How would you revise the following sentences to avoid sexist language?

a. The competent technician knows his equipment.
b. If your secretary continues to type poorly, report her to the manager.
c. Each salesman should keep his records as accurately as possible.

5. Revive the comatose verbs in these sentences:

a. The judge's ruling is applicable to all businesses.
b. We insist on the examination of your bank account.
c. Have perseverance in the accomplishment of your task.
d. Your laboratory has received permission to carry out experiments on live vegetables.
e. Please present a summary of your findings.

6. Find a short sample of organizational writing that violates one or more of the principles of URBAN writing. Revise it and write a paragraph explaining your revision's advantages.

7. If your instructor chooses, take part in the Decco Corporation exercises that follow over the course of the semester.

DECCO CORPORATION

P.O. BOX 1574 · LONG BEACH, CA 90815 · PHONE (213) 529-0990

TO: , Director, Training and Development

FROM: , Vice President, Human Resources

SUBJECT: Communication Training Seminars

DATE:

In our telephone conversation last week, you proposed offering a
series of seminars on effective communication for all Decco employees. I am interested in the idea, but I need more information
before I can commit the necessary resources.

What evidence do you have that communication training actually
improves performance, and what topics would be covered? I need a
response by next week.

....

Assignment 1

DECCO CORPORATION

P.O. BOX 1574 · LONG BEACH, CA 90815 · PHONE (213) 529-0990

TO: , Director, Training and Development

FROM: , Vice President, Human Resources

SUBJECT: Outside Consulting Services for Training Services

DATE:

Thank you for the information you provided on the importance of communication training. You've sold me on the idea of a series of seminars for our employees.

Please draft a letter for me to send to Staley & Associates, 30 East Hunter Avenue, Newport, CO 80901, to request a training proposal. I've spoken with their principal consultants, and they're interested in working with us. Plan on six seminars and the budget range we discussed.

I'd like the letter to go out by next week.

Assignment 2

DECCO CORPORATION

■ ■
P.O. BOX 1574 · LONG BEACH, CA 90815 · PHONE (213) 529-0990

TO: , Director, Training and Development

FROM: , Vice President, Human Resources

SUBJECT: Letter of Acceptance from Consulting Company

DATE:

Attached is the letter of acceptance from Staley & Associates.
I'm pleased with the way you've handled this assignment, and I'm
looking forward to a positive training experience for Decco employees!

STALEY & ASSOCIATES   COMMUNICATION CONSULTANTS

(Date)

(Instructor)
Vice President, Human Resources
Decco Corporation
P.O. Box 1574
Long Beach, CA 90815

Dear   :

Thank you for your recent letter confirming our agreement to conduct a series of six seminars on "Communication That Works," covering:

Seminar 1	Listening Conscientiously
Seminar 2	Writing Effectively
Seminar 3	Speaking Powerfully
Seminar 4	Communicating Interpersonally
Seminar 5	Meeting Efficiently
Seminar 6	Managing Conflict

We're looking forward to the opportunity to work with your employees at Decco Corporation. We know from our experience with organizations around the country that our "Communication That Works" series can really make a difference!

Sincerely,

Robert S. Staley J.

Robert Stephens Staley II, Ph.D.
Principal Consultant

Constance Courtney Staley

Constance Courtney Staley, Ph.D.
Principal Consultant

---

30 E. HUNTER AVENUE • NEWPORT, COLORADO 80901 • (111) 444-4567

DECCO CORPORATION
....
P.O. BOX 1574 · LONG BEACH, CA 90815 · PHONE (213) 529-0990

TO: _____, Director, Training and Development

FROM: _____, Vice President, Human Resources

SUBJECT: Report on Communication at Decco

DATE:

As a result of our work on the communication seminar series, I've become very interested in the subject of communication in organizations. Undoubtedly, there are many areas in which we could improve communication here at Decco.

To help us target one of those areas, I'd like you to prepare a report on some aspect of communication that you believe is important, but underemphasized, at Decco. I'll expect not only research, but also your recommendations that pertain directly to our company.

If I like what you do with this assignment, I'll let you present your ideas to all Decco managers. I'd like to meet with you sometime soon to hear about possible topics. Stop by my office soon to arrange a convenient time.

Assignment 3

....

Notes

1. For example, see Henry H. Beam, "Good Writing: An Underrated Executive Skill," *Human Resource Management* 20 (Spring 1981): 2–7.

2. H.W. Hildebrandt et al., "An Executive Appraisal of Courses Which Best Prepare One for General Management," *The Journal of Business Communication* 19 (Winter 1982): 5–15; James C. Bennett and Robert J. Olney, "Executive Priorities for Effective Communication in an Information Society," *The Journal of Business Communication* 23 (Spring 1986): 13–22; J. David Hunger and Thomas L. Wheelen, "A Recruiter's Question: How Does the Bachelor's Degree in Business Compare to the MBA?" *Human Resource Management* 19 (Fall 1980): 2–15; Bruce B. MacMillan, "Writing Your Way to the Top," *Marketing Communications* 11 (May 1986): 76–77.

3. Bennett and Olney, "Executive Priorities," 13–22.

4. Based on information extracted from the "Dartnell Target Survey," Dartnell Institute of Business Research, Chicago, March 1987.

5. Edward P. Bailey, Jr., *Writing Clearly* (Columbus, OH: Charles E. Merrill, 1984), 25–27. We highly recommend Bailey for some of the most useful descriptions available of the reading and writing processes.

6. Ilena De Vos, "Getting Started: How Expert Writers Do It," *Training and Development Journal* 42 (October 1988): 18–19.

7. See Buck Joseph, "Business Writer's Block," *Supervisory Management*, October 1985, 25–31; this article is a comprehensive discussion of writer's block in business and the professions—including causes, effects, and, most important, "ways to get unstuck."

8. E.B. White quoted in Kenneth Roman and Joel Raphaelson, *Writing that Works* (New York: Harper & Row, 1981), 4.

9. Bailey, *Writing Clearly*, 64–65.

10. Benjamin Franklin's *Poor Richard's Almanac* contains many concise and memorable expressions.

11. James Suchan and Robert Colucci, "An Analysis of Communication Efficiency Between High-Impact and Bureaucratic Communication," *Management Communication Quarterly* 2(4) (May 1989): 454–484.

12. MacMillan, "Writing Your Way," 76.

13. Adapted from Paul R. Timm, *Managerial Communication*, 2nd ed. (Englewood Cliffs, NJ: Prentice-Hall, 1986), 279.

Chapter 3 ✎→ **Reading Efficiently in Organizations: A Self-Teaching Exercise** 🖎 The

modern executive drowns in a flood of information. He or she is a decision maker, and every decision has a host of inputs. Pressure groups must be heard. Data must be evaluated. Recommendations must be accommodated and fiats absorbed.

And they are all embodied in vast stacks of paper.

✉ — *Thomas A. Easton* ✍ ▌t's true.

We're surrounded by information. According to one source, the amount of available information doubles every four to five years. Any weekday edition of *The New York Times* contains more information than you would have come across in an entire lifetime in seventeenth-century England.[1] Staying afloat in this vast sea of data is no easy task.

Regardless of your career field, the way in which you gather, assimilate, and dispense information will play a key role in your organizational success. The average worker spends up to two hours per day reading charts, graphs, forms, computer screens, and manuals.[2] As you move up the career ladder, you will be required to spend increasing amounts of time reading books, professional journals, newspapers, proposals, reports, feasibility studies — you name it, you'll be reading it.

In fact, according to a survey of 3,000 executives conducted by Chicago's Dartnell Institute for Business Research, the average corporate executive spends as many as four months each year in reading and answering correspondence.[3] Fully 83 percent of CEOs reported that they "did not have time to keep up with the reading in their field."[4]

THE IMPORTANCE OF EFFICIENT READING

Throughout your career, you'll read for a variety of reasons: for *survival*, for *advancement*, and simply for *fun*.[5]

Reading for survival includes memos and reports from superiors and subordinates, letters sent by customers and outside organizations, and trade journals in your particular field — everything you need to know to do your job well. If you are a training specialist, you'll want to keep a watchful eye on journals such as *Training* and *Training and Development*. If you're in the marketing business, you'll need to stay tuned to *The Journal of Marketing Research* and *Marketing News*. And, of course, if you're a health care specialist, you'll need to keep abreast of medical breakthroughs in the *New England Journal of Medicine* among a host of others.

Reading for advancement pertains more to future than current events. Perhaps even more demanding, your reading in this category will include publications recommended by your boss, information you must know to move up the organizational ladder, and material to help you polish your skills and remove your deficiencies.

Reading for fun, on the other hand, includes business literature that results from fascination rather than obligation — for example, you never miss an issue of *Computer World* even though its contents are unrelated to your work.[6]

With all of these demands on your time, reading efficiently will be to your advantage. A reading expert once calculated that if every American older than fifteen were trained in reading techniques for one month, the hours saved — figured at the modest rate of fifty cents per hour — would save the nation $5 billion.[7] Of course, you won't have a month to spend on this topic in class, but we believe the "eyes-on" approach in this chapter will help. Think about these general guidelines before we start.[8]

1. Successful organizational communicators find time to read. They sometimes close the door and eat lunch at their desks while reading, or they take an extra hour before or after the normal workday. Reading is not viewed as simply "entertainment" or a pastime; it is a necessary and legitimate work activity.

2. Select reading material that suits the amount of time you have available. If you are to be at a meeting that starts in ten minutes, don't begin perusing the company's 150-page annual report. Instead, look at the two-page journal article you've been meaning to skim. Although breaks sometimes are necessary if the reading task is long, too many interruptions can disturb comprehension.

3. Before you begin a reading task, glance over the material. Look at division headings, opening paragraphs, and the synopsis. In other words, get the lay of the land first; it always helps to look at the road map before you begin the trip. You may even decide that your time would be better spent reading something else.

4. Have you ever read an entire page of something only to turn to the next page and realize you have no idea of what you just read? Unfortunately, reading on automatic pilot is something we all do, but we need to create ways to conquer this habit. Highlighting passages sometimes involves us more in the reading process. And reading while standing may help you to focus your attention on what you're reading. Despite back problems, John F. Kennedy often read while standing at a lectern to improve his concentration (he is reputed to have read at the remarkable rate of 1,000 words per minute).[9]

5. Read when distractions and noise are at a minimum; have your phone calls held, use earplugs if necessary, and find a quiet, well-lit spot.

6. If you find you can't manage the amount of information you need to process, consider an alternative. Delegate some of your reading tasks to a subordinate, asking him to skim and summarize articles for you. Subscribe to a news service or a news data base. Or hire someone to help you.

7. Attitude makes a difference. If you expect to learn something

and you feel positive about the reading tasks in front of you, you *will* be a more productive reader.

Throughout this chapter, we'll ask you to participate in reading exercises so that we can make some important points, and so that you can measure your reading speed and comprehension. These exercises are based on short articles that you'll find interesting from *Business Week Careers*, a publication for students. Each article is written at a similar level of difficulty and contains useful information to help prepare you for your chosen career. After each exercise, we'll ask you a few short questions. When you've finished answering, you can find the correct answers in the answer key at the end of this chapter.

....

Pretest

Before we continue our discussion of reading, let's pause for a pretest to check your reading speed and comprehension right now. Read the following article, "Blueprint for Career Planning," at your normal rate, and time yourself with an athletic stopwatch, a digital wristwatch with a built-in stopwatch, or a watch with a second hand. At the end of the chapter, locate the words-per-minute chart (Table 3.1) to find out how you did. (The average reading rate for this article is 250 words per minute. You should aim for a minimum comprehension score of 70 percent.)

After you read the pretest article and answer the comprehension check questions, calculate a *reading efficiency score* by multiplying your number of words per minute (from the words-per-minute chart) by your comprehension score. For example, if you read the pretest article at 280 words per minute and answered 8 of 10 questions correctly on the comprehension check, your reading efficiency score would be 224:

$$(\text{words per minute})\,(\text{percent correct answers}) =$$

$$(280)\,(80\%) = 224.$$

Keep this *baseline* reading efficiency score in mind as you progress through our discussion. We'll ask you to check your reading rate and your comprehension after each reading selection. Try the techniques we suggest and then take the posttest at the end of this chapter to measure improvement in your reading efficiency.

Blueprint for Career Planning

Marilyn Moats Kennedy

Don't wait. Start now to master career planning skills which, once acquired, will serve you throughout your working lifetime.

Graduation from college confers a degree, but not a career plan. Career planning is either not taught in most colleges or is taught by people with little real business experience. They can tell a graduate which are the hot fields (by "hot" they mean positions in specific disciplines in which companies are recruiting and hiring people), but typically have few resources and less interest in helping someone decide what kind of industry or job he or she should be looking for. This is especially true for the student who wants a job in business but was not an undergraduate business major.

A good example of this type of situation is Bob Seevers. He got his degree in history with a minor in accounting but didn't really know what he wanted to do. The university's accounting department assumed he would work for a public accounting firm so he could be licensed as a certified public accountant. Seevers, however, didn't think licensing was necessary unless he wanted to spend his life in public accounting.

Seevers went to every campus recruiting interview regardless of the company or the job. He also went to interviews his parents lined up through their friends, but nothing seemed right. The day after graduation Seevers finally realized what was keeping him from getting a job. It was his indecision.

Even though Seevers had been an excellent student, he had not considered what was most important in his job search. He had only the vaguest idea of the possibilities for using his skills. He knew that historians got PhDs and taught and some banks hired them. He also had a good idea of what went on in public accounting firms and in accounting departments in companies, but not enough to make him feel secure in choosing one over the other. Seevers needed a plan and he needed more information.

Don't wait to begin serious career planning until after graduation. You can and should start now to master the skills which, once acquired, will serve you throughout your working lifetime — even if you change directions frequently. In the current unpredictable economic climate no one can expect to spend his or her entire career with one company. It's difficult to predict which *(continued)* companies will be prosperous in ten years. Most important, it's difficult to predict at 22 what will be of greatest interest to you at 32 or 42. Career planning is a necessity.

Career planning means applying the same research and analytical techniques to your skills and interests as companies apply to their management problems. It means building contacts with people who can help you. Most important, it involves periodically evaluating your strategies to see if you are going in the direction you planned. At the simplest level, career planning answers four questions.

- What skills do I have that I want to use?
- What kind of organization do I want to work for? Are there organizations I would be unhappy or uncomfortable working for?
- What are my goals? Do I want to be a doer or a manager? How high would I like to rise? Would I like to run my own business someday? Am I interested in the fast track or do I have other personal goals?
- How can I build contacts with people who can help me over a lifetime?

Let's examine these areas one at a time.

Skills

What are your skills? A skill is something that you can do or something you know well. We separate "knowledge about" skills from "how-to" skills because it helps you analyze them more easily.

When you look at your major in college you're looking at what we call "knowledge about" skills rather than "how-to" skills. Although a new graduate in English literature has learned a great deal about the subject area, there is a limited practical application for that knowledge. More important are your "how-to" skills. What you do on a job has less to do with what you studied in college than it does with your "how-to" skills.

Ask yourself what "how-to" skills you have. Are you good at persuading people to do what you want them to do? You may have some ability in selling or marketing. Do you enjoy analysis and problem solving? Do you sometimes puzzle over problems and work out solutions even though they aren't your problems and no one has asked you to? The skills you employ when no one is telling you what to do are the ones that, combined with your "knowledge about" skills, should be the foundation of your career.

What did you learn in your college activities? What do these activities tell you about your skills? Think carefully about the roles you played in extracurricular activities.

It is important in your career to concentrate on the skills you most enjoy using rather than the ones people tell you are your best or the most sought-after in the job market. Here's why. If you know that computers are the rage and that most people who go into the information systems fields do well financially, the temptation to choose a computer career is strong. Consider, however, how uncompetitive you will be in this area if you are there merely because it is popular while co-workers think computers the most fascinating and exciting field in which to work. You would quickly be identified as a disinterested hanger-on, not someone in the mainstream. In order to be competitive you have to use the skills which are more than just an interest, but approach being a passion.

How do you find those skills — especially if what you've studied doesn't appear to lend itself to definitions? Start with a thorough reading of *What Color is Your Parachute?* by Richard N. Bolles. Bolles clearly explains how to look for your practical how-to skills. This self-analysis will do more for building your career foundations than two days' worth of vocational interest tests because it will force you to make choices.

Obviously this goes against the common wisdom that says as you start your career you should leave your options open. If you don't make some upfront skills choices how will you know you've found a good opportunity? You have to know what you're looking for. That's why the process of making skills choices is so important.

Most new graduates spend much of their job-hunting time writing resumes. The best-kept secret in career planning — and it should not be a secret — is that if you know what you're looking for and the skills you want to use, nothing can keep you from getting a job. If you don't know what skills you want to use nobody can help you. A rough estimate is that you should spend 40% of your job-hunting time on skills analysis. Where do I want to work? What style and values would I like the people I work with and for to have?

Selecting an organization

Many otherwise savvy people say, "I can get along with anyone. I'm very flexible." That's not true. Even at 18 you had certain values and preferences. If you don't take these into account in both career planning and job hunting you'll get less satisfaction from your work than you might. Before you begin any serious job search ask yourself the following questions.

- Do I like working for a large structured organization or do I prefer a more informal organization? Do I see myself speaking directly with top management or moving through the channels?
- Do I want to work for a nonprofit organization instead of a business? There are differences in style.
- At this point in my career do I want a formal training program or an opportunity to learn by doing?
- Do I want a staff job (cost center) or a line job (profit center)?
- What kinds of people do I get along with best? Do I like to be part of a group or work on my own?
- Do I need to work for a company with a name? Will it bother me if when I talk about my organization people say, "Who?"

In other words, make choices before you seriously job hunt. You do this to narrow the number of things you'll examine at one time. Making these choices means that the answers become part of your long-term career plan. If, on your first job, you find that too much structure, or too little, dampens your spirit you'll know that your next company needs to be looser or vice versa.

(continued)

Define your goals

Despite the economy you need three-to-five-year goals. Otherwise you may keep your first job long after you've stopped learning. What do you want to learn that will help you move on to a second or third job? Do you think you might eventually be interested in managing people? Are any of the jobs you might consider springboards to management or are they stepping-stones to greater excellence in providing the same service?

In the past, companies have talked about career ladders. This is especially inappropriate in times of business uncertainty because if the business is retrenching or going into bankruptcy neither a ladder nor a path will be useful. Instead you have to think of yourself as moving over a much wider range than in the past. Think in terms of flexibility if you're going to develop a career plan. For instance, if you are interested in publishing consider the different kinds of publishing.

Your education doesn't stop at graduation. Your goals must include ways of keeping up with the state-of-the-art in your chosen field in terms of both technical knowledge and people skills. At the beginning of a career it's difficult to imagine that you could fall behind. In highly technical fields, however, this could easily happen in fewer than five years.

Develop lifetime contacts

If you ask successful people what has helped them most in their careers many will say, "contacts." By this they mean knowing people with influence who have put them in touch with others in influential positions who helped them further their career goals. Some people call this networking, others contact building, still others connecting. However you describe the process the basic principle is this: your future career will depend as much on who you know as what you know. This should cause no cynicism on your part because the people you need to know are available for you to meet! The inner circle is certainly not closed to you.

The people who can help in whatever field you choose are the ones in your industry or skill group who check in regularly at the monthly meetings of trade and professional associations. Fortunately, these trade associations are all over the country, some throughout the world. The first place to look for career information is at these meetings. The people who can tell you about jobs before they're posted are there. They are also the ones who can suggest contacts to give you information. If you make up your mind now, before you're working full time, that you're going to explore the trade and professional associations in your area of interest you'll begin to build the kind of working network needed to help insure against unemployment—or at least shorten the length of it.

The reason networking is such an important part of career planning is that it can provide the latest information. What happened at the office today is a topic of conversation. Who's coming and who's going is also mentioned.

More jobs are passed around at these meetings than most people realize. Best of all, the only qualification for attending is an interest in the subject. Once you've decided which areas are most interesting you're ready to attend the meetings. The college library should have a copy of *Gale's Guide to Trade, Business and Professional Associations*. It's an excellent reference book because it provides names and national headquarters addresses for thousands of these organizations. Call the headquarters for the name of the contact in your area. People are generally friendly and welcome newcomers at meetings as potential members. Building contacts can shorten the time it takes to get a job and later to change jobs.

Six Career Planning Tips

1. Listen to everyone who offers advice. If it seems sensible, check it out. Beware of anyone who suggests that one career plan fits all needs. There's nothing more personal to you than your career plan. There is no way to issue career plans in general.

2. Flexibility doesn't mean not making choices. It means looking for more than one path to the same end result.

3. Ignore anyone who tells you that in this economy you should be grateful to get anything. That's your life someone is talking about! You should be making more careful choices than in better economic times because you may feel the need to stay with a job longer than in the past.

4. Never miss an opportunity to talk with anyone, at whatever level, in a field or a specific organization that interests you. If you sell that person with your interest and enthusiasm, who knows what door he or she may open or what ways she or he might think of to help? Sell everybody on what you're trying to do.

5. Find people who graduated two to five years ago with your major. What are they doing now? What do they like or dislike about the choices they made? What advice do they have for you?

6. Don't be swayed from trying to do the thing you've identified as potentially the most satisfying or what you always dreamed of doing. For example, although it's difficult to break into network television or investment banking, the beginning of your career is the time to try.

Finally, remember that career planning takes time in the beginning. Once you've laid the foundation it will be a matter of keeping up what you've begun. Without a career plan you'll always be dependent on others for direction. Who of us wouldn't rather be in control and independent? The responsibility for the success or failure of your career is in your hands.

Marilyn Moats Kennedy is the founder and managing partner of Career Strategies, located in Evanston, Ill. She specializes in writing about careers.

For additional information

Jobs 82/83 by William N. Yeomans. Perigee Books. 332 pages; $6.95.
Job & Career Building by Richard Germann and Peter Arnold. Ten Speed Press. 256 pages; $6.95.
The Dewar's Guide to Career Development. Dewar's Career Guide, Suite 1100, 110 East 59 St., New York, N.Y. 10022. 39 pages; $1.00.

Pretest Check

Circle your response for each question. Then check your answers and compute the number of questions you answered correctly, allowing ten points for each correct answer.

1. Career planning is:
    a. best begun after graduation when you've completed your major field of study.
    b. what you learn in college.
    c. researching and analyzing your skills and interests.
2. In career planning, it is important to:
    a. make a career plan now and stick to it.
    b. periodically evaluate your strategies to see if you are going in the direction you planned.
    c. listen to what your professors tell you about what kind of industry or job you should be looking for.
3. Which of the following is one of the four questions that career planning answers?
    a. What salary would I like to make?
    b. What do I expect to be doing in ten years?
    c. What are my goals?
4. According to Kennedy, the best kept secret in career planning is:
    a. if you know what you're looking for and the skills you want to use, nothing can keep you from getting a job.
    b. evaluating your skills isn't a difficult job.
    c. selecting an organization to work for is harder than you think.
5. *Networking, contact building,* and *connecting*:
    a. are three skills you need to know in career planning.
    b. all relate to the same career-planning skill.
    c. relate to the impenetrable "inner circle."
6. Which of the following is *not* a tip offered by the author?
    a. Seeking advice from people who graduated two to five years ago is a good idea.
    b. If you run into roadblocks, don't give up your original goal. The beginning of your career is the time to try for your "dream" job.
    c. "It's who you know, not what you know that counts" is an inaccurate statement.
7. According to the author, you should:
    a. ignore people who tell you to take any job in a poor economy.

      b. plan to spend most of your initial career-planning time writing the best resumé you can.

      c. be able to remain in your chosen career forever if you follow the right career planning.

8. Networking's real value as a career-planning technique is that it:

      a. can provide the latest information.

      b. helps you get around the country to professional meetings.

      c. ensures against unemployment.

9. Which of the following is a true statement?

      a. Only plan your goals one year at a time because the economy changes from year to year.

      b. Concentrate on the skills you enjoy using, not on what other people believe you're good at.

      c. Selling everyone on your career plans will cause others to perceive you as a boring person.

10. When you begin your career planning, you should:

      a. focus on your "how to" rather than your "knowledge about" skills.

      b. plan to spend your career at one organization.

      c. decide on one pathway to your goals and stick to it.

THE READING PROCESS

You first learned to read a long time ago, right? Perhaps you remember sitting with your fellow "Bluebirds" or "Redbirds" in school and feeling the exhilaration of taking your turn at what seemed like a mysterious and magical process. Chances are you've been relatively satisfied with the skills you developed because you've been using them for many years. By now they're second nature. Research tells us that the average adult reads at a rate of approximately 250 words a minute, depending on the difficulty of the material. That same adult, however, is capable of reading 500 words per minute — and, with practice, 750, then 900, and even 1,500 words per minute.[10]

We have several purposes in this self-teaching exercise: to help you understand the reading process, to identify reasons why you may not read as efficiently as you could, and to give you a means of measuring and improving your reading speed and comprehension — right before your very eyes. In other words, this exercise is intended to produce immediate results as well as long-term awareness that will benefit you in your future career.

Let's begin our discussion with a brief explanation of the reading process. When we read, a great deal more goes on than most of us are aware of. As an analogy, consider watching a motion picture:

Just as the motion picture is made up of many still pictures flashed before us rapidly, so our reading is a series of visual impressions carried to our brain in a rapid sequence. We stop for each glance and then move on for another glance at another word or phrase. Reading rate, then, is a combination of the amount we see at each glance [or eye span], the length of time we hesitate for each eye fixation [rate of perception], and the speed with which the eye can move and focus on another unit of material. . . . The potential maximum reading speed of any individual is unknown.[11]

Few of us have had specialized training in improving our reading efficiency; but still, why don't we reach our potential as readers? What slows us down? See if any of the following problems apply to you.[12]

1. **Lip reading**—pronouncing each word audibly or inaudibly. Suggestion: Place a finger over your lips to break this habit.
2. **Individual word reading**—concentrating on each word rather than the ideas behind the words. Suggestion: Try to grasp the meaning of whole phrases at a time.
3. **Generic reading**—failing to adjust your reading rate to the difficulty and purpose of the material. We'll talk more about reading flexibility later.
4. **Head rotating**—moving your entire head as your eyes sweep each line. This is a tiring habit. Suggestion: Hold your head in your hands and move only your eyes.
5. **Word halting**—stopping for unfamiliar words. If you can't determine a word's meaning from its context, look it up *after* you've finished reading instead of breaking your rhythm. And, of course, if word halting is a frequent problem for you, you may need to take steps to build up your vocabulary.
6. **Tunnel vision**—becoming so fixated on the words that you overlook headings, italics, bold print, and other cues about importance. Suggestion: Preview material so that you know what to expect.
7. **Backtracking**—rereading individual words, phrases, and sections to ensure understanding. Unfortunately, this practice can become habitual. Suggestion: Concentrate on moving forward

with comprehension. Don't yield to the temptation to backslide.

8. **Reading on automatic pilot** — we already discussed this problem; concentration, of course, is the remedy.

READING TECHNIQUES

Now that we've identified potential problems, let's consider ways to improve reading efficiency. We mentioned the idea of *reading flexibility*. Just what does that mean?

Earlier, we discussed three major reasons why you'll read as an organizational communicator: for survival, for advancement, and for fun. Of course, we could be more specific. Not all the materials you read for survival or for advancement will require the same level of concentration. Some will be long and difficult; others will be short and simple. Reading for fun, on the other hand, typically requires less thought investment, and yet you may work quite hard at it, because you're reading out of your own fascination. What all this means is that you should read different materials differently. According to actor, comedian, and reading expert Dr. Bill Cosby, *previewing*, *skimming*, and *clustering* are reading techniques worth considering.[13]

Previewing

Previewing quickly to get a bird's-eye view of divisions, headings, and so forth is a good idea whenever you begin reading anything longer than a memo or letter. But it's a particularly good idea if you're about to take on a challenging reading assignment in the survival or advancement category. For example, you need to read lengthy personnel reports on each of the seventy-five people in your division of the company, and you're on a tight schedule. Although previewing the entire stack may limit your comprehension by 50 percent, you'll need only 10 percent of the time you'd normally take. But be sure to flag reports that deserve more time later. Here is Cosby's advice on previewing: *carefully read the first two paragraphs, next read the first sentence only of each successive paragraph (likely topic sentences), and finally read the entire last two paragraphs.* You won't know everything in each report, but you also won't waste time reading unnecessary material. Previewing, in other words, is a valuable time-management technique.

....

Skimming

Skimming is worthwhile for the same reasons, even though you'll again come up short on comprehension — approximately 50 percent — in half the time. Skimming works best for light reading (from the entertainment category, for example) or for material that you're rereading. *To skim: Use your eyes like magnets; think of them sweeping across each line, picking up a few words per line.* Again, you sacrifice comprehension for time, but sometimes it's worth the bargain. Try skimming the paragraph below. You'll get the gist of it in just a few seconds.

The Personnel Department at Widefield Electronics
announces an opening in the Data Management Division.
No management experience is necessary.
Opportunities for advancement are excellent.
Send your resume with two letters of reference
to Widefield Electronics, 1410 Hartford Avenue,
Denver, Colorado 80101.

....

Clustering

Cosby's third suggestion seeks to increase your eye span by *clustering*. Rather than plodding along word by word, train your eyes to focus on groups of as many as three or four words at once. With practice, clustering can help improve speed *and* comprehension. Here's how your eyes might divide the paragraph above by clustering.

The Personnel Department at Widefield Electronics
announces an opening in the Data Management Division.
No management experience is necessary.
Opportunities for advancement are excellent.
Send your resume with two letters of reference
to Widefield Electronics, 1410 Hartford Avenue,
Denver, Colorado 80101.

RECOGNIZING ORGANIZATIONAL PATTERNS

Now that we have discussed "mechanical" techniques to improve your reading, we want to focus on the internal mechanics of *what* you read. You'll be a more successful reader if you can climb into your writer's mind and use her clues to help you find your way. We'll discuss the four most widely used organizational patterns in business and professional publications. But before we focus on entire articles, we want to work on a smaller scale by directing your attention to paragraphs, the building blocks of articles and books.

Paragraphs are an arbitrary convention: They help the reader break long, complicated matter into manageable chunks. As you attack these chunks of information, try this three-part strategy:[14]

1. Determine the paragraph's subject or *topic*.
2. Identify the statement, generalization, or *main point* the author is trying to make about the subject.
3. Locate the *evidence* offered to support the main idea.

Let's try this strategy in the article "Business in the Year 2001."

Looking back from the year 2001, I can still recall how apprehensive some of us felt in the 1980s, when robots and automated factories were just starting to displace substantial numbers of people. Even now, it seems incredible that we got through to the turn of the century intact, despite the enormity of the underemployment and dislocations suffered by millions of workers, white-collar as well as blue-collar. Older men and women were especially hurt. Often they resisted retraining at a time when the flexibility to adapt to change was becoming clearly vital; other times, they were the unwitting victims of top management's growing use of computers, which made middle managers increasingly superfluous.[15]

Now see whether you agree with our analysis.

Topic: The turn-of-the-century transition in business
Main point: The transition was difficult.
Evidence: a. Workers were fearful of automation.
       b. Underemployment and dislocations were problems for millions of people.

c. Older workers refused to retrain to meet demands for change.

d. Middle managers became superfluous.

Although analyzing paragraphs may seem tedious work, this skill is worth practicing. Learning to understand paragraphs quickly will increase your overall speed and comprehension when it comes to longer works you'll need to read.

Perhaps our best advice to help you with the reading tasks you will face in business or your profession is this: Watch for the four organizational patterns most often used in business writing: *problem–solution, persuasive, informative*, and *instructional*.[16] Many writers of business and professional articles follow these organizational patterns. Once you're familiar with the limited kinds of patterns used, it will become easier to make sense of what you read.

To understand what we mean, look at the numbers below for ten seconds and then try to reproduce them on another sheet of paper:

9113652460144

To be most successful at recalling this string of numbers, you would have capitalized on recognizable patterns: 911 (emergency), 365 (days in the year), 24 (hours in a day), 60 (minutes in an hour), 144 (number in a gross). Similarly, when you are faced with a reading task, you will read with greater speed and comprehension if you break the material into smaller meaningful units. Decide which pattern you face in a given article and fit information from the article into the pattern you have assigned. It may help to think of filling a *file drawer* with *folders* of information, with each folder representing a component of the particular pattern you've identified. Once you learn to recognize these four patterns and their essential components, you'll become a more efficient reader.

....

Problem–Solution Pattern

Much business and professional writing concerns problems and proposed solutions. If you were to thumb through a current business periodical, you'd most likely find articles on topics such as "the problem with appraisal systems" or "why exit interviews don't work" in which the author identifies a *problem*, describes its *effects*, speculates on its *causes*, and presents a possible *solution*. Typically, the problem is discussed first, the solution is discussed last, and causes and effects (in either order) are

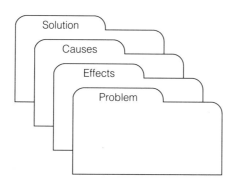

Figure 3.1 The Problem–Solution Pattern

discussed in between. Returning to our file-drawer analogy, the *problem–solution* organizational pattern contains four components you must search for (see Figure 3.1). When you have extracted the information to fill these four folders, you will have grasped the essence of the article.

Here's an example of an article that follows a problem–solution pattern. It discusses a problem that students face today: Those who wish to succeed in today's sophisticated business world must develop a variety of technical competencies. Read the article, time your reading, and then check your comprehension.

Technical Skills You Need to Succeed

Steven S. Ross

The important business tools you need for the future — and how to acquire them — are described in this must-read article.

Ten years ago, young women going into business were routinely asked if they could type. Just as routinely, most replied that it didn't matter if they could or not — they were not going to waste hard-won business degrees by becoming secretaries or executive assistants. Men, of course, were never asked about typing in those days. That's what executives had secretaries for.

Today every executive should be familiar with a typewriter keyboard, not for routine correspondence, but to use the computers and computer terminals that are becoming as common as telephones on executive desks in many companies.

Typing ability is only one small example of the technical skills managers will need in the years ahead. The computer alone has created the demand for businesspeople to handle simple programming chores, understand the statistical implications of raw data on everything from a marketing survey to coal production in China, and to be able to query a data base.

International competition and labor dissatisfaction have forced U.S. firms to look for graduates with skills in manufacturing operations. Public pressure has forced companies to pay attention to government regulators. Financial upheavals and recurring recession have placed a new emphasis on financial analysis.

"As obvious as it sounds, people do expect to get promoted in a company," says Thomas R. Horton, president of the American Management Assns. "Look at the job pyramid. A young grad comes in with knowledge of computer science, accounting, maybe a little history and political science. The grad needs the occupational courses to get in. To move up, though, the history and political science become more important. But if you don't get them now, you never will. Two weeks in Aspen isn't going to do it for you."

The emerging management style of "task teams" has placed a premium on the management generalist, too. Some teams are designed for permanently servicing a given market. Others are meant to solve a specific problem or exploit an opportunity, then are regrouped to do something else. Thus it's not enough to know one area well — like computers or marketing statistics.

"We have a new program for our major accounts, where we bring together a team of operations people, sales, customer service, and billing," says Sue Loucks, in charge of training at US Tel, a large telephone interconnect company based in Dallas. "Everyone has to know a little about everyone else's business, so we started two-week team training programs last July 1." Many of the firm's customer service people are former Braniff employees — skilled in interpreting complex pricing schedules and understanding about the promises (and pitfalls) inherent in advanced technology.

"When I went through grad school there was a fantasy that somehow we were going to land jobs at major industrial or investment banking firms and be set for the rest of our days," says Jerome Gordon, president of Lutine Corp., a New York-based financial consulting firm specializing in the insurance industry. "That fantasy is an absolute lie. In fact, there is an enormous acceleration of the pattern of job changing — inside companies or from firm to firm — among young execs with the express purpose of garnering a range of experiences and approaches to management."

Which of these "technical" skills (in contrast to more broadly based "people" skills such as intuition and the ability to listen) are most important? And where do you get them? The accompanying box summarizes the consensus of people in business and academia who were consulted for this article. The list is not simply the product of wishful thinking — of people who want perfection in every manager.

"It's not the genius who necessarily has to be broad-based," says Gordon, but the nongenius. "In investment banking, you have to put twenty deals down on the table to get two to work. You don't put them down one at a time. Careers require the same kind of thinking.

"People in the middle ranks of their class should start immediately and shrewdly to accumulate a variety of work experiences they can build on, to increase their value to competitive organizations," Gordon adds. "The more narrowly pigeonholed you are, the less likely you are to progress."

But Horton, who spent three decades at IBM before coming to the American Management Assns., warns that "the moving around takes a commitment to lifetime learning. Otherwise you simply get mediocrity rather than excellence in all areas."

The learning comes through formal courses, seminars, a sensitive boss, or rotation through the ranks. "At IBM we did that to excess, sometimes," admits Horton. "No one would cooperate with these 'crown princes' who were being rotated through the chairs."

With those cautions in mind, therefore, let's explore the skills you'll need to succeed in the years ahead.

Mechanical skills

Typing and spelling were at the top of everybody's list. "It was bad enough for a manager to make a fool of himself to his boss in a memo," said one personnel expert for a manufacturing company. "But
(continued)

now the damn fools can't retrieve their electronic mail from the computer in the morning because they can't type in their code numbers properly."

Even worse, simple typing errors such as the transposition of two numbers can produce erroneous and hard-to-check data from computer models. The problem is less acute for typing straight text, however, because many word processing programs are now equipped with "spelling checkers" that go through a memo or report and flag or correct errors.

Being a facile typist can improve a person's image inside a computerized company, too. Some bright people who nevertheless would not have the personality (or ability to think fast enough on their feet) to be noticed in "live" meetings have dominated computerized teleconferences held through New Jersey Institute of Technology's Electronic Information Exchange System.

They allow people from around the world to compose their messages on terminals, wire them to NJIT, and pick up messages from others at the same time.

Informational

The ability to write clear, concise, well-organized prose is the most important of all informational skills. Studies have shown that engineers and managers spend 40% to 60% of their time communicating their ideas and findings to others. "Good language skills help people frame logical and mathematical problems better, too," says Horton.

His views were confirmed by a recent Educational Testing Service study on lack of problem-solving skills among American high school and college students. They were reasonably good at basic mathematical computations, but were usually unable to reduce "word problems" to simple equations for solving.

Where does one learn to write? Ideally before one gets to college. But while in college, students should opt for at least one course that stresses frequent, short papers — perhaps one a week — from an instructor who will offer positive advice on style. One or two long term papers won't teach students anything except library research skills, because content is more important than writing ability and any criticism of writing style takes place too late — often after the course is over.

Managerial use of data bases has been increasing greatly. The reason is simple: knowledge is power. And the fastest way to obtain knowledge (or at least good information) is often to use a computerized data base. The computer can sort through information and present it in a way you can easily digest and use.

Data bases come in two varieties — internal "management information systems," developed for keeping a specific company's records, and external systems that often provide summaries of materials that have already been published (usually in a magazine, journal, newspaper, or conference proceeding). A few data bases provide only citations; that is, names of articles, authors, titles and the publications in which the articles appeared. Some advanced data bases offer full text of such articles.

Many data bases also provide new information — material that has never been published elsewhere. A few combine information from many articles on such subjects as oil production, mergers, and chemical technology and place the information into carefully footnoted tables. Some will read information directly into your own tables, set up the way you want them on a microcomputer.

One warning from Horton: "Most MIS people seem to be from another planet. They are math majors, or whatever, hired to serve corporate departments they've never been in, such as accounting or sales."

He looks with favor upon the approach of Celanese and some other companies, which train operating personnel from other departments as programmers. "That might become a trend, and a good career path," he says.

"People in specialized areas such as computer science or majoring in MIS must make sure they are getting more than a stress on hardware and programming software," says Joel Goldhar, dean of Illinois Institute of Technology's management school. "The emphasis must be on use; they need not only to understand how information systems work, but how they affect decision-making."

"Better software may make current MIS skill levels obsolete or unnecessary in a few years," argues Lynn Appelbaum, who handles public affairs for New York University. "This more sophisticated software makes systems easier to use and might reduce the expertise required for interaction with the technology."

These information-gathering skills have a direct bearing on statistical skills as well. "The most important thing you have to know in statistical work, espe-

cially to evaluate things like market research, is exactly how the data were gathered," says Goldhar. "Nonspecialists don't have to know how to crunch the numbers. But they do have to know where biases and errors could have been made, and how sensitive their decisions are to those possible errors."

Goldhar recommends one solid course in statistics, perhaps combined with a marketing sequence. Statistical skills are difficult to learn from books; make up for lack of college training with intensive seminars. Some good seminar programs run a full week or more, and include hands-on experience with microcomputers for manipulating data statistically.

"Government is an abstraction in the typical mind," says Gordon, "an abstraction filled with two kinds of characters: political appointees and civil servant/bureaucrats. The former can be manipulated and the latter are engaged in paper-shuffling and gaming activities that don't amount to much for the private sector."

The abstraction is false, Gordon says. "For a whole group of industries, the regulators at federal, state, and local levels can limit action and affect markets." That's especially true for financial services such as insurance and for manufacturers who must comply with environmental and occupational safety laws.

But what about deregulation? "Don't kid yourself," says Gordon. "Deregulation of financial services at the federal level has led to increased scrutiny by the states. And environmental regulators are not going to go away. It is only the wealthy who can afford the luxury and

(continued)

leisure time to make use of nature. Thus, they are natural proponents for environmental protection. Even the current administration recognizes that environmentalists often come in three-piece suits. As income levels rise, this group increases in numbers."

A business law course that spends a few weeks on regulatory matters (most concentrate on contract law) is therefore a useful asset for new grads. After that, a close eye on newspapers and business magazines will help managers keep track of general regulatory trends. Trade association bulletins also help (but you'll have to ask the boss for them; they tend to be distributed only to top management within a company). Lower-level managers also increasingly qualify for subscriptions to high-priced industry newsletters and data bases.

"Companies first set up departments to watch Washington," says Horton. "Then they developed environmental staffs. Now firms are looking more closely at international affairs." Those staffs tend to be made up of small groups of very bright, scholarly people, Horton says. But their decisions affect many levels of corporate planning. Should the company invest in new energy-conservation equipment? The answer may depend more on what the CEO thinks will happen in the Middle East next year than on relative capital costs vs. fuel costs now.

There's also the matter of foreign trade, and of dealing with managers from other cultures. "A relative of mine, a chemical engineer, says he cannot stretch the truth a bit with the Japanese on delivery schedules, specifications or product performance," says Gordon. "What we consider innocent hype, they consider an outright lie."

Outside of living abroad and learning from your mistakes, it is difficult to gain a world view if you haven't had one in college, Horton says. "A good reading program is a must," he says. For specific matters, such as specifications on trademarks, international taxation, export laws, or counterfeiting, the American Management Assns. and other groups offer seminars. "But they are for specific topics, not for gaining an overall view of a culture," Horton warns.

Financial

At least one accounting course is a must. The object is not to turn all managers into bean-counters, but to give them an understanding of such things as the tax consequences of their actions. In addition, it is vital that all levels of the company speak the same "language" when it comes to financial statements. Are the expenses listed under "July," for instance, in a publishing venture for the July issue or for that calendar month? Is the income recorded from a consulting client the "cash in" or the income "earned" by fulfilling the client's contract?

Such distinctions often seem like minor abstractions to the nonaccountant. Not knowing them, however, can lead a firm to the brink of disaster — or over the brink.

No graduate should expect to get all knowledge of accounting out of a single course, though. Each industry has specific "generally recognized accounting practices," or accounting rules to live by.

Companies should make sure their new managers understand those rules.

Managers should also be familiar enough with microcomputers to be able to use a simple "spreadsheet" program such as VisiCalc. Such programs require little more skill than using a calculator. But they are much more efficient. Using them, a manager can build a sheet of numbers on the computer screen. Unlike a manual spreadsheet, however, the computer permits the manager to add extra lines, or insert extra columns. And repetitive calculations can be made automatically. This can turn a spreadsheet into a model for playing "what if" games at your desk.

Operational

Plant managers a few years back had inferiority complexes. If a banker lived on one side, and a financial vice-president on the other, chances were that the plant manager would be considered the dolt of the neighborhood. No more. "The fact of the matter is that if you don't have a decent manufacturing system and don't maintain a good quality level, you will end up killing your market," says Gordon.

No corporate strategy is complete without manufacturing expertise, Goldhar says. "Computers in manufacturing are revolutionizing the factory. That's no news to anybody. But the impact is that it opens up strategies that weren't possible before. It's been said that we've been best at producing long runs of products, over long periods of time, and getting costs down by amortizing equipment and simply learning to make an

item more efficiently." Manufacturing experts call it "getting down the learning curve."

"Now we don't get a chance for long runs. And the numerically controlled machine tool doesn't care. It can make a dozen identical items, or one each of 12 items as long as it has been programmed," says Goldhar.

Result: the learning curve for the company as a whole is at least as important as the learning curve for a particular product. "We have to move ideas from market research to R&D, through engineering and the factory, and out the door to marketing and distribution faster than ever before," says Goldhar. "To be a product manager, to move something through the system, will be the skills in greatest demand in the 1990s."

Specifically, those skills include a basic understanding of manufacturing technology for your industry, an understanding of microeconomic impacts (what effects costs might have on your product or a competitor's), and a feel for quality.

The trend in industry today is away from "inspecting in" quality, and toward designing the manufacturing and marketing system to "build quality in." That's not a job left entirely to technical people, however, because "quality" is not the same as "durability." Instead, it is best defined as "fitness for use" or "value for the price, in the customer's eyes."

A solid college course is necessary for a basic understanding of the statistical and managerial theories involved. Managers heading for manufacturing companies might consider taking part-time or full-time MBA or MS programs in

(continued)

manufacturing management. They're offered by a growing list of colleges, including Vanderbilt (one of the pioneers), Rensselaer Polytechnic Institute, Illinois Institute of Technology, University of Texas at Austin, Carnegie-Mellon, and the University of Pennsylvania's Wharton School.

Is all this too much to ask of a new manager? What about the average student?

"What average?" asks Goldhar. Most managers cluster around the norm. Creativity, which comes from stimulation on the job, can really make the difference. "There's no such thing as a noncreative person. Lots of people are in environments that don't allow them to be creative. But ability and creativity are widespread in society. It's a matter of developing creativity, and being in a position where such skills are required."

You can greatly increase your employment opportunities by learning the necessary technical skills in school, at home, or on the job.

Steven S. Ross is an Assistant Professor of Journalism at Columbia University, specializing in national and computer-assisted reporting.

For additional information

The Official MBA Handbook or How to Succeed in Business Without a Harvard MBA by Jim Fisk and Robert Barron. A Wallaby Book published by Simon & Schuster. 237 pages; $4.95.

The Computer Careers Handbook by Connie Winkler. Arco Publishing Inc. 142 pages; $7.95.

Computer Careers by Joyce Lain Kennedy and Connie Winkler. Sun Features Inc., Box 368, Cardiff, Calif. 92007. 30 pages; $3.50.

Data Exchange in PC/MS Dos by Steven S. Ross. McGraw-Hill. 411 pages; $24.95.

Technical Skills and How to Acquire Them

Mechanical

Typing	Self-paced instruction
Spelling	Use a pocket dictionary

Informational

Writing	College course; job; seminars
Data base queries	College library; seminars
Government regulation	College course; reading
Statistics	College course; seminars
World view	Travel; reading; seminars

Financial

Basic accounting	College course
Computer programming	Manuals for using computer "spreadsheets"

Operational

Plant management	On-the-job; college courses; seminars
Quality assurance	College course; on-the-job
Microeconomics	On-the-job; college courses

Comprehension Check: Problem–Solution Pattern

1. What *problem* does the author of this article describe?

2. What are the *effects* of the problem?

3. What are the *causes* of the problem?

4. What is the *solution*?

Persuasive Pattern

In addition to describing problems and proposing solutions, much business and professional writing uses a related pattern to convince you to do, say, or believe something. When an author uses a *persuasive pattern*, she will make an *assertion*; *support* the assertion with facts, figures, testimonials or other evidence; and then discuss expected *outcomes* (although expected outcomes often are implied rather than explicitly stated). In this case, you have three folders to fill (see Figure 3.2).

As a result of your reading, you may simply agree with the author, take whatever action the author is advocating, or disagree with the author's assertion. But by anticipating these three components of persuasive articles, you can increase both reading comprehension and efficiency. Read the following article and see whether you are persuaded that the author is right about the importance of job satisfaction. As before, time your reading and check your comprehension.

Figure 3.2 The Persuasive Pattern

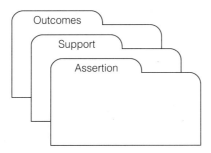

The Importance of Job Satisfaction

By Marilyn M. Kennedy

Your personality, your likes and dislikes, all come into play. Advice on what to do to make good career decisions.

Before graduation, Martha Bowen was in the fortunate position of having three job offers from consulting firms. She accepted the most prestigious firm's offer and she's not happy. It was clear from day one that her free-wheeling style and bubbly personality were at odds with the company's staid posture. The carpeting was gray, people wore gray suits, and she felt like she was living in a black-and-white movie.

One of the offers she turned down was from a smaller, less formal firm that she liked, but her parents and friends told her she "couldn't turn down" the larger, better-known firm. It was, they said, "The chance of a lifetime, and look at the money!"

Burt Walker went with a Big Eight firm because his accounting professors said, "You'll never forgive yourself if you don't." He's unlikely to forgive himself anyway because he's not doing well. Burt is overwhelmed by the size and scale of every audit he's assigned. He hates the extensive travel and his boss, the product of a private college, seems to think Burt's state university education is a handicap to be overcome.

Earl Williams, who grew up on Chicago's South Side, took a job in a remote area of northern California. The job was a fine opportunity and the community was reputed to be a nature lover's paradise. Once he settled there, however, Earl missed Chicago far more than he'd anticipated. He was one of only 10 minorities in the company and one of fewer than 50 in the town. The locally popular Mexican cuisine was not soul food.

With the best intentions, all these people made mistakes in choosing a first job that might have been avoided. They listened to parents, friends, and teachers whose advice was well-intentioned but disastrous. After all, more experienced professors, placement professionals, and friends were trying to help. But they blocked out the negative messages from their intuitions and made what appeared to be rational choices. Unfortunately, by being logical and unemotional, they found themselves in jobs they should have rejected. They should not have ignored their feelings and doubts, because what we sometimes call intuition is often a rational response to our past experiences.

Martha refused to acknowledge the importance of her style and effervescent personality even though after she'd taken the office tour during the interviewing process, she told her roommate it was "drab" and "stuffy."

A friend of Burt's had gone to work two years before for the same accounting firm he'd chosen. She had left after 18 months, claiming she'd never been happy a day there.

Earl's parents didn't want to throw cold water on his romantic notions about living near the mountains and redwoods, but his mother did remind him that his one experience at a wilderness scout camp had been so disagreeable that he'd begged to come home after one week.

Remember, if you hate your first job, even if you perform well, it's going to be an ego-rattling disappointment. It can also undermine your self-confidence. Every job you have between the first one and retirement may not be perfect, but that's no reason not to do everything possible to make each one a satisfying experience. Before making a "logical" decision about your first job, consider these vital issues.

Who are you?

You have likes, dislikes, values, peculiarities, social and cultural needs, and a bundle of complex and competing interests. Before you go on an interview — or a second interview — and long before you accept a job offer, you should look inward and get in touch with yourself.

The best way to begin is through a process of elimination. Most people are clearer on what they dislike than on what they like. Start by listing everything you dislike about the following categories: 1) people; 2) work environments; 3) geographical locations; 4) size of organization or size of the work unit.

Mine your memory and think through all your past work experiences. Think of the vacations you've had to places you've traveled and list what you liked or disliked about them and why. Have you ever said, "This is a great place to visit but I'd hate to live here"? If you've lived in several different places, which one did you like the most, the least?

Your lists should be as exhaustive as you can make them—especially when you're considering your people preferences. Had Martha done this, her list of phobias would have included: 1) people who are snobbish and keep reminding others that they went to a prep school; 2) people who lack a sense of humor; 3) low energy people; 4) intense people who can't see that, as Noel Coward said, "Work should be more fun than fun." She might have continued with 10 or 15 more dislikes. Had she made her "shopping" list before she went on her site tour, there is little chance she'd have taken the job, especially when she saw the people were almost as drab as the environment!

Campus recruiters sometimes sense that a prospect is a bit uncomfortable with some aspect of the company and may ask outright, "Have you ever lived in a small town?" The recruiter may note the answer and others who interview a candidate may pick up on it. Earl was asked several times if he was sure he'd like living in a small town. Being a polished interviewee, he managed to overcome the company's doubts even though he honestly hadn't addressed his own.

Burt had more than enough notice that the public accounting firm he'd chosen had a well-known reputation for

(continued)

ruthlessness, but he didn't consider how much that would affect him on a day-to-day basis. It's easy to discount someone else's experience when you're not in touch with your own values. Within three weeks Burt was saying (to himself), "But that's not how I treat the client."

Work environment matters

There's been controversy lately about the effect of bullpen arrangements, partitions, and private offices on concentration and productivity. Think about your study habits: Do you work best in a library with many people around you? Are you able to concentrate better in a room with fewer visual distractions? How do you prepare for finals? Has it been your practice to study with others or alone? Studying is work. You already have work habits and preferences although you may not have identified them as such.

If you know you need a fairly self-contained work area to do your best, wouldn't it be detrimental to both productivity and satisfaction to pick a place that hummed with people working at closely packed desks? This has been a problem for some accounting, data processing, and engineering people. It's not insurmountable. You can learn to function well in a different environment but you should know going in that you'll have to make the effort to adjust.

Working with like-minded people

This is important to job satisfaction. Woe to the person who says, with consummate naivete, "I can get along with anyone." Yes, but at what price? Being

the only whatever you are can contribute to an uncomfortable sense of being different. If you're aware of the situation before you begin a job you can be mentally prepared to deal with it. Still, especially on a first job, having a few similar souls around you can be helpful.

Even more important than the more obvious areas of compatibility is compatibility of style. A true loner, accustomed to taking an assignment and returning when the work is completed will have a hard time adjusting to consensus-style management or even participative management. The endless meetings during which people try to work out problems and get commitments to common goals through discussion will be numbingly tedious — and unnecessary as well.

A young banker described just the opposite experience on his first job: "I was given an assignment and sent away. I felt totally abandoned and lonely. My boss never even asked casually how I was getting along until one week before the project was due." A loner would have found that heaven, the ideal environment. Someone who needs more people contact would have had the same reaction as the banking neophyte.

When you have a clear fix on the kind of people you're comfortable working with and the style you work best with, you'll want to find out about both during interviews. Ask, "What's the background of most of the people in the department?" or, "Are meetings an important part of getting the job done?" Neither question is aggressive and will help you find out what you need to know in a neutral way.

Don't dismiss first impressions

Listen to your gut feelings. If the campus recruiter makes you uncomfortable, the size or scale of the company's operation seems overwhelming, or the idea of being 30 miles from downtown five days a week strikes you as bleak, don't dismiss those thoughts. First impressions can be false but frequently they are honest. You may change your mind, but you should do so on the basis of further input, not because you tell yourself, "I shouldn't feel that way." Negative feelings cannot be controlled or even effectively suppressed. They can change in response to new data. They should alert you to the need for further investigation.

Virtually every job seeker who made a wrong choice will admit that part of the problem was that he or she rode roughshod over feelings that were honest and important. Admitting that they'd done so when it was too late made them feel even more distressed when the job failed to be satisfying.

A firm's name and reputation have little effect on job satisfaction. Of course, drawing a "Wow, you work for IBM!" from friends may be pleasant, but what if IBM's style — and it has a very definite style — makes you miserable? Do you think being miserable at IBM or Arthur Andersen would be less miserable than being at the Mighty Mouse Computer Co.?

Miserable is miserable — no matter whose name is on the brass plate. Telling yourself you can "stand anything for a year so I can put it on my resume" is foolish. Wouldn't satisfying, developmental, successful experiences almost anywhere look as good? Prestige and job satisfaction rarely compute if the rest of the work situation isn't positive.

Ultimately, your work satisfaction will depend on a combination of circumstances, some of which are within your control. The more care you take as you go through the screening process, the better off you'll be in the long run. Your own feelings and experiences are the only definitive ones, and have the most to do with how satisfied and successful you'll be once you're on the job.

Marilyn Moats Kennedy is founder and managing partner of Career Strategies in Evanston, Ill.

For additional information
Thank God it's Monday! by William E. Diehl. Fortress Press. 192 pages; $5.95, paperback.
Thank God it's Monday: How to Turn Work into an Adventure by Robert M. Randolph. Institute for Business Planning Inc. 249 pages; $15.95.

....

Comprehension Check: Persuasive Pattern

1. Which of the following is the author's main assertion?
   a. Listening to the advice of friends and relatives on which job offer to accept can be a mistake.
   b. It's important to realize that no job is perfect.

c. Your own feelings and experiences are the best indicators of how satisfied and successful you're likely to be once you're on the job.

d. Hating your first job is an ego-rattling disappointment.

2. What is the author's evidence for this assertion?

a. People who take jobs based on others' recommendations and ignore their own perceptions often suffer disappointment.

b. Most job seekers who made the wrong choice admit they ignored important feelings of reservation.

c. A firm's name and reputation have little effect on the job satisfaction of individuals.

d. All of the above.

3. If you agree with the author's assertion, you would probably:

a. Listen to your own feelings in choosing an organization to work for.

b. Take a job with a prestigious company primarily for the boost it will give your resume.

c. Realize that although the job is less than perfect, it's important to do your best.

d. Leave an organization as soon as possible if you are unsatisfied with your job.

Informative Pattern

When an author is not describing problems and solutions or convincing you of something, he may be presenting information. He may want to describe the new payroll system, the benefits of time management, or the profit outlook for the next quarter. Using this *informative pattern*, the author most likely will present a *series of subtopics*, one after the other. You will have as many folders to fill as there are subtopics (see Figure 3.3).

You'll see what we mean when you read the following article, "Ten Reasons People Get Fired," which includes information on ten subtopics. Time your reading and answer the questions on comprehension.

Figure 3.3 *The Informative Pattern*

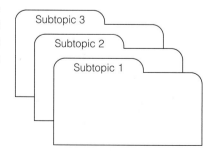

10 Reasons People Get Fired

Marilyn Moats Kennedy

How to avoid the most common job traps that snare the unwary employee and cost 10% of new hires their jobs.

When Rose Smith was fired after only six months with an accounting firm, she was stunned. What could make the firm decide that quickly that she was not the employee they wanted? Ted Rogers had the same experience when he was told he "wasn't working out" in the management training program. His boss expressed his sorrow and disappointment, but Ted hardly felt better.

After you've been through months of interviewing, being told that you aren't "working out" will not make your first job experience a happy one. Yet about 10% of new hires are either fired or strongly encouraged to resign within the first six months of their being on the job.

To minimize the risk of learning from bitter experience, you should be aware of the most frequent reasons new employees don't "work out"; that way, you will be better able to make sure that you don't find yourself in this category. Here is a list of the 10 most common reasons that cause people to be fired from their jobs.

First on the list is failure to fit in. In every company, top management has a collective perception of what the organization values in its employees. Some companies think of them as one big, happy family. They hire family members, award scholarships to the children, and sponsor company sports teams.

At the opposite end of the spectrum are companies that encourage employees to be autonomous, with dozens of variations in between. It's unlikely that a job description will say, "The candidate must have graduated from a Midwestern college, like to bowl, and be able to get along with old Mossback in bookkeeping," but these may be important criteria for fitting in. You must find out what they are.

Carol Shorr, president of MKM Consultants Inc., a Chicago recruiting firm, says, "If I had to name the single, most frequent reason new employees were fired, it would be inability to fit in with the corporate culture."

Corporate culture is simply another way of describing top management's

(continued)

perceptions. To get a feel for a company's culture, try to talk to present and past employees and watch people at work during the interviewing process.

If you make a mistake in your choice and are fired because you don't fit in, don't assume your fledgling career has suffered a knockout blow. The company may have done you a favor. Most of the people who are fired because they don't fit the company's culture would probably have had to go through a prolonged and difficult period of readjustment to adapt, and even then may never have really fit in. If you are not comfortable with the people and the company you work for, you're better off looking for another job.

This was Rose's problem. The accounting firm wanted serious, fast-track people. Rose was more interested in her new apartment, meeting new people, and exploring the city than in working 90 hours a week. She did it, of course, when she had to, but it was obvious to her boss that she lacked the enthusiasm for overtime that he considered essential for new auditors.

2 Over-selling yourself and your qualifications is the second reason. Companies don't make every hiring decision rationally. Recruiters and personnel people, even line managers, can be charmed by a particular candidate who does not actually fit the company's job requirements.

One data processing manager for a medium-sized consulting firm said, "I really liked one of the young men we interviewed. He was interested in everything, had done his homework on us,

and had a lot of poise. He sold me on how quickly he could learn.

"I hired him. The problem was, he didn't have the technical skills we needed. He was floundering at the end of the first week. I felt bad because I'd known from the start that there was barely a 50/50 chance that he would succeed. I shouldn't have let my emotions cloud my judgment."

Sometimes the applicant can over-sell. Betty Harper, a liberal arts graduate, got a copy-editing job with a magazine, in part because she had done some editing for her college magazine. It was her dream job, but, unfortunately, the pace in the office was much too fast. Betty had not lied about her experience; however, she failed to take into account the much slower tempo of the college magazine. Though over-selling her experience got her the job, it could not help her keep it.

3 Bad chemistry with the boss can also result in a job situation with an unhappy ending. Limited experience with bosses can make it difficult to adjust rapidly to different styles of supervision. If your new boss likes people to take orders rather than ask questions, and you like to ask questions, that difference in style could be an insurmountable obstacle.

Personnel people who place new hires can often be wrong about who will work out with a certain boss. There are so many subtleties that determine whether two people will be compatible that "bad chemistry" is often difficult to predict. It's not necessarily fatal if you don't like the boss, as long as the feeling isn't mutual!

4 Rigidity and/or unmanageability on the job can also lead to being fired. Dan Martin was the brightest recruit in the commercial credit program at the bank. Unfortunately, he never tired of telling his boss and coworkers about his college successes and his summers spent working for the bank in his home town.

Whenever he was told about the bank's approach to a particular problem or transaction, he talked about what his hometown bank had done. He used his own approach before trying what the program called for. He argued about everything, but always, he said, "as the loyal opposition." He viewed himself as willing to learn; his boss saw him as rigid and unable to change.

Ted had a similar problem in his management training program. The trainers expected him to try the standard approach first, but he wanted to see if he could find another way. The result was unnecessary arguing about things that shouldn't have become issues at all.

5 Lack of necessary skills is another problem that can lead to termination. Lois Arrand had excellent grades in college. However, she got through school because of her excellent 24-hour memory. She would cram at the last minute and forget what she had learned soon after the exam.

When it came to actually writing computer programs, she couldn't do it. At first, several of her coworkers helped her out. She'd ask how to do something, and they would essentially do the work for her. In a month, there was no one she could go to for help. Coworkers expected her to carry her share, which, unfortunately, she couldn't do.

A skills failure happens most frequently when someone has had the requisite courses but has not understood the logic underlying what he or she has studied. This phenomenon is most often seen with technical skills, but it can also affect other areas.

According to Peter W. Hom, professor of management at Arizona State, lack of people skills is a serious stumbling block for many new hires. Professor Hom, who has extensively studied the turnover rate for new hires, says, "College graduates are frequently hired as supervisors when they have had little or no experience in this area. Typically, a company's management training program is not thorough enough in training people how to motivate or delegate."

People skills come with experience, it's true, but how can a new hire get experience? If you know your job will entail supervision of subordinates, find out what kind of training program the company offers and what kind of continued support you will get. Begin reading up on the principles of supervision. Talk to experienced supervisors to find out how they delegate responsibility and motivate subordinates.

Above all, do not underestimate the level of skill you will need from the start. Don't figure you'll have no people problems because you managed a
(continued)

McDonald's or were head counselor at summer camp. Supervising adults and dealing with different types of people, many of whom may be a number of years older than you, will be different — and difficult. Most importantly, be sure the company intends to provide the followup training and support.

6 Office politics can sometimes result in losing a job. Nothing is more unfortunate than being the victim of a power play that no one could reasonably anticipate. For example, suppose a new worker is hired and several coworkers go out of their way to be friendly. The new hire is delighted. What he or she can't know is that these people are enemies of the new worker's boss and are lining up the new worker as a potential ally.

This drawing of battle lines happens frequently during a reorganization, a merger, or another major internal change. A boss may not realize that the new subordinate has been led astray. Instead it may be assumed that the new worker understands the issues and really sides with these people against the boss.

Another form of political trouble can result from expressing an opinion critical of the company or your boss before sorting out the issues. This happened to Joe Robertson, a new salesman, when he let the secretary — a direct conduit to the boss — hear him complain about all the confusing red tape and paperwork in the job. He was quoted to his boss in detail.

Had he politely asked the boss to explain the correct and most straightforward way to do a particular kind of re-port, Joe might have positioned himself as someone trying hard to learn the company's system. His backstairs criticism was seen as political.

If you're fired for political problems, they will not usually be identified as such. The catch phrase is "didn't work out." Bosses are often quicker to fire for political sins than for skills problems. The best way to avoid such situations is to circulate for the first six months among all of the groups in the office and to express no opinions other than to remark that you've barely found your way to the coffee pot and washroom.

7 Refusal to conform to unspoken rules is another reason people get fired. Most of the people in the office wore conservative suits, but Will Jefferson liked brighter colors and the most fashionable styling. His boss saw Will's actions as deliberate rebellion against the company's unspoken policies.

Because the company had no written dress code — new hires were supposed to "fall in" with what they saw others wearing — it was difficult for the boss to confront the issue of Will's attire. The more the boss thought about it, the angrier he became. Will was fired for a minor infraction after the boss blew up over the accumulated aggravation. Sadly, Will never did understand why he was fired.

8 You can also get fired for failing to be a team player. Logic isn't the only operative principle in the workplace. When Mary Louise Ritter told a coworker that she always exercised from 5 p.m. to

6 p.m. at the health club and, therefore, wouldn't be joining the others for a drink on Friday night, she thought that was a reasonable explanation for her absence.

Unfortunately, her boss and coworkers interpreted her behavior as a rejection of sorts. If she liked them, she'd want to have a beer with them on Friday evenings and discuss the week's happenings. The group began to exclude her from the grapevine and she began to hear about things late. Decisions were made and ideas exchanged at those Friday night sessions. Mary became isolated and, since she lacked several key pieces of information, her work suffered. She now has the firmest thighs of any current job hunter not looking for work as an aerobics instructor, since she was fired from her job.

9 One reason for getting fired that is out of your control is business dislocation. When the company recruited Cheryl Logan in early May as an administrative assistant, she was elated. When she started work on July 1 as scheduled, she discovered that there had been a company-wide 10% reduction in June.

Her boss, nervous about the changes taking place within the company, kept giving Cheryl vague answers when she asked what was happening. On August 1, Cheryl was let go because the company had decided it didn't need administrative assistants anymore. Department heads were going to have to do their work without them. This was technically a layoff, but Cheryl felt as bad as if she'd been fired for poor performance.

When businesses are forced to make cutbacks, it's often the new hires who are the first to go. Being laid off will have no long-term effect on your career, but it can be emotionally devastating to you.

10 Poor judgment. Bill Marks approached his first assignment with great zeal. He was asked to put together a simple marketing study, much like those he'd done as an intern. Unfortunately, because he believed he understood the assignment, he had waited until a day before it was due to begin. To his chagrin, he had to ask for an extension when he discovered the assignment had a few twists that required research. The study was three weeks late. The next assignment, about which he felt very confident, was also late. His boss said, as he fired Bill, that he considered it very important to "know one's own limits."

A company will often fire new employees during their probation period if there are any doubts about whether they will be able to perform the job for which they were hired. At that early stage, no explanation is necessary other than "It's not working out." Once an employee has completed probation, firing must be documented.

To prevent a mismatch that results in being fired, be sure to research the company carefully. Talk to present and former employees about the company's mode of operation, values, management style, and profitability.

Keep in touch with your new boss before you report for work, especially if

(continued)

there's a gap of four weeks or more. Much can happen in that time. Although firings do occur, and some are not preventable, many can and should be averted by avoiding the above situations whenever possible.

To sum up, the first six months on a job are extremely important. During this period you'll be watched closely by coworkers and company executives. They'll notice how well you do your work, how cooperative you are, and how you get along with others.

Present a cheery, can-do attitude and perform each task to the best of your ability. What you are doing is creating an image — and you want it to be a positive one. Too many people start new jobs without being aware of the politics and subtleties of the office.

As a new person on the job, take the time to notice what goes on around you. Determine the person in the office with power. Don't go to lunch every day with the same people. If you are perceptive, you'll learn the politics of the department and the company. Such knowledge can help you progress on the job.

Marilyn Moats Kennedy is founder and managing partner of Career Strategies in Evanston, Ill.

For additional information
How to Manage Your Boss by Christopher Hegarty with Philip Goldberg. Ballantine Books. 276 pages; $3.50, paperback.

Comprehension Check: Informative Pattern

Cite as many of the ten subtopics and main ideas as you can from this article.

Subtopics

1.
2.
3.
4.
5.
6.
7.
8.
9.
10.

Instructional Pattern

The fourth organizational pattern that you will encounter in reading business and professional literature is the *instructional pattern.* Here an author will take you *step by step* through a process to teach you something — how to fire an employee, how to prepare a presentation, or, in the example that follows, how to write persuasive cover letters. In this case, each step in the process described contains information to fill a folder. Look at Figure 3.4 and then read the following instructional article. As before, answer the questions that follow to check your comprehension.

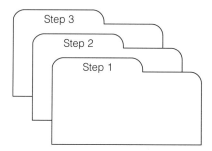

Figure 3.4 *The Instructional Pattern*

Nine Steps to a Persuasive Cover Letter

Pamela E. Berns

It's an important part of your total sales package, so take the time to make it special. Use it as an opportunity to bring your resume to life and to demonstrate your enthusiasm as well as creativity.

People often describe you as an articulate, ambitious, and experienced individual. You have worked hard to produce a dynamite resume. However, while a postage stamp and neatly typed address may be enough to get your resume to a prospective employer, it will require a great deal more to convince him or her to ask you to come for an interview. That's the function of a cover letter.

More than just a brief introduction to your resume, the cover letter is a very important part of your total sales package. It must make your resume stand out among scores of others before you can even begin to compete for the job you're after. The cover letter is your chance to tell an employer why you are so uniquely qualified for the job. Your enthusiasm and creativity can come through in a way that is often not possible on a resume. Here are nine steps to a persuasive cover letter—the kind that will get your foot in the interview door.

1 Start with a bit of self-analysis. You have the advantage of knowing everything there is to know about your product. Your task is to decide which facets you wish to present and in what light. Keep in mind that an effective cover letter should not exceed one page.

Consider the case of Steve. Steve had been employed in strategic planning at a broadcasting company and always had seen his future in media. He was laid off rather abruptly, however. As he sought new ways to package his experience in a seemingly limited marketplace, he discovered in himself talents and inclinations that led him into a whole new field. He now has a challenging position with a financial consulting firm specializing in mergers and acquisitions.

Steve's newly discovered strengths were always there. It was simply a matter of stepping back and adjusting his focus. By placing himself in his prospective employer's shoes he was able to zero in on the precise qualifications needed for his new job.

Take a good look at your resume and brainstorm. Pick out the highs, especially the accomplishments, of your career to date and jot them down. Try to fill in the blanks your resume leaves open. Use the cover letter to breathe life into a resume's declarative, chronological statements.

Reprinted by permission of Pamela E. Berns, New York City.

Ask yourself what you would want to know about this applicant if you were the one doing the hiring. Does your educational and vocational history include any memorable successes or contributions? Have you had any noteworthy experiences that are especially relevant to the job you're presently seeking? Do you possess any skills or talents that are uniquely useful for this job? Can you pinpoint a particular detail in your background or a positive aspect of your personality that makes you stand out from other applicants?

If you're trying to break into journalism, use your cover letter to describe how you founded your college magazine. If your input on a company project contributed to profits, bring it to the reader's attention. And give the figures to back it up. If you began your advertising career as an art director and have now decided to enter the business side, use your creative perspective to gain some valuable points over the MBAS.

2 Narrow your appeal. When you feel you've listed everything you can think of, it's time to start adjusting your focus. Look at your list. You'll probably be quite impressed by your own qualifications. Select the two or three most relevant or impressive facts and organize them so that they will have the greatest impact on your reader.

Take the risk of patting yourself on the back in order to demonstrate high self-esteem and spirit. After all, most employers want to hire people who have confidence and enthusiasm.

Consider this excerpt from an inquiry about a position as assistant to the CEO of a Fortune 500 company. The writer goes beyond simply informing the reader of her pertinent skills and background to reveal special insight into the unspoken essentials of the job:

As the assistant to the provost of a major New York teaching medical center, I am relied upon heavily for my administrative and supervisory skills. A crucial component is my ability for tact and discretion, as I am privvy to all confidential matters in dealing with upper-echelon personnel at the medical center.

Another way to enhance the information listed on your resume is to focus on one achievement and give it extra dimension. By doing just this, the writer of the following letter painted a self-portrait of a dedicated professional who possesses a wealth of appropriate knowledge and understanding.

Because my career includes five years in nonprofit and community environments, I feel I can make significant contributions to your organization as you establish a new residential facility for community corrections. I have worked with all age groups (from preschoolers to senior citizens) and have established supportive, as well as mutually rewarding, relationships. I have been especially successful with delinquent young people.

3 Accentuate the positive. Remember the old riddle, "Is the glass half-full or half-empty?" The answer depends entirely on how you look at it. It's the same when your "market research" ends up leaving you with that eerie feeling that you lack all relevant experience. Take heart; even limitations can be construed

(continued)

as genuine advantages. So many of us find ourselves caught in the catch-22 of needing the experience to get the job, but needing the job to get the experience in the first place.

Calm down. After all, if you're interested in the job you must have some related experience, however remote it may seem. A Washington, D.C., news bureau chief advises recent college graduates to focus on the practical experiences they've had in school. "If you participated in any internships, talk about details, not your grades. Tell me about the stories you covered for your campus radio station."

He also points out that lack of experience can give an applicant the advantage of appearing open-minded and free of bad habits. At a company where employees are trained in a particular style or philosophy, enthusiastic willingness as a trainee can turn out to be a better selling point than years of work experience.

Of course it never hurts to do a little homework. To get information about the inside workings of the industry you're after, read industry trade publications and business magazines, and contact trade associations. You'll probably find that your own experience is more relevant than you thought—you just didn't have the right words for it.

4 Eliminate the negative. There are four pieces of information you should leave out of your cover letter: personal problems; the fact that you can't get along with your boss; your beef about the way things are run at your current place of employment; the fact that you've been fired.

At some time in your life at least one of these will be the motivating factor behind a job search. However, nobody is interested in inheriting your personal problems. Nor does your prospective employer care to become the new target of your insubordination. (Your boss may truly be at fault, but what guarantee does the stranger reading your letter have that you're not always on the warpath?)

If you've been let go for bad performance, you do yourself no good to broadcast it. However, if you were part of a massive layoff plan, your pink slip takes on a different hue. If you feel it helps to build your case, then talk about it. If the layoff has been in all the papers, you need merely to mention it. If the information is less public, you may want to give an explanation.

5 Respect your reader. One of the best ways to convince a prospective employer of your interest is to show you've taken the time to learn something about the company. Betsy Rosini, manager of staff advisory services at Chemical Bank, says that evidence that someone has taken time to research the job or her department automatically increases her interest in the applicant.

Here are some approaches you might want to try: *Congratulations on landing the Mercedes account. I believe my experience in automotive advertising would be a great asset to this new assignment. Or, The strength and diversity of your ac-*

counts would seem to offer a stimulating environment in which I could make good use of my varied skills and talents.

If you're replying to an ad, the name of the company may not always be revealed. However, you should pay attention to the details it does provide. What are the job requirements, both explicit and implicit? Be sure to address them positively and concretely. If the ad calls for an energetic, articulate individual with good typing skills, don't write about your analytical abilities and supervisory skills. And be clear about the person or company to whom you're writing. Don't boast about all the contributions you can make as an employee of the Garland Agency when the position is available with the firm Garland represents.

One final point about respecting your reader. It's important that you appear self-confident. However, it's equally important that you don't appear arrogant or condescending, which can sometimes be the result of just a little too much confidence. To Rosini, "flowery language, puffery, and bombast" are automatic turnoffs.

6 Concentrate on what you can do for the employer. Perhaps the greatest mistake you can make is to fill your letter with the way in which this job will boost your career. Certainly it's to an employer's advantage to offer a position to someone whose future will be enhanced by it; what better way to guarantee peak performance? However, there's a job to be done, and it's the person who shows a commitment to doing it who will be hired.

When you list your qualifications, do so in terms of what you can give, not what you will get. Use words like "offer" and "contribute" over "growth potential" and "career opportunity." Suggest that both parties will benefit through your employment. Phrases like "mutually rewarding" and "mutually beneficial" are quite effective.

7 Write an attention-getting introduction. Every day we open mailboxes filled with sales letters. The number we actually read is small, however. If the writer hasn't grabbed us early, the sales pitch is doomed to fail.

In your cover letter, the opening has three basic functions: to invite, inform, and entice. Be precise about the job for which you're applying. Explain how you heard about the job; if it was through a personal reference, tell the reader about it immediately.

If you don't know whether there is a position available, but are merely making a general inquiry, try to be specific about the type of job you're after. This will enable the prospective employer (or recruiter) to focus his or her search.

Be creative. If you're applying for an advertising job, write the headline. If profits are the name of the game, and you've been a winner, put it in the first few sentences. If you want to catch your reader's attention, you're going to have to show him or her early on why you're the perfect person for the job.

(continued)

8 Close the deal. If openings are the most important parts of selling letters, closings can't be far behind. A good finale looks forward and tells the reader what action will be taken in the future.

If you intend to follow up with a phone call, let your reader know when he or she can expect to hear from you. If you would like the person to contact you, give your phone number and the times of day when you can be reached most easily.

The following conclusion, from a letter written shortly before Christmas, resulted in an interview just after the New Year.

I would like to meet with you, at your convenience, to discuss the possibility of a mutually beneficial employment. You can reach me at work on (212) 222-2222 or at home on (212) 333-3333. I am looking forward to hearing from you. Happy holidays.

9 Don't forget the finishing touches. Before you send your letter, double-check the name, title, department, and address. Be especially careful about Jr.'s, PhD's, Inc.'s, and Co.'s. Be sure you have proofread your letter for typos, misspellings, and improper grammar. Read your letter over and make sure that it is concise. Take out extraneous words, tighten up your sentences, and be sure your punctuation is correct.

Keep paragraphs short. Nothing will put off a reader more than large blocks of type. Leave adequate margins all around the page. This is easier on the eyes and gives the reader a place to make notes.

Finally, be careful to choose high-quality paper. Stay away from paper that is flimsy and almost transparent. As a general rule, color should be limited to white, ivory, or light gray. Although appearances might not be everything, they are a sure way to gain or lose your prospect's respect and interest even before he or she starts to read what you've sent. Your written correspondence should contribute to a professional, polished image.

Consultant Pamela E. Berns, a former advertising account executive, conducts workshops and seminars on business writing.

For additional information
Getting To the Right Job by Steve Cohen and Paulo de Oliveira. Workman. $6.95, paperback.

Comprehension Check: Instructional Pattern

List as many as you can of the nine steps in writing a persuasive cover letter.

1.
2.
3.
4.
5.
6.
7.
8.
9.

Posttest

Reading often is an overlooked communication skill in business and professional communication texts. We're convinced that you can become a more efficient reader if you assess what slows you down; practice reading with flexibility; and learn to recognize problem–solution, persuasive, informative, and instructional organizational patterns.

Refining your reading skills now will serve you well later as an organizational communicator. Think of it this way. Assume you have one hour of reading to do each day in your first position. If you can increase your reading speed by just one hundred words per minute without any loss in comprehension, then you will be able to read one hour's worth of reading in forty minutes. Now multiply the twenty minutes you save by five days per week, fifty weeks per year. By increasing your reading speed a modest 100 words per minute, you've already saved 416 hours during your first five years on the job.

Even though our focus here has been on efficient reading, we hope you've also learned about career planning, technical skills, job satisfaction, the reasons why people get fired, and writing a persuasive cover letter. We have one more important topic for you to read about: negotiating your first salary. Using the strategies we've shown you, read the closing article. Measure your speed and comprehension, compute your reading-efficiency score, and compare your posttest and pretest scores.

The Fine Art of Salary Negotiations

Marilyn Moats Kennedy

The person who gets the best offer is rarely the most qualified. The winner is the candidate best prepared to negotiate. Here's how to do it.

What salary should you ask for on that first job? This can be a difficult question, especially if your work experience has been limited, if you don't have a degree in the field you're applying for, or you don't have contacts in the field.

But you've been to an interview with a company you like. The job looks good, and the manager seems to be someone you could work with and for comfortably. You're hoping for an offer. The problem is you have no idea what salary to mention if you're asked what you have in mind. The tendency is to assume that whatever the company offers is the going rate and should be accepted. This is not true. Once you are in the working world you're expected to know the rules, even if they've never been explained.

As with everything else, there are strategies to the fine art of successful salary negotiation. Even if this is your first full-time job, you must be prepared to negotiate for money. Therefore you need to know how salaries are set and the role you play in the negotiation process. And don't forget the fringe benefits. They are part of salary negotiations.

When a prospective employer says to a candidate, "What salary do you have in mind?" that person is playing a game. The employer is testing to see if the candidate knows the going market rate. Employers know the market rate. They want to see if the prospect knows. For instance, suppose the employer knows that most companies pay between $26,000 and $28,000 for a BA in accounting.* If the prospect, when asked for a range, says, "$24,000 to $26,000," the employer can offer him or her $25,000, the middle of the candidate's range. The candidate will think he or she is getting more than the minimum salary and the employer will save $1,000.

If the job hunter agrees, only to find that fellow employees doing the same work are making at least $1,000 more, he or she will be upset. If the new employee goes to the boss and says, "I'm being paid less than other people doing the same job," the boss is likely to reply, "But we're paying you more than you asked for." Both statements are true. Unfortunately, the now angry new employee is unlikely to be either motivated or effective after such an experience.

Long before you reach the final interview or the job offer you need to know

Reprinted by permission of the author.

the kind of job you're interested in and the salary it pays in a specific geographic area. Here's how to get this information.

- Call your college placement office and ask if companies have been recruiting for the kind of job you're interested in. Ask what salary range was mentioned. Describe the job in detail, including the kind of work you want to do. Job titles are frequently misleading. A management job in one company is a staff job elsewhere — and that affects the pay scale. Most important, describe the size of the company in sales volume and mention the industry. Ask the placement counselor if requests have been received for people to fill the kind of job you're applying for in the past few months. If so, what was the salary range mentioned?

- Get the names of several personnel agencies who place people in your target job and industry. The placement office may suggest several agencies. A better source is friends who are several years older who've used such agencies. Call the agencies, speak to a placement person and repeat the job description and questions you asked above.

- Find a friend or friends in a Fortune 500 company which has a job-posting system. This is a program in which announcements of all job openings are posted on bulletin boards or in the company newsletter so that employees can apply for them first. Ask friends to check the listings for jobs similar to the one you want.

- Locate a friend in a nonprofit organization such as a hospital or university or both and ask the same question as those in the paragraph above.

- Check the want ads in the Sunday edition of your town's newspapers. Some of them will include salary range. If not, and there's a telephone number, call the next day. Try to find the salary range the company has in mind. Your personal salary survey should include five to ten different sources.

Why do you need this information? Because the second part of salary negotiations is when the prospective employer says, (if you name the correct salary range), "What makes you think you're worth that kind of money?"

The answer to that question is not, "I think I'm worth it," but, "The market in this area for this job is X to Y dollars. I expect to be paid the market rate." This is better than trying to justify an argument or prove your superiority to other candidates. It also tells the employer that you have taken the time to get the facts.

The game being played is really, "Can you guess what I'm thinking?" or "Can you guess the cards I'm holding?" The employer's job is to hire the best possible talent at the most reasonable price.

Employers have something else working for them, too. For most people salary information is the last frontier of privacy. If you ask someone at a party about his or her love life you are more likely to hear the dreary details than if

(continued)

you ask how much money he or she earns. That person will fall in the onion dip rather than answer the question. The subject is taboo because, at gut level, most people believe they are what they earn. Fighting that conspiracy of silence requires some creativity if you're not to become both better paid and a social outcast at the same time.

The best way is to be honest. You would never ask a friend exactly what he or she earns. Instead you'd say, "As you know, I'm applying for a job at Bachmann Enterprises as — give a brief description and title if it helps clarify what the job involves. I've been doing my own salary survey because I expect the interviewer to ask me what salary I want the next time we meet. Here's the information I have. Describe what others have told you from job postings, employment agencies, and contacts. What do you think? Are these people on target?"

At that point your friend is likely to indicate whether the range you have in mind is high or low based on his or her experience. You have not intruded on your friend's privacy and, in addition,

---

7 Keys to Salary Negotiation

••

1. The candidate who has the most information impresses the prospective employer on two levels: preparedness and follow-through — both important qualities.

2. Quiet, insistent repetition is the most effective technique you can use in negotiating for money. When the person raises an objection, say, "I understand that. However, here's why I think this salary range is right, (proper), (correct)." Never say, "I don't agree" or "That's wrong."

3. Keep your salary discussion with a prospective employer focused on the issue of market rate. It is difficult to explain as a beginner why you are the best candidate for the job. It's easier to be convincing with the market rate argument.

4. Research indicates that 80% of the people who turn down the first salary offer get a second offer even if it's only a few hundred dollars higher.

5. Ask yourself, "What would make this employer want to pay me the market rate? Are there skills I haven't sold properly?"

6. Do I have any examples I can give which will help my case? For instance, are there people I know doing the same job elsewhere for the salary I want?

7. Have I given the prospective employer the idea that I'll work for any sum just to get a job? If you have, keep in mind that the employer may remember this fact at your first salary review and decide to give you a below average increase.

you may have provided him or her with valuable information.

When you have a salary range in mind it's time to discuss benefits. It's not good form to bring up benefits until you're sure you want the job and a firm offer has been made. That doesn't mean that benefits aren't negotiable. They are. It's a matter of timing. The two benefits new workers tend to want are graduate school tuition reimbursement or assistance and more vacation than is usually allotted to an employee. If either or both are on your agenda, it's important to find out if they are available and what benefits you might exchange for them.

It is also important to ask in detail about the company's health insurance policy. A serious accident could bankrupt you if your insurance coverage isn't adequate. Get the facts from the personnel department before you decide.

Your best bet in thinking about salary negotiation is to keep in mind that though there has been a recent recession you are building a salary history which spans many years. Don't be panicked by a climate of fear which presses you to take whatever you can get. The economic climate will improve and you'll have to live with the results of your decision long after its cause has disappeared.

One of the ironies of salary negotiation is that the person who gets the most money, the best offer, or more benefits, is rarely the most qualified candidate. The winner is the candidate best prepared to negotiate. Make it your business to know the market rate in your field. It can pay off in a higher salary on that important first job.

Salary data updated from Statistical Abstract of the United States, 1990, *Bureau of the Census, U.S. Dept. of Commerce, Library of Congress, Washington D.C., 161.*

Marilyn Moats Kennedy is the founder and managing partner of Career Strategies in Evanston, Ill. She specializes in writing about careers.

For additional information
Higher Salaries: How to Get Them by Joyce Lain Kennedy. 24 pages: $3.50. Sun Features Inc. Box 2000-H, Cardiff, Calif. 92007.
Salary Strategies: Everything You Need to Know to Get the Salary You Want by Marilyn Moats Kennedy. Rawson, Wade Publishers, Inc. 242 pages; $12.95.

....

Posttest Check

Circle the correct response for each question. Then check your answers and compute the number of questions you answered correctly; each correct answer is worth ten points.

1. When a prospective employer asks you what salary you have in mind:
   a. he or she is playing a game.
   b. he or she expects you to know the current market rate.
   c. he or she is following company policy.
2. Before you reach the final interview stage, you should:
   a. get information for a personal salary survey from one or two sources.
   b. ask a good friend in the work force what he or she is earning.
   c. check on salary ranges at your college placement office for the kind of company in which you're interested.
3. The two benefits most new workers want are:
   a. time off and a good pension plan.
   b. reimbursement or assistance with graduate-school tuition and more vacation than is usually allotted.
   c. day care and extended vacations.
4. According to the author:
   a. The person who gets the best job offer is rarely the best qualified candidate.
   b. You should offer to accept any salary just to get that first job.
   c. You should focus your salary request on why you are the best candidate.
5. Which of the following is true?
   a. Regardless of your fears, you should not hesitate to turn down an initial offer if you believe it is too low. Research indicates that a second offer probably will be forthcoming.
   b. You shouldn't expect to receive a market-rate salary on your first job.
   c. You shouldn't provide a prospective employer with examples of other people who do the job you want for the salary you want. This may be perceived as intimidation.
6. The best way to negotiate for money is by:
   a. forceful but polite argument.
   b. quiet but insistent repetition.
   c. letting the prospective employer make the first move.

7. According to Kennedy:
   a. You should discuss benefits early in the negotiation process because they are one part of a total salary package.
   b. Once you're in the working world, you're expected to know the rules about salary negotiations.
   c. Health insurance is a benefit included in every job.
8. During salary negotiations, you should:
   a. adequately sell your skills so that the prospective employer will want to offer you the current market rate.
   b. be informed. The candidate who knows the score demonstrates preparedness and follow through.
   c. a and b.
9. When you are collecting information for your personal salary survey, you should *not*:
   a. call several people at random in the company you want to work for and ask them about starting salaries.
   b. call friends in a Fortune 500 company that posts jobs openings and ask them to check salary listings for jobs similar to the one you want.
   c. check local want ads.
10. When you have an interview with a company you like and are hoping for an offer:
    a. you should realize that many companies don't negotiate salaries.
    b. you should understand how salaries are set and what role you should play in the negotiation.
    c. you should inflate or fabricate offers you've had from other companies. This is standard practice.

CHAPTER SUMMARY

We began our discussion of reading with a summary of the kinds of reading you'll find yourself doing in organizations: reading for *survival*, for *advancement*, and for *enjoyment*. We also presented guidelines for your consideration, suggestions that range from finding time to read within the organization to approaching reading tasks with an expectant, enthusiastic attitude.

Next we turned our attention to the *reading process* itself. We pointed out potential pitfalls that can slow readers down: *lip reading, individual* word reading, generic reading, head rotating, word halting, tunnel vision, backtracking, and reading on automatic pilot. We also discussed reading techniques that centered on reading flexibility. Previewing, skimming, and clustering are techniques worth practicing.

We concluded our discussion of reading with advice on the value of recognizing organizational patterns. Four patterns are used most often in business writing: problem–solution, persuasive, informative, and instructional. Learning to recognize these patterns and their components can be invaluable in better time management.

MEASURING SUCCESS

1. The chapter described three reasons why organizational communicators read: for survival, for advancement, and for fun. Perhaps the same motivations hold true for you now as a student. What materials do you read out of necessity, what do you read to better yourself, and what do you read for enjoyment? Think about your reading habits over the last six months or year and list as many items as you can in each category.

2. The chapter identified eight problems that could be slowing down your reading rate. Do any of these problems apply to you? Do certain problems appear more frequently with particular types of reading material? If so, go beyond the general suggestions we've provided and write an action plan — specific steps you can take to improve your reading.

3. Find a recent edition of the Wall Street Journal and try the skimming and clustering techniques we've described. Locate an article of interest to you and skim it by sweeping your eyes across each line, picking up a few words per line. Afterward, summarize the article in a paragraph and check your summary against the original article. Locate a second article of interest and practice widening your eye span by clustering words together. These techniques take conscientious practice but are well worth your effort. After trying the clustering technique, check your comprehension by returning to the article you read.

4. Peruse recent editions of business periodicals such as Personnel, Training and Development, and Supervisory Management to find examples of the four organizational patterns described in this chapter. After you locate good models of the four patterns (file drawers), identify the com-

ponents of each article (information to fill each folder). For example, for the persuasive example you select, identify the author's *assertion, evidence*, and *expected outcome*.

Decco Exercise Assume your boss has asked you to design and teach a three-hour information seminar titled "Improving Reading Skills" for interested company employees. In a brief memo to the boss, summarize your ideas on this program's content.

....

Answer Key

Pretest: "Blueprint for Career Planning"

1. c
2. b
3. c
4. a
5. b
6. c
7. a
8. a
9. b
10. a

Problem–Solution Pattern: "Technical Skills You Need to Succeed"

1. Today's business world requires extensive and broad-based technical skills.
2. Specialization and "pigeonholing" are less valuable to organizations; lifetime learning is a requirement.
3. The problem is caused by the pervasiveness of computers, international competition and labor dissatisfaction, expectations of promotion, emerging management styles of "task teams," the widespread nature of job changing, and so on.
4. Students about to enter the business world must develop *mechanical, informational, financial*, and *operational* skills to succeed.

Persuasive Pattern: "The Importance of Job Satisfaction"

1. c
2. d
3. a

Informative Pattern: "Ten Reasons People Get Fired"

1. Failure to fit in
2. Overselling yourself and your qualifications
3. Bad chemistry with the boss
4. Rigidity, unmanageability, or both on the job
5. Lack of necessary skills
6. Office politics
7. Refusal to conform to unspoken rules
8. Failure to be a team player
9. Business dislocation
10. Poor judgment

Instructional Pattern: "Nine Steps to a Persuasive Cover Letter"

1. Start with self-analysis.
2. Narrow your appeal.
3. Accentuate the positive.
4. Eliminate the negative.
5. Respect your reader.
6. Concentrate on what you can do for the employer.
7. Write an attention-getting introduction.
8. Close the deal.
9. Don't forget the finishing touches.

Posttest: "The Fine Art of Salary Negotiations"

1. a
2. c
3. b
4. a
5. a
6. b
7. b
8. c
9. a
10. b

MINUTES: SECONDS	PRETEST: "BLUEPRINT FOR CAREER PLANNING" (2400 WORDS)	PROBLEM SOLUTION: "TECHNICAL SKILLS YOU NEED TO SUCCEED" (2900 WORDS)	PERSUASIVE: "THE IMPORTANCE OF JOB SATISFACTION" (1780 WORDS)	INFORMATIVE: "10 REASONS PEOPLE GET FIRED" (2630 WORDS)	INSTRUCTIONAL: "9 STEPS TO A PERSUASIVE COVER LETTER" (2300 WORDS)	POSTTEST: "THE FINE ART OF SALARY NEGOTIATIONS" (1630 WORDS)	SECONDS
:30	4800	5800	3560	5760	4600	3260	30
:40	3600	4350	2670	3945	3450	2445	40
:50	2800	3480	2136	3156	2760	1956	50
1:00	2400	2900	1780	2630	2300	1630	60
1:10	2057	2486	1526	2254	1970	1400	70
1:20	1800	2175	1335	1972	1725	1220	80
1:30	1600	1933	1187	1753	1530	1090	90
1:40	1440	1740	1068	1578	1380	980	100
1:50	1310	1582	971	1435	1255	890	110
2:00	1200	1450	890	1315	1150	815	120
2:10	1108	1338	822	1214	1060	750	130
2:20	1029	1243	763	1127	986	700	140
2:30	960	1160	712	1052	920	650	150
2:40	900	1087	667	986	862	610	160
2:50	847	1024	628	928	812	575	170
3:00	800	967	593	877	767	543	180
3:10	758	916	562	831	726	515	190
3:20	720	870	534	789	690	490	200
3:30	686	829	509	751	657	466	210
3:40	655	791	485	719	627	444	220
3:50	626	757	464	687	600	425	230
4:00	600	725	445	659	575	408	240
4:10	576	696	427	632	552	391	250
4:20	554	669	411	608	531	376	260
4:30	533	644	396	586	511	362	270
4:40	514	621	381	565	493	350	280
4:50	497	600	368	545	476	337	290
5:00	480	580	356	527	460	326	300
5:10	465	561	345	510	445	315	310

Table 3.1 Words-per-Minute Chart

MINUTES: SECONDS	PRETEST: "BLUEPRINT FOR CAREER PLANNING" (2400 WORDS)	PROBLEM SOLUTION: "TECHNICAL SKILLS YOU NEED TO SUCCEED" (2900 WORDS)	PERSUASIVE: "THE IMPORTANCE OF JOB SATISFACTION" (1780 WORDS)	INFORMATIVE: "10 REASONS PEOPLE GET FIRED" (2630 WORDS)	INSTRUCTIONAL: "9 STEPS TO A PERSUASIVE COVER LETTER" (2300 WORDS)	POSTTEST: "THE FINE ART OF SALARY NEGOTIATIONS" (1630 WORDS)	SECONDS
5:20	450	543	338	494	431	304	320
5:30	436	527	324	479	418	296	330
5:40	424	512	314	465	406	288	340
5:50	411	497	305	452	394	280	350
6:00	400	483	297	439	383	272	360
6:10	389	470	289	427	373	264	370
6:20	379	458	281	416	363	257	380
6:30	369	446	274	405	354	251	390
6:40	360	435	267	395	345	245	400
6:50	351	424	260	385	337	239	410
7:00	343	414	254	376	329	234	420
7:10	335	403	248	367	321	227	430
7:20	328	395	243	359	314	222	440
7:30	321	387	237	351	307	217	450
7:40	314	378	232	343	300	213	460
7:50	307	370	227	336	294	208	470
8:00	300	362	223	329	287	204	480
8:10	294	355	218	322	282	200	490
8:20	288	348	214	316	276	196	500
8:30	282	341	209	309	271	192	510
8:40	277	335	205	303	265	188	520
8:50	272	329	202	298	260	184	530
9:00	267	323	198	292	255	181	540
9:10	262	316	194	287	251	178	550
9:20	257	310	191	282	246	175	560
9:30	253	305	187	277	242	172	570
9:40	248	300	184	272	238	169	580
9:50	244	295	181	268	234	166	590
10:00	240	290	178	263	230	163	600

Table 3.1 Words-per-Minute Chart (continued)

MINUTES: SECONDS	PRETEST: "BLUEPRINT FOR CAREER PLANNING" (2400 WORDS)	PROBLEM SOLUTION: "TECHNICAL SKILLS YOU NEED TO SUCCEED" (2900 WORDS)	PERSUASIVE: "THE IMPORTANCE OF JOB SATISFACTION" (1780 WORDS)	INFORMATIVE: "10 REASONS PEOPLE GET FIRED" (2630 WORDS)	INSTRUCTIONAL: "9 STEPS TO A PERSUASIVE COVER LETTER" (2300 WORDS)	POSTTEST: "THE FINE ART OF SALARY NEGOTIATIONS" (1630 WORDS)	SECONDS
10:10	236	285	175	259	226	160	610
10:20	232	281	172	255	222	157	620
10:30	229	276	170	251	219	155	630
10:40	225	272	167	247	216	153	640
10:50	222	268	164	243	212	150	650
11:00	218	264	162	239	209	148	660
11:10	215	260	159	235	206	146	670
11:20	212	256	157	232	203	144	680
11:30	209	252	155	229	200	142	690
11:40	206	249	153	225	197	140	700
11:50	203	245	150	222	194	138	710
12:00	200	242	148	219	192	136	720
12:10	198	238	146	216	189	134	730
12:20	196	235	144	213	186	132	740
12:30	193	232	142	210	184	130	750
12:40	190	229	140	208	182	128	760
12:50	187	226	139	205	180	127	770
13:00	185	223	137	203	177	125	780
13:10	182	220	135	200	175	124	790
13:20	180	217	134	197	173	122	800
13:30	178	214	132	195	170	121	810
13:40	176	211	130	192	168	119	820
13:50	174	209	129	190	166	117	830
14:00	172	207	127	188	164	116	840
14:10	170	204	126	186	162	115	850
14:20	168	201	124	183	160	114	860
14:30	166	199	123	181	159	112	870
14:40	164	197	121	179	157	111	880
14:50	162	195	120	177	155	110	890
15:00	160	193	119	175	153	109	900

Table 3.1 *Words-per-Minute Chart (continued)*

Notes

1. Richard Saul Wurman, *Information Anxiety* (New York: Doubleday, 1989), 32.

2. Anthony P. Carnevale, Leila J. Gainer, Ann S. Meltzer, and Shari L. Holland, "Workplace Basics: The Skills Employers Want," *Training and Development Journal* 42 (October 1988): 25.

3. R. Alec Mackenzie, *The Time Trap: How to Get More Done in Less Time* (New York: McGraw-Hill, 1972), 72.

4. MacKenzie, *The Time Trap,* 77–78.

5. Francesca Turchiano-Bumcrot, "Successfully Reading Large Numbers of Reports." In John Louis DiGaetani, Ed., *The Handbook of Executive Communication* (Homewood, IL: Dow Jones–Irwin, 1986), 462–468.

6. Turchiano-Bumcrot, "Successfully Reading," 463–464.

7. James I. Brown, *Efficient Reading* (Boston: D.C. Heath, 1962).

8. Turchiano-Bumcrot, "Successfully Reading," 466–468.

9. Kit Morgan, "The ABCs of Better Reading Power," *Executive* 26 (May 1984): 63.

10. Lyle L. Miller, *Personalizing Reading Efficiency: Seek the Ideas Behind the Words,* 2nd ed. (Minneapolis, MN: Burgess, 1981), 13; Morgan, "The ABCs," 60.

11. Brown, *Efficient Reading,* 12.

12. Miller, *Personalizing Reading,* 13–14.

13. Bill Cosby, "How to Read Faster." In William I. Gorden and John R. Miller, *Managing Your Communication — In and For the Organization* (Prospect Heights, IL: Waveland Press, 1983), 6–7.

14. Richard P. Santeusanio, *Developing Reading Skills for Business and Industry* (Boston: CBI, 1981), 37–38.

15. Otis Port, "Business in the Year 2001," *Business Week's Guide to Careers* 1 (Fall–Winter 1983): 53.

16. Our discussion of organizational reading patterns is adapted from Santeusanio, *Developing Reading Skills,* 50–51, 87–88, 150–151, and 196–197.

Timed reading selections in this chapter include:

Marilyn Moats Kennedy, "Blueprint for Career Planning," *Business Week's Guide to Careers* 1 (Fall/Winter 1983): 60–61.

Steven S. Ross, "Technical Skills You Need to Succeed," *Business Week's Guide to Careers* 1 (Fall/Winter 1983): 24–28.

Marilyn Moats Kennedy, "The Importance of Job Satisfaction," *Business Week's Guide to Careers* 4 (Spring/Summer 1986): 118, 120, 124.

Marilyn Moats Kennedy, "Ten Reasons People Get Fired," *Business Week's Careers* 4 (September 1987): 39–41.

Pamela E. Berns, "Nine Steps to a Persuasive Cover Letter," *Business Week's Careers* 5 (September 1987): 115–116, 118.

Marilyn Moats Kennedy, "The Fine Art of Salary Negotiations," *Business Week's Guide to Careers* 1 (Fall/Winter 1983): 62–63.

Part III 🖋️ The Spoken Word

Chapter 4 ✏ **Preparing a Successful Presentation**

A mighty thing is eloquence . . . nothing so much

rules the world. — Pope Pius II (1405–1464)

Picture this. You graduated recently from

your college or university and landed a good

position with a major corporation. After six

successful months working almost exclusively

on a priority project, your supervisor asks you to prepare a presentation for a group of high-level managers. You are asked to report not only your progress but also your plans for completing the project and implementing your results.

This is the chance you've been waiting for, an opportunity to demonstrate your enthusiasm and competence to your new colleagues and superiors. The excitement you feel, however, may be tempered by the slightest twinge of anxiety you feel as a junior employee who has been asked to present information to senior managers. You may even be tempted by the flight half of the "fight-or-flight" syndrome. At worst, you may tell yourself, perhaps you could go into some other line of work.

If you've already faced a similar challenge, you probably know what we're talking about. In Chapter 2, we dealt with the problem of writer's block, or the "tyranny of the blank page." In some ways, speech anxiety is a similar phenomenon; in both cases, anxiety immobilizes and prevents peak performance. The difference, of course, is that writer's block occurs in the privacy of your office, while speech anxiety occurs in the public context of the conference room. In our next chapter, we'll present new ways of looking at the problem of speech anxiety as well as practical antidotes.

According to the *Book of Lists*, public speaking is the number-one fear in the United States.[1] It is more frightening for most of us than death, sickness, deep water, financial problems, insects, or high places. We often have speculated on the box-office sensations Hollywood could create if it only knew what terrifies us the most. Imagine a major movie thriller not about threatening aliens, towering infernos, or killer tomatoes but instead a nail-biting "edge-of-your-seater" titled *PODIUM*. Unfortunately, it appears that what we fear most is one another.

Because presentational speaking is one of the most *pervasive*, most *popular*, and most *problematic* forms of communication in organizations, now is the time to begin preparing for the inevitable. We must take

BLOOM COUNTY   by Berke Breathed

responsibility as communicators and realize that *we* are the ones who push the panic button, who react negatively to an *opportunity* to demonstrate our competence, and thus to experience success. One expert uses an equation you may remember from science classes to create a helpful and pertinent analogy.[2]

Ohm's Law:

$$\text{Current at point of use} = \frac{\text{Power source}}{\text{Resistance}}$$

Similarly:

$$\text{My level of communication excellence} = \frac{\text{Creative potential}}{\text{Fears, resentments, prejudices}}$$

In other words, to some extent, whether we are successful communicators is simply a matter of choice; the barriers are self-imposed. Most of us realize intuitively that speaking publicly is one of the most immediate and direct representations of who we are — even more so than our writing. How prepared, articulate, and composed we are during a presentation all connect directly to our intelligence, reputations, and sometimes sensitive egos. Within organizations, we also can identify very real connections between communication competence and pragmatic outcomes such as career advancement. Because we live in a time during which corporations are downsizing and more people are technically qualified (or overqualified) for fewer choice positions, it stands to reason that those who can best communicate their competence will be the most successful.

The information in this chapter may be applied to both *internal* presentations (such as delivering a briefing, proposal, or evaluation within your organization) and *external* presentations (addressing a civic, educational, or parent group as a representative of your organization or as a private citizen). We believe that what follows is good advice for both types of presentations, but you'll notice that we focus more attention on the first category. Most likely, your internal presentations to your business or professional subordinates, peers, and superiors — those for and with whom you work — will most affect your organizational success. And that is our concern here.

PRESENTING FACTS AND IDEAS ORALLY

We have identified presentations as pervasive and popular within business and the professions. Why is this so? In organizational contexts, presentations offer the following distinct advantages over other forms of communication.

- *Immediate response.* Presentations allow you to find out what others think of your ideas on the spot, whereas others may take weeks or months to read and respond to written reports.
- *Maximum control.* As speaker, you control the information that you disclose. *You* are the "expert" in charge. When you send a letter or memo, you relinquish control to your reader (who simply may deposit your hard work into "file thirteen").
- *Visual and auditory impact.* Rather than the mere visual impact of writing, speaking allows those who are present to listen to your words and watch you deliver your presentation.
- *Less work.* Listening to a presentation often is easier and faster than deciphering a lengthy report.

We also have identified presentations as problematic. Consider the following disadvantages:

- *Transitory nature.* Presentations are here one moment and gone the next. If you are lucky, your audience will remember 50 percent of what you have said by the time you finish. A written report, on the other hand, becomes a permanent record for later reference.
- *Cost.* The expenses of artwork, arrangements, and materials can become staggering, and the salaries of those who attend could be better spent on more "productive" work.
- *Unwieldiness.* For extremely large groups, presentations are an awkward way to present information. If you must reach all 5,000 employees in your company, a letter or memo simply is more efficient.
- *Sender control.* If a speaker is a competent communicator, then sender control is not a problem. But if the speaker moves too slowly or too quickly, or if the message is poorly organized, underdeveloped, or oversophisticated, then the audience probably can do little to change the situation. Writing, on the other hand, is more receiver-controlled: The reader determines the appropriate pace for processing the information in a document.[3]

These are the advantages and disadvantages you must consider when deciding whether you will put together a presentation or a paper. Of course, much of the information about organization, tone, and style in Chapter 2 also applies to presentational speaking. The URBAN method, in particular, can serve as an excellent checklist in preparing a successful organizational presentation. Just as when you write a memo or report, you want listeners to your presentation to Understand, Remember,

Believe, and **A**ct so that you can **N**ote results. On the other hand, presentations also are a breed unto themselves and deserve specific strategies to ensure success.

THE STEPS TO SUCCESS

Regardless of why you put together a presentation, following certain preparatory steps will mean success. Business and professional presentations typically are designed with particular *purposes* in mind: to *inform, persuade, entertain*, or *inspire*. Obviously, these categories overlap to some extent. In a successful informative presentation, you must persuade your audience that what you're saying is both true and important. A persuasive presentation most definitely will contain information. In many, if not most, business presentations, persuasion is the bottom line, and this is where we will direct your attention. But to simplify matters initially, consider the following situations in which you may well find yourself.

- *Informing*. You may be asked to give a briefing or short report that will give busy executives and supervisors predigested information.
- *Persuading*. You may be required to prepare an oral proposal, which generally accompanies a written report, to persuade your superiors to approve a new policy.
- *Entertaining*. You may wish to present an award, "roast" a retiring colleague, or serve as an emcee for the company social event of the year.
- *Inspiring*. You may be asked to motivate a group of subordinates as they begin a new task or anticipate difficult change.

Typically, you will have one primary purpose in mind when you begin preparing a presentation. However, if you've been asked to deliver a presentation on the company's five-year plan to all employees, you may have all four purposes in mind. You'll want to *persuade* employees that the company is on solid financial footing, *inform* them about the business decisions to be made over the next five years, *entertain* them or at least deliver an interesting and enjoyable presentation, and *inspire* them to continue working hard for the company's success.

If you are assigned a speaking task on the job, or if you volunteer, how should you proceed? What are the steps to success? We have identified six fundamental steps from many excellent sources as well as from our own experience over many years.[4] The six steps to success are: (1) clarifying your objective, (2) analyzing your audience, (3) developing your game plan, (4) collecting and organizing your information, (5) choosing your visual aids, and (6) preparing your notes.

Step 1: Clarify Your Objective

Clarify the objective of your presentation. What result are you seeking? At the outset, you will choose no doubt from among the overall purposes just discussed: to persuade, inform, entertain, or inspire. More specifically, however, *what* do you want your listeners to know, believe, or do when you are finished? Although one of your objectives always will be to deliver an outstanding presentation, remember that it is merely a means to the actual end you seek.

For example, imagine that you and your colleagues in the human resources department have just completed a study on employees' preferences for day-care options for their children. Now you must prepare a presentation to senior managers on your findings. Step 1 will include considering your range of possible objectives and then targeting one.

You could simply inform managers of the results of your study, in which case your objective would be to simply increase their knowledge. However, instead you might want to persuade them to approve an in-depth cost analysis of the options that you present (building an on-site facility, contracting with local nursery schools, or using licensed in-home care facilities). On the other hand, if you want to present your findings and then recommend building an on-site facility, you could try to persuade your listeners to approve soliciting architects' bids. In each case, your objective would be to reach a consensus by the end of the meeting. Or you could simply ask them which course of action should result from the study. Whether your purpose is to inform or to persuade, your targeted *objective* is different in each case, from simply increasing your listeners' knowledge to reaching a consensus to requesting suggestions for a specific next step (see Table 4.1).

We cannot overemphasize the importance of Step 1. Defining your goals carefully and specifically will help you in several ways:

- You will be forced to clarify in your own mind the issue that prompted the presentation.
- You will be better able to establish a central idea or a statement

Table 4.1 *Day-Care Presentation Objectives*

PURPOSE	DESIRED OBJECTIVE
Inform	Increase knowledge
Persuade	Reach consensus: approve further study or recommended action Solicit suggestions for next step

of the single most important fact, attitude, or belief that you want your listeners to have.
- You will be required to limit the content of the presentation to what is *critical* to achieving your specific objective.
- You will pave the way to making important tactical decisions about such issues as formality and timing.
- You will indirectly define your own criteria for success based on whether you meet your objective.

Accomplishing this step early, when possible, also can reduce your anxiety because you become more comfortable with your ideas. Think about the objectives of your presentation while you walk to the grocery store, while you stand in line at the movies, while you fill your car at the service station. As the saying goes, "The more you sweat *beforehand*, the less you will have to sweat *during* your presentation." Mark Twain once remarked that it takes three weeks to prepare a good ad-lib speech. We wonder what guidelines he might have provided for those in business and the professions who speak to important people about "high-stakes" issues. In our business and government careers, we have seen presentations in which the stakes were literally high enough to make or break an organization.

Step 2: Analyze Your Audience

Analyzing your audience is not new advice. If you ever have taken a basic course in speech making, you recognize this fundamental law of public speaking. However, in preparing for a presentation in business and the professions, where costly decisions and months or years of work may be at stake, Step 2 has added significance. After you have determined who is likely to be present, you must ask yourself four critical questions:

Table 4.2 *Audience-Analysis Matrix*

	KNOWLEDGE	INTEREST	ATTITUDES	POWER
Sue Nurlator				
Phil A. Buster				
Mal Praktiss				
Holly Tosiss				
Bill Klector				

1. What do they already know about my topic?
2. What would they like to know; or rather, what do they *need* to know?
3. What are their attitudes about me, my position, and my proposal?
4. What capabilities or decision-making powers do they have?

In other words, you must consider the audience members in terms of their *knowledge, interest, attitudes,* and *power.*

Even if you aren't sure who will attend, you still must find the answers to these questions; the process will simply require more detective work. After all, your goal is to achieve a presentation that is likely to be successful by focusing on your audience rather than on yourself, an *audience-conscious* rather than a *self-conscious* presentation.

During this planning stage, you may wish to create a matrix with these four categories across the top and key audience members listed on the left.[5] Table 4.2 shows a sample audience-analysis matrix.

What you must determine ultimately is *how* each listener characteristic will affect your presentation. If you know who will attend or if the group is small, then consider each person's characteristics. Of course, if you do not know who will attend or if the group is large, then you'll need to think less about individuals and more about the group as a whole. It may help to consider these facets of your audience: knowledge, interest, attitudes, and power.

Knowledge. During your preliminary analysis, you must discover how much your audience knows about your topic. If you are not certain of everyone's level of expertise and cannot find out, then provide slightly more information than listeners need rather than slightly less. A brief summary that brings everyone to a common level of knowledge also may be helpful. But if your audience members have widely divergent levels of expertise — engineers who design the product versus consumers who buy the product — then you may need to give separate presentations. Assessing audience knowledge will affect such pragmatic decisions as the amount of jargon you can use safely. Audience members are likely to turn off if they cannot understand your language. Acronyms, for example, can be real time-savers; but if you use too many too rapidly or unintelligibly, then your presentation may be perceived as little more than alphabet soup. The rule we suggested earlier for business writing also works for business speaking: speak (and write) at your conversational *best*.

Interest. This assessment may be even more important than determining your listeners' prior knowledge. To make an accurate determination, consider their needs — organizational, departmental, and personal, both long-term and immediate. Again, if your listeners have divergent needs, you might give a summary presentation to everyone and then give a series of specialized presentations based on a stated agenda so that audience members can elect to hear what they need to hear.

Attitudes. You must not only consider what your listeners know and want to know but also recognize that they will respond with both head and heart to your message. How are they likely to feel about the ideas you are proposing? Will your proposal help them and their departments? Hurt them and their departments? Do your ideas represent an increased work load for them? In other words, assessing not only attitudes but also what is behind them will provide you with a clearer picture.

Power. This last point is especially important. The audience may have a favorable attitude toward you and your message after your presentation is over; but if your listeners have no power to implement your proposal, or influence those who do, then you have given your presentation to the wrong people. If you are proposing a new budgeting cycle for the company, then make sure the director of finance attends your presentation. Tailor your presentation to the decision-making capabilities of your listeners and make certain you've included the decision makers whose approval you need.

Step 3: Develop Your Game Plan

To ensure success in a business or professional presentation, this is one of the most important questions you can ask yourself: "How can I best begin planning my presentation with this blueprint in mind: formality, timing, physical arrangements, attendees, and key players?" Assuming that you are preparing an important persuasive presentation, let's look at examples of what we mean.

Formality. How formal should your presentation be? Should you wear jeans and sneakers and hold a relaxed conversation with your audience or wear a pin-striped suit and use elaborate visuals? Both kinds of presentation require thoughtful preparation, but you should consider several factors when making this decision.

To begin with, what is the precedent? What does the organizational culture dictate? If the organizational culture values informality and your superiors are of the "manage by wandering around" persuasion, then it may be inappropriate for you to go overboard and deliver a highly formal presentation when others have not done so in the past.

Beyond this initial consideration, Meuse suggests that you consider five issues: stakes, audience opposition, complexity, audience size, and repeat performances.[6] When the stakes are extremely high, when the audience is likely to oppose your ideas, when the material is highly complex, when the audience is large or enormously influential, and when you will have to repeat the presentation to several different groups—*then* a formal presentation is in order. When the stakes are not high, when the audience is on your side, when the material is not difficult, when the audience is small, and when you are giving a single performance—*then* the presentation safely can be less formal. Obviously, many variables enter into the picture; however, when the time comes, you probably will be able to weigh these factors and make the right decision.

Timing. Successfully timing your presentation is important. To do this, you must understand what is going on in your organization, your field, and the marketplace. Most experienced communicators prefer to give presentations on Tuesdays, Wednesdays, and Thursdays to avoid Monday morning doldrums and the Friday afternoon "TGIF" syndrome. They also understand the human-energy curve and aim for "peak" hours rather than times when listeners are "unfocused," such as early in the morning, or have "bottomed out," such as late in the day. On the other hand, if a potential client will make a decision on Monday, then a presentation on Tuesday is too late.

Beyond decisions on what time and which day, effective speakers make certain that key decision makers can be present, and they decide on the optimal amount of time for the presentation. This latter consideration, of course, partly depends on the amount of information you must cover; however, remember Shakespeare's advice, "Brevity is the soul of wit"; or the well-known rule of thumb, "Be sincere; be brief; be seated." Or remember the horrible fate of President William Henry Harrison: In 1841 he delivered the longest inaugural address in U.S. history — 9,000 words in more than two hours — into a freezing Northeast wind. He caught cold and died of pneumonia a month later. We don't mean to imply that this might happen to you; it could be worse!

Most experts agree that listeners have an endurance limit of approximately 1½ hours at a stretch. We do not suggest that you omit necessary detail or race through your presentation. We suggest, however, that you be efficient and considerate of your listeners' time. Complex subjects and voluminous material may have to be broken into a series of short, easily digestible presentations.

Physical Arrangements. We have discussed the *when* of your presentation, but what about the *where*? Believe it or not, you should consider such factors as the size, shape, acoustics, temperature, and air circulation of the presentation room. A room that is too large for your audience can make you sound as if you were speaking in a vault and thus erode your confidence. On the other hand, a crowded room can make participants feel claustrophobic and eager to leave. Although we'll wait until Chapter 5 to discuss such details as arranging the seats, lectern, and equipment, all of these factors will fit into your overall strategy for success.

Attendees. Who should attend your presentation? Obviously, those who have the power to make things happen. Of course, those who "need to know" and those who will be affected by the content of your presentation also are natural audience members. Often the decision about who will compose your group of listeners is made for you by your superiors or by the nature of your presentation.

Perhaps we should rephrase the question. Who should *not* attend your presentation? Individuals who oppose your ideas? Troublemakers? Although you might prefer to exclude these individuals, this is rarely possible, usually because you will *need* their cooperation to implement your ideas. Sometimes it is possible to invite a primary group to attend the presentation and send written summaries to a secondary one. Our upcoming discussions on predetermining support and responding to hostile questions will provide sound advice on this subject.

Key Players. Predetermining support for your objective is an often overlooked and yet critical dimension of strategy development. Many presentations are "killed" in the conference room simply because a speaker neglected this aspect of preparation. Sometimes you can do a great deal to ensure success by giving what might be called *minipresentations* to key players before the actual presentation. If you are advocating what you suspect will be an unpopular, controversial, or highly innovative idea, then you might consider giving a synopsis of the presentation to your immediate boss or several individuals at that level, incorporating their suggestions and giving a series of minipresentations up the chain of command. This is excellent preparation for your real presentation, and you are less likely to be surprised at your listeners' reactions. Lobbying individuals beforehand allows you to preview your ideas, test the waters, and refine your strategy.

You may be thinking, "This sounds good, but scouting the territory in advance is not foolproof. What if I am surprised through sabotage — one of my key players has a hidden agenda? This person sided with me during a preliminary interview, but is raising serious objections during my presentation." In this case, you must rely upon all the communication skills you can summon. You may have to firmly but politely call your adversary on the carpet: "Randolph, when we discussed this proposal in your office last week, you supported the idea 100 percent." No, predetermining support is not foolproof. Nothing is. But we cannot overemphasize its importance. Eventually, however, this aspect of preparation should become second nature to you.

Not doing your homework, on the other hand, can have devastating results. One of us once witnessed a presentation on a controversial subject made by a small group of officers to an Air Force general and his staff. Shortly into the presentation, the general, who disagreed vehemently with what he was hearing, stood up and took over the podium, had his aides bring in a new set of charts, and proceeded to give his own presentation. When asked why they hadn't followed the advice given in this chapter, the original presenters replied that they knew the general disagreed with their perspective, but that they had thought they could win him over during the presentation. They learned an important lesson the hard way: *during* a presentation may be too late.

The politics of presentations are an important aspect of preparation. We advise you to use the summary checklist in Table 4.3.

Step 4: Collect and Organize Your Information

You have set the stage by clarifying your presentation's objective, analyzing your audience, and developing a game plan geared to success. The backdrop is ready. Now comes the critical part of the process: "building" your presentation's content by selecting and arranging "blocks" of information.

The most useful analogy for this step of the process is to think of yourself as a GUIDE. Again, your audience comes to you with prior

Table 4.3 *Presentation Strategies*

1. Consider presenting your proposal to each decision maker individually before presenting it to them as a group. Decision makers rarely enjoy surprises when it comes to important decisions. Speakers, on the other hand, rarely enjoy surprises when it comes to how their ideas will be received.

2. Consider the best time of day to present your proposal.

3. Consider having someone else deliver the actual presentation, particularly if your role in the presentation could have politically undesirable results. In some instances, you may need to find a powerful champion to represent you. In other words, *who* speaks may be as important as what is said.

4. Consider the right location in which to make your presentation (off the premises rather than on, conference room rather than boardroom).

5. Consider coupling your proposal with another that you know will be a sure winner. The momentum of other green-light decisions may carry over to your presentation.

6. Consider sending the decision makers a written draft for critique before giving your presentation or submitting the final proposal — or better yet, ask for their suggestions in person. People rarely walk away from things in which they are invested.

7. Consider having a compromise position ready, a point to which you can fall back without losing everything.

8. Consider a new approach to funding your proposal (a grant, going over budget, cost-sharing with other units, changing the rules).

9. Consider whether the decision makers really are ready for your proposal.

10. Consider whether risking disapproval of this program may start a chain of events that multiplies the loss to your unit. Better to lose the battle and win the war!

Adapted from C. R. Bell, *Influencing: Marketing the Ideas that Matter* (San Diego, CA: University Associates, Inc., 1982), 157–158. Used with permission.

Table 4.4 *The GUIDE Checklist for Presentations*

• •

[G]	Get your audience's attention
[U]	"You"—Don't forget yourself
[I]	Ideas, ideas, ideas!
[D]	Develop an organizational structure
[E]	Exit gracefully and memorably

knowledge, attitudes, and beliefs about you and your proposal—hence the need for audience analysis discussed in Step 2. You are not communicating in a vacuum. Rather it is your task to *guide* listeners through the maze of ideas they already have to the new knowledge, attitudes, and beliefs you wish them to have.

Guides have particular tasks to perform and particular responsibilities to uphold. If you were to serve as a guide for prospective freshmen and their parents visiting campus, no doubt you would do some serious thinking about what these tasks and responsibilities are. Picture yourself in front of the university's administration building with a group of people assembled around you, their guide. You will want to get and keep their attention to achieve your *purpose*: informing them about your school. You would not want to turn left suddenly and leave them wandering down the wrong path. Are you beginning to see the analogy? More specifically, you can use our GUIDE checklist, which uses the word *guide* as an acronym (see Table 4.4).

[G] Get Your Audience's Attention. To guide your listeners, you must get their attention immediately in the introduction to your presentation. How can you prepare to do that successfully? Consider the following methods, which are illustrated through introductions from significant presentations by nationally known figures.

Relate the topic to your listeners.

When I was an assistant district attorney in Queens it used to make me terribly nervous to get up and argue a motion in front of one judge. So you can imagine how I feel standing up here in front of hundreds of judges.

Of course, I am not here today to argue. But I am here to plead a case. My case is that women in leadership positions make

a real difference in the way our society works. And I believe that women like us must continue to make that difference.
—Geraldine A. Ferraro (Delivered to the annual meeting of the National Association of Women Judges, New York City, 9 October 1982)[7]

State the significance of the topic.

It took 50 million years to move from the spoken language to writing; 5,000 from writing to printing; 500 years from printing to radio and the telephone—and just about 50 years ago we entered the telecommunications era with those fuzzy little black and white pictures on a tiny screen.

Today, there are more television sets in the world than telephones (700 million versus 550 million), which is just one small measure of the magnitude of the impact of this new medium.
—John F. Budd, Jr., Vice-President, External Relations, Emhart Corporation (Delivered to the Financial Communications Society, New York City, 27 May 1983)[8]

Arouse the curiosity of your listeners.

Good morning, ladies and gentlemen. In Frankfurt, it's called *Personalberater*; in Milan, *cacciatore di teste*; in Tokyo, *Kubikari-Zoku*; and in Paris, *un chasseur de tetes*. In English, of course, it's headhunter. Many of my fellow consultants are a bit self-conscious about the term and prefer the more formal terminology, executive recruiter. But over the years, I've come to see the popular phrase as colorful, descriptive, and accurate; we *are* hunters, skillful hunters in search of talented heads.
—Lester Korn, Chairman and CEO of Korn/Ferry International (Delivered at the Business Week Conference for Senior Human Resource Executives, New York City, 14 November 1983)[9]

Begin with a compelling quotation or paraphrase.

Whether you view change pessimistically, as Alvin Toffler did in *Future Shock*, or optimistically, as John Naisbitt does in *Megatrends*, one fact stands out. Nothing in this world is permanent except change. And nowhere is that statement more true than in the retail industry.
—William A. Andres, Chairman and CEO, Dayton Hudson Corporation (Delivered at the Young President's Organization Retailing Seminar, New York City, 6 March 1983)[10]

Tell a joke or an anecdote.

> W.C. Fields was one of the great American philosophers in the vein of Will Rogers and Fred Allen. In addition to his crackerjack line calling Mae West "my little chickadee," he was an active speaker on the lecture circuit. The Toast Mistress, excited at booking the red-nosed Fields, asked him to speak at her club meeting. He gruffly turned her down. But surely you believe in clubs for [bankers]? Certainly, he said—when all other means of persuasion fail.
> —Herbert S. Gruber, President of Walter E. Heller and Company, Southwest, Incorporated (Delivered to National Association of Bank Women, Pompano Beach, Florida, 11 May 1983)[11]

You may instead elect to *startle your listeners*, *question them*, *tell a story*, or *ask a rhetorical question*. Regardless of which method you select, remember that a well-designed introduction must do more than simply get the audience's attention. Obviously, getting its attention is crucial. If you fail to do that, then whatever else you accomplish will be pointless. In addition to getting your audience's attention, your introduction should do the following:

1. Motivate your audience to continue to listen
2. Establish your qualifications, particularly if you are not known to all listeners
3. Develop rapport with your audience
4. Preview what you will say in the body of your presentation by letting the audience in on your central idea.

Whatever you do, don't begin with a comment like, "I really wasn't given much lead time to get ready for this presentation" or "Max here probably knows more about this subject than I do." Such suicidal openings quickly kill a presentation. Instead, enhance your credibility by including in your opening a statement like, "When the chairman asked me to speak with you today, he asked me to be sure to include. . . ." Such a statement communicates that you and your ideas have the support of powerful people.[12]

Finally, please note that *although introductions occur first, they generally are best composed last*. Because one of the most important functions of an introduction is to preview the main points of your speech, you must have a clear sense of the body of your presentation before you can compose an effective introduction.

[U] "You" — Don't Forget Yourself. With all of this talk about objectives, audiences, and strategies, we must not exclude the most immediate source of your presentation — YOU. Although your presentation should be focused on the needs of the audience, this doesn't mean that you should leave yourself and your personality out of your message. Words alone do not create the total impression; merely reporting information is not enough. Even in a formal business or professional presentation, you will be most successful if you work from the inside out. Sounding like a robot with a computerized voice will do nothing to enhance your reputation as a speaker or to help your audience process the content of your presentation. Your goal should always be to develop a comfortable style that's easy to listen to. The presentation represents who you are and how you think. Capitalize on that idea. Be yourself, don't play a role, and let your wit and personality shine through.

One expert puts it this way: The only difference between the words *poise* and *pose* is the *I* in the middle.[13] Chances are your listeners are at least mildly interested in both you and your ideas (otherwise they probably wouldn't be there), and chances are they will come to respect both if you deliver what you promise and are confident in your delivery. The importance of this principle will be discussed further in the next chapter, including several details relating to the nonverbal messages you send as a speaker.

[I] Ideas, Ideas, Ideas! One effective way to generate ideas is *brainstorming*. Create a list of all the possible points you might want to make during your presentation and write them as conclusions that you want your listeners to accept. For example, imagine that because of your training and expertise in business-letter writing, you have been asked by your boss to prepare a presentation for a group of poor writers in your organization. After reviewing recent pieces of correspondence produced by the group, you brainstorm about the main ideas you might want to communicate, creating a list that looks something like this:

1. Trim unnecessary words.
2. Make sure grammar and punctuation are perfect.
3. Define technical terms.
4. Use appropriate letter formats.
5. Find the appropriate level of formality.
6. Identify your reader.
7. Organize your thoughts.
8. Edit everything you write.
9. Ask for a specific response from your reader.
10. Get to the point quickly.
11. Avoid jargon.

12. Write at your conversational best.
13. Avoid vague abstractions.

For the typical business or professional presentation, experts agree that a maximum of five main points is about all that most listeners can process at one time. After considering your list for awhile, using redundancy and relevancy as your criteria, you decide that only five of the points above are critical:

1. Identify your reader.
2. Get to the point quickly.
3. Write at your conversational best.
4. Ask your reader for a specific response.
5. Edit everything you write.

Let's look at a second example. You are preparing a presentation to convince upper management that the new Model X computer would be a sound investment. After deliberation and research, you decide on three reasons to make such an investment:

Buying the new Model X computer would be a wise investment for these reasons:

1. It offers the upgraded capabilities the company needs.
2. It is priced more reasonably than its competitors.
3. It includes a reliable service contract.

You decide that fewer main points would not tell the whole story and more would be overkill.

Or let's look at a third example. Imagine that your organization is having trouble with absenteeism. Your boss wonders whether flextime is the answer. (In case you're not familiar with the term, employees in the flextime system select their work hours. As long as they work a forty-hour week, they have some freedom in determining their work schedules. For example, one employee may choose to work from 7 A.M. to 3 P.M. while another works from 10 A.M. to 6 P.M.) The boss asks you to survey employees on the causes of absenteeism and present the results to upper management. As you tabulate the results, you see that responses can be grouped into three major categories:

1. Employees experience problems with child care.
2. Employees experience problems scheduling personal appointments.
3. Employees experience problems with stress and burnout.

In this case, the number of main points to include has been determined for you. Typically, however, it's better to generate more ideas than you think you'll need so that you can select the best ones. In other words, from the many ideas you have in your head at the outset, you must decide what is relevant and what is critical to meeting your objective. As you formulate your main ideas, keep the following guidelines in mind.

- *Main points should be parallel if possible.* The last example above uses a parallel structure; all main points are full sentences with similar construction. A nonparallel structure might look like this:

  1. Child care.
  2. Employees have trouble scheduling personal appointments.
  3. Some people experience stress and burnout.

- *Main points should each include a separate, single idea.* The flextime example also follows this principle as each main point sticks to one crucial idea. Crowded main points, on the other hand, might look like this:

  1. Employees experience problems with child care and are often late because of traffic problems.
  2. Employees experience problems scheduling personal appointments, as well as suffer from stress and burnout.

- *Main points should cover relatively equal amounts of time in your presentation.* If you found enough material to devote three minutes to the first point above, but only a half-minute to the second, then you'd better rethink your approach.

Now that you have begun to make decisions about which main ideas to include, you have constructed a skeletal version of your presentation. Earlier we used the term *central idea.* What do we mean? The central idea is a concise statement of your presentation's thesis, major thought, or residual message. It is the one statement you would make if you were allowed only one, and thus it includes the main points of your presentation. Be sure to write your central idea as a declarative sentence and include a version of it in your presentation's introduction. In the example above, the central idea might read: *"Absenteeism in our company is caused by the problems our employees experience with child care, personal appointments, and stress and burnout."*

How can you best communicate your main points as they begin to take shape, and what evidence can you put forward to make them interesting, clear, and believable to your listeners? How do you make those kinds of decisions? You make "educated" decisions based on research: You read company documents, interview key people, check library sources, or design your own survey or other research tool.

In other words, to ensure that your main ideas "work," you must use a variety of supporting materials. Ideas rarely stand on their own merit. Supporting materials in your skeletal presentation add *interest*, *clarity*, and, most important, *evidence*. The three most widely used forms of supporting materials are *examples*, *statistics*, and *testimony*. Let's look at how a single main point can be developed by using these supporting materials.

Examples

Main point: Decco Corporation has had its most profitable year since 1988.
Supporting example: Last year we reached two new markets, Puerto Rico and Guam, adding an additional $750,000 to profits.

Examples include *stories* and *illustrations*, *hypothetical events*, and *specific cases*. They can be powerful, compelling ways to dramatize and clarify your main ideas *if* they are relevant, representative, and reasonable.

Statistics

Main point: Decco Corporation has had its most profitable year since 1988.
Supporting statistics: Corporate profits reached the $200 million mark last year, our largest profit margin since 1988, representing a 13 percent increase over the previous year alone.

Statistics obviously are widely used forms of evidence in business and professional presentations. Statistics, of course, have received "bad press": Numbers can be manipulated, and the unscrupulous sometimes lie with statistics. Even so, statistics typically are the "meat" of organizational presentations. Make sure they are clear, concise, and comprehensible to your listeners.

Testimony

Main point: Decco Corporation has had its most profitable year since 1988.
Supporting testimony: According to the editor of *Fortune* magazine, if Decco Corporation has another year like the last one, it will be on the road to becoming one of the fortunate Fortune 500.

Testimony provides you the opportunity to quote outside experts, paraphrase reliable sources, or generally demonstrate the quality of individuals who agree with you and your main points. When you elect this method of support, make sure the testimony is accurate, qualified, and unbiased.

Finally, because your audience members are unique individuals, you most likely will add interest, clarity, and evidence to your presentation by varying the types of support you provide.

[D] **Develop an Organizational Structure.** Beyond developing your ideas through supporting evidence, you also should develop an overview of your presentation — its organizational structure. You'll be able to choose from a variety of structural formats, depending on the nature and the objective of your presentation: *problem–solution, cause–effect, question-and-answer, chronological, spatial*, and *topical.*

For example, if you are giving a presentation to upper management on the feasibility of building an on-site day-care facility at your organization, you probably would want to use a *problem–solution* format. You would describe the problem, present the pros and cons of several solutions, and finally identify your proposed solution as the best option. As you might expect, this type of format is extremely common in business and professional presentations.

A similar organizational pattern frequently used in business and professional settings is the *cause–effect* format. Imagine that you are a financial expert addressing the state board of realtors on tax revisions. You might identify a decrease in housing sales in the local area, a leveling off of housing prices, and a sharp increase in the volume of houses on the market (*effects*) as the results of new tax legislation that is disadvantageous to the potential real-estate buyer (*cause*). You may elect to work in either direction — from cause to effect or from effect to cause. Again, the nature of business and professional presentations causes this format to be widely used.

Or perhaps you must give a very different kind of presentation. As chief of your corporation's research-and-development division, you must present a new product developed by your engineers, the *Thingamajig*. You could elect to use a *question-and-answer* format, posing a series of questions and then answering them on the spot: What is the Thingamajig? Why was it developed? How does it work? What advantages does it have over similar products? How will it be marketed? Here you must be sure to ask *all* of the necessary questions and answer them in a logical, orderly fashion.

A second organizational format that would be possible in the previous example is the *chronological* pattern. In this case, you could describe the process of using the Thingamajig, beginning with how the customer starts it, what happens next, and so forth until it is turned off. The five-point example given earlier (page 163) in which you were asked to give a workshop on effective writing also is organized somewhat chronologically, from identifying your reader to editing the final product. Obviously, chronological patterns work best when you are discussing processes, development, and history.

Sometimes business and professional presentations are organized using a *spatial* pattern. For example, imagine that you are giving the key presentation at a national convention for your company's salespersons. You might compare marketing success by geographical sector, discussing the West Coast, the East Coast, and the Midwest before finishing with the South.

Finally, the most logical organizational pattern for your presentation sometimes is a *topical* format. The other patterns don't fit; instead you are discussing three reasons, four concepts, or two changes. Keep in mind, however, that merely throwing together several items does not a topical pattern make. Your main points must be related thematically if a topical format is to be used effectively.

Whichever organizational pattern makes sense for the nature and objective of your presentation, keep in mind the following rules of thumb.

- *Don't mix and match; select one format and stick with it.* The human mind works best within patterns. And when an initial pattern suddenly shifts, or when no pattern exists at all, listeners demonstrate a remarkable tendency to adopt undesirable behavior: They may grow hostile, bored, or cynical; they may challenge you when you least expect it; they may sleep; and, finally, they may generalize from your obvious inability to organize, finally losing all confidence in your work.
- *In general, begin with your most important ideas.* Perhaps the most widely voiced criticism of business and professional speakers is that they begin by spending too much time on secondary information. For some reason, many of us seem to feel the need for preliminary chitchat, just as we often do in writing business letters. With busy listeners (or readers), this won't work. When you get to the conference room only to find that your speaking time has been halved, or when two minutes into your presentation the boss breaks in — "Can you get to the heart of the matter, Jones? We're all busy here" — then you may realize only too late the importance of this fundamental rule.

Some experts use the bull's eye analogy in Figure 4.1 to represent the idea visually, reminding speakers to start with the bull's eye and move outward based on time and interest.

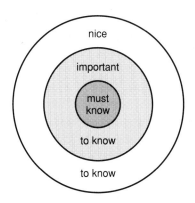

Figure 4.1 *Bull's Eye Analogy for Presentations*[14]

What we're talking about is similar to the difference between a *deductive* and an *inductive* approach. A deductive approach begins with a generalization and then points to specific examples—from general to specific. An inductive approach is the reverse and begins with a series of specific facts that build to a general conclusion—from specific to general. In business and professional presentations, a deductive approach often is preferable. The most likely exception to the rule occurs when you are presenting highly controversial ideas. The audience may not buy your first main point immediately; instead, you may need to build to it in a careful and considered manner, following the inductive approach.

Regardless of which organizational pattern you select, the main structure of your presentation probably will look something like the following:

    I.   Introduction
        A.   Get your listeners' attention
        B.   Motivate continued listening
        C.   Establish your qualifications
        D.   Develop rapport with your listeners
        E.   Preview your central idea
   II.   Body
        A.   First main point
            1.   Subpoint one
                a.   Evidence
                b.   Evidence
            2.   Subpoint two
                a.   Evidence
                b.   Evidence
                c.   Evidence
        B.   Second main point
            1.   Subpoint one
                a.   Evidence
                b.   Evidence

  2. Subpoint two
    a. Evidence
    b. Evidence
 C. Third main point
  1. Subpoint one
    a. Evidence
    b. Evidence
  2. Subpoint two
    a. Evidence
    b. Evidence
III. Conclusion
 A. Signal the close of your presentation
 B. Review your central idea

Actually writing an outline may be one of the most useful ways to prepare. Many experts suggest that a useful preliminary step in writing a final outline is to list each main point and subpoint separately on 3″ × 5″ or 5″ × 7″ cards. This allows you to work on a large surface, such as the floor, and arrange, rearrange, add, and delete cards until you reach the most effective format. Then simply number the cards and use them to prepare your final outline (see Figure 4.2).

As you organize your presentation, remember that your overall purpose is to GUIDE your listeners. That means you must not neglect connectors between your main points. Returning to our original analogy, if you were a campus guide, you would find ways to keep your followers together with you between the new art gallery at one end of the campus and the football stadium at the other. As a speaker you can accomplish the same thing by using *transitions* to guide your listeners from one point to another. You can do this in several ways, but let's look at three: internal summaries, internal previews, and signposts:[15]

- *Now that we've looked at* the three problems associated with absenteeism. . . . (*internal summary* of where the presentation has been)
- *The first half of my presentation* has identified four major issues surrounding increased PC training. . . . (*internal summary*)

- I've described a difficult problem, but I won't stop there. *Consider what we could do about it.* . . . (*internal preview* of where the presentation is going)
- So much for last year's financial profile. *Now what does the future hold?* (*internal preview*)

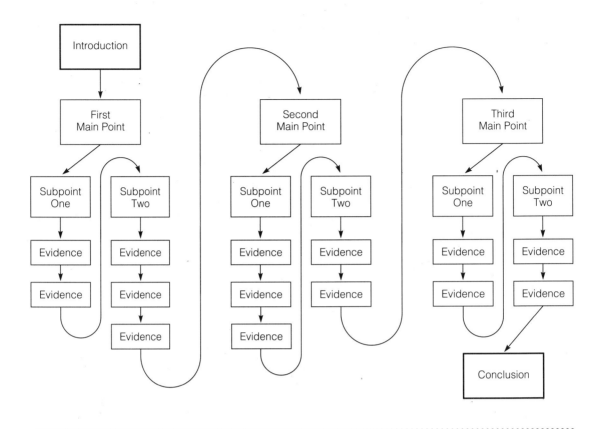

Figure 4.2 *Arranging A Presentation Outline*

- The *first* factor to consider is. . . . The *second* important factor is. . . . (*signpost*)
- The *most important point* I'll make today is. . . . (*signpost*)

Transitions make the difference between keeping your listeners "with" you and losing them at an important juncture.

[E] Exit Gracefully and Memorably. A man named Lord Mancroft once commented, "[A] speech is like a love affair. Any fool can start it, but to end it requires considerable skill." We agree. Most of our suggestions about introductions also apply to conclusions; that is, you can effectively conclude your presentation by *relating the topic to your listeners, stating the significance of the topic, ending with a quotation or paraphrase, telling an anecdote, making a startling statement, asking a question, telling a story, referring back to your introduction, reinforcing your central idea, issuing a challenge,* or *providing an appropriate "hook"* — a call for action, a suggestion to approve the proposal, a next step. At the very least, you'll most likely want to signal the close of your presentation and review your central idea.

Whatever else you do, go out with style, impact, and dignity. Don't leave your listeners asking, "So that's it?" Subtly signal that the end is in sight (without the tired "So, in conclusion"), summarize your major points, and then conclude. Should you thank your listeners at the end of your presentation? Good question. Our best advice is to use your own intuition. A "thank you" can come across as perfunctory and insincere or as an honest expression of appreciation, depending on you and the rapport you've developed with your listeners.

One final note: Your presentation won't be over when you sit down. Remind yourself to find answers you promised to locate, follow up on commitments you made, send memos to people who need to know the results, and thank instrumental people who helped you.

Step 5: Choose Visual Aids

One of the disadvantages of presentations mentioned at the beginning of this chapter is that they are *transitory*, here one moment and gone the next. Your listeners will have only one chance to catch what you say; and as Chapter 6 will show, listening is rarely anyone's strongest communicative "suit." The question is, What can we do to surmount this potential threat to the success of our presentations?

The answer is to combine channels. Capitalize on the fact that most of us tend to be *aurally deficient* but *visually proficient*. Listening to complex material often is difficult; visual aids raise both comprehension and recall. According to one study, when visual aids are added to aural presentations, we can absorb 35 percent more information—and recall 55 percent more over time.[16] For this reason, the *audio + visual* presentation is the standard in business and the professions.

To make these truths work for you, you must prepare carefully. Using visual aids can increase audience interest, comprehension, and retention, as well as sharpen your professional image—but not as an unqualified rule. As with everything else we've discussed, the secret to using visual aids successfully lies with you as the speaker. Let's consider how you can select the appropriate medium, and how you can create visuals that will help you meet your objective.

Many of the questions already discussed also are important in selecting the audiovisual medium you will use for your presentation. What is your objective? How formal will the presentation be? How large is your audience likely to be? How much time and resources do you have available? Let's begin by looking at a basic division between *projected* and *material* media. In general, projected visuals are suitable for large groups, and they tend to add to your professionalism as a speaker. If overdone, however, they can detract from what should be the center of attention — you. Projected visuals also come with the risk of mechanical breakdown. In general, material media, such as chalkboards and flip charts, can be more spontaneous and less formal, but they are often less impressive as well.

Projected Media. Although an array of choices is available to you in this category, you will find that most business and professional speakers rely almost exclusively on *overhead projectors* and *transparencies* because their advantages often outweigh their disadvantages. When considering the use of transparencies, think about these pros and cons.

Pros

1. You need not totally darken the room.
2. You can prepare transparencies easily and inexpensively on most copy machines.
3. You can change your information at the last moment if needed.
4. You need not relinquish eye contact because you can continue to face your listeners at all times.
5. You can highlight important points as you talk by using overlays or special felt-tip pens.
6. You can transport transparencies easily in your briefcase.
7. You can most likely obtain a projector anywhere you need to speak.
8. You can communicate complex material because transparencies allow you more space for information than do most other media.
9. You can hand out hard copies of your transparencies to audience members if you wish.
10. You can write on blank transparencies and create new visuals on the spot.

Cons

1. The projector is bulky to store and transport if you must provide your own.
2. Bulbs occasionally burn out (so be sure you have a spare).
3. Because of the arrangement of the room, some audience members may have difficulty seeing.

4. Distortion can be bothersome and distracting.
5. Transparencies generally are less effective for highly formal presentations or presentations to extremely large groups.
6. Transparencies can lose their impact if overused within a company.

If the nature of your presentation calls for more sophisticated visual aids, you may elect to use *35-mm slides*. You or a photographer from your company's audiovisual department can take slides in color or black and white of whatever you need. Although slides can become expensive, especially if you are shooting color artwork prepared by a graphics specialist, they typically are more formal and impressive than transparencies. Again, you'll want to consider these advantages and disadvantages.

Pros

1. You can operate the projector by remote control from a speaker's podium.
2. You can preprogram slides with narrative or sound effects if you wish.
3. You can impress your audience with high-quality images.
4. You can mix photos and graphics easily.
5. You can transport or store slides easily.

Cons

1. Slides occasionally "hang up" in the projector, causing embarrassing gaps in your presentation.
2. Slide-projector bulbs occasionally fail.
3. Slides generally require a darker room than do transparencies.
4. Slides require more lead time to prepare.
5. Slides may require an assistant to control the room lights and help out with equipment "glitches."
6. Slides do not easily lend themselves to displaying complex information.
7. Slides don't allow highlighting.
8. Slides may be considered too "glitzy" in informal organizations or for small groups.

When appropriate, *videotapes* and *films* can add not only interest but also excitement to business and professional presentations. This is the medium to use if you want to show people, events, or processes in action. But again you must weigh the following factors.

Pros

1. Videotapes can show events either as they happen via closed circuit or as they already have happened through record and playback capability.
2. Videotapes can be reproduced and reused easily.
3. Videotapes and films can be edited.
4. Videotapes and films are visually exciting.

Cons

1. Videotapes and films often are of inferior quality if not produced by professionals.
2. Videotapes require several monitors for large groups.
3. Videotapes and films often are expensive to produce.

Computer-generated media are some of the technological wonders of the information age discussed in Chapter 1 and explored still further in Chapter 12. Now software packages can help you to produce *drawings* or *diagrams* (Figure 4.3), *word charts* (sometimes called "agenda" or "we-are-here" slides; Figure 4.4), *statistical tables* (Figure 4.5), *line graphs* (Figure 4.6), *pie charts* (Figure 4.7), *pictograms* (Figure 4.8), and *bar graphs* (Figure 4.9 on page 178).

Certain hardware systems also can create on-the-spot images as generated by your computer. By fitting a plastic cone over the computer monitor, you can allow an instant-exposure camera to click away. Some equipment will allow you to connect a camera system directly to your

Figure 4.3
Drawing

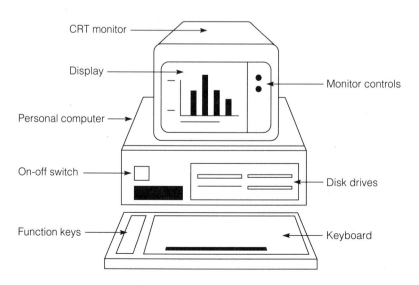

Figure 4.4
Word Chart

G Get Your Audience's Attention

U "You"—Don't Forget Yourself

I Ideas, Ideas, Ideas!

D Develop an Organizational Structure

E Exit Gracefully and Memorably

Figure 4.5
Statistical Table

Salary Offers to Degree Candidates

[Average beginning salaries based on offers made by business, industry, government, and nonprofit and educational employers to graduating students]

Field of Study	Bachelor's	Master's	Doctor's
Accounting	$25,290	$28,874	N/A
Business	22,274	33,903	N/A
Marketing	22,523	34,462	N/A
Civil Engineering	26,735	30,723	37,214
Chemistry	26,698	32,157	43,215
Mathematics	26,789	31,498	37,500
Physics	28,296	29,889	42,632
Humanities	23,010	25,799	N/A
Social Science	20,205	23,814	N/A
Computer Science	28,557	35,823	50,049

Source: College Placement Council

Figure 4.6
Line Graph

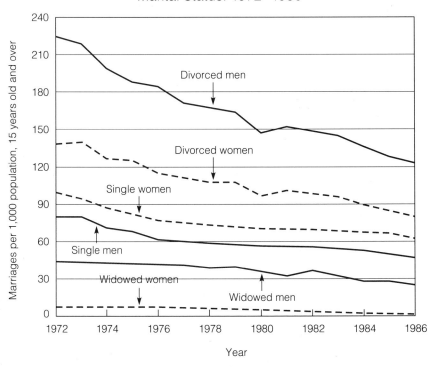

Marriage Rates by Previous
Marital Status: 1972–1986

Source: U.S. Bureau of the Census

Figure 4.7
Pie Chart

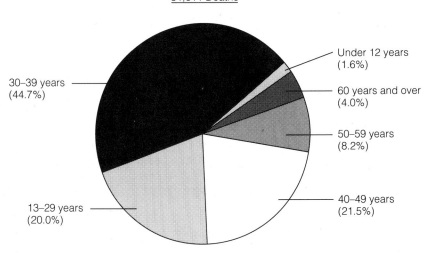

Distribution of AIDS Deaths
by Age: 1982–1988

51,611 Deaths

Source: U.S. Bureau of the Census

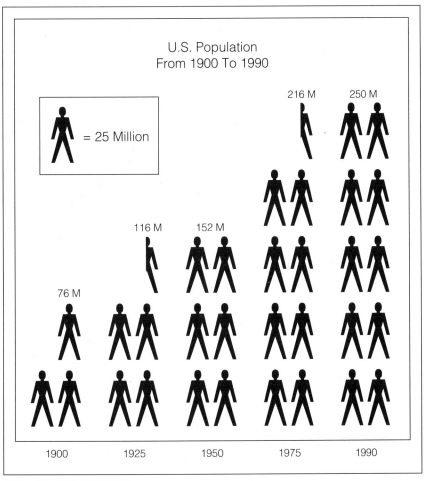

Figure 4.8
Pictogram

U.S. Population
From 1900 To 1990

= 25 Million

216 M
250 M
116 M
152 M
76 M

1900   1925   1950   1975   1990

Source: U.S. Bureau of the Census

personal computer (PC) (just like a monitor) and create color slides. Computer-image *projectors* simply plug into your computer and project the image you've created on your monitor directly onto a screen. As you type in new facts and figures, the projected image on the screen changes for everyone to see. The realm of opportunities, already staggering, continues to increase daily. The advantages and disadvantages of these systems are similar to those we've already discussed, but the results are more professional, more immediate, and sometimes more compelling.

Overhead transparencies (created by computer-software packages), 35-mm slides, films, and videotapes are the most frequently used projected media in business and professional presentations. Other media such as opaque projectors are used occasionally, but they are rarely worth the inconvenience. But whatever the medium, it's safe to say that most presentations in the business and professional world rely to some extent on projected media.

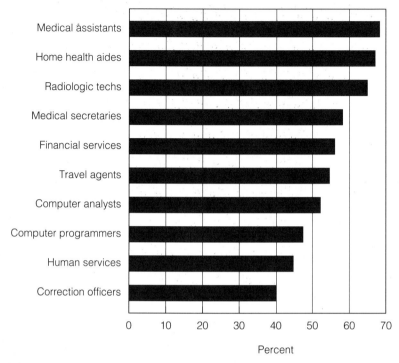

Figure 4.9
Bar Graph

Projected Change in Employment for 10
Fastest Growing Occupations: 1990–2000

Source: U.S. Bureau of the Census

Material Media. As with projected media, each type of material media has advantages and disadvantages worth considering.

The *chalkboard*, for example, offers spontaneity. If you plan to solve problems during or after your presentation, you can list, add, and subtract ideas as they surface. Blackboards (or whiteboards) almost always are available, and you needn't prepare your visual aids in advance. Most of these factors also work against you, however. Erasures produce smudges and messiness, and it's difficult to save what you've written. Blackboards don't work well for complicated diagrams, and you break contact with the audience each time you turn to write. Unless you have a specific reason to use a chalkboard, don't. Your professional image usually is better enhanced when you use some other medium.

Flip charts, on the other hand, achieve a higher level of professionalism. Pictures, charts, and diagrams can be prepared attractively on posterboard before your presentation. You can make pencil notations on them during your presentation, and you needn't lose contact with the audience as you refer to your visuals. You can even remove charts to display them one by one if you want your listeners to make comparisons. On the negative side, flip charts often are expensive, work well only with small groups, are cumbersome to store and transport, and are more or less permanent; last-minute changes are messy and often impossible.

Easel pads have advantages and disadvantages that are similar to those of flip charts. Artwork can be prepared in advance, and you only need to turn the page to show your next chart or graph. Like chalkboards, however, easel pads have a casual quality that makes them primarily suitable only for informal presentations to small groups.

Handouts deserve a special note of caution. They provide your listeners with hard copies of your major points and elaborations on those points, but if you pass them out during your presentation, you run the risk of losing your audience to the printed word. You may distribute handouts after your presentation as references for later use, but at that point they really aren't visual aids. To use them as visual aids, our best advice is to distribute them early, wait until the audience has had time to give them at least a cursory look, and then move them through the information at your own rate.

Magnetic, flannel, or *Velcro*™ boards have unusual advantages, particularly if you want to display process or change — the stages of production that an item undergoes, for example. But not all organizations have this kind of equipment.

Models and *actual objects* also are required by particular circumstances. If you wish to propose a new wing of the hospital in which you work, a model floor plan might be your most effective visual aid. Or sometimes it's possible to demonstrate the real object — a new computer, for example — or transport your audience to see the real object — a newly opened branch office. The difficulties with such visual aids are obvious, but sometimes there is no better way to get your point across.

As you select visual aids and the information they will display for your presentation, consider these rules of thumb:

1. Make visuals clear and easy to follow — use readable lettering and don't crowd information.
2. Limit each visual to one main point.
3. Introduce each visual before displaying and explaining it.
4. Allow your listeners sufficient time to process visuals.
5. Proofread carefully — misspelled words erode credibility.
6. Display each visual only while you discuss its content.
7. Maintain eye contact with your listeners while you discuss visuals. Don't make the mistake of talking to your visual aids.
8. Paraphrase visuals — don't read every word aloud.
9. Make sure everyone can see your visuals — position yourself so that you're not obstructing the audience's view.
10. Make your visuals appear as professional as possible. They are an important part of your image as a speaker.

"But is showing you this toy and telling about it the whole story? Let's take a look at its sales record, as illustrated by this chart, which compares it with other toys in its price class."

···

Step 6: Prepare Your Notes

You have accomplished the first five steps to success by *clarifying your objective, analyzing your audience, developing your game plan, collecting and organizing your information*, and *choosing your visual aids*. Your remaining task is to *prepare notes* for your presentation. In your role as an effective guide, what you do now is create a clear map to follow as you speak.

There are many useful ways to do this, but one option to *avoid* is writing out the content of your presentation word for word. If you are like most speakers, you will find having an entire text before you an irresistible temptation, and you will end up reading much more of your presentation than you had originally planned. Of course, you will rationalize by telling yourself that much of your material was so important that you dared not risk forgetting it.

But such rationalization is nothing more than an excuse for reading your presentation. In many instances, the members of your audience have little idea of what you had planned to say—how can they "miss" what they didn't know to expect? Of course, if your presentation is to be televised, if the content of your presentation will be printed, or if you must adhere to a strict time limit, then you may be required to read from text. If so, be well rehearsed so that you can use as much vocal expressiveness and eye contact as possible.

A second option to *avoid* is memorizing your presentation and eliminating notes altogether. Comedian George Jessel once said, "[T]he human brain is a wonderful organ. It starts to work as soon as you are born and doesn't stop until you get up to deliver a speech." Remember, your memory can fail you. And even if it doesn't, your presentation may sound "canned." Risking this option with the kind of high-stakes presentation we've been discussing is dangerous. On the other hand, it is a good idea to memorize the introduction and conclusion so that you can maintain eye contact and therefore build rapport with your listeners.

We've suggested two routes you shouldn't take; what *should* you do to prepare notes for your presentation? We have distinct ideas about what works.

When we discussed the "D" of our GUIDE principle, *develop an organizational structure*, we suggested that you outline your presentation, preferably in full sentences, point by point, following the skeletal example we provided. From this full-blown outline you prepare notes to use during your actual presentation. These notes, however, will be minimal so that you can speak extemporaneously. In this case, you rehearse thoroughly in advance, but because you are speaking from brief notes, your choice of words for each presentation will be slightly different, which allows you to sound prepared but natural in your delivery.

One choice for presentation notes is to use 3″ × 5″ or 4″ × 6″ cards because they are small and unobtrusive. (But remember to number them. Nothing is more flustering than dropping the entire stack as you make your way to the podium.) Other speakers prefer 8½″ × 11″ paper or putting notes in a ring binder to be turned in order without being dropped. In other words, no one method is best, so experiment and choose what works best for you.

As you prepare notes, one of your most challenging tasks will be merging the *audio* and *visual* channels of your presentation smoothly. You want one channel to complement the other; you don't want the visual channel to overshadow the audio channel so that listeners fix solely on the charts or slides you're showing. On the other hand, you don't want the audio channel to do all the work when visual aids can make difficult facts or ideas easier for your listeners to grasp. Integrating what you have to say with what you have to show doesn't just happen naturally as you speak; this, too, is another aspect of preparation.

Combine the two channels in your notes. In some organizations, this will be accomplished initially by using a storyboard, a layout of the presentation in a series of sketches of visuals with the accompanying verbal message. Typically, cards or papers that display sketches of visuals are placed in cardholders or hung from magnetic strips on the wall so that presenters and other key people can integrate verbal and visual material.

Those who use storyboards to prepare presentations find them to be highly effective aids.[17]

We suggest that you prepare your notes by beginning with notecards or paper that has been folded in half. Write a key word outline on the left side of your cards or paper; on the right side, draw rough sketches of your accompanying visuals. This forces you to integrate the audio and visual channels. You will be able to see, for example, gaps in the visual channel—places where you will need to add visual interest to keep your audience listening (see Figure 4.10).

After you have become a more experienced speaker, you may want to experiment with other methods of preparing notes. Eventually, you also may want to let your visuals serve that purpose. You can always write notes to yourself on transparency frames, for example, or lightly pencil in items you want to remember on charts that you display, or provide handouts of key points that also serve as your basic outline. As you become even more proficient, you may find you no longer need notes. The ability to deliver an entire talk without referring to any notes at all can be quite impressive. At first, however, you will be better off building a repertoire of successful experiences through careful and deliberate preparation.

A Footnote on Collaborative Presentations

Presentations often are given in organizations by teams of two or more people rather than solo "performers." You may find yourself working as part of such a team, with each person assigned to prepare or deliver (or both) a particular piece of the presentation.

Obviously, team presentations have certain advantages over individual presentations. Generally, they are more interesting to watch and listen to because they make use of each contributor's perspective and areas of expertise without one person's style becoming tiresome.

In some ways, however, collaborative presentations are more difficult to plan and execute smoothly. More than one (and sometimes conflicting) opinions must be considered, more time is needed to coordinate schedules and dry runs, and basic questions must be tackled early on. For example, should the team presentation consist of a series of individual presentations or will the material be integrated? How compatible are the presenters' styles? And who should be assigned which portion?

Despite these challenges, team presentations are the preferred modus operandi in some organizations. This may be the case in the organiza-

VERBAL CHANNEL	VISUAL CHANNEL
I. Introduction	1. Title slide
A. Average American manager:	

1. 18–26% time managing conflict
        2. 2 days/week in meetings
        3. 4 hours/day reading (at executive levels)
        4. up to 60% listening	

B. As a manager, communication is what you do most; it should be what you do best!	
C. Communicating successfully on the job	2. "Success is . . ."

1. Your success
        2. Your staff's success
        3. Your organization's success	

II. The Communication Process	3. Model of communication
and so on	

Figure 4.10 *Audiovisual Presentation Script*

tion you join. Still, all of the advice we've provided thus far on presentations by single individuals applies — and then some.

This chapter began by asking you to imagine your first speaking opportunity in your new organization. When that opportunity actually arises — and it surely will — you'll find our six steps helpful in preparing a successful organizational presentation.

CHAPTER SUMMARY

Chapter 4 began by noting two truths about public speaking. First, the *Book of Lists* describes public speaking as the most prevalent fear in the United States; and second, for the most part, barriers toward conquering this fear are self-imposed. However, because they contain inherent advantages, presentations are *pervasive* and *popular* forms of communication in organizations. Therefore, it is important to prepare now for the inevitable. Presentations also are somewhat *problematic* in organizations; that is, they contain inherent disadvantages. The presentational speaker must capitalize on the advantages of presentations while working to minimize or circumvent the disadvantages.

When preparing a business or professional presentation, following certain preparatory steps can help to ensure your success. First, you must decide on the general purpose of your presentation: to *persuade*, *inform*, *entertain*, or *inspire*. Following this initial decision, you should follow our six-steps-to-success model:

1. *Clarify your objective.* What do you want your listeners to know, believe, or do when you are finished?
2. *Analyze your audience.* Discover beforehand audience members' *knowledge*, *interest*, *attitudes*, and *power*.
3. *Develop your game plan.* Develop strategies in terms of *formality*, *timing*, *attendees*, *physical arrangements*, and *key players*.
4. *Collect and organize your information.* Use the GUIDE checklist as you prepare the content of your presentation:

   [G] Get your audience's attention
   [U] "You" — Don't forget yourself
   [I] Ideas, ideas, ideas!
   [D] Develop an organizational structure
   [E] Exit gracefully and memorably

5. *Choose your visual aids.* Choose between *projected* and *material* media based on your needs and goals.
6. *Prepare your notes.* Integrate the audio and visual channels; experiment with methods of preparing useful notes.

Following these six steps should allow you to prepare successful presentations by using an approach that will serve you well in your business or professional career. But preparing a presentation is only half of the picture. In the next chapter, we discuss techniques for delivering what you've worked so hard to prepare.

MEASURING SUCCESS

1. According to Kenneth Tynan (1927–1980), a critic is someone "who knows the way, but can't drive the car." You may or may not agree, but it would be valuable for you to assume the role of critic with regard to the information presented in this chapter. In a current volume of *Vital Speeches of the Day* in your school library, find the text of a speech on some aspect of business or the professions that interests you. Using the GUIDE principle, critique the speech. How did the speaker get the audience's attention, insert him- or herself, generate ideas, develop an organizational structure, and exit gracefully and memorably? Even though you weren't there, how successful do you think the speech was?

2. Imagine that you are now an old hand in the position you landed after graduating from your college or university. A new employee who has been directed to hurriedly prepare a presentation for top management comes to you for advice. Knowing this person has only a few days to prepare for a very important task, what advice would you offer?

3. Consider the following three situations and decide which kind of visual aid you would use and what kinds of information you would want to communicate to your listeners. Provide one or more rough sketches for each situation.

   a. You are an architect preparing a presentation to university officials for a competitive bid on a new dormitory.
   b. You are a design engineer for a toy manufacturer preparing a presentation on a new product that you believe will sweep the market during the next Christmas season.
   c. You are director of training and development in a large corporation preparing a presentation for the board of executives proposing an innovative training program for all company employees.

4. Write a paragraph introduction for each of the situations presented in Exercise 3. Label each introduction according to its purpose (startle

your listeners, arouse their curiosity, tell a joke or anecdote, and so on). Remember that introductions should *capture your listeners' attention, motivate them to continue to listen, establish your qualifications, develop rapport,* and *preview the rest of your presentation.*

5. Earlier in this chapter we gave an example of a situation in which you were proposing that your company purchase a new computer because it "offers the upgraded capabilities the company needs, is priced more reasonably than its competitors, and includes a reliable service contract." If, as the company's director of data analysis, you were preparing a presentation on this proposal, what sort of *game plan* would you develop for the following key players who would be present at your presentation?

> Miles N. Miles, President (conservative, opinionated, about to retire)
> Clair Voyensze, Vice-President (innovative, visionary, proponent of change)
> Lin Chin Pardee, Director of Research and Development (direct, volatile, argumentative)
> Sandy Soyell, Director of Public Relations (newly appointed, energetic, liberal)
> Bob Katze, Director of Marketing (cautious, rigid, supporter of the status quo)

 Decco Exercise A representative from corporate headquarters whom you once met briefly must come to your division to give a presentation to middle managers on a new company-benefits policy. In writing, the representative asks you for advice about giving presentations in your division. Write a return letter itemizing your major points of advice.

·················

Notes

1. David Wallechinsky, Irving Wallace, and Amy Wallace, *Book of Lists* (New York: Bantam, 1978), 469.

2. Kenneth Wydro, *Thinking on Your Feet: The Art of Thinking and Speaking Under Pressure* (Englewood Cliffs, NJ: Prentice-Hall, 1981), 83.

3. For a more extensive discussion of the advantages and disadvantages of presentations, see Leonard F. Meuse, Jr., *Mastering the Business and Technical Presentation* (Boston: CBI Publishing, 1980).

4. For example, see Meuse, *Mastering*; T. Leech, *How to Prepare, Stage, and Deliver Winning Presentations* (New York: AMACOM, 1982); P.R. Timm, *Functional Business Presentations: Getting Across* (Englewood Cliffs, NJ: Prentice-Hall, 1981). Two of our favorite treatments of public speaking are found in the 1980 edition of *Together: Communicating Interpersonally* by John Stewart and Gary D'Angelo and *Speaking Up* by Janet Stone and Jane Bachner. Both books have greatly influenced our thinking on speechmaking.

5. Leech, *How to Prepare*, 61.

6. Meuse, *Mastering*, 8–9.

7. Geraldine A. Ferraro, "Who Will Fight for the Worth of Women's Work?" *Vital Speeches of the Day* 49 (1982): 70.

8. John F. Budd, "Video, A Corporate Communication Tool," *Vital Speeches of the Day* 49 (1983): 592.

9. Lester Korn, "Selecting Chief Executives," *Vital Speeches of the Day* 50 (1984): 204.

10. William A. Andres, "Meeting the Challenge of Managing Change," *Vital Speeches of the Day* 49 (1983): 470.

11. Herbert S. Gruber, "Banking on Women," *Vital Speeches of the Day* 49 (1983): 587.

12. Walter Kiechel III, "The Big Presentation," *Fortune*, 26 July 1982, 99.

13. Wydro, *Thinking*, 113.

14. Meuse, *Mastering*, 28.

15. Stephen E. Lucas, *The Art of Public Speaking* (New York: Random House, 1983), 150–151.

16. Stephen S. Pride, *Business Ideas: How To Create and Present Them* (New York: Harper & Row, 1967), 172.

17. Leech, *How to Prepare*, 105–109.

Chapter 5 ✑ Delivering a Successful Presentation

✎ *A speech is a solemn responsibility. The man who gives a bad thirty-minute speech to two hundred people wastes only a half hour of his own time. But he wastes one hundred hours of the audience's time — more than four days — which should be a hanging offense. —Jenkin Lloyd Jones* ✎

Mark Twain once resorted to mild sarcasm when comforting a terrified friend before he rose to give a speech: "Just remember — they don't expect much." Needless to say, Twain wasn't referring to the kind of business and professional presentations we have been discussing. Here's what *Fortune* magazine has to say about the importance of successful presentations:

> Let us in no way minimize the opportunity, or the danger, involved. The 30 minutes an executive spends on his feet formally presenting his latest project to corporate superiors are simply and absolutely the most important 30 minutes of that or any other managerial season. The game isn't show-and-tell; it's gladiator time, career death or career glory, the Big P — for presentation.[1]

In fact, a reciprocal relationship exists between your presentational success and your eventual organizational success. As one Fortune 500 chief executive noted, "there are the people who do the work and the people who present it. . . . Often it's the presenters who get the credit, and the promotion."[2] The more speaking you do, the more visible are your communicative talents.

Likewise, the higher you climb on the organizational ladder, the more speaking you will need to do both inside and outside the organization. Many top executives, for example, make $10,000 to $15,000 per speech and can accept only 25 percent of the speaking invitations they receive. In just one year, Lee Iacocca of Chrysler received 2,500 invitations to speak and accepted only 30.[3] Former President and Mrs. Ronald Reagan, Oliver North, and Dan Rather each made $25,000 or more per speech (see Table 5-1). Of course, corporate executives frequently rely on speechwriters to prepare their speeches, but their own presentational skills — how they deliver speeches — remain fundamentally important to their success.

In other words, your presentational skills not only help you achieve your organizational goals, but you also increasingly use your presentational skills as you realize those goals. For both junior and senior organizational communicators, presentations have important results.

As you launch your career, realize that senior managers use presentations to evaluate the abilities of junior employees. Listening to a corporate "fledgling" explain a revised benefits policy, disclose an innovative marketing strategy, or propose a new product line provides a wealth of information. Not only is the presenter's competence immediately apparent, but so are her commitment to the project and her communicative talents. Simply put, for junior employees their organizational "fit" is of-

Table 5.1 *How Much Speakers Charge*

AMOUNT	SPEAKER
$50,000	Ronald Reagan
$30,000	Nancy Reagan
$25,000	Oliver North, Walter Cronkite, Tom Peters, Sam Donaldson, Tom Brokaw, Dan Rather
$20,000	Jerry Ford, Alexander Haig, Donald Regan
$18,000	William Safire
$17,000	Mike Ditka, Pat Riley, Walter Payton, David Stockman, Charles Osgood
$15,000	George Will, David Brinkley, Lou Holtz
$14,000	Howard Baker
$12,500	Howard K. Smith, Buck Rogers (ex-IBM executive), Art Linkletter, Willard Scott
$10,000	Patrick Buchanan, Jimmy Carter, Vladimir Posner (Soviet spokesman)
$ 8,000	Arthur Laffer, Joe Thiesman, Bart Starr, Hugh Sidey
$ 7,000	Dr. M. Scott Peck, author of *The Road Less Traveled*
$ 6,000	Peter Hanson, author of *Joy of Stress* Frank Cappiello (*Wall Street Week* regular)
$ 5,000	Barry Asmus (economist), Jerry Brown

Reprinted by permission of the *San Francisco Chronicle*.

ten assessed through the spoken word. Cultivating presentational skills now can put you ahead of the game considerably.

The last chapter dealt with the mechanics of preparing a sound presentation. This chapter will examine the fine points of delivering a successful presentation.

REHEARSING YOUR DELIVERY

As we mentioned in Chapter 4, if you find the notion of speaking before others to be an exciting challenge, and if you already have enjoyed many speaking successes, then you are off to a good start. On the other hand, all this discussion about speech making may raise your anxieties rather than lower them.

Along with Paul Sweeney, we believe that "true success is overcoming the fear of being unsuccessful." Because we want to lower your anxieties rather than inadvertently raise them, allow us to provide information that you may not have considered.

Once you begin speaking, your anxiety is likely to be short-lived. According to a study conducted by researchers at the University of Rhode Island, anxiety levels are highest immediately before and during the first two minutes of a presentation.[4] If you can make it past that preliminary obstacle, you are on your way to channeling your nervous energy.

The audience generally is unaware of your anxiety. Even though your heart seems to be pounding audibly and your knees feel as if they are knocking visibly, rarely is this the case. *You* are the one concentrating on clues to your anxiety, not your listeners. Chances are much better than fifty-fifty that they are rooting for your success — not your demise — as a speaker.

Some anxiety is beneficial. Anxiety indicates ego involvement — it means that your presentation is important to you. Apathy, on the other hand, would not bode well for the presentational speaker. Think of your nervousness as *energy* and harness it to propel you before and during your presentation. Of course, this is easier said than done, but the more opportunities you have to speak, the more this principle will become second nature.

Practice is the best preventative. The best way to reduce your fears is to prepare and rehearse *thoroughly*. World famous violinist Isaac Stern is reported to have once said, "I practice eight hours a day for forty years, and they call me a genius?!" The same principle applies to successful presentations.

As you rehearse, form an image of success rather than of failure. In one sense, even thinking about your presentation beforehand is a form of practice. If you focus solely on all the possible mistakes you might make, not to mention the negative reactions these might evoke from your superiors, you are defeated before you've given yourself a chance. Remember that for some people, a pessimist is a man who looks both ways before crossing a one-way street, while an optimist is a driver who thinks the empty space at the curb won't have a hydrant beside it. We're not discouraging realism—we're cautioning you against excessive worry, which can be nonproductive and sometimes paralyzing. And while the admonition "stay calm" is rather like the suggestion "be spontaneous," frame of mind does make a difference.

Practice your presentation aloud several, perhaps even many, times beforehand, harnessing that energy-producing anxiety. Begin a few days before your target date and continue until you're about to go "on stage." The point is not to memorize your presentation, but to become familiar with your material—so familiar that you can almost hear a tape recording of your presentation in your head during your actual delivery. Of course, this is difficult if your presentation contains a great deal of complex information, but at least you will have a clear sense throughout of what comes next. When you rehearse aloud, you're using *external* spoken language rather than *internal* spoken language. Thinking through your speech and talking through your speech produce very different results.[5]

Practice before a "pseudoaudience"—your subordinates, your partner or spouse, your dog, even the mirror. Talking to something or someone helps to simulate the distraction that listeners cause. Practice in the designated room, if possible. Not only will this increase your confidence but also it may give you a subconscious boost by helping you use visual stimuli around the room as cues. You may even want to wear the clothes you plan to wear for your presentation. Precreate the setting. Beginning this shadowboxing process early allows enough time to make changes if something isn't working. Also consider audiotaping or videotaping yourself to pinpoint mistakes and reinforce strengths. When it comes to business and professional presentations, both pseudoaudience and taped dry runs are invaluable. And, of course, having your pseudoaudience critique you will give you some idea of needed changes. Many successful presenters use such critiques not only to allay anxiety but also to strengthen content and delivery. When a multimillion dollar contract is at stake, one does not wing it.

POLISHING YOUR NONVERBAL SKILLS

Rehearsing is not enough to ensure success; make sure that you are rehearsing correctly. In other words, if you are a newcomer to presentational speaking, you may end up rehearsing bad habits that probably will do more harm than good. Many of these habits are nonverbal. We want to focus your attention, then, on the nonverbal aspects of delivery. Why? Because these aspects typically are an important source of your dynamism and credibility as a speaker. Chapter 4 discussed the difference between *poise* and *pose*—the *I* in the middle. Nonverbal aspects of presentations are the heart of that "I"; they are how you project confidence, enthusiasm, and energy. We'll describe the nonverbal aspects of superior delivery, and your instructor will demonstrate actual techniques in class. As you rehearse, keep this information in mind.

....

Movements

Many speakers have great difficulty deciding where to put the appendages at the ends of their limbs—namely, their hands. Sound familiar? We seem to need to occupy our hands somehow and so, when speaking, we often jingle the coins in our pockets, fidget with a pen or paper clip, or smooth unruffled hair. These are examples of nonverbal behaviors called *displacement activities*, or "agitated fill-in actions performed during periods of acute tension."[6] Although these normal human behaviors serve as *unconscious* masks to cover underlying turmoil, they also can *consciously* irritate listeners. Displacement activities result from unconscious displacement *wishes*, your mind's way of saying through your body, "I sure wish I were somewhere else!" Beyond these irritating movements, other distracting hand placements for speakers include the "lectern clench," the "fig-leaf" position, the "reverse fig-leaf" position (behind the back), the "singer's clasp," and the "mortician's grip."[7] (See Figure 5.1.)

The best way to avoid such "manual" distractions is to allow your hands to hang comfortably at your sides so that they can take over their

Figure 5.1 *Distracting Hand Placements*

normal function during communication — gesturing. Natural, spontaneous gestures would be optimal, but you'll probably want to refine your normal tendencies. For example, you may naturally tend toward over-gesturing or undergesturing. Women, for example, typically use smaller and less frequent gestures than do men.[8] We certainly do not recommend that women take on an exaggerated "John Wayne" nonverbal style to command attention, but it may be helpful to risk somewhat more dynamic gestures when speaking before others. On the other hand, if you normally are a hyperactive gesturer, then you may wish to tone down your natural tendencies so that your audience isn't lost by your thrashing. Whatever you do, make sure to vary your gestures. One gesture, used repeatedly, can be annoying to an audience. And even though we recommend rehearsing gestures, they must finally appear natural. Stylized or mechanical gestures are even more distracting than no gestures at all.

Now that your hands are under control, what about posture and movement during your presentation? Obviously, you will want to stand erect; don't lean over the lectern if you use one. And plan to move comfortably around the room without pacing nervously. If you are using visual aids, this will happen naturally — as you walk to the flip chart to turn a page, for example. If you use a microphone, then ask for the lapel, lavaliere, or wireless variety so that you needn't remain in one spot restricted by an electronic leash. Some experts even suggest that you change positions between major points to punctuate your presentation. The unconscious message is: "I've finished with that point; let's shift topics." Whatever you do, face your audience as much as possible, and don't be afraid to move toward it while you speak. Approaching your listeners can communicate your involvement and your interest in their needs. Besides, they won't move toward you.

....

Face and Eyes

If we had to select one dimension of nonverbal communication that has more impact than any other, it would be the eye contact you use — or avoid — with your audience. Volumes have been written on this subject because eye contact is the cement required to build rapport with an audience. The eyes are not only the window to the soul but also the door to audience members' heads and hearts. Look at individuals, meet their eyes, and move actively from one face to another. Some speakers make the mistake of looking only at people who wield power; others sweep the room mechanically like a robot; still others fake eye contact by gazing at an imaginary audience projected on the back wall. Instead, it's much better to make contact with as many listeners as you can by looking at individuals as directly and engagingly as possible. Making eye contact with listeners in a relaxed, confident manner also will help you read the reactions of individuals and establish speaker command.

Your overall level of facial activity also is important. A smile often can warm up your listeners, although you should avoid excessive or inappropriate smiling. If you smiled through a presentation on record financial losses for the company, then your listeners would receive a mixed message.[9] In general, an appropriate level of facial liveliness is more likely to evoke a positive response from your audience than a deadpan expression. And because we often are unaware of our precise expressions, seek feedback from your pseudoaudience on your facial expressions.

Voice

Vocal quality and paralanguage also are crucially important in business and professional presentations. *Vocal quality* includes such characteristics as breathiness, nasality, and throatiness. We should also point out that these qualities can be perceived differently in men and women. According to one classic study in this area, women with breathy voices are seen as petite, pretty, and shallow, while men who display this characteristic are perceived as young and artistic. Women who have throaty voices, on the other hand, are viewed as unintelligent, ugly, and lazy; throaty men are seen as realistic, sophisticated, and mature.[10] Vocal quality, then, reflects the overall pleasantness or unpleasantness of your voice.

Paralanguage is *how* you say something rather than *what* you say. It's the difference between saying "This proposal is worth reviewing" and exclaiming "**THIS** PROPOSAL is WORTH **REVIEWING!**" This category of nonverbal behavior includes voice pitch, rate of speech, volume, articulation and pronunciation, and fillers or verbalized pauses.

Pitch. As audience members, we tend to react to someone whose voice is pitched too high or too low. We're often put off by it, sometimes amused, occasionally even offended. So learn to work primarily within the average range of pitch for natural speaking. Don't feel that you'll be more forceful if you always speak in a deep voice — you won't, especially if that depth isn't natural for you. And don't feel that people will like you more or protect you if you speak in a high voice — they're more likely to wonder what you're afraid of. Instead, project the confidence and enthusiasm you already feel by varying your pitch within your natural range.

Pitch variation is crucial in at least two ways. First, extended changes in pitch—a deepened voice during a particularly serious passage or a raised pitch to underscore excitement—emphasize the feelings that underlie certain portions of your speech. Second, varied pitch within specific words and sentences animates speech, enlivens delivery, and energizes a topic and an audience. Few experiences are more boring than listening for twenty minutes to a speaker whose voice remains on one note the entire time—especially if the note is flat.

Rate. Either extreme in speaking rate–very fast or very slow–hurts. If you consistently speak too quickly, runningeverythingtogether, either your listeners won't understand your words or they won't follow your arguments. And if you drag out your delivery word—by—excruciating—word, you either put them to sleep or antagonize them. Once again, practice a delivery rate that mirrors normal conversation. But, as in normal conversation, remember to vary that rate, both to engage your audience and to achieve specific effects. You reflect excitement by speeding up, just as you emphasize a serious point by slowing down. And if you want people to pay particular attention at a specific place in your presentation, then use a sudden deceleration—and watch your audience hang on every word.

Volume. Which is worse, **TOO LOUD** or *too soft*? We think they are both counterproductive. Given the acoustics of your room, the size of your audience, and the effectiveness of your public-address system (if you need one), establish a middle range that is pleasant and clear. Until you've done enough presentational speaking to make such judgments naturally, practice and feedback will be important. Try the room with a listener stationed at various points. Will your voice carry to the back row? Are you too loud in front?

Beyond finding the most useful volume level, however, you should consider varying your volume for the same reasons you vary pitch and rate: to engage your listeners and to produce special effects. And think of the effects you have to play with by combining changes in all three variables. Don't confine yourself merely to variations that are either high pitch–rate–volume or low pitch–rate–volume. Experiment with the emotional effect of a moment in which your voice raises in pitch, slows down, and drops in volume. Or try lowering pitch, speeding up, and dropping your volume. You'll find the results startling—and useful.

Articulation. A poorly articulated word, such as *gonna* for *going to*; a mispronounced word, such as *nucular* for *nuclear*; or a misused word can erode credibility quickly. George Plimpton once remarked that he always began a speech by thanking the person who introduced him to the audience for his or her "fulsome" introduction—that is, until he learned that *fulsome* means offensive and insincere.

Fillers. Verbalized pauses or fillers such as "uhm," "uh," "like," and "you know," are nonfluencies that can become distracting. Their overuse attests to the discomfort generated by a lack of words. Believe it or not, you can use silence to your advantage by pausing at appropriate moments and allowing your listeners to reach a particular conclusion or realize an emotional response.

The best way to appraise your vocal qualities is to tape record yourself and honestly assess the results. The truth is that most of us don't enunciate as carefully as we could. Often we don't realize the importance of controlling regional dialects or reducing unpleasant vocal qualities because we don't hear ourselves as others do. Sounding like a "native" may be fine when you address other "natives," but listeners from other parts of the country may have trouble deciphering your message.

Earlier we suggested that you elicit feedback from your pseudoaudience about your facial expressions. Because we usually are less in tune with our nonverbal than our verbal behaviors, this is good advice for many of the aspects of nonverbal behavior we've discussed.

Personal Appearance

How should you dress for your presentation? This is where chameleon-like qualities come in handy. Watch and listen for what successful speakers do and then follow their example. If you're speaking to corporate officers in Miami, Los Angeles, or New York, dress as they do. Naturally, you will want to enhance your professional image, so when in doubt, err on the side of formal but comfortable attire. (You don't need the added distraction caused by a binding waistline or a choking collar.) If you're slightly overdressed, your listeners undoubtedly will make allowances because you are the speaker. They may interpret your formal appearance as a positive indication of their importance in your eyes.[11]

Naturally, a neat appearance is important. Well-groomed hair, well-applied makeup for women, and either a well-trimmed beard or clean-shaven face for men are all requirements. The image you want to convey is one of professionalism, preparedness, and success—being at your nonverbal best. Remember the words of Lawrence J. Peter, author of *The Peter Principle*: "Competence, like truth, beauty, and a contact lens, is in the eye of the beholder."

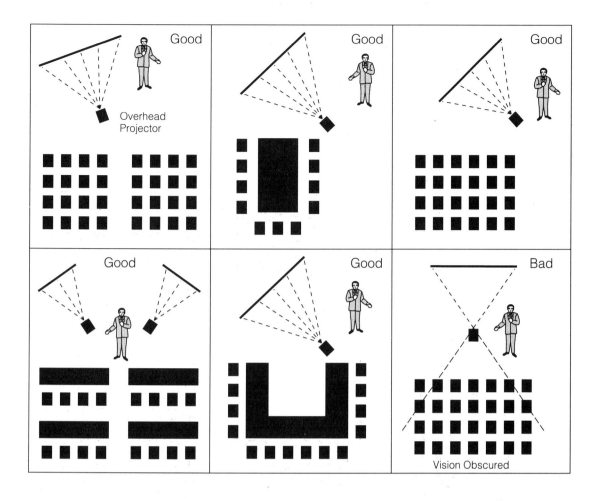

Figure 5.2 Physical Arrangements[12]

CONSIDERING PHYSICAL ARRANGEMENTS

Rehearsing for success also includes such tasks as inspecting the facilities and equipment beforehand and considering the arrangement of tables, chairs, and visual aids. For example, based on your objective, the formality of your presentation, the type of visual aids you will use, and the size of your audience, what room arrangement makes sense? The arrangement depicted at the top left in Figure 5.2 probably would be the best choice for a large, formal presentation, while the arrangement at the top center would work for a smaller, less formal presentation, particularly if your goals included a discussion or meeting afterward. Research indicates that, if given a choice, audiences often prefer a U-shaped arrangement such as the one at bottom center.[13]

As you work to ensure a successful presentation, consider the following checklist.

1. Take complete responsibility for the adequacy of the physical arrangements for your presentation. "The price of greatness is responsibility," as Winston Churchill once noted. Even if you are speaking away from your corporate or professional building, and even if the arrangements coordinator there has assured you that all systems are go, check out each detail yourself.
2. Make a detailed checklist beforehand so that you don't omit important considerations.
3. Be specific about the type of equipment you request. The word *projector* could refer to an overhead projector, a slide projector, or an opaque projector.
4. Test your equipment well in advance so that you can be sure that visuals can be seen from various points in the room and that equipment is in good working order.
5. If you use a projector, carry a spare bulb (and handkerchief—bulbs can be hot) and know how to insert it. Murphy's Law (see page 209) is real, and it attacks everyone from time to time.
6. Test the public-address system in advance. Actually use the microphone under working conditions to see that it meets your needs.
7. Locate the electrical outlets, the light switches, and the temperature controls in advance and know how they work.
8. Arrange seats and tables so that audience members will be comfortable and can see and write easily. Make sure the entrance to the room is not toward the front because latecomers will distract your audience.
9. If your presentation is away from your usual facility, then find out what will be happening in adjacent rooms. The awards ceremony for a large organization may be noisy competition.
10. Book your presentation room well in advance, and verify the reservation at least once. Arriving early and finding another meeting in progress can be very unnerving.

RESPONDING TO AUDIENCE QUESTIONS

A successful business or professional presentation often is not over until after you've responded to audience questions. This is when your listeners have an opportunity to clarify troublesome points, probe for additional information, and react in general to your message. This also is the time when you may feel most vulnerable, as if it were "open season" on you the speaker. For many of us, in fact, this part of the presentation process provokes as much, if not more, anxiety than preparing and delivering the actual presentation. Why? Probably because we fear being attacked by nitpicking or hostile listeners and thus appearing uninformed and foolish. But such fears are usually exaggerated.

First, remember that you are ready by the time you reach the "stage." You have accumulated the knowledge you need, you have skillfully arranged that information, you have predetermined the support you have from key players, and you have rehearsed your delivery to build confidence. Obviously, you can't anticipate every possible eventuality, but nevertheless you are well prepared.

Second, remember that as speaker you still have control of the situation, and you still have choices and strategies available to you as a communicator. Let's look at rules of thumb that will help you to set up desired responses from listeners and handle questions effectively.[14]

1. *Be as ready as possible.* Predict in advance the kinds of questions your presentation will elicit and prepare appropriate responses.
2. *Stay alert.* Realize that the question-and-answer period is part of the presentation. Don't relax too soon; sometimes you can win or lose your argument here.
3. *Announce format and limits.* Tell listeners at the presentation's outset whether to expect a question-and-answer period and what format you will use. Questions throughout your presentation, as opposed to afterward, can help to eliminate confusion, although you risk having your presentation degenerate into a free-for-all. You also can indicate both a time limit and topic limits at the beginning of the question-and-answer period: "We have ten minutes remaining for any questions you may wish to raise. I'll be happy to entertain questions on the development of the new model, but marketing strategies will be announced at a future meeting."

4. *Allow audience members an opportunity to leave.* Not everyone will have time for or be interested in this portion of the presentation. If appropriate, allow listeners an opportunity to leave before you field your first question.

5. *Predict questions and questioners.* Watch audience members' nonverbal behaviors during your presentation for cues about what questions may originate and from whom. A puzzled expression on someone's face at a particular point in your presentation may lead you to anticipate both a questioner and a question.

6. *Start the questioning yourself, if necessary.* If you ask for questions and none are forthcoming, suggest a few areas for exploration to your listeners: "Many of you may be concerned about the work distribution on this project." Make sure the questions you pose for yourself are difficult ones; otherwise, you may look like a phony. Or you may try humor: "I assume nobody wants to ask me about . . ." and then ask a particularly difficult or challenging — perhaps even a hostile — question. "Planting" questions in the audience is another option, but this sometimes is transparent to audience members. If you repeatedly fail to generate questions from listeners in presentation after presentation, you may be doing something wrong. Determine what aspect of your style may be putting people off and correct it.

7. *Repeat the question before answering.* When a question is posed by an audience member, particularly in a large group, rephrase and repeat it before answering. This practice has three benefits: It assures you that everyone has heard the question, it ensures that you understand the question before you begin an answer, and it buys time for thought.

8. *Respond to the entire audience.* Don't answer by speaking only to the questioner. The rest of the audience also may be interested, so speak to the group as a whole. As an audience member, it's annoying to feel you're missing something important that is going on in another part of the room.

9. *Be brief.* Keep your answers succinct. Your listeners probably don't have time for a series of additional presentations. Delay complex, time-consuming answers until later.

10. *Don't bluff an answer.* Generally, if you do not know the answer to a question, then offer to find out. This response is usually best; the audience will see through an outright bluff.

11. *Be courteous.* Never embarrass an audience member for asking what you consider to be an irrelevant question. You should be

courteous and respond always, even if only to say, "That's an interesting question, but it goes beyond my area of expertise on this project. I'd prefer to limit our time to the project's development." Also, don't refer a difficult question to an unsuspecting audience member who may not be prepared to answer right then.

12. *React to statements as well as questions.* If an audience member makes a statement, instead of asking a question, respond in some way. Don't let silence fill the room. Instead, say something like, "Well said, Jack," and move on.

13. *Remain in control.* As speaker, it is your duty to keep the line of questioning on track. If someone asks you a completely "off the wall" question, then you may wish to shift the topic skillfully to an area you know well; for example, "That's an interesting question, Terry. But the first thing we have to consider is this." People we perceive as brilliant often have cultivated an ability to direct conversations toward their own areas of expertise.

14. *Don't allow someone to dominate.* If one audience member attempts to dominate the question-and-answer period, then you will have to take back the reins and do so skillfully. Interrupt, paraphrase the question, provide an answer, and move on to another questioner; for example, "I see that several people in the front row also have questions. Let's hear from some of them."

15. *Defuse hostile questions.* We have discussed the necessity of analyzing your audience and predetermining support from key players. Despite these precautionary measures, you still may be asked a hostile question. A good strategy to follow is to first *paraphrase* the question by asking, "Do you mean X?" rather than asking weakly, "What do you mean?" Do this especially if you are sincere about uncovering the questioner's intent. This technique also ensures that you understand what is being asked. Second, *defuse* the question by dividing it into manageable parts; for example, "Your question addresses several broad issues; I'll respond to X"; then give an honest response. Maintaining both your sense of humor and a non-defensive posture also helps.

16. *End on a high note.* You can end the question-and-answer period with the usual "I have time for one more question," although this approach is risky. For all you know, the last question may be from the one person who is looking for an opportunity to deflate your presentation. It also is anticlimactic

to end with the weak trailer, "Well, since there aren't any more questions. . . ." Instead, wait until you have given a particularly articulate answer, summarize the question-and-answer period, and then conclude. This method guarantees that you will leave your audience with a good impression.

IMPROMPTU SPEAKING IN ORGANIZATIONS

A recurring theme in both this chapter and Chapter 4 has been reducing anxiety through preparation. As we have said, anxiety is a common reaction to the prospect of public speaking, a reaction that may be heightened by the high stakes that often accompany business and professional presentations. But think about that reaction's validity for a moment.

First, when you come right down to it, all speaking is *public* speaking. Chances are that whenever you speak, you do so in public. Few of us do much speaking in *private*. In other words, let's redefine public speaking as a continual way of life rather than as a "one-shot" event.

Second, most of your organizational speaking will not require the extensive preparation and high-pressure format that we've discussed. Most speaking will be impromptu minipresentations given on the spot with little or no preparation. You will give impromptu presentations when a colleague in a meeting asks your opinion on a pending decision, when a subordinate stops you in the hall to find out your position on a proposed change, or when your boss asks you to defend your views on a new company policy. Of course, because this kind of speaking is so pervasive, it shapes your image as a successful communicator. For this reason, you must think about how you *can* prepare for impromptu speaking and communicate at your best.

When you know that you will be expected to express your thoughts publicly, use our steps-to-success model to prepare. For example, imagine you are invited to a meeting of high-level managers to discuss a new management training program and you suspect that you will asked to give your viewpoint. The following are steps you can take to achieve success.

> *Step 1. Clarify your objective.* What is your communicative goal? Are you for the idea or against it? Do you simply want to inform your listeners or do you want to persuade them to side with you on the issue? What is the single most important message you want to get across?
>
> *Step 2. Analyze your audience.* Who else will be there? What

positions are those individuals likely to take on the issue to be discussed?

Step 3. Develop your game plan. If the stakes are high and the outcome of the meeting is important to you, seek out key players and test the waters beforehand.

Step 4. Collect and organize your information. Go with ammunition in hand. Know what you're talking about, structure your facts for maximum clarity and impact, and bring whatever evidence might strengthen your case.

Step 5. Choose your visuals. Although few of us cart around an overhead projector, we still can use a blackboard, a note pad, or even our hands to make a point.

Step 6. Prepare your notes. Jot down a few notes so that you can stay organized as you talk. Whether or not you are persuasive, you will convince others of your competence and your commitment to the group's goals. In other words, our suggestion is to make impromptu speaking as *nonimpromptu* as you can.

Of course, you won't always have enough lead time to use this step-by-step model. Sometimes you will be put on the spot without prior warning; what do you do then?

Probably the best suggestion is to use Step 4: Organize your information and structure your facts for maximum clarity and impact. Caught off guard, most of us ramble on at length toward some unforeseen conclusion, an ineffective strategy used by default.

According to some experts in this field, sounding articulate when asked for an immediate response is not a matter of quick thinking; it's a matter of selecting one response quickly from all the possibilities that pop into your head at once.[15] In other words, being decisive is the key. And after you commit to a particular response, you must arrange your message so that listeners can grasp your main points easily.

There are many ways to arrange your thoughts, but one of the most popular uses what is called the PREP formula.[16] A shortened acronym for *preparation*, this formula requires that you give your:

Point of view (that is, provide an overview — a clear, direct statement or generalization)

Reasons why (give the broad reasons why you hold this point of view)

Evidence or examples (present specific facts or data that support your point of view)

Point of view restated (restate your position to make sure you are understood clearly)

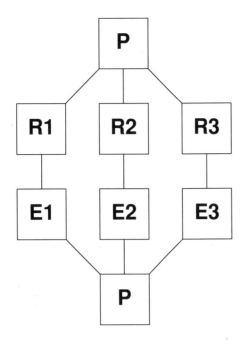

Figure 5.3 *The Branched PREP Response*

Let's examine the PREP formula in action:

BOSS: "Do you think we should hire the last interviewee?"

YOU:

P "Yes, I do. She is an extremely qualified applicant."
R "She is exactly the kind of employee we need."
E "She has six years of experience, excellent letters of refer-
   ence, and superb oral communication skills."
P "Therefore, my vote is yes. She's exceptionally qualified for
   the job."

Of course, your answer sometimes may be more complicated. When it is, you may resort to a branching PREP response, one something like that in Figure 5.3.

Imagine the following scenario in which you come up with three reasons rather than one:

COMPANY PRESIDENT: "What do you think of the proposed plan to establish flextime in the company?"

P   "I've been doing some thinking about flextime,
J. R., and I'm in favor of the idea—for three reasons."

R1   "First, flextime would improve company morale."

E1   "The people in my division are constantly asking for time
off for personal appointments, and from time to time they
exhibit symptoms of stress from work overload. Flextime
would give them more personal control over their own
schedules."

R2   "Second, flextime would increase productivity."

E2   "We'd avoid some of the production bottlenecks we're experiencing now—which could result in a 10% greater output."

R3   "And last, flextime would reduce traffic congestion around
the plant during the rush hour—a factor that influences
not only morale but also safety."

E3   "With more than six hundred vehicles trying to enter and
exit two access roads at the same time, driver frustration is
at an all-time high. And let's face it, that leads to the kind of
accidents we've seen out there all too often. Flextime would
stagger incoming and outgoing traffic and improve the situation tremendously."

P   "For these reasons, I think flextime is a good idea. I'm for it
100 percent."

The end result of using a device such as the PREP formula is that you
sound logical, organized, and competent, a result that contributes to
your effectiveness as a successful communicator.

HANDLING (AND MINIMIZING) MISTAKES

We cannot leave the topic of presentational speaking without asking,
"Yes, but what if . . .?" We have stressed planning, organizing, preparing,
checking, and rehearsing—all of which are positive, proactive steps that
help to ensure success. But despite the precautions you have taken, what
if calamity strikes? What if the projector goes up in smoke? What if the
audience continues to laugh even though comedy is not your goal? What
if you knock over the lectern? What if you trip and fall into the flip
chart? In other words, What if your worst nightmare comes true? What
then? Fair questions.

Even though such misfortunes aren't all that common, Murphy's Law — "Whatever can go wrong, will" — continues to lurk. Most of us have experienced this truth in many different contexts. Table 5.2 is a humorous summary of how Murphy's Law operates in business and professional presentations. Of course, we can express this truth another way: No presentation is ever perfect. We think this generalization should be more reassuring than threatening.

But let's return to our continuing theme of reducing anxiety through preparation. As with everything else we've discussed, thinking through these challenges in advance is the answer. That such fears haunt us attests to the difficulty of moving from a *self-centered* to an *audience-centered* presentation.

You might begin by asking yourself what your worst fears are. When we conduct informal polls with students or businesspeople to discover the mistakes they fear most, we always find two major categories: internal fears and external fears. If we look at these categories in more detail, we may realize that many mishaps are controllable if not preventable.[17]

....

Internal Fears

Internal fears relate directly to you in your role as speaker. Some of them surround your psychological condition, some pertain to your physical state, and some concern your actual behaviors. *Psychological difficulties* such as losing your train of thought or going completely blank are remedied easily through preparation: Always bring notes. Slips of the tongue, however, are not remedied as easily. Spoonerisms are an example. These slips are named for the Reverend Spooner of Oxford Univer-

Table 5.2 *Murphy's Law and Presentations*

••

1. Visual aids packed with luggage that is headed for Cleveland will end up in Detroit.

2. An upside-down slide or transparency will not be projected correctly until every other incorrect position has been tried.

3. In a major two-speaker presentation, the other speaker will be hit by Asian flu thirty minutes before the presentation is to begin.

4. A person can hold a coffee cup hundreds of times without incident until he is the next presenter — then he spills coffee all over himself.

5. A loose jacket button on a male presenter will pop the first time the speaker points at the screen — and the button will go into the boss's coffee.

6. Stockings worn by a female presenter for three weeks will shred immediately before the presentation.

7. The one time that the presenter fails to check the projector bulb is just after the last person burned out the bulb — and didn't replace it.

8. The pointer that has always been there, won't be.

9. In a visual that discusses Murphy's Law, the speaker and the audience will discover simultaneously that the *w* in "Law" has been typed as a *y*.

10. If a presenter must have a specific type of equipment, such as a cassette recorder, a reel-to-reel recorder will be delivered.

11. Whenever a speaker says, "As all of you can see . . . ," half the audience can't.

12. While scrambling to get to a meeting across town, the harried presenter, who is, of course, first on the schedule, suddenly will remember that she forgot to put gas in the car . . . just before it starts to cough . . . while driving on the freeway.

Adapted from T. Leech, *How to Prepare, Stage, and Deliver Winning Presentations* (New York: AMACOM, 1982), 181. © 1982 Thomas Leech. Reprinted by permission of the publisher.

sity, who often unknowingly transposed the first letters of words in sequence: "You have hissed my mystery lesson; you have tasted the whole worm," meaning "You have missed my history lesson; you have wasted the whole term." Spooner once embarrassed everyone else around him by referring to Queen Victoria as the "queer old dean." True, slips of the tongue can be embarrassing, but they also are frequently amusing. Chances are you should pat yourself on the back for providing your listeners with a moment of fun, and then forget about it.

Physical difficulties are more problematic because they are less easily controlled. Some of the wavering in your voice can be removed by learning to project from your diaphragm, just as you would in singing lessons. You can mimimize the effects of trembling hands by holding small cards rather than gripping 8½″ × 11″ paper at the bottom so that the upper half of the page quivers visibly as your hands tremble. And you can always hide knocking knees behind a lectern, table, or projector cart. But it's more difficult to control your body if it wants to do you in completely. You must learn to control your idiosyncrasies and prepare for them as best you can. If you are bothered by nausea before a presentation, then eat lightly (if at all) beforehand, and find the restroom closest to your presentation site. In the worst possible case, you can make a swift exit and return when you've composed yourself. You also can minimize the physical effects of stress through brief exercise — for example, by walking back and forth in a hallway. Generally, problems of this nature are relatively rare, and they decrease in severity as you become a more experienced speaker.

External Fears

External fears relate to your audience or your equipment, factors that are outside of you. They can be controlled to the extent that you plan, prepare, and safeguard against them. *Audience problems* such as hostility can result if your presentation is missing its mark. For example, if you cover too much information too quickly, an audience may become frustrated, which can breed hostility. If you have neglected to analyze your audience beforehand, then you may be giving it old information and in effect wasting its time, which also can lead to hostility. These are mistakes you can guard against. A solitary eccentric listener who is playing out some personal vendetta, however, is another matter. But using the techniques in this chapter, you now have some ideas about how to respond. And, of course, as we've discussed, *equipment problems* usually are controllable if you plan ahead.

More often than not, things will go smoothly and your preparation will pay off. Whatever minor misfortune does strike, the most important factor is not that it occurred, but that you as the speaker handled and minimized the problem. Don't forget, your listeners have been in your position and probably have some empathy for what you're going through. Accentuate the positive; rely on your wit; use the opportunity to emphasize your humanness. Your recovery is what they are most likely to recognize; your success is what they are most likely to remember.

CHAPTER SUMMARY

In this chapter, we focused on six aspects of delivering a successful presentation:

- rehearsing your delivery,
- polishing your nonverbal skills,
- considering physical arrangements,
- dealing with audience questions,
- impromptu speaking in organizations, and
- handling (and minimizing) mistakes.

In the section on rehearsing your delivery, we pointed out that anxiety typically decreases as you continue speaking, that the audience generally is unaware of your nervousness, that some anxiety is beneficial, and that practice is the best preventative. Practice aloud, practice thoroughly, precreate the setting, and form an image of success.

Polishing your nonverbal skills includes eliciting feedback on your movements, face and eyes, voice, and personal appearance. Make sure your gestures are as natural and as varied as possible. Your eye contact should be directed at individuals around the room, and your facial expressiveness should be lively and engaging. Many possibilities exist for variation in your voice — variation that can add interest and special effects to your presentation. You should be neat and well-groomed, modeling your appearance after other effective speakers within the organization.

Considering physical arrangements is another important element in delivering a successful presentation. We discussed arranging tables, chairs, and equipment and provided a ten-point checklist to help you plan ahead. Checking each detail in advance is your responsibility as speaker.

Often business and professional presentations are not over until after you've finished responding to audience questions. Even though the prospect of a question-and-answer session can make you feel vulnerable, remember that this portion of the presentation is at least as important as your speech itself. We provided sixteen suggestions on preparing yourself to respond adequately.

Most of the speaking you do will not require the extensive preparation and high pressure format discussed in Chapters 4 and 5. Instead, impromptu speaking in organizations will be a daily occurrence. When you're asked to give an opinion or answer a question, the result will be a brief, impromptu presentation without much time for preparation. Often it's possible to predict the need for such a presentation; if so, rely on our steps-to-success model to prepare. If you're caught off guard, try the PREP formula to enhance your image as an organized and competent communicator.

We closed this chapter by asking, "Yes, but what if . . .?" questions. What are our worst fears? Typically, such fears can be categorized as internal (psychological or physical) or external (audience or equipment). Handling and minimizing mistakes is challenging and important because your recovery is what the audience is likely to remember.

In the next chapter, we take a close look at listening, the *receptive* skill that complements speaking as a *productive* skill. Research indicates that most of us need to become better organizational listeners.

MEASURING SUCCESS

1. Create a critique sheet to use for evaluating in-class presentations. Which aspects of verbal and nonverbal behavior from Chapters 4 and 5 should be incorporated to give classmates feedback about their presentational speaking success? Your instructor may ask you to do this as a group exercise.

2. Sketch what you believe would be effective room arrangements for the following presentations. Include such items as tables, chairs, visual aids, and a lectern.

  a. a presentation to three managers on a new proposal
  b. a presentation to fifteen department heads on a policy change
  c. a presentation to all three hundred of the company's employees on a new benefits package

d. a presentation on a cooperative project to forty executives from other corporations in the city.

3. According to Lawrence Peter, "There's only one thing more painful than learning from experience, and that is not learning from experience." We want you to gain experience in responding to challenging questions and statements. Assuming that the following questions are posed to you during hypothetical question-and-answer sessions, compose effective responses. To respond, create whatever background context you need.

a. "If women would stay at home where they belong, we wouldn't be discussing a million dollar on-site day-care facility."
b. "I'd like to know where you got your information. I haven't heard any of this stuff before."
c. "Don't you think the real solution is to drop this project before we invest too much in it?"
d. "What's your opinion on the other side of this issue? There are obviously some arguments you didn't mention in your presentation."
e. "I agree with everything you've said so far, but I'd like further information on the ramifications of the operations effects this project will set in motion in future years."
f. "I'd like to know more about the project's work distribution, the reporting schedule, and the assignment of supervisory responsibilities."

4. Using the PREP formula, create minimal notes for impromptu presentations on the following:

a. Public speaking should be part of your company's management training program.
b. Communication training programs help your employees to develop their speaking and writing skills.
c. Listening is the primary communication problem in your company.

5. Identify the three presentational speaking mistakes that you fear most and discuss possible responses that would minimize each problem in your audience's eyes and ears. In what ways are these mistakes less traumatic than you might imagine, and how could you possibly use them to your advantage?

Decco Exercise Select one of the three statements in Exercise 4 and write a one-page summary of your position for your boss, giving a rationale for your views.

··············

Notes

1. Walter Kiechel III, "The Big Presentation," *Fortune*, 26 July 1982, 98.

2. Kiechel, "The Big Presentation," 98.

3. Keith H. Hammonds, "Big Bucks for the Big Names in Business," *New York Times*, 11 September 1983, p. F15.

4. Winifred W. Brownell and Richard A. Katula, "The Communication Anxiety Graph: A Classroom Tool for Managing Speech Anxiety," *Communication Education* 32 (1984): 243–249.

5. Frank X. E. Dance and Carol C. Zak-Dance, *Public Speaking* (New York: Harper & Row, 1986), 141–143.

6. Desmond Morris, *Manwatching* (New York: Harry N. Abrams, 1977), 179.

7. Thomas Leech, *How to Prepare, Stage, and Deliver Winning Presentations* (New York: AMACOM, 1982), 234.

8. P. Peterson, "An Investigation of Sex Differences in regard to Non-Verbal Body Gestures," *Proceedings of the Speech Communication Association Summer Conference*, Austin, TX, 1976.

9. Some research indicates that women are socialized to smile too frequently and inappropriately. For example, see M. Parlee, "Women Smile Less for Success," *Psychology Today* 12 (March 1979): 16.

10. D. W. Addington, "The Relationship of Selected Vocal Characteristics to Personality Perception," *Speech Monographs* 35 (1968): 492–503.

11. Popular books of the 1970s such as John T. Molloy's *Dress for Success* (New York: P. H. Wyden, 1975) and *The Woman's Dress for Success Book* (New York: Warner, 1977) have brought mixed reactions. Many experts now perceive more freedom of dress, particularly for women. Although conservatism and neatness still count, we think that today's executive woman can use style and color effectively to create her professional image.

12. For a thorough treatment of this subject, see The 3M Meeting Management Team, *How to Run Better Business Meetings: A Reference Guide for Managers* (New York: McGraw-Hill, 1979).

13. J. Heston and P. Garner, "A Study of Personal Spacing and Desk Arrangement in the Learning Environment." Paper presented at the annual meeting of the International Communication Association, 1972.

14. For an excellent discussion of question-and-answer strategies, see Janet Stone and Jane Bachner, *Speaking Up: A Book for Every Woman Who Wants to Speak Effectively* (New York: McGraw-Hill, 1977), 119–135.

15. Stone and Bachner, *Speaking Up*, 154.

16. Kenneth Wydro, *Thinking on Your Feet: The Art of Thinking and Speaking Under Pressure* (Englewood Cliffs, NJ: Prentice-Hall, 1981), 64–69.

17. Stone and Bachner, *Speaking Up*, 38–48.

Chapter **6** ⌁ **Listening Consci-**

entiously in Organizations

If working people were taught to listen effectively,

the efficiency of American business could be doubled.

— Robert L. Montgomery **N**ow that you

have begun to read this chapter, **STOP**! Hand

this book to your roommate, a friend, or some-

one close by and ask this person to read

the first portion of the chapter (in upside-down print) aloud to you. Using all possible resources and techniques, listen as carefully as you can. When you're done, we'll ask you a few simple questions.

R. Danforth has been at Remco's California headquarters for the past six years. As head of the Research and Development Division, this individual has been successful in heading up the production of five new products during that time and supervising the preliminary plans to develop four more. The average income of personnel in the division is now $39,000 per year, an increase of $7,000 over the average when the new head took over. Working under the head of the R & D division are the division directors: Marion Smithfield, Director of Testing; Al Klein, Director of Plans; and Rich Helms, Director of Market Research. In all, 36 employees currently work for these directors.

Now answer the following questions based on what you have heard.

1. Who is the head of the research and development (R&D) division at Remco?
2. How long has this person occupied the position?
3. What is the name of the person who heads the market research division at Remco?
4. Before the new head of R&D took over, what was the average salary in the division?
5. Who is the highest-ranking person mentioned?
6. All told, how many people work in the R&D division?
7. In what city is Remco located?

An exercise such as this one typically tends to reinforce what we all probably know intuitively but are often slow to admit—most of us are poor listeners. In fact, we are much quicker at characterizing others as poor listeners than we are at admitting this about ourselves. Let's look at the preceding exercise as a measurement of your listening skills. Here are the correct answers to each question.

1. *Who is the head of the R&D division at Remco?* The correct answer is *R. Danforth*. If you remembered the name at all, you may have answered Mr. Danforth even though there is no indication that Danforth is a man. Only a first initial was provided, so Danforth could be a man or a woman. You also may have

confused Danforth with other names in the paragraph or simply have gotten the name wrong. If you answered correctly, congratulations.

2. *How long has this person occupied the position?* The paragraph tells us that R. Danforth has been at Remco for six years, although we are not told how long she or he has been head of the division. Although a good guess would be six years or less, the correct answer is that *this information is not provided.*

3. *What is the name of the person who heads the market research division at Remco?* This answer *is* provided in the paragraph: *Rich Helms.*

4. *Before the new head of R&D took over, what was the average salary in the division?* Although you heard the information needed to answer this question, you must put together several facts to calculate the correct answer. You were told that the current average salary is $39,000, an increase of $7,000 over the average when the new head took over, which makes the correct answer *$32,000.*

5. *Who is the highest-ranking person mentioned?* This is a straightforward question with an easy answer. If you said *R. Danforth,* you are correct.

6. *All told, how many people work in the R&D division?* Again, the necessary information is provided, but you must put together several pieces of information to answer correctly. Thirty-six employees work for three division directors under the division head, R. Danforth; this is a total of *forty people.*

7. *In what city is Remco located?* Remco is located in California, although *the exact city is not mentioned.*

Now score your answers. Don't be surprised if you scored three or fewer correct. And although you were instructed to use helpful resources and techniques — which might include taking notes, using a tape recorder, and asking your reader to repeat portions of the paragraph — you probably listened "passively."

Although this exercise may seem unusually difficult and unrealistic, throughout your career you'll find yourself in similar circumstances: Time is short, the boss is in a hurry, and you'll be doused with facts and instructions that you must listen to and act upon. Before you read the rest of this chapter, continue your self-analysis by filling out the questionnaire in Table 6.1.

Table 6.1 *Listening Self-Analysis*

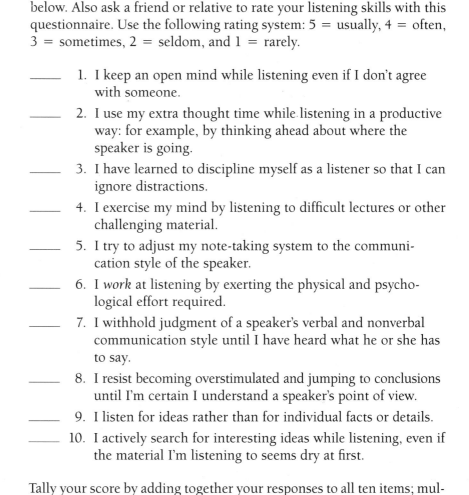

Reflect on your own listening habits and respond to the ten questions below. Also ask a friend or relative to rate your listening skills with this questionnaire. Use the following rating system: 5 = usually, 4 = often, 3 = sometimes, 2 = seldom, and 1 = rarely.

_____ 1. I keep an open mind while listening even if I don't agree with someone.

_____ 2. I use my extra thought time while listening in a productive way: for example, by thinking ahead about where the speaker is going.

_____ 3. I have learned to discipline myself as a listener so that I can ignore distractions.

_____ 4. I exercise my mind by listening to difficult lectures or other challenging material.

_____ 5. I try to adjust my note-taking system to the communication style of the speaker.

_____ 6. I *work* at listening by exerting the physical and psychological effort required.

_____ 7. I withhold judgment of a speaker's verbal and nonverbal communication style until I have heard what he or she has to say.

_____ 8. I resist becoming overstimulated and jumping to conclusions until I'm certain I understand a speaker's point of view.

_____ 9. I listen for ideas rather than for individual facts or details.

_____ 10. I actively search for interesting ideas while listening, even if the material I'm listening to seems dry at first.

Tally your score by adding together your responses to all ten items; multiply that number by two. Consider the resulting score to be an approximate percentage of time that you spend listening at your best.

Adapted from Ralph G. Nichols, "Listening is a 10-Part Skill," *Nation's Business* 45 (July 1957): 4. Copyright 1957, U.S. Chamber of Commerce. Reprinted with permission.

THE IMPORTANCE OF LISTENING SKILLS

Research indicates that we use our listening skills more frequently than we speak, write, or read. A well-known and now classic study conducted in 1926 demonstrated that people spend 42.1 percent of their total verbal-communication time listening; 31.9 percent speaking; 15 percent reading; and 11 percent writing.[1] More recent research corroborates these early findings; in fact, the percentage of time we spend listening is represented in newer studies as more than half of our total communication time — 54.93 percent in one study and 52.5 percent in another.[2]

Relating more specifically to business and professional communication, two researchers asked a cross-section of businesspeople how they divided their communication activities during the normal work week. Respondents reported spending 32.7 percent of their time listening; 25.8 percent speaking; 22.6 percent writing; and 18.8 percent reading.[3] Executives report that listening takes as much as 63 percent of their typical workday.[4] In other words, study after study underscores both that we are communication receivers more often than we are communication producers and that we receive more information through listening than we do by reading. Within the organization, your listening skills will contribute both directly and indirectly to your image as a successful communicator.

Perhaps the best way to get our point across is to remind you of certain national and global disasters that occurred because of failures to listen. Although you probably were not around, you may know about what happened on Sunday evening, October 30, 1938, when radio stations across the United States broadcast Orson Welles's Mercury Theatre production of H. G. Wells's *The War of the Worlds*. Although an announcer introduced the play, newspapers listed it in the day's programming, and three separate statements about the play's fictional nature were made during the broadcast, Americans failed to listen and panic spread across the country. People assumed that an alien invasion was in progress. Many suffered from shock and hysteria, families fled their homes, and thousands called radio stations, newspapers, and police departments for help.[5]

Or perhaps you remember or know about one of the worst disasters in aviation history in April 1977 when two Boeing 747 jetliners collided on the ground in the Canary Islands. As the two planes prepared for takeoff, the control tower ordered KLM flight 4805 to taxi east the length of the runway, turn 180 degrees, and wait for takeoff clearance. Pan American flight 1736 was told to follow three minutes behind, turn off at the "third intersection" (Ramp C-3) and report back when it had cleared the runway. The Pan Am pilot decided not to count the first ramp, Ramp C-1, as an actual intersection because other aircraft were blocking it, so he proceeded to Ramp C-4, which he believed to be the "third intersection." For some reason, the KLM pilot did not wait for clearance as he had been instructed and began his takeoff. Visibility was only one-quarter mile.

As the Pan Am pilot finally saw the approaching plane through the fog roaring at full power, he shouted into his microphone, "What's he doing? He'll kill us all." As the two planes collided at Ramp C-4, 576 lives were lost. Afterward, a team of 70 investigators described the listening errors involved: "If both pilots and the tower controllers had fully heard—and understood—one another, the KLM pilot would never have sent his craft hurtling toward takeoff before the Pan Am plane was off the runway."[6] Because both crews were tuned to the same radio frequency and were able to hear one another's conversations with the air-traffic controllers, a failure to listen obviously played a key role in the worst tragedy in aviation history.

Listening errors with results of this magnitude have produced a great deal of interest in what is often overlooked—our most "natural" communication skill. All of us have been listening "naturally" since early childhood, long before we could speak, write, or read; therefore, listening must be a "natural" skill. After all, we've functioned adequately this long, right? Not necessarily.

Research is quick to point out that the average person listens at only 50 percent efficiency, losing another 25 percent of what has been heard over the next 48 hours.[7] Just as in the two examples above, the results of poor listening skills in business and the professions also can be devastating:

> With more than 100 million workers in the country, a simple $10 mistake by each of them, as a result of poor listening, would add up to a cost of a billion dollars. And most people make numerous listening mistakes every week.
>
> Because of listening mistakes, letters have to be retyped, appointments rescheduled, shipments rerouted. Productivity is affected and profits suffer.[8]

In other words, as we've discussed in terms of writing and speaking, your listening skills will shape others' views of you as an organizational communicator. This is true regardless of the fact that listening, like reading, is a receptive rather than a productive skill and therefore is less overt. Peter Drucker, a management expert and widely read author, takes a firm position on the subject, placing the burden of responsibility squarely on the receiver: Communication is the act of the recipient.[9] And although both listening and reading are receptive processes, becoming a better reader does not automatically make you a better listener. Listening sometimes is called our most important communicative skill.[10]

Allow us to show you evidence that relates specifically to business and professional settings. DiSalvo reviewed twenty-five studies and reported that effective listening was identified repeatedly as the most important skill needed by those entering the work force.[11] According to a recent survey by Smith, administrative managers believe that active listening is the most critical skill for management.[12] Downs and Conrad, who studied seven hundred middle managers, reported that listening was identified as the most important skill for subordinates and the fifth most important skill for supervisors.[13] Fortune 500 executives at the vice-presidential level ranked poor listening skills as the second most serious problem having negative impact on communication in their organizations.[14] In another study, organizational personnel ranked listening as one of two major areas in which they believed they needed additional training.[15] We could go on, but we've made our point.

Unfortunately, not only do most individuals take listening for granted but also so do many organizations. In a study of forty-five companies, Carstens found that although listening consistently surfaced as *the* most important communication skill, only nine of the surveyed companies provided training to improve listening.[16] Sperry Corporation is a notable exception, having launched seminars for its 80,000 employees around the world and a corporate advertising campaign to promote good listening habits.[17] Companies such as IBM, Ford, Honeywell, and Bank of America are following suit. But because of the relationship between your listening habits and your success as an organizational communicator, you must begin sharpening your skills now.

BARRIERS TO EFFECTIVE LISTENING

If listening constitutes our most frequently used communication skill, why are most of us "underskilled" as listeners? As we've suggested, part of the problem is that we take our listening skills for granted. We assume that listening and hearing are the same activity; in fact, listening is a tremendously complex process.

Listening Stages

Active listening, or listening at your best, is defined by one of this country's premier listening experts as a four-stage process: sensing, interpreting, evaluating, and responding.[18] According to Steil and his colleagues, listening and hearing are not equivalent; obviously, however, good listening begins when you *sense* the speaker's message. Sensing is the process of receiving the speaker's sounds through the auditory system and registering them in the brain. After the message has been sensed, a second stage occurs when you accurately *interpret* the message or assign meaning to the sounds you receive. Third, if you are listening actively, you *evaluate* the message by weighing evidence and sorting fact from opinion. To complete the process, you *respond* by providing feedback or taking action.

For the listening process to be effective, these four stages must occur in the order we've described. In fact, listening errors often are caused by skipping stages — for example, by jumping to the evaluation stage too early or by listening "out of order" and responding before interpreting and evaluating the message. Errors can occur throughout the listening process. However, errors at any stage become obvious at the response level because responses are external and observable, while sensing, interpreting, and evaluating take place within the listener.

Let's think about what these four levels mean by analyzing the kind of listening problems that occur in actual organizations. Read the following paragraphs and from the clues provided you, determine the origins of the listening errors.

- *Situation A.* On Wednesday afternoon, Frank Peters hung up the phone and walked down the hall to the shipping department. Frank's boss had just asked him to verify that a $20,000 order had been processed and was ready for shipment by next Thursday's deadline. As a result of the conversation, Frank told the shipping supervisor to put a rush on the order; it had to be out by 5 P.M. the next day no matter what. A partial shipment went out the next day to a confused and angry customer. Taking this story at face value, was Frank guilty of an error of sensing, interpreting, evaluating, or responding?

(In our view, Frank's error was largely one of *interpretation:* He mistook a routine follow-up inquiry as an expression of urgency and panic, misinterpreting the words "next Thursday's deadline.")

- *Situation B.* Janet Stone was nervous. She had now been with XYZ Corporation for six months and the time had come for her first formal performance evaluation. Although she enjoyed her job, she was shy and found dealing with her officemates sometimes difficult. Janet felt weak in her interpersonal skills. As she listened to her supervisor outline her superior writing skills, her impressive computer skills, and her technical expertise, Janet decided she had probably better turn in her resignation tomorrow. In which of the four stages of listening did Janet go wrong?

(Janet's listening error was one of *evaluation*—and one prompted by her own insecurity. She assumed that her boss's omission of praise in the area of interpersonal communication represented a general lack of regard for her overall performance.)

- *Situation C.* Just as Jack O'Keefe began to search for a missing report he needed, one of his most valued employees asked Jack if he had a few minutes to confer. "Sure, fire away!" Jack replied. The employee described an intolerable situation in the department that was leading him to consider another job offer. As he flipped through the stacks of papers on his desk, Jack responded, "Great idea! You've got my go-ahead." Was Jack's error one of sensing, interpreting, evaluating, or responding?

(Jack committed a *sensing* error: Preoccupied with his own concerns, he didn't even *register* his partner's message.)

- *Situation D.* Ellen Preston listened intently to the applicant who sat across from her as he summarized his experience and success in sales. Ellen liked what she was hearing, but she decided to remain cool and detached. At the conclusion of the interview, Ellen said, "Thanks for your time. I'll get back to you." When she phoned the applicant the next afternoon with a job offer, she discovered that he had assumed a lack of interest on her part and already had accepted a position with her company's leading competitor. Where did Ellen go wrong?

(Ellen's error falls into the *response* stage: She sensed the message, interpreted it correctly, evaluated it favorably, but delayed the appropriate response.)

Preoccupation, Pressure, and Priorities

When you finally begin the career for which you're now preparing, you no doubt will be frustrated at times by the multiple demands made by superiors, subordinates, and peers. And even though pressing deadlines, urgent quotas, and the proverbial bottom line often will induce stress, such inconveniences constitute part of the price we pay to be part of an interesting and dynamic organization. Both internal and external barriers will interfere with your ability to listen at your best consistently.

Three internal barriers — that is, distractions that come from within — are critical: *preoccupation, pressure,* and *priority.*[19] Let's look at these barriers to effective listening as they apply to business and professional settings.

Imagine the following scenario. You are a manager in a large company, and employee Jim Gates asks for your help in unraveling a challenging departmental problem. Despite your best intentions, your listening is limited by your *preoccupation* with a difficult meeting that you must run that afternoon, the *pressure* you feel about a personnel decision you must make by Friday, and the *priority* you place on finishing a report that is due tomorrow morning. With such competing stimuli, how can you possibly be "psychologically" present as an active listener? Dialogue that should be occurring with someone else is occurring within you, and your role as listener becomes secondary. In *The Empathic Communicator,* William Howell labels this kind of distraction "internal monologue" (IM), a phenomenon that "happens frequently to everyone. People want to concentrate fully on a topic, but their minds wander. If they are in an emotional state, the power of irrelevant thoughts is multiplied. Their attention is divided between what they should be doing and a stream of [internal] distractions."[20]

Perhaps the best strategy to use in the example above would have been to admit honestly to Gates that you're not able to give him your full attention at the moment, but you want to schedule a time when you can.[21] By doing so, you take control of the situation, express commitment to your role as listener, and communicate your belief that what he has to say is important. This strategy is far superior to your learned tendency to *pretend* to listen. "After all," you think, "I can always ask Jim for a memo summarizing our conversation, read it when I have more time, and respond then." By postponing your "listening," however, you lose your ability to clarify particular points on the spot, and you sacrifice valuable time — both yours and Jim's.

Of course, other barriers to effective listening are *external* distractions. Your conversation with Gates may be interrupted by six phone calls, four visitors, and the whir of construction machinery outside. In some ways, external distractions are easier to control than internal ones because you may be able to remove yourself from the distractions: You can meet with Gates in the company conference room, over lunch away from the building, or on a park bench across the street. Of course, you probably cannot move out of your office permanently. However, it's to your advantage to control those external distractions that you *can*. Your failure to "turn off" external distractions is frustrating and offensive to your conversational partner, and your interpersonal relationships suffer as a result.

Memory

Although talking generally about internal and external barriers to effective listening is important, several other specific factors are worth considering. For example, beyond pressure, preoccupation, and priority, are there other reasons why we don't always *concentrate* as well as we should? And how does *memory* fit into the picture?

According to a recent study, business students ranked internal distractions as the most serious barrier to effective listening on the job. Businesspeople already on the job, however, described environmental distractions as the most serious barrier. Both study groups ranked inattentiveness as the third most troublesome barrier.[22] And what causes inattentiveness or a failure to concentrate? Listeners often concentrate more on the people involved or the situation itself rather than on message content. Consider the elements identified by Erving Goffman as they relate to your own communication experiences.

- *Self-consciousness*: Wondering how well you're performing as a communicator; this may lead you to rehearse your next response.
- *Interaction consciousness*: Observing how well the interaction itself is going.
- *Other-consciousness*: Concentrating on your conversational partner's characteristics, idiosyncrasies, or point of view.[23]

These "attention saps" inevitably destroy or distort the information transfer between you and your conversational partner.

We mentioned earlier that listeners tend to recall only 50 percent of what they have heard immediately afterward and lose another 25 percent in the following 48 hours. That prompts us to explore another variable that is related directly to how well we listen: memory. Although there are conflicting theories about the structure of human memory, one school of thought tells us that our memories consist of three information repositories: the *sensory register, short-term memory* (STM), and *long-term memory* (LTM).

The sensory register is a repository for raw and immediate stimuli that enter through the sensory channels. Visual-image storage is thought to last only several hundred milliseconds, while auditory information can last as long as three to four seconds. Information selected for attention is transferred to STM; all other information is lost.

Short-term memory keeps information for greater periods, perhaps from twenty seconds to one minute, and longer if we rehearse a particular piece of information. Even so, there appears to be a limit to the amount STM can hold: approximately seven units or chunks of information. Rehearsal also helps to transfer information to LTM, although interruption or distraction can cause us to lose information before it reaches LTM — within sixty seconds, in fact.[24] Overall, experts tell us that we forget information because of several other factors, which are listed below.[25]

- *Fading:* If we don't use information frequently, we tend to lose it.
- *Distortion:* If a piece of information is very similar to another stored bit of information, it loses its distinguishing characteristics and becomes distorted.
- *Suppression:* Information that is unpleasant is sometimes forgotten.
- *Interference:* Previously learned information can interfere with what we're trying to learn now, and what we learn later can interfere with what we already have learned.
- *Processing breakdown:* We cannot recall part or all of a message because of poorly organized storage or retrieval techniques.

Let's see how these factors operate. If your boss told you some bit of information six months ago that you've never had the opportunity to use, then that message probably has begun to *fade*. If you're being briefed on changes in a long-standing company program and the new information is similar to the old, then it may become *distorted*. If you've been told during a painful confrontation with a superior that your performance in a particular area is subpar, then you may *suppress* that message. If you're used to a particular word-processing system and your firm switches to a new one, then you may find yourself repeatedly asking for instructions because of *interference* from the old system. And if you have no strategy to help you remember the names of people you have just met, then you most likely are experiencing *processing breakdown* (not to mention the embarrassment of forgetting someone's name after two minutes of conversation). In other words, memory failure can be explained in many ways. But if you want to improve your auditory memory, many books are available to help you.

What about the positive end of the spectrum? What are we most likely to remember? Research tells us that we tend to remember better if what we hear is meaningful, interesting, unusual, well organized, and reinforced visually.[26] (This may help to explain a potentially low score on this chapter's introductory listening quiz. Why? The paragraph read to you basically was meaningless, uninteresting, ordinary, unorganized, and nonvisual.) And although a chapter on listening is probably not the best place to discuss speaking again, keeping the profile of the "memorable message" in mind may encourage us to construct messages that help our listeners overcome their listening barriers.

LISTENING ACTIVELY TO SUBORDINATES, SUPERIORS, AND PEERS

So far in this chapter, we've emphasized poor listening and its effects: "Humans listen before they speak, speak before they read, and read before they write. Thus, failure to refine our listening skills impairs the entire process of human communication."[27] We've also offered reasons why poor listening occurs: The listening process is complex, we take listening for granted, and a continuous stream of internal and external barriers interferes with even the best of intentions.

Now that we understand the challenge involved, let's focus on strengthening our listening skills as organizational communicators. When you think about the communication situations in which listening at your best will make a difference — during meetings, performance appraisals, interviews, training sessions, negotiations, and presentations — you realize that listening is the sustaining heartbeat of business and the professions.

Within the organization, or in any social situation, for that matter, you will find yourself playing the role of listener in a variety of types of conversations: phatic, cathartic, informative, persuasive, and entertaining.[28] Good listeners learn to adapt, because the requirements for effective listening vary from one situation to another.

Phatic Communication

Although not the least important, the simplest kind of communicating in which you'll engage is *phatic* communication, or what often is called "chitchat." Informal hallway conversation — "How's it going?" "Nice day, huh?" "Hey, how are you?" — is rarely given a second thought.

Regardless of its trivial nature, phatic communication still serves several critical functions in organizations. It helps us form new relationships, cement existing relationships, tune in to the informal network, and create a comfortable organizational climate. Phatic communication can help you stay abreast of what's happening in the organization and how people feel about it. And even though you would not want to spend too much time on phatic communication, by abstaining you probably will be seen as cold, withdrawn, and aloof. Furthermore, you may be "left out in the cold" in terms of important organizational scuttlebutt.

In some cultures, phatic communication may play an even more critical role than the one we've just described. Organizational consultant Peter Drucker describes the importance of phatic communication in the Japanese organization:

> Very few CEOs of large Japanese companies have *any* time available for managing their companies. All their time is spent on relations, even the time spent on internal company business. . . . The top people spend their time sitting, sipping cups of green tea, listening, asking a few questions, then sitting some more, sipping more cups of green tea, listening, asking a few more questions. . . . In all these sittings they do not necessarily discuss business, surely not their own business. Indeed, to a Westerner their conversation at times appears quite pointless. . . . Their aim, of course, is not to solve anything but to establish mutual understanding. When there is a problem, one knows where to go. . . . When either crisis or opportunity arrives, these immobile sitters are able to act with amazing speed, decisiveness, and at times ruthlessness, for the purpose of all this sitting is not to produce mutual liking, agreement, or trust. It is to produce an understanding of why one does not like another, does not agree, does not trust.[29]

In U.S. organizations, phatic communication is worth listening to, because it not only brings social benefits but also leads to more substantive communication.

Cathartic Communication

Often your role as an organizational communicator will require you to listen to the *cathartic* communication of customers, peers, subordinates, and even superiors. We sometimes communicate to vent emotions, relieve stress, and dispel anxiety. Here the role of listener is complex. As Ptah-Hotep, author of the oldest existing book on human communication, wrote more than 3,000 years ago: "An official who must listen to the pleas of his clients should listen patiently and without rancor, because a petitioner wants attention to what he says even more than the accomplishing of that for which he came."[30]

Speculate on how you might respond as a listener in the following emotional situations.

1. "I just can't stand working for Ron. He's as chauvinistic as they come. Maybe I should just quit and look for another job."
2. "After I've worked here for fifteen years, you give 'my' promotion to a new college graduate with three weeks' experience? I don't know why I keep killing myself for this company."
3. "Give me a break! My supervisor just keeps piling on more work. Believe me, it doesn't pay to do a good job around here. Once they know you're conscientious, they start to take advantage of you."
4. "My wife just filed for divorce, my father's in the hospital recovering from a heart attack, my mother passed away last month, and you think my performance on the job has been subpar?!"
5. "I don't know what to do. Everyone in my division goes right over my head with their problems. I have no credibility with them whatsoever even though I've done everything by the book."

Listening with sensitivity to cathartic communication requires three basic skill sets: attending skills, following skills, and reflecting skills.[31] *Attending skills* involve listening with your entire body, giving your physical attention by leaning toward your conversational partner, facing him or her squarely at eye level, uncrossing your arms and legs, and selecting an appropriate distance for conversation, which is approximately three feet in our culture. You should maintain eye contact, move in response to your partner, and avoid distracting movements.

Following skills include offering "door openers" or invitations to communicate, such as "You look upset" or "Something's on your mind — I'd like to hear about it." You also should provide brief indicators of encouragement such as "Oh?" "Right!" or "Really?" to communicate your interest. Bolton suggests that you ask occasional open-ended questions such as "What are your thoughts on . . .?" You also can encourage communication simply by remaining silent.

Reflecting skills require that you repeat back what you have just heard to verify your accuracy before you act, challenge, or respond, as well as to check your perceptions of the feelings behind another person's words. By paraphrasing, summarizing, or reflecting meanings or feelings, you can help others verbalize their thoughts and feelings and encourage them to work through their own problems.

You probably already use attending, following, and reflecting skills to some degree, but cultivating your expertise in this area will most likely pay off if and when you work in a supervisory or managerial position. As a listener, you can do a great deal to create a supportive rather than a defensive climate for communication.

Perhaps a classic study by Jack Gibb explains this best. Gibb identified several ways to reduce defensiveness in interpersonal relationships by describing six characteristics of defensive communication and six characteristics of supportive communication.[32] When people perceive threats, they tend to respond defensively. A defensive response from one partner often produces a defensive response from the other, and a destructive circular pattern results. The solution is found by listening and responding supportively to foster productive communication. Let's return to the second situation above and contrast these two listening modes. Consider what follows to be a series of hypothetical conversations between a boss and an employee.

EMPLOYEE: "After I've worked here for fifteen years, you give 'my' promotion to a new college graduate with three weeks' experience? I don't know why I keep killing myself for this company."

BOSS:
1. a. *Defensive* climate using ***evaluation*** to blame or judge: "You know, if your work is as good as you think it is, you'd probably have been promoted years ago."
   b. *Supportive* climate using ***description*** to explain perceptions in a neutral manner without demanding change in another and to request more information: "I sense your anger and frustration. Tell me more about your reaction."

2. a. *Defensive* climate using ***control*** to change others' attitudes, influence their behavior, or restrict their options: "If you

want my support for the next promotion that comes along, you'd better think seriously about how you handle this situation."

   b. *Supportive* climate using a **problem orientation** to communicate a willingness to share a concern or work through a problem collaboratively: "Let's sit down and talk through this problem. I understand your concern."

3. a. *Defensive* climate using a **strategy** that relies on gimmicks or deceit to manipulate others: "The president tells me there may be an even better opportunity looming on the horizon. He's probably going to be asking me to suggest qualified candidates soon."

   b. *Supportive* climate using **spontaneity** straightforwardly, openly, and honestly: "I'd like to help you understand the rationale behind my decision."

4. a. *Defensive* climate using **neutrality** to communicate a lack of concern or cold disinterest: "Look, do whatever you like. The decision has already been made."

   b. *Supportive* climate using **empathy** to express understanding, caring, and acceptance: "I understand how deeply disappointed you must feel."

5. a. *Defensive* climate using **superiority** to make others feel inadequate: "As a top executive in this company, I have difficult decisions to make every day. This one wasn't the first and it won't be the last."

   b. *Supportive* climate using **equality**, respecting others as unique human beings and expressing a willingness to work together with mutual respect and trust: "I want you to know that I respect your feelings. You've done good work, and perhaps we can think about alternative ways to reward your service."

6. a. *Defensive* climate using **certainty** to express a "know-it-all," dogmatic, and inflexible attitude: "I make the decisions around here. That's the way it is and that's the way it's going to stay."

   b. *Supportive* climate using **provisionalism**, the willingness to investigate, explore, and reconsider: "I'd like to hear your perspective. I know I'm not infallible."

In volatile situations, listening often challenges our communicative skills to the limit. *Stress listening*, as it has been called, requires a sympathetic and analytic ear. Communication expert Jon T. Powell offers the following suggestions to help supervisors cope with angry confrontations with their subordinates.[33]

1. *Avoid sharing anger.* Maintain a calm and straightforward but sympathetic manner.
2. *Respond constructively.* If possible, channel the employee's emotion by avoiding smiles and small talk, maintaining eye contact, preventing outside interruptions, providing an informal setting, asking the individual to sit, and showing respect.
3. *Ask questions.* Help the employee understand the problem by asking questions in a patient, guiding, and step-by-step manner.
4. *Separate fact from opinion.* Because emotions often cloud the distinction between fact and opinion, help the employee sort through the situation and discern the difference.
5. *Avoid hasty responses.* Anger may cause an employee to spew short and disorganized blasts of words. But don't respond in kind. Wait until you hear the whole story. As Powell reminds us, "Haste and objectivity rarely go hand in hand."
6. *Consider the employee's perspective first.* Communicate empathically that you understand by summarizing the employee's concerns and relating the problem to his or her past work experiences; then move toward workable solutions.
7. *Help the employee find the solution.* Too often our typical responses during stress listening include *advising* ("In my view, Jones, what you need to do here is . . ."), *judging* ("Let's face it, Jones, your problem is the result of an unwise decision"), *analyzing* ("I see three different problems here, Jones, each with important considerations"), *interrogating* ("Well, Jones, did you do X? How about Y? And, of course, I hope you didn't forget Z!"), or inadvertently *trivializing* the problem to placate the employee ("Jones, I'm sure there's really nothing to worry about. Just cheer up!").[34] In such stressful situations, reactions like these, no matter how well intentioned, probably will heighten rather than defuse the listener's frustration, insecurity, and anger. Taking Powell's suggestions to heart, however, may help no matter what organizational role your conversational partner has: client, peer, subordinate, or even superior — even if *you* are the problem!

We have just described what communication expert Paul Friedman calls *soft listening*.[35] To understand the listening process, it's important, Friedman says, to distinguish between two primary states of awareness, soft and hard, each of which is appropriate in a particular situation. When we listen in a "soft" mode, we are more sensitive, more inclusive, and more patient listeners who delay conclusions until we collect a complete set of impressions. In organizations, soft listening is appropriate for the kinds of interpersonal problem-solving situations that we have just described.

A "hard" listening mode, on the other hand, means that we are more tenacious and more selective listeners who are concerned more with controlling, achieving, efficiency, and effect. Hard listening is more appropriate with informative and persuasive communication in organizations.

Informative Communication

In whatever career field you select, much of your time will involve listening to messages to understand and retain information. Of course, that is the primary type of listening you engage in as a student. But your responsibility for listening to informative communication certainly will not end with your college days. According to John Naisbitt in his best seller *Megatrends*, information is our foremost national commodity.[36]

When it comes to listening to *informative* communication, what factors must be considered? Let's look at suggestions from the work of Ralph Nichols, a pioneer in listening research.[37]

Capitalize on Thought Speed. One of the most significant barriers we face is universal: We listen three to four times faster than speakers deliver messages. We are what Nichols calls "tortoise talkers" and "hare listeners." Consequently, we spend our spare time with various distractions: deciding whether to have pizza, sushi, or hamburgers for dinner; worrying about how well we did on yesterday's algebra exam; or eavesdropping on a nearby conversation.

What should we do with leftover time while we're being presented with information? According to Nichols, we should use that time to *think ahead* ("Where is this speaker going? What does she want me to understand?"), *weigh the evidence* ("What does this have to do with me? How can I use this information?"), *review what we have heard* ("What has he said so far? What kind of case is he making?"), and *listen between the lines* ("What points are missing? What does her nonverbal communication tell me?"). "Not capitalizing on thought speed is our greatest single handicap," Nichols writes. "The differential between thought speed and speech speed breeds false feelings of security and mental tangents. Yet, through listening training, this same differential can be readily converted into our greatest asset."[38]

Listen for Ideas. When listening to information, many people create their own hurdles by feeling obliged to remember every fact offered by a speaker, and soon they are bogged down in detail. The best advice here comes from previous discussions about speaking and reading: Learn to recognize organizational patterns. Is the speaker using a topical, cause–effect, or chronological pattern? Listen for previews in introductions, summaries, and conclusions, and transitional devices throughout: internal summaries ("Now that we've looked at. . . "), internal previews ("I've discussed a difficult problem, but I won't stop there. Consider what we could do about it. . . "), and signposts ("The most important point I'll make today is. . . "). Supplement your understanding with significant detail to support the main points you discern; don't waste time on irrelevant digression and insignificant extras.

Devise Note-Taking Systems to Match Speaking Styles. Often the best way to retain information is to take notes, although effective note taking is trickier than it sounds. Perhaps you've noticed that each of your professors has a highly individual speaking style. Some present interesting and orderly lectures, some ramble from one idea to another as if they are free associating, and some read from yellowed lecture notes of days long gone. Each organizes and presents material differently. Such stylistic variations challenge the best note-taking skills, but the key is to develop several systems rather than a single generic one. Outlining works well if the speaker's material is well organized; writing short paragraph summaries every few minutes rather than taking continuous notes may help you focus on listening rather than writing; even visual representation — drawings or color coding — may work. Experiment now so that you can carry these skills with you into the organization.

Persuasive Communication

Listening to *persuasive* communication requires the use of evaluation. Based on the speaker's credibility, the validity of the arguments presented, and the emotional appeals used, listeners decide whether to "buy into" what they hear. Because much of what you listen to in your career will be persuasive in nature, let's examine more specifically what it means to use critical listening.

Speaker credibility typically is determined by such factors as position or title, expertise, trustworthiness, and dynamism. For those you know and work with regularly in the organization, you develop a more or less stable perception of their credibility. That perception may fluctuate somewhat based on the topic under discussion, but experience probably will help you find some people more believable than others. With new or one-time-only speakers, you make an assessment based on the kinds of factors just described.

You also assess the appropriateness and acceptability of the speaker's *message content*. The discussion on presentational speaking distinguished between *inductive* reasoning (moving from specific facts to a general conclusion) and *deductive* reasoning (moving from a general conclusion to specific cases). As a listener, you should determine which line of argument the speaker is using. Ask yourself the following: "Is the evidence adequate, sound, and representative (inductive)? Is the speaker's generalization true? Is the proposed specific case an example of the cited generalization (deductive)? Or is the speaker guilty of faulty or circular reasoning?"

Your final consideration as a critical listener is assessing the speaker's intent and honesty, as well as your own susceptibility to the *emotional appeals* being used. If a speaker is discussing your company's financial vulnerability and advocating a merger with another corporation (appealing to your fears of job insecurity, economic instability, lowered standard of living, and so on), then you must decide whether the emotional appeals outweigh the logic of the argument and whether the speaker has ethical motives.

To the four types of communication discussed thus far, we now add communication that is used to *entertain*. When a colleague retires and close friends are asked to "roast" her, when the year-end banquet is emceed by the company comedian, or when a brass quartet plays for the company noontime "brown bag" series, then you have the opportunity to listen appreciatively. And while everyone does not agree on what is entertaining, this kind of communication captures our attention relatively easily.

BECOMING A BETTER ORGANIZATIONAL LISTENER

Throughout this chapter, we've woven together practical suggestions for improving your listening skills. As we conclude our discussion of listening, consider two final suggestions.

First, AIM to listen.[39] Good listening is a blend of **a**ttention, **i**nterest, and **m**otivation.

- Attention: Poor listeners pretend to listen while allowing their minds to wander; good listeners work at listening, exerting the effort required to pay attention.
- Interest: Poor listeners usually decide early that the subject or the speaker is not interesting and tune out; good listeners actively search for useful information even if the speaker or material is dull.
- Motivation: Your listening success depends on your level of motivation. Good listeners realize the personal and professional benefits to be had from listening well.

In short, the only person who can improve your listening skills is you, and attention, interest, and motivation constitute the basic formula for success.

Second, learn to "listen by objectives." You may be familiar with management-by-objectives (MBO), a system in which performance objectives result from collaboration between employees and supervisors. One rationale behind MBO is that performance improves when expectations have been outlined in advance. "Listening by objectives" has equally advantageous results. Let us show you what we mean.

- As you prepare for an important meeting, think about your *listening goals*. Are you interested in a particular person's perspective? Do you need to know how specific issues will be handled? In other words, set your own agenda for the meeting so that you create listening expectations that you can meet.
- If you are interviewing candidates for a new position in the company, *prepare* to listen. Read, learn as much as you can about each applicant beforehand, and ask questions. Focusing your attention in advance is good preparation for the actual listening that you will do during the interview.
- To manage your time as effectively as possible, *prelisten* to presentations.[40] Find out in advance about the speaker, the topic, the intended audience, and the presentation's main idea. This preliminary work may take some time, but you may reap one of two possible rewards: You may save yourself the frustration of attending a useless presentation or, if you decide that attending the presentation will be time well spent, you will be ready to listen by objectives.

CHAPTER SUMMARY

The message of this chapter has been that listening skills are at a premium in organizations. *The importance of listening skills* is something we all take for granted, but few of us realize that listening is a complex, four-stage process that involves *sensing, interpreting, evaluating,* and *responding.* As an organizational communicator, you can expect to spend more time listening than speaking, writing, or reading. Unfortunately, most people listen only at approximately 25 percent efficiency. Because listening is critical to personal and organizational success, many organizations now offer their employees training in listening skills.

The *barriers to effective listening* in organizations are many, and listening at your best is often a challenge. At times, *internal* barriers such as preoccupation, pressure, and priority will intervene. You also must contend with *external* barriers — telephone calls, drop-in visitors, and noisy construction work. Both internal and external barriers threaten your listening success. Learning to overcome listening barriers and understanding the role your auditory memory plays in recalling information are keys to overcoming listening barriers.

Next we discussed *listening actively to subordinates, superiors, and peers.* We examined five types of organizational communication: phatic, cathartic, informative, persuasive, and entertaining. Good listeners learn to listen with flexibility because the requirements for effective listening vary by situation.

Phatic communication helps us form new relationships, cement existing ones, and create a comfortable organizational climate. Listening to phatic communication is important because it leads to more substantive communication.

Listening to *cathartic communication* requires "soft" listening — creating a supportive rather than a defensive communication climate by using *attending, following,* and *reflecting skills.* We provided seven suggestions for stress listening in confrontive situations with employees.

Listening to *informative communication,* on the other hand, requires "hard" listening. We can become better listeners in informative situations by capitalizing on thought speed, listening for main ideas rather than details, and devising note-taking systems to match speaking styles.

Listening to *persuasive communication* requires additional skills: assessing speaker credibility, evaluating the appropriateness and acceptability of the speaker's message content, and discerning any emotional appeals being used. Finally, listening to *entertaining communication* often captures our attention easily.

Chapter 6 closed with two additional suggestions for *becoming a better organizational listener:* AIMing to listen and listening by objectives.

MEASURING SUCCESS

1. Keep a listening log for twenty-four hours. Divide your day by hours as in the example below. Identify the *amount* of listening you do and the *content* (symbolized by a word or phrase) of what you listen to. Then calculate the overall daily percentage of your time spent listening. Use the example below as a guide.

	TIME	ACTIVITY	APPROXIMATE TIME LISTENING (%)	CONTENT
A.M.	7–8			
	8–9			
	9–10			
	10–11			
	11–12			
P.M.	12–1			
	1–2			
	2–3			
	3–4			
	4–5			
	5–6			
	6–7			
	7–8			
	8–9			
	9–10			
	10–11			
	11–12			
			Total:	

2. Name three people to whom you listen in each of the five types of communicative situations described in this chapter.

COMMUNICATION TYPE				
PHATIC	CATHARTIC	INFORMATIVE	PERSUASIVE	ENTERTAINING

1.

2.

3.

For each person named, list three suggestions to improve your listening.

3. Try this experiment. During one class this week, keep track of each time your mind wanders and you no longer listen to your professor or class discussion. In each case, jot down what internal or external barrier to effective listening captured your attention. Note how many times and how frequently you "tune out."

4. Make an interview appointment with a business or professional person on campus or in your community. Ask about the importance of listening skills in her or his career field in terms of *who* is listened to, *what* the topics are, *when* the most important listening takes place, *where* the listening happens, and *how* (in what ways) it is important. Probe for specific examples.

5. Use the following chart to speculate on how others would grade your listening. In each case, give yourself the grade you think each would assign (A, B, C, D, or F) and list three adjectives you think these individuals might use to describe your listening skills.

	GRADE	ADJECTIVES
a. mother	_____	_____, _____, _____
b. father	_____	_____, _____, _____
c. brother	_____	_____, _____, _____
d. sister	_____	_____, _____, _____
e. boss	_____	_____, _____, _____
f. boyfriend or girlfriend; husband or wife	_____	_____, _____, _____

g. *favorite teacher* _____ _____, _____, _____

h. *minister* _____ _____, _____, _____

i. *roommate* _____ _____, _____, _____

j. *best friend* _____ _____, _____, _____

 Decco Exercise We devoted much of Chapter 6 to listening to cathartic communication, a form of listening that is problematic for many managers and supervisors. Imagine yourself as Decco Corporation's director of training and development and create three confrontive opening statements from employees. Discuss how you might respond when you are listening at your best.

Notes

1. Paul Tory Rankin, "The Measurement of the Ability to Understand Spoken Language" (unpublished Ph.D. dissertation, University of Michigan, 1926), *Dissertation Abstracts* 12 (1952): 847–848.

2. Elyse K. Werner, "A Study of Communication Time" (M.A. thesis, University of Maryland, College Park, 1975), cited in Andrew Wolvin and Carolyn Gwynn Coakley, *Listening*, 3rd ed. (Dubuque, IA: Wm. C. Brown, 1988), 13; and Larry Barker, Renee Edwards, Connie Gaines, Karen Gladney, and Francis Holley, "An Investigation of Proportional Time Spent in Various Communication Activities by College Students," *Journal of Applied Communication Research* 8 (November 1980): 101–109.

3. J. Donald Weinrauch and John R. Swanda, Jr., "Examining the Significance of Listening: An Exploratory Study of Contemporary Management," *The Journal of Business Communication* 13 (February 1975): 25–32.

4. William F. Keefe, *Listen, Management!* (New York: McGraw-Hill, 1971), 10.

5. Robert L. Montgomery, *Listening Made Easy* (New York: AMACOM, 1981), 3–4.

6. "What's He Doing? He'll Kill Us All!" *Time*, 11 April 1977, 22.

7. Lyman K. Steil, Joanne Summerfield, and George DeMare, *Listening: It Can Change Your Life* (New York: John Wiley, 1983), 58.

8. Lyman K. Steil, "Secrets of Being a Better Listener," *U.S. News and World Report*, 26 May 1980, 65.

9. Peter F. Drucker, *Management: Tasks, Responsibilities, Practices* (New York: Harper & Row, 1974), 483.

10. Gary T. Hunt and Louis P. Cusella, "A Field Study of Listening Needs in Organizations," *Communication Education* 32 (October 1983): 393.

11. Vincent S. DiSalvo, "A Summary of Current Research Identifying Communication Skills in Various Organizational Contexts," *Communication Education* 29 (July 1980): 283–290.

12. "The 20% Activities That Bring 80% Payoff," *Training/HRD* 15 (June 1978): 6.

13. Cal W. Downs and Charles Conrad, "Effective Subordinancy," *The Journal of Business Communication* 19 (Spring 1982): 27–37.

14. James C. Bennett and Robert J. Olney, "Executive Priorities for Effective Communication in an Information Society," *The Journal of Business Communication* 23 (Spring 1986): 13–22.

15. Thomas E. Harris and T. Dean Thomlison, "Career-Bound Communication Education: A Needs Analysis," *Central States Speech Journal* 34 (Winter 1983): 260–267.

16. Susan Mundale, "Why More CEOs Are Mandating Listening and Writing Training," *Training/HRD* 17 (October 1980): 37.

17. Steil, "Secrets," 66.

18. Lyman K. Steil, Larry L. Barker, and Kittie W. Watson, *Effective Listening: Key to Your Success* (Reading, MA: Addison-Wesley, 1983), 21–23.

19. Thomas E. Anastasi, *Listen! Techniques for Improving Communication Skills* (Boston: CBI, 1982), 10.

20. William S. Howell, *The Empathic Communicator* (Belmont, CA: Wadsworth, 1982), 70.

21. Anastasi, *Listen!*, 9–14.

22. Kittie W. Watson and Larry R. Smeltzer, "Barriers to Listening: Comparison between Business Students and Business Practitioners" (paper presented at the Fourth Annual International Listening Association Convention, St. Paul, Minnesota, 4 March, 1983), cited in Wolvin and Coakley, *Listening*, 200.

23. Erving Goffman, "Alienation from Interaction." In R. Wayne Pace, Brent D. Peterson, and Terrence R. Radcliffe, Eds., *Communicating Interpersonally* (Columbus, OH: Charles E. Merrill, 1973), 144–153.

24. Adapted from Wolvin and Coakley, *Listening*, 73.

25. Adapted from Wolvin and Coakley, *Listening*, 191.

26. Guy R. Lefrancois, *Psychology for Teaching*, 4th ed. (Belmont, CA: Wadsworth, 1982), 143–151.

27. Florence I. Wolff, Nadine C. Marsnik, William S. Tacey, and Ralph G. Nichols, *Perceptive Listening* (New York: Holt, Rinehart & Winston, 1983), 24.

28. Steil, Summerfield, and deMare, *Listening*, 66.

29. Peter F. Drucker, "Behind Japan's Success," *Harvard Business Review* 59 (January–February 1981): 83–90.

30. Steil, Summerfield, and deMare, *Listening*, 73.

31. Robert Bolton, *People Skills* (Englewood Cliffs, NJ: Prentice-Hall, 1979), 32–61.

32. Jack R. Gibb, "Defensive Communication," *Journal of Communication* 11 (September 1961): 141–148; Wolvin and Coakley, *Listening*, 249–250.

33. Jon T. Powell, "Stress Listening: Coping with Angry Confrontations," *Personnel Journal* 65 (May 1986): 27–29.

34. Ronald B. Adler and Neil Towne, *Looking Out/Looking In*, 4th ed. (New York: Holt, Rinehart & Winston, 1984), 237–242.

35. Paul Friedman, *Interpersonal Communication: Innovations in Instruction* (New York: NEA, 1978), 84–90.

36. John Naisbitt, *Megatrends: Ten New Directions Transforming Our Lives* (New York: Warner, 1982).

37. Ralph G. Nichols and Leonard A. Stevens, *Are You Listening?* (New York: McGraw-Hill, 1957).

38. Ralph G. Nichols, "Listening Is a 10-Part Skill," *Nation's Business* 45 (July 1957): 4.

39. George R. Bell, "Listen and You Shall Hear," *Association Management* 36 (March 1984): 105–106.

40. Anastasi, *Listen!*, 78–79.

Chapter 7 ✑ Communicating Interpersonally in Organizations

People have one thing in common: they are all different. —Robert Zend

Think about it. Over the course of your career, you'll work with hundreds of different people—men, women, bosses, subordinates, colleagues, customers, contacts, and clients.

As we all know, organizations are not just desks, conference rooms, and computer terminals. In fact, despite our recent technological revolution, human interaction still forms the basis for what goes on in business and the professions. According to John Naisbitt, the more "high tech" we introduce into our corporations, the more important our "high touch" or interpersonal needs seem to become.[1] People are what organizations are all about.

If you're in your early twenties, experts estimate that you will change jobs ten times during your career.[2] Each move will come with not only a change of scenery but also a new cast of characters. Each person will have his own personality, her own communication style, his own work habits. How will you fit in? How successfully will you be able to form work relationships? How satisfying will these relationships be? When it comes to one-on-one communication on the job, just what should you expect? As one expert puts it:

> As the people are, so will the organization be. Each organization is different, not necessarily because of differing goals, or objectives, or tasks, or products produced, but because of a myriad of people with differing personalities, personal expectations and goals, and attitudes about work. . . . The result of having people work together may be as dramatic as having an office love affair, notoriously played out, between the supervisor and supervisee, or it may be as sad as a well-known case of two state bureaucrats who worked together for years and did all of their communicating to one another by formal memo because they couldn't stand talking to one another. . . . Interpersonal relationships in organizations can also be beautiful and fun, and can lead to productive results.[3]

Perhaps the best way to start exploring these questions is by looking inward. What kind of communicator are you now? What kinds of satisfying relationships have you cultivated as a college student? What kinds of experiences have helped shape you into the person you are?

These are important questions. As the opening epigram asserts, each of us is unique. Why so? To some degree, our varying backgrounds are responsible. For example, if you are the last child in a rural family of eight children, you probably will relate differently to others than would the only child of a professional couple in the city. Factors such as these affect independence, intimacy, and dominance in work relationships.[4]

The goals of this chapter are to explore interpersonal communication in organizations from a variety of perspectives. We'll touch on working *with* others, working *over* others, and working *for* others; however, many of the principles discussed apply whether you communicate up, down, or across the organization. We'll also introduce archetypes of people you can expect to meet and provide you with sound advice on sensitive personal matters.

INTERPERSONAL RELATIONSHIPS ON THE JOB

Nowhere are interpersonal relations more complex and continuous than in the laboratory of human interaction known as the work environment. — Donald Sanzotta

Put yourself in the following situations.

Scenario 1

It's your first day on the job, and you feel somewhat overwhelmed. You've spent all morning setting up your desk and rearranging the furniture in your office, and you've worked up quite an appetite for lunch. Suddenly you're hit by a wave of panic. You realize you have no one with whom to eat lunch, and the idea of walking into the large company cafeteria alone is too threatening to face. Just then your attractive new secretary asks you to join her for a bite at a cozy pub down the street. You're male, single, and uninvolved. Good idea or not? Good question.

Scenario 2

You've worked under the same boss for the last five years. Although the two of you have never seen eye to eye, you've coexisted peacefully for most of that time. The two of you, however, have some deep-seated ethical differences. An incident arises in which you simply cannot tolerate an unethical decision that your boss has made; it's the last straw. You see three alternatives for yourself. Should you confront the boss, report him to higher authorities, or leave the company quietly?

Scenario 3

Over the last few weeks, one of your most promising employees begins to miss work, make costly errors, and badmouth you to other employees. You suspect that personal problems outside the office, possibly involving alcohol and drug abuse, are to blame. As a manager who is concerned about the welfare and productivity of your employees, how should you proceed?

Scenario 4

A friend in another department confides to you that she is diverting departmental grant monies for an extended research project from one account to another to stretch the department budget. She rationalizes that bending the rules is in everyone's best interest. You disagree sharply with your friend's judgment. What should you do?

Scenario 5

During a difficult appraisal interview with an employee whose performance has declined over the last six months, the subordinate becomes hostile. He shouts accusations and storms out of your office. You are caught off guard and have no clue about how to reopen lines of communication. How would you handle this situation?

Throughout your career you will be faced by perplexing situations such as these with superiors, subordinates, and peers. Communicating interpersonally is a "way of life" in organizations, as opposed to a focused activity in which you engage from time to time, such as writing a letter or preparing a formal presentation. Whatever else you do, you'll communicate interpersonally, almost nonstop. Chances are good that 70 percent to 80 percent of your time in the organization will be spent in face-to-face interaction.[5] Some managers are alone approximately one-third of each day, but never for longer than one-half hour at a time.[6]

Not only is interpersonal communication inescapable, but also your abilities in this area are of paramount importance. A recent organizational survey of 428 personnel administrators ranked interpersonal skills as the *most important* requirement for successful job performance.[7] Or in case you didn't catch the negative motivation in Chapter 1, 85 percent of people fired lose their jobs because they lack human relations or interpersonal skills.[8] One organizational consultant puts it this simply: "The people who master relationship skills will probably enjoy their jobs more and do better in their careers than the people who ignore them."[9]

More and more, every sector of business and the professions is realizing the value of interpersonal communication skills. Recent research indicates, for example, that what we value most in a physician is the ability to communicate well. In fact, we value this ability over other important skills such as thoroughness, interest, promptness, and efficiency.[10] Most of us value high-quality interpersonal exchanges regardless of whether we're complaining to a department store's customer-relations representative, interviewing for a new job with a personnel director, or visiting the dentist for a six-month checkup. On the other hand, as you know from day-to-day interactions with roommates, friends, family members, and romantic partners, communicating at your interpersonal best is not always easy.

COMMUNICATION STYLES IN ORGANIZATIONS

I will pay more for the ability to deal with people than any other ability under the sun. —*John D. Rockefeller*

According to one viewpoint, understanding interpersonal communication *styles* is key to understanding organizational communicators. In the following sections, we will examine various theories about communication styles.

Open, Blind, Hidden, and Closed

In *Communicating for Results*, Hamilton and Parker identify and describe four interpersonal communication styles used in organizations: *open, blind, hidden,* and *closed.* Their categories are based on the Johari Window, a tool for understanding the *self* — the open self, the blind self, the hidden self, and the unknown self. You may have been introduced to this tool in an introductory communication course. Two variables separate the four communication styles used in organizations: feedback and disclosure. *Feedback* is defined as others' responses to our behavior, attitudes, work, and self-presentations in various forms. *Disclosure* is our sharing of ideas, opinions, and feelings with others.

Open and hidden communicators solicit more feedback from others; closed and blind communicators are less inclined to do so. Open and blind communicators disclose more while closed and hidden communicators refrain from this kind of communication (see Figure 7.1). Understanding the profiles of the four styles strengthens your ability to adapt your style to that of your communicative partner and thus build more productive working relationships.[11] According to Hamilton and Parker's

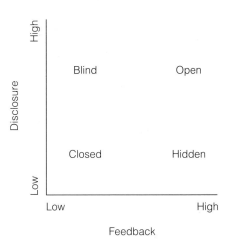

Figure 7.1
Communicator
Styles

theory, all of us have a style preference for use under normal conditions and a fallback style we use under stress.

Open Communicators. Interpersonal communication is perhaps easiest for *open communicators* because they genuinely like people. They are flexible, using a balance of both *disclosure* and *feedback* — that is, give and take — as interpersonal tools. An open communicator is likely to let you know how he thinks a project is going and also ask for your feelings on it. Although being too open is possible in certain organizational settings, and open styles may not be valued by everyone (particularly closed and blind communicators), open communicators have many positive qualities. Typically, they are trusting, friendly, productive, and dependable. They accept criticism graciously, are willing to look at all sides of an issue, and strive for consensus during conflict. As you might suspect, being an open communicator is not always easy. If this style fits you, you sometimes may find yourself frustrated because others are less open than you are, and you may become impatient with an organization's imperfections. The best way to interact with open communicators is by being an open communicator yourself.

Blind Communicators. *Blind communicators* have exaggerated estimates of their overall abilities and communication skills. Much more inclined toward disclosure than feedback, they prefer telling to being told. Although they can indeed be knowledgeable, they also typically are overconfident, authoritarian, and egotistical. Because they view themselves as more important than their communication partners, they can be critical, demanding, competitive, controlling, and stifling. Control is an issue for blind communicators; they feel they must have it.

The best blind communicators also can be organized, loyal, and dependable. They let you know where you stand, although as managers they can be difficult to work for. (To paraphrase Chevy Chase in the early "Saturday Night Live" television programs, the blind manager's motto is: "I'm the boss and you're not.") Winning challenging work assignments, receiving accolades for jobs well done, and taking the lead probably will be difficult if you work for a blind manager. When interacting with a blind communicator at any level in the organization, it's important to do your best, handle criticism gracefully, and appeal to your counterpart's expertise.

Hidden Communicators. *Hidden communicators* are motivated by one of two factors: a basic mistrust of people or an intense desire to be accepted by others. They disclose little of themselves but seek constant feedback to find out what's going on among the ranks or how others perceive them. Hidden communicators are so named because they hide their feelings and thoughts. Interestingly, they often are well liked and well spoken; however, often under the surface is someone who is manipulative, suspicious, and two-faced. Working for a hidden communicator is difficult because she may wrongly suspect you and your motives and you never know where you stand. Because she will not disclose fully, you must watch her nonverbal behavior for clues. Whether as superior, subordinate, or peer, interacting with a hidden communicator requires tact, insight, and sometimes caution.

Closed Communicators. *Closed communicators* basically are non-communicators. Motivated by anxiety, fear, and insecurity, they use little disclosure and rarely request feedback. Often seen by others as aloof, their real problem usually is low self-esteem. Because they typically prefer to work alone, they can be productive in that capacity. However, they often perform as "hands-off" leaders, preferring to follow the book. If you work for a closed manager, find out the answers to questions from other senior-level managers, downplay your good ideas in front of the boss, and don't expect to receive his support if you get into trouble. Interact carefully with all organizational communicators who use the closed style; remember, you probably are dealing with a fragile ego.

Although no one fits any one of Hamilton and Parker's profiles exactly, we all have certain tendencies as communicators. No doubt you recognize characteristics of people you know in one or more of the four profiles. All four communication styles have positive and negative points. Knowing your own tendencies and being aware of your communication choices are important considerations for business and professional communicators.

Figure 7.2
Social Styles

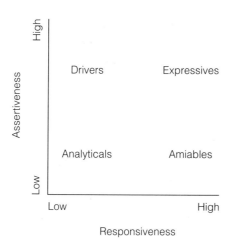

High

Assertiveness

Drivers   Expressives

Analyticals   Amiables

Low

Low   High

Responsiveness

Analyticals, Drivers, Amiables, and Expressives

A second theory for understanding interpersonal communication styles derived from the work of three researchers in the mid-1970s who devised an instrument called the Social Style Profile.[12] Closely related to communication style, a person's social style is measured by three traits:

- *assertiveness*, or ability to communicate his own needs,
- *responsiveness*, or willingness to meet others' needs, and
- *versatility*, or ability to adapt to other styles and situations.

By using two of these characteristics—assertiveness and responsiveness—the Social Style Profile classifies four types of communicators. *Analyticals* are people who are low in both traits. *Drivers* are high in assertiveness and low in responsiveness; *amiables* are low in assertiveness and high in responsiveness; and *expressives* are high in both traits. Figure 7.2 shows relationships among the four styles.

What does all this have to do with communicating interpersonally in organizations? Understanding the communication styles of others is helpful if we wish to make our interpersonal communication as productive as possible, whether hiring a new employee, establishing goals for subordinates, or developing the potential of those around us.[13] Most of us favor one style, although we may have characteristics that overlap.

Analyticals. People who are analyticals (low in both traits) are oriented toward thought and data analysis. Described by some as "cold fish," analyticals are detail-oriented, conscientious, and critical of themselves and others. They value logical solutions, persistence, industriousness, objectivity, and perfectionism. Managing an analytical employee requires that you keep your distance, provide structure, and reduce ambiguity. Written instructions, for example, may be more effective with analyticals than would transferring the same information during an informal chat. Capitalize on analytical employees' dedication to task, but help them develop more interpersonal sensitivity.

Drivers. Drivers (high in assertiveness, low in responsiveness) are action-oriented people who are thorough, efficient, and decisive. Usually, they know what they want and are not afraid to go after it. As skilled organizers and planners, drivers normally make things happen in organizations. However, they may alienate colleagues and subordinates because they are perceived as insensitive and brusque. Drivers make autocratic leaders, imposing their will on those they lead. When managing drivers, keep your communication tone slightly impersonal, praise their task-oriented talents, allow them free rein on challenging projects, give them authority when results count, and help them cultivate their people skills.

Amiables. Amiables (low in assertiveness, high in responsiveness) tend to be somewhat shy but friendly and warm individuals. They are more people-oriented than task-oriented and often fill "counselor" roles within the organization. At the extreme, however, their interpersonal strengths also can become interpersonal weaknesses. To keep everyone happy, they may say what others wish to hear or avoid taking a stand. The lack of conviction behind their words may result in a failure to follow through, thus eliciting their superiors' disappointment. When managing amiable employees, address their personal interests—ask about their family members, for example. Provide them with plenty of positive feedback and capitalize on their relationship skills by assigning them tasks that require interpersonal finesse. Amiables perform best in jobs with low leadership demands, low risk factors, and high need for interpersonal communication skills. The challenge in developing amiable subordinates is in cultivating their dedication to task.

Expressives. Expressives (high in both traits) are oriented toward both people and tasks. Social in nature, expressives often are known for their abilities to entertain and motivate. They can amuse others for hours with their embellished stories of everyday events or motivate others to begin challenging projects. Expressives are dreamers and have short attention spans. They like to be involved in everything, which sometimes leads others to perceive them as overbearing meddlers. Because of a competitive nature, starting, not following through, is the expressive's strong suit. Expressive employees should be placed in highly interactive roles and given stimulating, challenging work. Large projects should be broken down into smaller tasks to ensure completion, and their competitive natures should be challenged.

Although interpersonal communication obviously is more complex than the categories and schemes presented here, perhaps knowing something about communicator styles and related social styles will help you become a more effective superior when you step into a leadership role as well as more effective when interacting with peers.

MANAGING UP

Working with people is difficult, but not impossible. — Peter Drucker

Answer the following multiple-choice question.

Which of the following is the most important predictor of job satisfaction?

a. receiving a comfortable salary
b. winning recognition and prestige
c. being challenged by interesting work
d. developing a satisfying relationship with the boss.

If you selected (d), then you are correct. According to Gerald Goldhaber, an organizational communication scholar, "The most important contributor to job satisfaction is the quality of the relationship employees have with their supervisors."[14]

A recent study found that three factors — communication climate, communication with immediate supervisor, and personal feedback — are most closely related to job satisfaction and job performance. In other words, if the organization's communication climate is positive, if communication with one's immediate supervisor is open and regular, and if personal feedback is forthcoming, then employees are likely to be satisfied with their jobs and perform well. The study also found that perceptions of communication with top management heavily influence employees' job satisfaction and job performance, and that these findings remained consistent across five different studies conducted in various regions of the United States.[15]

Although salary, prestige, and challenge obviously will affect how you feel about the positions you hold during your career, the kind of relationship you have with your immediate superior may well be the primary determinant of your satisfaction level. And if you have the extreme good fortune to like, admire, respect, and communicate productively with every boss you encounter, you will be in the minority.[16] No doubt, you'll have more than one *demanding* boss to contend with; but you also may come across one or two whom you find to be truly *difficult*.[17]

Being able to tell the difference between the two is important. A *demanding* boss is simply one who constantly pushes you to do your best, one who has high performance expectations for employees. A *difficult* boss lacks at least one of three things: the appropriate *level* of respect for employees, a *willingness* to communicate this respect, or the *interpersonal communication skills* to do so.

History holds many examples of difficult bosses. Henry Ford, for example, was reputed to be a classic tyrant who made life miserable for his employees. A generation later, we can point to the career of Lee Iacocca, widely recognized as one of the all-time best managers in the automobile industry. In 1978, *Time* magazine reported, "After weeks of futile maneuvering to save his job, Lee Iacocca, 53, the hard-driving, cigar-chomping president of the world's fourth largest manufacturing company, found himself quite bluntly sacked by his equally toughminded boss, Chairman Henry Ford II. It was the culmination of months of behind-the-scenes quarreling between two of the auto industry's most respected — and often feared — executives."[18]

Today's organizational behavior experts would likely point to such figures as Ted Turner, chief executive of Turner Broadcasting System, Inc., who is said to hold brusque, irate meetings. According to inside reports, several years ago one of his vice-presidents suffered a heart attack in Turner's office.[19] Unfortunately, the incidence of difficult leaders is higher than one might think. In one study, three-fourths of highly successful Fortune 100 executives in three companies reported having had at least one intolerable boss over the course of their careers.[20]

According to one expert, the bottom line is that "most executives were never taught relationship skills, and most subordinates never learn them."[21] In fact, because this issue is so important and because you may well have between eight and twenty bosses during your career — some of whom may stretch and challenge your interpersonal communication skills — we want to focus your attention on superior–subordinate communication.[22] Many books and articles have been written on this subject, everything from popular, self-help books with titles such as *Problem Bosses: Who They Are and How to Deal with Them* to scholarly articles on "Managing Up."

Popular literature on the subject of communicating with one's boss often provides tongue-in-cheek typologies of difficult bosses. Writing in *Fortune*, Walter Kiechel III described the "Attack of the Obsessive Managers," the hard-driving, detail-oriented boss who is "usually more concerned that his people make sure of every detail than he is that the details add up to anything of value to the business":[23]

> At companies where cost cutting has become the watchword, the obsessive manager may well be crawling out of the woodwork and into the limelight. Watch him pounce: "Ah yes, Gengerschneck, in reviewing your latest expense report I noticed that you took an $8 cab ride from the airport when a bus was available for a mere $3 . . . So what if it was four in the morning?" See him interact with subordinates: "This concludes our weekly 2 P.M. meeting. In 15 minutes we'll get together for our weekly 4 P.M. meeting to discuss the results of our 2 P.M. meeting." Hear his battle cry: "Is everybody *busy*?"

Another executive, whose career spanned 38 years and 23 different bosses (one every 1.65 years), describes archetypal behavioral profiles of difficult bosses that produce smiles of recognition: Fred Faultfinder, Max Minutiae, Stan Stubborn, Bill Bully, and Stanley Smoothy. Beyond simply establishing categories, however, popular literature also provides facetious advice on how to deal with each type — the men as described and their female counterparts. For example, when faced with an obsessive Fred Faultfinder boss, this executive suggests practicing "The Theory of the Obvious Error." The advice is this: Omit an obvious and important bit of information from a document that requires the boss's signature. He will take the bait, spot the error immediately, and ask you to fix it. After you do, he will sign off on the entire report immediately. According to this theory, if you work for a Fred Faultfinder, incorporating an obvious intentional error actually speeds up the entire work process![24]

More substantive literature suggests that the key to productive superior–subordinate relationships is to "manage up" or use what is sometimes called "reverse management." For generations, U.S. business has applied downward management. Executives at the top instruct senior-level employees, who pass the word down to mid-level managers, who inform first-line supervisors, who then disseminate information to the rank and file. The principles of management, or so we think, work vertically from the top down.

What *is* managing up? Reverse management, or managing up, simply is initiating communication with your boss in key areas of mutual concern to cultivate a productive superior–subordinate relationship.

Reverse management is neither manipulation to get what you want from your boss nor a threat to the boss's power. Instead, managing up is an essential requirement to becoming an effective subordinate.[25] And because virtually everyone in the organization is someone else's subordinate, the principles of reverse management are widely applicable. In fact, an increasing number of companies now offer their employees reverse-management training.[26]

Why is reverse management finally receiving the attention it deserves? Several reasons come to mind. For example, downsizing in today's corporations means that fewer people are available to do the same amount of work. Competition in today's world has stiffened and our competitors around the world have entered the global marketplace. Factors such as these underscore the need for improved communication between superiors and subordinates.[27]

Why manage *up*? Because it is difficult, if not impossible, for *one* boss to initiate the kind of productive communication we're talking about with *many* employees. The burden of responsibility thus falls on you, the subordinate. What should you communicate *about*? The following are three communication suggestions for reverse management: (1) clarify job content and performance expectations, (2) take the initiative, and (3) keep the boss informed.[28]

Clarifying Job Content and Performance Expectations

You cannot expect to be a good subordinate unless you know what your superior expects of you and how you can meet those expectations. Surprisingly, many employees expect jobs to "unfold" as time goes by instead of taking the initiative to clarify expectations at the outset. You may labor for months, thinking you're on target, only to find at the conclusion of your efforts that the boss had another idea of what the finished product should look like.

First, when your supervisor assigns a new project, get her to explain all the related tasks—who to see, where to go, what to do, when to finish, and so on. But also make sure you understand the *context* in which you operate. What is the history of the project? Has it been attempted before? Are you taking over someone else's initial efforts?

For example, if you are asked to develop a new communication training program for company managers, then you better know what kind of training they already have completed, how they responded to past programs, and how they assess current training needs. If you fail to find the answers to these essential questions, you may create a technically perfect training program and still fail miserably. Redundant and irrelevant programs, no matter how high their quality, will surely be received poorly by managers who completed similar training the year before you joined the company.

Second, rather than simply asking questions, demonstrate your competence to the boss by offering *your* understanding of your responsibilities, and then asking her for a response. Asking "What should I do?" may make you sound weak and dependent, but providing a list of your perceptions and then asking her for additions, deletions, and corrections portrays you as a responsible employee with initiative.

Third, in addition to reaching mutual agreement on the bottom-line expectations for your position, you must renegotiate specific expectations as your tasks change with special assignments.

....

Taking the Initiative

Initiative — the appropriate amount — should be a topic of communication between you and your boss. How closely does he expect the two of you to cooperate during a particular project? How much help may you ask for? Again, some bosses want to be involved; others only want a finished product. They may prefer that you find answers to questions by asking other senior people in the organization or knowledgeable peers. In particular, should you:

- Wait for instructions?
- Ask for instructions?
- Recommend a plan of action and then act if given the go ahead?
- Usually act on your own but immediately report whatever action you take?
- Always act on your own and report routinely?[29]

Boss A prefers employees who have the ability and foresight to stay one step ahead of her. With many different projects and people to manage, she appreciates employees who can work independently. She values resourceful employees. When a previously discussed option fails to materialize, such employees seek other avenues until they are successful, instead of dropping the task because they have reached what appears to be an impasse.

Boss B, on the other hand, prefers to remain in total, or almost total, control of his employees. In his view, employees who are self-directed create problems by overstepping their bounds. These two bosses represent two ends of a continuum.

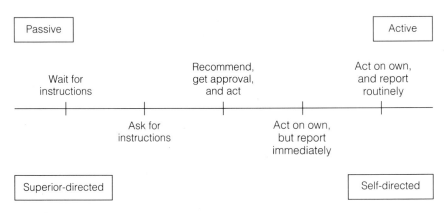

Figure 7.3
Initiative Continuum

Where on the initiative continuum in Figure 7.3 should your relationship fall? What is your preference, what is your superior's preference, and how can the two of you find a comfortable compromise? Your superior may have a general preference, but her views also may vary depending on the particular project underway. Factors such as the importance and visibility of the task you are assigned may affect your degree of autonomy. For example, on internal projects within your own department or within the company, you may be given freer rein than on those in which you operate between departments or between organizations.

Keeping the Boss Informed

While running to the boss to report every minor occurrence is not a good idea, regular communication with your superior is essential, whether the news you provide is good or bad. Withholding negative information may seem like the best course of action, but it can have devastating results. Consider the following examples as reported in the *Wall Street Journal.*[30]

> The president of a large machinery producer ordered work to begin on a new kind of photocopying machine. Though those with direct responsibility for the machine knew the job would take two years, a report to the president stated that the machine could be developed in a matter of months. . . . Working day and night, the staff managed to construct a prototype to meet the truncated timetable. The president inspected it and left with assurances it was "ready to roll." Hardly had he left the lab, when the prototype burst into flames and was destroyed.

The chief executive of an electronics company on the West Coast discovered that shipments were being predated and papers falsified to meet sales targets that his managers knew were unrealistically high. At least 20 persons in the organization cooperated in the deception, but it was months before anyone at the top found out.

Although these examples were extreme enough to merit national attention, similar events take place daily on a smaller scale. Rationalizations such as "She has plenty of other things to worry about," "He'll fly off the handle," or "We'll hope for the best" are poor excuses for abandoning the direct, forthright approach to superior–subordinate communication.

You also must know *how* the boss prefers to be informed. You may assume a telephone conversation will suffice, but she may expect a detailed written report. The problem is that many subordinates fail to see a situation from the boss's perspective. She, too, is a subordinate who reports to her superior. She has deadlines to meet, others' expectations to fulfill. If she assumes a project is well underway and then finds otherwise too late to take another course of action, she may suffer the consequences with her own boss.

The best superior-subordinate relationships are reciprocal: The boss benefits from your productivity and high-quality work, and you benefit from the boss's direction and rewards. You enhance her reputation within the organization and vice versa. When your alliance is based on trust, mutual respect, and loyalty, both of you will benefit within the organization. For these reasons, it is important to look out for her welfare as well as your own. Communicate your successes as well as failures. In other words, do all you can to make working with you pleasant and enjoyable, and demonstrate your appreciation of the boss's effort and support.[31]

Another pragmatic reason to use managing-up communication principles has been identified by a study conducted at the University of Colorado. According to researchers there, communication skills are key to organizational advancement.[32] But another study that compared how women professionals evaluated their own communication skills with how their supervisors rated these same skills found little agreement. In general, women as a group rated themselves as more skilled than supervisors as a group rated them.[33] Previous studies with male subjects yielded similar results.[34] Taking responsibility for cultivating a productive relationship with one's superior may be important not only to *become* an effective subordinate but also to be *perceived* as one by the boss. Communication between subordinates and superiors must go both ways.

Reverse management is an important concept, one to think about as you prepare for your future career. Actually carrying out the principles we've described, however, requires considerable interpersonal finesse and some time and experience on the job. But even as a new employee, you'll find that communicating with your superior about expectations, initiative, and progress will contribute greatly to your job satisfaction.

One final discouraging but realistic point must be made: Not all bosses are "manageable." If your superior is so difficult to work for that your communication overtures repeatedly are ignored and you cannot function productively in the organization, a well-considered resignation may be the only logical alternative. At the very least, however, working for a difficult boss will teach you valuable lessons about communication, superior-subordinate relationships, and yourself. Those who have survived intolerable bosses report two important lessons: first, how to cope with adversity; and second, how to do things better by watching someone else do them wrong.[35] We don't mean to imply that all bosses are difficult people—quite the contrary. However, now is a good time to begin thinking proactively about the possible communication challenges that await you.

PERSONAL PROBLEMS ON THE JOB

Thus far, we have been discussing interpersonal communication on the job. Enlarging your repertoire of skills by developing an awareness of communicator styles has been our primary focus. At this point, however, we shift our attention to the *personal* effects of *interpersonal* communication choices. The maze of choices you'll face and the ramifications of those choices make life in the organization interesting, to say the least.

Throughout your career, you will be faced with challenging personal and interpersonal choices. Consider, for example, the issue of loyalty: more specifically, *loyalties* to yourself, your superior, your peers, your subordinates, the department or division in which you work, the organization itself, your spouse, your family, and the ideals you hold in high esteem. As an organizational communicator, your loyalties in one area at times may directly challenge those in another.

When your boss offers you a promotion that requires relocation to corporate headquarters halfway across the country and your spouse wants to invoke his veto power, then you will be faced with a difficult decision. Should loyalty to your boss, who may have been instrumental in securing your promotion, and the company, who wishes to reward your hard work, override your loyalty to your spouse and his corresponding career loyalties? When your boss bends the rules and engages in what you believe is unethical behavior, then you may be forced to choose between loyalty to your boss and loyalty to your own ideals. When an interesting colleague of the opposite sex vies for your personal attention, then you may be required to choose between your own needs for companionship and ego gratification and your department's reputation and smooth operation.

Making the right decision, or at least the best decision possible, is easier now in the abstract than when you are faced with these types of stressful situations. In the final section of this chapter, we want you to look ahead to some of the personal problems that you may face as business and professional communicators. Learning to balance your loyalties and prioritize them are important challenges to think about now.

....

Loyalty to Self

Romantic Relationships on the Job. Like the average American, you will spend eight hours or more on the job five or more days of every week. Spending a minimum of forty hours per week in close contact with your co-workers will provide a natural opportunity for romantic relationships to develop. The ever-increasing number of women entering the work force has resulted in more travel with and more interaction and socialization between the sexes. Attraction is a natural and inevitable result. In one recent study, 86 percent of 175 respondents reported that they had been exposed to one or more romantic relationships on the job.[36]

Why then is the prevailing sentiment against such "indiscretions"? The interoffice affair serves as raw material for many a movie script, television episode, and letter to "Dear Abby." Why is the general public alarmed by and critical of intimate relationships that originate in the workplace? On the surface such views may appear antiquated; nevertheless, the bias is real and, from our point of view, often justified. Society looks askance at the woman who ascends unusually swiftly up the corporate ladder, and she often is suspected of "sleeping her way to the top." Society also deplores the powerful man who uses and manipulates female colleagues to get information or to simply keep women in their place.

The most recent example of public outrage about a romantic relationship on the job was aimed at Bill Agee, CEO at Bendix Corporation in Southfield, Michigan, and his executive assistant, Mary Cunningham, who quickly ascended the ranks to become vice-president for corporate and public affairs and finally vice-president of strategic planning. Company rumors leaked to the national media, and the couple became the target of public criticism. The two maintained that "they built a professional trust that developed into a love relationship."[37] In their defense, Cunningham wrote *Power Play: What Really Happened at Bendix*, in which she states:

> Men and women who work together will fall in love. And why should this surprise anyone? People who work together come to know each other in a way that is far more meaningful by most standards than meeting in a singles bar. To put these people off-limits to one another is unrealistic.[38]

Part of society's bias is based on the fact that romantic relationships on the job affect not only the two people involved but also the work groups to which they belong, the departments in which they work, and sometimes the entire organization. The informal channel — the heartbeat of any organization — is the vehicle for the changes and problems produced by interoffice romance. The formal channel, on the other hand, usually ignores such problems. According to a survey of Fortune 500 companies, only 6 percent of respondents reported that written policies or orientation programs addressed romantic relationships at work. The historical approach of ignoring workplace relationships seems to be giving way, however, to increased openness and counseling for employees.[39] In a recently conducted survey, 53 percent of professional women expressed the belief that office romance is not beneficial, although 71 percent said that a romantic indulgence is not professionally risky "if the couple acts professionally."[40]

In truth, however, intimate workplace relationships usually are disruptive, uncomfortable for everyone involved, and generally not worth the trouble. As the epigram by Lord Mancroft in Chapter 4 stated, "A speech is like a love affair. Any fool can start it, but to end it requires considerable skill." The intensity of work relationships may make attraction between co-workers inevitable, but cooling and broken relationships also may make some people uncomfortable enough to leave their jobs prematurely. And when a relationship is over, saying goodbye to a romantic partner you see everyday at the office isn't easy.

If you do consider cultivating a romantic relationship on the job, keep the following guidelines in mind.[41]

1. First, analyze your organization's corporate culture, its collective personality. Some organizations are young, liberal, and progressive, while others are older, conservative, and tradi-

tional. In some companies, intra- or interoffice romance may be seen as a matter of course; in others, the same behavior may be viewed as a serious breach of professionalism. In other words, look carefully before you leap.

2. Understand that others will know what's going on. Secret alliances don't remain secret for long, particularly when others are indirectly involved by virtue of close proximity. Think about how this realization may affect your credibility and therefore your reputation within the organization.

3. Play by the rules. Getting involved with a boss, a subordinate, or someone already spoken for is understandably off limits. A relationship with a corporate peer, on the other hand, particularly with one in another department, usually is better received.

All other things being equal, our best advice is to resist on-the-job temptation and establish romantic liaisons elsewhere. The conflicts generated in a romantic relationship at work between your organizational loyalties and your personal loyalties may be hazardous to your job.[42]

Machiavellianism. A second practice through which self-loyalty eventually can produce disastrous results is that of stepping over others to get to the top. Despite today's focus on the "me generation" and "looking out for number one," extreme competitiveness at others' expense generally will produce negative reactions from co-workers. We'll discuss this idea in relation to the topic of power in organizations in Chapter 10.

The term *Machiavellianism* comes from the name of a sixteenth-century Florentine writer, Niccolo Machiavelli, who produced in 1513 one of the world's most famous books, *The Prince*. Because of the ruthless principles he advocated, Machiavellianism now has negative connotations. Being described as a "high Mach" or a highly Machiavellian person usually is not a compliment:

A definition of the twentieth-century Machiavellian administrator is one who employs aggressive, manipulative, exploiting, and devious moves in order to achieve personal and organizational objectives. These moves are undertaken according to perceived feasibility with secondary consideration (what is necessary under the circumstances) to the feelings, needs, and/or "rights" of others. Not that Machiavellianism is "right" or even particularly "bright," but it exists in today's leadership and needs to be recognized as such.[43]

In one study, highly Machiavellian managers were found to report more job strain and less job satisfaction than did their less Machiavellian counterparts.[44]

According to experts, leaders become Machiavellian for the following reasons.[45]

1. *Ambition*: They are motivated by personal impatience about getting ahead.
2. *Organizational constraints*: They decide that roadblocks in the system require the use of underhanded techniques.
3. *Failure*: The use of direct and forthright methods has proven unsuccessful.
4. *Operationality*: Machiavellian techniques have achieved results.
5. *Ignorance*: They know of no other way to get what they want.
6. *Personality*: They have highly compulsive personalities or strongly avoid conflict.

Still, some experts advocate the use of Machiavellian techniques in today's organization: An "executive-politician must use caution in taking counsel . . . avoid too close superior–subordinate relationships . . . not hesitate to be ruthless when expedient . . . limit what is to be communicated . . . learn never to place too much dependence on a subordinate unless it is clearly in the latter's personal advantage to be loyal . . . and give outward evidence of status, power, and material success."[46]

Dealing with Machiavellian bosses or co-workers is difficult business; you may even want to read *The Prince* to understand their motivation and devise productive communication strategies. Machiavelli's techniques clearly conflict with the communication principles advocated by today's participative-management movement, the communication principles used in today's excellent companies, and the communication principles suggested throughout this text. Be pragmatic—yes. Be prepared—yes. Be informed—yes. Know the organization's political climate—yes. But when your loyalties to yourself and your own organizational advancement mean sacrificing your loyalties to your colleagues and their goals, you may well jeopardize the long-term contribution you can make and your own eventual success.

....

Loyalty to the Organization

Stress and Burnout. *Stress* will be a part of whatever you do, but how you handle organizational stress is worth thinking about. Overcommitment to the organization and undercommitment to your family and other outside relationships that help you relieve stress may affect your long-term happiness and productivity. Although commitment to the organization for which you work obviously will contribute to your success and satisfaction, you also must balance your loyalties between your personal life and your professional life.

Formally defined as "an adaptive response, mediated by individual characteristics and/or psychological processes, that is a consequence of any external action, situation, or event that places a special physical and/or psychological demand upon a person," stress is a fact of life we cannot escape.[47] It's that feeling in the pit of your stomach when you have two unannounced papers to write, an exam to study for, and that long-awaited date with the person of your dreams — all scheduled for the same evening.

Stress can be positive (having three excellent job offers to choose among) or negative (losing someone you love). Organizational stress, however, has three basic causes: *personal, social,* and *organizational.*[48]

Theoretically, some people are more susceptible to stress because of personal factors such as age, personality, and disruptive changes in their lives. Social factors such as family problems, finances, and negative social attitudes also can play a role. One expert notes, for example, that today's employee is more likely than his counterparts in past generations to resist change, to challenge authority, and to feel that hard work pays off.[49]

Within the organization itself, your stress level also will be affected by the nature of your job and its work load, your role in the organization, your career progress, your work relationships, and the structure and culture of the organization. Some cultures, for example, are more stressful than others, and a mismatch between your personality and the collective personality or culture of your organization can make matters worse. In other words, personal, social, and organizational factors combine to raise overall levels of professional stress.

According to John Howard, co-author of *Rusting Out, Burning Out or Bowing Out: Stress and Survival on the Job,* three main characteristics of today's society produce the stress we face in daily living: hassles, helplessness, and hurriedness.[50] *Hassles* represent "the gradual grind of a million annoyances" — bad weather, pollution, commuting, traffic jams, arguments, taxes — and although each individual annoyance produces only a small amount of stress, collectively they may affect us more adversely than a single major traumatic event. They lower our threshold of tolerance and wear us down over time. If you are like the average person, you probably will have experienced several hassles by the time you reach the office each morning.

Helplessness is the feeling we have when we compare our own sense of power (or powerlessness) to the power of big business, big government, and big unions, among others. We feel too small to effect change and thus frustrated and stressed. On-the-job helplessness results when you are given a title and a level of responsibility but not the authority to go with it.

Hurriedness results from living in a fast-paced society and working in a fast-paced organization. We try to schedule more and more in less and less time, producing stress symptoms that are characteristic of the classic Type A personality. According to one study, 60 percent to 70 percent of managers and professionals exhibit Type A characteristics. And note these results: When managers keep daily diaries of their activities, the average length of one activity is seven minutes. In fact, 70 percent of managers' daily activities last no longer than seven minutes, and 40 percent of these seven-minute activities are judged to be highly urgent.[51] Research also indicates that women, particularly those in junior and middle management, have the highest occupational stress levels of any managerial or supervisory group in the work force—and 50 percent more stress than their male counterparts regardless of managerial level.[52]

How should we cope with these stress producers in our lives?[53] Reducing hassles requires foresight, planning, building in hassle-free time, and cultivating supportive relationships. The antidote to helplessness is taking more initiative, perhaps by concentrating on one area of your life in which you can exercise more control. Combatting hurriedness requires learning and using techniques of time management. Activity and hurriedness are not synonymous. Learning to slow down in *attitude* (as well as practice) may be key to survival. Beyond these practical techniques, exercise, hobbies, meditation, and biofeedback are potential ways to cope with excess stress.

Failing to cope adequately with organizational stress may lead to another serious problem that plagues many American workers: *burnout*. One writer reports that recent management-workshop participants were asked to draw pictures to express their feelings. One depicted a skid-row bum lying in a gutter; one showed a stick figure being crushed by a vise; and one showed a dry well. All of these images—failure, pressure, and emptiness—depict elements of professional burnout.[54] According to current projections, burnout is responsible for approximately 20 percent of the costs of high turnover, absenteeism, and declining work-force productivity.[55]

Candidates for burnout typically are idealistic and self-motivated people who experience a great deal of job-related stress and aim for unrealistic goals.[56] Symptoms of job-related burnout include the following:[57]

1. *Fatalism*: the feeling that you lack control over your work
2. *Boredom*: a lack of interest in the work you are doing

3. *Discontent*: a dislike for what you are doing
4. *Cynicism*: the feeling that your work is unimportant or without meaning
5. *Inadequacy*: the feeling that your work does not measure up to that of others
6. *Failure*: the feeling that your work is of poor quality
7. *Overwork*: the constant feeling that you cannot get everything done
8. *Nastiness*: rude or unpleasant behavior toward colleagues
9. *Dissatisfaction*: the feeling that you are not recognized or rewarded for your work
10. *Escape*: the desire to get away from it all.

The burnout process takes time, occurring gradually (as shown in Figure 7.4) and continuing in a self-perpetuating cycle (as shown in Figure 7.5). In fact, experts describe five stages of burnout.[58]

Stage 1: The honeymoon. Beginning a new career is an exciting challenge. Learning to adapt to your new environment absorbs an enormous amount of valuable energy, but during this period you also must learn to adapt to stress. If you fail to do so, then you may move to Stage 2.

Stage 2: Fuel shortage. For many people, Stage 2 begins with a vague realization that the honeymoon is over. Enthusiasm for the job begins to

Figure 7.4 *Path to Professional Burnout*[59]

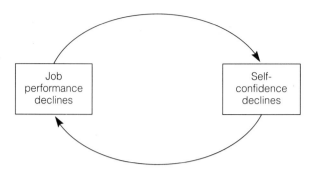

Figure 7.5 *Self-Perpetuating Nature of Burnout*[60]

fade, and job dissatisfaction, inefficiency, fatigue, sleep disturbances, and escape activities may begin to bother you.

Stage 3: Chronic symptoms. Stage 3 of job burnout begins with pronounced and recognizable physical and psychological symptoms: chronic exhaustion, physical illness, anger, and depression. This may be when you first realize that you are in trouble.

Stage 4: Crisis. By Stage 4, symptoms become critical. Pessimism and frustration take over, and as a victim of burnout, you are obsessed with escaping.

Stage 5: Hitting the wall. This stage is analogous to that of a marathon runner who "hits the wall." When muscles are depleted of their energy source, glycogen, runners become dehydrated, their temperatures soar to 106° or 107°, and their blood volume decreases. Muscle paralysis, fainting, and collapse can occur. Hitting the wall as a victim of professional burnout probably means that alcoholism, drug abuse, or heart disease have emerged as serious problems.

Fortunately, burnout can either be treated before the onset of later stages or prevented altogether. The remedy is in cultivating high-quality interpersonal relationships, balancing competing loyalties, and devising effective means to cope with organizational stress.

Loyalty to Ideals

Ethical Considerations. Occasionally you may find yourself in situations like those described in Scenarios 2 and 4 early in this chapter. Your personal sense of ethics may lead you to disagree with a colleague's or boss's actions. These situations can be difficult enough if the relationship is between peers, but if the relationship is between you and your supervisor, your choices may have complex consequences. Locking horns with your boss over ethical issues puts you in a vulnerable situation. She may become threatened by your position, and the results may affect your relationship and your job tenure. You are the only person who can decide how to handle these difficult situations, and you may have to think long and hard about the best course of action.

Newspapers are littered with stories of corporate ethics gone awry: bribes, kickbacks, embezzlement, falsified records, suppressed evidence, unsafe products knowingly marketed. According to one expert, "the hard truth is that corporate misconduct, like the lowly cockroach, is a plague that we can suppress but never exterminate."[61] Four commonly held rationalizations account for many of the unethical actions taken by organizations:

> A belief that an unethical activity:
> • is not "really" illegal or immoral,
> • is in an individual's or corporation's best interest,
> • is safe because it will never be found out, or
> • is acceptable because if it helps the company, then the company will condone it and protect the participant.[62]

Recently, ethics has become a prominent topic in business and the professions. The American Medical Association has reported that 90 percent of major U.S. hospitals have active ethics committees or staff ethics consultants. For the first time ever, Harvard MBA students must complete a new required course, "Decision Making and Ethical Values." Fortune 500 companies are calling on philosophers and theologians to help them draft formal ethics codes. Manhattan's Trinity Church now runs an outreach center that helps large corporations such as Standard Oil and Champion International develop sound and responsible corporate policies. Stockbrokers, bankers, analysts, and managers meet over brown-bag lunches to discuss the ethics of corporate takeovers, plant closings, and insider trading.

Why this sudden interest in ethics? To some extent, the reasons are pragmatic. One recent article states,

> In the wake of the scandals in Wall Street, Chicago's commodity market and defense contracts, there is an awareness that the company which acts responsibly can avoid fines and jail sentences, reduce court suits that entail costly legal and accounting fees, diminish the threat of more government regulation, increase company morale and attract a higher type, more loyal employee.[63]

According to a public-issues forum for two hundred CEOs, "There is a growing conviction that strong corporate culture and ethics are a vital strategic key to survival and profitability in a highly competitive era."[64]

Pragmatism, however, is not enough. The four rationalizations above all seek to justify unethical behavior on pragmatic grounds. Our sense is this: You must apply the same ethical standards in your professional life that you follow in your personal life.

CHAPTER SUMMARY

This chapter began with an important premise: "People have one thing in common: they are all different." Over the course of your career, you will come into contact with dozens of people. In fact, interpersonal skills often are named as the most important requirement for successful job performance. The quality of your interpersonal relationships on the job, particularly with your superior, also will affect your level of job satisfaction. Because people are what organizations are all about, cultivating your interpersonal communication skills is critical to both your survival and your success.

With diversity between and among people in organizations comes diverse communication styles. One way to examine communication styles is by looking at the variables of feedback and disclosure in identifying open, blind, hidden, and closed styles. We also may look at social styles through the variables of assertiveness, responsiveness, and versatility. Individuals can be described as analyticals, drivers, amiables, and expressives.

The chapter next explored managing up, or reverse management. Managing up is simply initiating communication with your superior in key areas of mutual concern to cultivate a productive relationship. Clarifying job content and performance expectations, taking initiative, and keeping the boss informed are important elements of managing up.

The chapter concluded with a discussion of personal problems on the job. How do we balance loyalties to ourselves, our superiors, our peers, our subordinates, our departments, the organization itself, our families, and the ideals we hold in high esteem? Are romantic relationships a good idea? Should we aim for success at the expense of others? How do we cope with stress and burnout? And just how important are ethical considerations?

Interpersonal relationships on the job will provide both your greatest enjoyments and your greatest challenges.

Our emphasis throughout Chapter 7 has been on communicating interpersonally in organizations. Early in the chapter we presented five scenarios of difficult situations. Focus now on the second scenario, which briefly discusses an ethical situation in which you and your boss do not see eye to eye. A full description of this situation is presented as a case study below. After you read "The Unethical Manager," we'll ask several questions.

The Unethical Manager

For the last ten years, you have been an employee of Smithson Corporation in Los Angeles, a highly reputable aeronautical engineering firm. You have worked your way up the ranks to your current position as assistant director of the marketing department. You have enjoyed your work, your spouse has launched a fine and successful career in a highly competitive field, you now have three school-aged children, and you recently have been able to afford to buy your first house. In general, things are going well.

For most of this time, Al Farnsworth has been your boss. Al is now ten years from retirement, and because of his many friends in high places, he probably will remain as director until then. You, on the other hand, are the most recent in a long line of assistant directors. Almost all previous assistant directors have left with negative feelings about Al. In fact, your relationship with Al has been difficult at times because of what you see as some fundamental differences between you.

You, for example, are highly competent and well liked by everyone; Al, however, is a weak leader. He is well spoken, what you might call a "smooth operator," and highly suspicious of each subordinate. Always afraid someone is after his job, Al keeps folders of secret information on everyone in the department in a locked file cabinet. Even though you are second in command in the department, you've noticed over the years that Al is never without his personal favorite, usually a new employee whom Al takes under his wing and uses as his confidant. The latest of these is Darin Kennedy, someone you judge to be a "brownnoser" and a "weasel." You've never been impressed with Darin's work, but because of his friendship with the boss, his career has progressed steadily. Most employees in the department, by the way, share your feelings about Darin.

Perhaps what bothers you most is that Al avoids conflict; in fact, his personal style is to promise anything to anyone and then do whatever he wishes. When you last asked Al for a raise to meet the demands of your expanding family, he agreed wholeheartedly. That was eight months ago, and nothing has happened in the meantime.

Perhaps the most important difference between the two of you is your ethical standards. Several years ago, you heard rumors that Al used his expense account to take business trips that were nothing more than visits to his mistress in another state. Al was just slippery enough to get away with it.

Last Friday, March 1, one of the department's bright new employees came to you with a serious concern. While standing in the mailroom, Carl overheard Darin bragging about the fact that he talked the boss into lying on his behalf. Because Darin was up for a promotion within the division — the next rung up the corporate ladder — he asked Al to include false information in his promotion folder. Although he had just finished the third of twelve courses in his MBA program, Darin asked Al to write in his performance evaluation that Darin had completed his MBA *cum laude*. Al agreed to do so to cinch Darin's promotion. Because Carl also was up for a promotion and was "playing by the rules," he found this piece of information personally distressing.

As assistant director, you told Carl that it was your responsibility to handle this problem; however, you now find yourself in a troublesome dilemma. You know that Al's action is blatantly wrong and clearly violates explicit company policy. On the other hand, you wonder how Smithson, a leader in its field and protective of its public image, would feel about a possible public scandal.

You see several possible solutions. You could report Al's behavior to his superiors; in fact, if you go behind Al's back, he may be fired, and you would be in line to take over his job. However, Al might be able to marshall support from his superiors, as he always seems to do when he's in trouble, by claiming that he was only trying to help a competent employee get a deserved promotion, and that you are trying to maneuver him out of his job.

A second option would be to approach Al, tell him the "rumor" you've heard and its possible negative consequences for him, Darin, and the entire marketing department. At the same time, you could offer to retrieve the promotion folder from the personnel department before it goes upstairs (where the decision will be made May 1) and repair the "mistake." You choose this second option.

After a worrisome weekend, you enter Al's office Monday morning, tell him what you've heard and offer to correct the false report. Al agrees immediately that the falsehood must be corrected. But he declines your offer of help and indicates that he will correct the inaccuracy himself after he discusses the problem with Darin.

Another week goes by. With the problem still weighing heavily on your mind, you approach Al the next Monday and ask if the problem has been taken care of. Al replies that he's working on it. Two weeks go by with no mention of the issue by Al. In the meantime, Carl asks you what's happening, as do several other people in the department who have now heard the story and are expecting you to solve the problem. Suspecting that, true to form, Al has decided to ignore the issue, you decide to retrieve Darin's folder from the personnel department and check to see whether the inaccurate information has been corrected. There, in black and white, is the lie—unaltered.

Group discussion questions

1. Of the four *communication styles* discussed in Chapter 7, which style best describes Al Farnsworth as a manager? Why? Describe the main characteristics of this style.
2. Does Al appear to have a backup style he uses under stress?
3. Which style do you use in this story? What evidence is there for your choice? What are the main characteristics of your style?
4. What advice does the chapter give about communicating with a boss like Al?
5. What should you do about the dilemma described above? Decide what your next steps would be and why.

 Decco Exercise Assume that the preceding case study took place at Decco Corporation and that the main character (the assistant marketing director), who is a good friend of yours, just came to you for advice on how to handle the situation. Write a memo for your files to document the contents of your conversation.

Notes

1. John Naisbitt, *Megatrends: Ten New Directions Transforming Our Lives* (New York: Warner, 1982).

2. Carol Teegardin, "Now It's Time for a Real Education," *Providence Journal-Bulletin*, 30 May 1989, pp. C-1, C-8.

3. Jerry W. Johnson, "Interpersonal Relationships in the Office," *Public Management* 66 (July 1984): 4.

4. Johnson, "Interpersonal Relationships," 5–6.

5. Rudi Klauss and Bernard M. Bass, *Interpersonal Communication in Organizations* (New York: Academic Press, 1982), 3; E. Brewer and J.W.C. Tomlinson, "The Manager's Working Day," *The Journal of Industrial Economics* 12 (1964): 191–197; C. M. Pavett and A. W. Lau, "Managerial Work: The Influence of Hierarchical Level and Functional Specialty," *Academy of Management Journal* 26 (1983): 170–177.

6. Rosemary Stewart, *Managers and Their Jobs: A Study of the Similarities and Differences in the Way Managers Spend Their Time* (London: Macmillan, 1967).

7. Dan B. Curtis, Jerry L. Winsor, and Ronald D. Stephens, "National Preferences in Business and Communication Education," *Communication Education* 38 (1989): 6–14.

8. Kathryn Martin, "Video Teaches Personal Skills to Students," *Colorado Springs Gazette Telegraph*, 8 September 1987, p. B-1.

9. Mark L. Goldstein, "Managing the Difficult Boss," *Industry Week* 233 (29 June 1987): 38.

10. David S. Gochman, George J. Stukenborg, Armando Feler, "The Ideal Physician: Implications for Contemporary Hospital Marketing," *Journal of Health Care Marketing* 6 (June 1986): 17–25.

11. Cheryl Hamilton and Cordell Parker, *Communicating for Results*, 3rd ed. (Belmont, CA: Wadsworth, 1990), 73–93.

12. S. Buchholz, W. B. Lashbrook, and J. R. Wenburg, "Toward the Measurement and Processing of Social Style." Paper presented at the International Communication Association Convention, Portland, OR, May 1976.

13. Barbara A. Schoeneberger, "Managing Multiple Personalities: Amiables, Analyticals, Expressives and Drivers," *Management World* 16

(February/March 1987): 40–41. The section on these social styles is adapted from Schoeneberger's article.

14. Gerald M. Goldhaber, *Organizational Communication*, 4th ed. (Dubuque, IA: Wm. C. Brown, 1986), 236.

15. J. David Pincus, "Study Links Communication and Job Performance," *IABC Communication World* 1 (November 1984): 27–28, 30.

16. Ron Zemke, "Working with Jerks," *Training* 24 (May 1987): 27–31, 33–34, 38.

17. Goldstein, "Managing," 37.

18. Normal C. Hill and Paul H. Thompson, "Managing Your Manager: The Effective Subordinate," *Exchange*, Brigham Young University School of Management, Fall/Winter 1978.

19. Goldstein, "Managing," 38.

20. Michael M. Lombardo and Morgan W. McCall, Jr., *Coping with an Intolerable Boss* (Greensboro, NC: Center for Creative Leadership, 1984).

21. Goldstein, "Managing," 38.

22. Goldstein, "Managing," 37.

23. Walter Kiechel III, "The Attack of the Obsessive Managers," *Fortune* 115 (16 February 1987): 127–128.

24. Harvey Gittler, "Bosses I Have Known (and Would Like to Forget)," *Industry Week* 233 (4 May 1987): 44–45.

25. J. J. Gabarro and J. P. Kotter, "Managing Your Boss," *Harvard Business Review* 58 (January–February 1980): 92–100.

26. Goldstein, "Managing," 39.

27. Goldstein, "Managing," 39.

28. Hill and Thompson, "Managing Your Manager," 297; Dean Tjosvold, *Working Together to Get Things Done* (Lexington, MA: Lexington Books, 1986), 153–154.

29. William Oncken, Jr., and Donald L. Wass, "Management Time: Who's Got the Monkey?" *Harvard Business Review* 52 (November–December 1974): 75–80.

30. John and Mark Arnold, "Manager's Journal: Corporate Cover-Ups," *The Wall Street Journal*, 5 June 1978, p. 18.

31. Hill and Thompson, "Managing Your Manager," 302–304.

32. Pamela Shockley-Zalabak, Constance Courtney Staley, and Donald

Dean Morley, "The Female Professional: Perceived Communication Proficiencies as Predictors of Organizational Advancement," *Human Relations* 41 (1988): 553–567.

33. Constance Courtney Staley and Pamela Shockley-Zalabak, "Communication Proficiency and Future Training Needs of the Female Professional: Self-Assessment vs. Supervisors' Evaluations," *Human Relations* 39 (1986): 891–902.

34. L. S. Baird, "Self and Superior Rating of Performance: As Related to Self-esteem and Satisfaction with Supervision," *Academy of Management Journal* 20 (1977): 291–300; H. G. Henemann, "Comparison of Self and Superior Ratings of Managerial Performance," *Journal of Applied Psychology* 59 (1974): 638–642; George C. Thornton, "The Relationship between Supervisory- and Self-Appraisals of Executive Performance," *Personnel Psychology* 21 (1968): 441–456.

35. Lombardo and McCall, *Coping*, 5–6.

36. C. Anderson and P. Hunsacker, "Why There's Romancing at the Office and Why It's Everyone's Problem," *Personnel* 62 (February 1985): 57–63.

37. Andrea Warfield, "Co-Worker Romances: Impact on the Work Group and on Career-Oriented Women," *Personnel* 64 (May 1987): 24.

38. Warfield, "Co-Worker Romances," 24.

39. Warfield, "Co-Worker Romances," 26.

40. Lisa Mainiero, *Office Romance: Love, Power & Sex in the Workplace* (New York: Rawson Associates, 1989), 279–280.

41. Mainiero, *Office Romance*, 259–264; Margaria Fichtner, "Heart Throbs on the Job," *Providence Journal-Bulletin*, 12 July 1989, p. G-3.

42. Lisa A. Mainiero, "A Review and Analysis of Power Dynamics in Organizational Romances," *Academy of Management Review* 11 (1986): 750–762.

43. Richard P. Calhoon, "Niccolo Machiavelli and the Twentieth Century Administrator," *Academy of Management Journal* 12 (June 1969): 211.

44. Gary R. Gemmill and W. J. Heisler, "Machiavellianism as a Factor in Managerial Job Strain, Job Satisfaction, and Upward Mobility," *Academy of Management Journal* 15 (1972): 51–62.

45. Calhoon, "Niccolo Machiavelli," 211.

46. Robert N. McMurry, "Power and the Ambitious Executive," *Harvard Business Review* 51 (November/December 1973): 144–145.

47. J. M. Ivancevich and M. T. Matteson, *Stress and Work* (Chicago: Scott, Foresman, 1980), 8–9.

48. Alan J. Dubinsky, "Managing Work Stress," *Business* 35 (July–September 1985): 30–35.

49. A. A. McLean, *Work Stress* (Reading, MA: Addison-Wesley, 1979), 12–14.

50. John H. Howard, "Hassles, Helplessness and Hurriedness—Coping in Turbulent Times," *Canadian Banker* 91 (April 1984): 34–37; *Rusting Out, Burning Out or Bowing Out: Stress and Survival on the Job* (Toronto: Financial Post Books, 1978).

51. Howard, "Hassles," 36.

52. M. J. Davidson and C. L. Cooper, "Occupational Stress in Female Managers: A Comparative Study," *Journal of Management Studies* 21 (1984): 185–205.

53. Howard, "Hassles," 36.

54. Donald P. Rogers, "Helping Employees Cope with Burnout," *Business* 34 (October–December 1984): 3–7.

55. Rogers, "Helping Employees," 5.

56. Oliver L. Niehouse, "Measuring Your Burnout Potential," *Supervisory Management* 29 (July 1984): 27–33.

57. Rogers, "Helping Employees," 4.

58. Robert L. Veninga, *The Work Stress Connection* (Boston: Little, Brown, 1981), 39–73.

59, 60. Rogers, "Helping Employees," 5. Copyright © 1984 by the College of Business Administration, Georgia State University, Atlanta. Reprinted by permission from *Business* Magazine.

61. Saul W. Gellerman, "Why 'Good' Managers Make Bad Ethical Choices," *Harvard Business Review* 64 (July–August 1986): 85.

62. Gellerman "Why 'Good' Managers," 88.

63. Hugh A. Mulligan, "Ethics Is In: From Wall Street to Madison Avenue, Ethical Standards Are Now in Demand," *Providence Journal-Bulletin*, 21 May 1989, p. B8.

64. Mulligan, "Ethics Is In," p. B8.

Chapter 8 ✎ Interviewing Confidently in Organizations

✎ *By our first strange and fatal interview . . .*

—John Donne, "On His Mistress" ✎

Seven years ago, Frank Nordo was hired at Decco Corporation after three job interviews. One day after joining the payroll, Frank was welcomed to the company during an orientation interview. Every six months thereafter, Frank sat down with his boss in performance-appraisal interviews and discussed his progress.

Soon, Frank moved into a supervisory role and began conducting such interviews himself in addition to counseling and disciplinary interviews. Occasionally, he even had to conduct exit interviews, either because Decco Corporation employees were moving on to even better jobs or because he had to inform them they were being laid off or even fired. And just this week, Frank Nordo experienced his final interview at Decco. He had accepted a job with another firm (an Asian competitor, SuperDecco Incorporated), and Frank's own exit interview was the end of seven years at Decco—years of productive work, it's true, but also seven years of interviews.

A survey by Robert Half International asked executives, "What is the most unusual thing you're aware of happening during a job interview?" Among the responses:

- He (the applicant) dozed off and started snoring during the interview.
- The candidate told me that her long-term career goal was to replace me.
- (The applicant) brought her large dog to the interview.
- She wore a Walkman and said she could listen to me and the music at the same time.
- Balding candidate abruptly excused himself. Returned to the office a few minutes later wearing a hairpiece.
- Job applicant challenged the interviewer to arm wrestle.
- (The candidate) interrupted to phone his therapist for advice on answering specific interview questions.
- (The applicant) announced she hadn't had lunch and proceeded to eat a hamburger and french fries in the interviewer's office.[1]

Interviews are a fact of organizational life. You'll usually begin your experience as part of an organization through one or more interviews. As an employee, you'll receive information on your progress in the organization through interviews, and you'll tell your supervisor how you think you're doing. As a supervisor yourself, you'll use interviews to praise, counsel, discipline, question, and even fire employees. Because interviews are omnipresent and crucial throughout modern organizational life, you should know how they work and what you can do to make them productive.

In any interview situation, you'll find opportunities to use many of the interpersonal skills we discuss in this book—skills such as speaking, listening, organizing, communicating nonverbally, and managing conflict. But no one has ever come up with a precise set of directions that will make your interviews perfect every time. Instead, you'll find your interviewing situations defined by a range of variables. Knowing about these variables and planning ahead can make your interviews more useful for *you*, your interviewing *partner*, and your *organization*. You'll also find that well-planned interviews can be pleasant and positive experiences.

THE INTERVIEW PROCESS

Interviews Defined

Interviews are conversations with a specified informational objective—not only for you and your partner but also for your organization. Although they sometimes involve several participants (for example, interviews conducted by a board or a panel), they usually occur between only two people. But whether involving two people or six, productive interviews are *purposeful* and *structured*. This means the best interviews are *prepared* and predictably *sequential*:

- We interview to achieve at least one and sometimes several specific purposes.
- We prepare both an agenda and our approach.
- We follow a structured agenda.
- We follow a fairly standard sequence of questions and answers.

Thus interviews are "prepared, structured interactions between two or more parties in which questions and answers are used to achieve relatively specific and mutually understood purposes."[2]

Interview Variables

Sometimes, especially as you start out in your organizational life, you'll find yourself the person being interviewed. You're the *interviewee*. During your college years, about the only interview that seems noteworthy is your employment interview, but throughout your life you'll find yourself in many other useful interview situations.

More and more, as you progress in experience and responsibility, you'll be in a position to interview others on behalf of your organization: You'll be the *interviewer*. Both cases carry responsibility: In the former case, it is primarily to yourself; and in the latter case, it is to your organization. This chapter discusses both cases, although often we concentrate on your role as interviewer. Understanding what an interviewer does (and why) will help you become a better interviewer, and it'll also make your occasional role as interviewee easier and more productive.

What are some of the other interviewing variables that you should be aware of?

- the *purpose* (or occasion) of the interview,
- the *stages* of the interview process, and
- the personal interviewing *styles* from which you will choose.

We've already mentioned many of the purposes served by interviews. The job interview is often called an *employment* interview. You also may participate in a broad range of interviews conducted for the purpose of appraising performance, airing grievances, counseling, disciplining, questioning, or saying farewell. We'll discuss some of these in detail later, but for now, keep these variables in mind as we discuss how to prepare and conduct an interview.

ORGANIZING THE INTERVIEW

Most interviews can be divided into four stages: planning, starting, continuing, and ending. Let's look at each stage to determine what you can do to make each interview as productive as possible.

Planning

Imagine looking at your schedule at 9:27 A.M. and realizing that at 9:30 you're to conduct an interview with a prospective employee. You know nothing about the person, except that you've heard she's from North Dakota and speaks Basque. You also remember having asked your secretary to bring you the MegaMerger file at 9:35, and you have an important board meeting at 9:45. You're tempted to reschedule the interview for the following day, but you remember that the applicant has driven three hours for this interview. What should you do?

The first bit of advice is this: Do *not* get yourself in such an awkward situation in the first place. Instead, *plan ahead.* If you are an effective interviewer, you'll get into the habit of planning each interview carefully. And each interview will be different. As you anticipate how to conduct each specific interview, you'll keep in mind the purpose of the interview, the interests and qualities of the person you're interviewing, and the best climate for a productive interview. Ask yourself, "*What* objectives do I want to accomplish in this interview?" Write out the answers so that you're sure you have reasonable and communicable expectations.

Once you've written the answers, ask yourself, "*How* can I best accomplish these objectives? What errors should I anticipate and avoid?" And learn not only from books but also from your own past. You've been in many interviewing situations before, whether with a supervisor, a subordinate, a teacher, a dean, an academic counselor, or an apartment manager. Remind yourself of your own interviewing successes and plan to capitalize on what you've learned. Remind yourself also of techniques or interchanges that weren't as successful as you would have liked and learn from them as well. Write out the answers to these questions, and use them to determine your approach, which should include the following:

- a useful *agenda,*
- an overall *strategy,* and
- the most appropriate *setting.*

Preparing an Agenda. Should you actually write out word for word what you'll say during the interview? In most cases, no. But you should plan your agenda carefully. And because the interview may take on a life of its own, your agenda is best committed to writing. What major points do you want to ask about or cover? What order will be most productive? Unless you've conducted similar interviews many times, a written agenda will be a valuable guide during the give and take of a lively interview.

> **Agenda for Performance-Appraisal Interview with Coakley**
>
> • Ask about Coakley's views on performance
> • Last month's contract negotiations: well done
> • This week's bond drive:
>   meeting held too late
>   missed Grimshaw, a key participant
> • Questions about next month's work schedule?
> • Restate key points of agreement
> • Schedule next performance-appraisal interview for 2 August

Preparing a Strategy. You will consider not only an agenda but also what strategy or approach will work best given the purpose of the interview and the person with whom you'll be talking. You should answer two questions immediately: (1) Should the interview be directive or nondirective? (2) Should it be oral or written?

1. *Directive or nondirective?* Sometimes you'll decide that the interview should be *directive*: You know exactly where you want the interview to go, what subjects you'll address, and what conclusions you'll reach. "Is the new hiring procedure working, Handel? Why or why not?" Or you may choose to be *nondirective*: You're most interested in bringing out the opinions, the personality, the character of the person you're interviewing. "How do you think your first two months here have gone, Porcaro?" You may choose to be directive or nondirective, or you may combine elements of both approaches, depending on your objectives and the interviewee's communication skills.
2. *Oral or written?* You also will decide whether the interview will be entirely *oral* or will begin with a *written* questionnaire. More and more, organizations are realizing the value of an objective, patterned (or structured) interview portion in which the answers to written questions provide a base of information about the interviewee before an oral interview. Especially in employment interviews, this technique saves time and provides consistent and necessary information that often is neglected in purely oral interviews.[3]

Preparing a Setting. You'll also decide ahead of time in what setting you'll conduct the interview. Will it be in a conference room or in your office? If in your office, will you sit behind your desk in an authoritative, business-like position, or will you move out from behind your desk and converse on relatively equal ground, sitting side by side or across a table from your interviewee?

These questions are best answered as you consider the most productive climate to establish for a particular interview. If formal authority is best and the interview will be directive, as in a disciplinary interview, then use the symbolic authority represented by the desk. But if the interview will be nondirective and involve a more open exchange of information, as in most employment interviews, then put yourself in a physical setting that promotes equality. Find a meeting place that is comfortable and private, and be sure that you can control the room for the length of the interview. If possible, have telephone calls and visitors delayed until the interview is complete.

One last point on setting: Some interviews may be conducted adequately by telephone. If being in the same room is too costly or if a face-to-face interview is unnecessary, then by all means reach out and touch your interviewee electronically.

Beginning the Interview

Interviews usually begin with two stages: building rapport and orienting the interviewee.

Building Rapport. Most conversations begin with an exchange designed to build rapport between the speakers. Much of that rapport is established through *phatic exchange*. Remember, phatic exchange is composed of the factually empty phrases and gestures we use to set each other at ease, to identify each other as people who can be trusted: for example, a smile, a handshake, or "How's it going?" or "Good morning, Stephanie." If these elements are missing at the beginning of an interview, what follows may well be strained or otherwise unproductive: "Sit down, Jones. Let me begin by asking how much longer you think you're going to be with us." If you begin an interview in this manner, then you'll have failed to establish rapport between you and your employee. As a result, Jones probably will spend more energy over the next half hour in worrying than in listening and contributing.

Rapport-building steps are important and should not evoke negative or overly authoritarian feelings. Imagine this opening:

"Come in, Jones. Sit down. And sit up. Straight. Now listen to me, and listen good. We're going to have a little relaxed interview here, see? I want you to loosen up and answer my questions straight out, no hesitation, no wasting time, no fooling around. Get me? And Jones, wipe that silly grin off your face. Interviewing is serious business. So let's get started."

How likely is Jones to contribute her own opinions or even to respond to your comments during the rest of the interview? Not likely at all. Why? Because the rapport you built was the sort found between a drill sergeant and a raw recruit. And what goes on between a sergeant and a recruit isn't usually called an interview.

The rapport you wish to build between you and your interviewing partner will vary according to your purpose. Generally, however, you'll seek to create a positive climate that encourages open communication. How? By making the interviewee feel valued and respected and by lowering the high level of tension and anxiety that may exist at the start of an interview. Your interviewee often will approach the interview anxious about the unknown and the uncontrollable. He may feel that even though much is at stake, he has little power to affect the outcome positively. These feelings restrict rather than free communication. The more you can reduce these tensions, the more information will flow and the more productive the interview will be.

You can reduce stress at the beginning of an interview by using the following techniques.

- Greet your subject with a friendly, firm handshake.
- In a direct and helpful manner, ask her to sit down.
- Engage for a moment in small talk about the weather, her trip in for the interview, or an interesting news item — all the while using a friendly tone and positive nonverbal cues such as smiles and nods.
- Make the interviewee feel welcome, and let her know that you're glad for this chance to talk about something important to both of you.

You might want to begin with something like this:

"Good morning, Miss Palumbo. How are you this morning?" (Listen closely to her reply, and follow as appropriate.) "I'm doing just great myself. How was your weekend?" (Again, listen and respond.)

Should you begin every interview this way? Certainly not. If discipline or bad news is your subject, then you had best get to the point in a more formal and authoritative manner. And sometimes too much small talk can increase people's anxiety; they're waiting for the actual interview to begin, and delay may make the wait worse. Be alert to these cases. But even in these instances, minimize stress and anxiety by treating the interviewee as you would want to be treated.

Orienting the Interviewee. Once you've established the sort of rapport you desire, move naturally to orient the interviewee to what's coming next. Let her know your objectives and how you'll seek to accomplish them through the interview. If you'll be taking notes, let the person know ahead of time that this is normal procedure. Otherwise a sudden flurry of note taking may be interpreted as writing down a mistake. In some instances you also may need to motivate the interviewee by revealing what is to be gained in the interview process.

One way to orient your interviewee is by giving him a prepared agenda well before the meeting. He thus will have time to think about his responses to the concerns that will be raised and also think through his own concerns. But be careful to leave room on the agenda for subjects the interviewee might wish to raise.

Continuing the Interview

After the rapport and orientation stages, continue with the actual work of the interview — the questions and responses, the giving and receiving of information. The climate of the interview — in fact, the actual productivity of the interview — will depend in large part on the types of questions that you ask.

Types of Questions. As you plan your interview, you'll want to take advantage of several kinds of questions, including closed, open-ended, blends of closed and open-ended, hypothetical, loaded, leading, and follow-up.

Closed questions. If you're intent on obtaining specific information or on determining the interviewee's knowledge in a narrow range of responses, then use questions that have *yes* or *no* answers or answers that are demonstrably right or wrong. For example, you might ask, "What was your previous salary?" or "Have you ever piloted a multiengine aircraft?"

Open-ended questions. If you're genuinely interested in evaluating the *person* you're interviewing rather than merely her answers, then don't ask questions easily answered *yes* or *no*, or with objectively correct answers. Instead, ask broad questions that allow the respondent freedom in determining how and what to answer. For example, ask "What are your views of our management policies?" or "Do you have any suggestions on how to improve our hiring practices?" The ultimate open-ended question perhaps is "Do you have any questions for me?"

The open-ended approach usually helps the interviewee be more relaxed, informative, and even creative. Thus you'll understand how the interviewee thinks and feels and see more clearly what she values. You'll show yourself to be interested in the interviewee as a person rather than as merely a source of right (or wrong) answers. You'll also gain more insight into the interviewee's interpersonal skills, language abilities, and even her judgment. However, keep in mind the disadvantages of open-ended questions: They take a great deal of time, require skill and insight on the part of the questioner, and often produce excess (and extraneous) information.

Blends of closed and open-ended questions. Perhaps the most normal and useful situation blends the two types of questions. If the interviewee answers your closed question, "Yes, I've piloted multiengine aircraft numerous times," then you can ask an open-ended question in response: "What's it like?" or "Why did you do it?" This blend most naturally mimics our day-to-day conversational patterns and thus best serves to put the interviewee at ease.

Hypothetical questions. If you're interested in discovering your interviewee's ability to react to a specific situation, then use a hypothetical question: "What if you had to tell an employee he was being laid off. How would you tell him?" Remember, however, that the interviewee might not actually react as he says he would. Instead, he may try to anticipate the "right" answer that you expect. But even with this disadvantage, hypothetical questions are extremely useful in prompting creative, open-ended responses, and thus in showing your interviewee's attitudes and abilities.

Loaded questions. If you're interested not in objective information but in an emotional response, then ask a loaded question — that is, one that implies a negative quality about the interviewee. Ask, for example, "What exactly are you trying to hide from us?" or "Why were you asked to leave your last job?" The interviewee may flash in anger or calmly set the record straight, and you'll have gained insight into his tendencies. Be careful, however, to use such questions carefully. They may turn off the interviewee so strongly that you'll have destroyed the rapport that is necessary for most productive interviews.

Leading questions. If you want to discover how far your interviewee will go in following your lead rather than in thinking for herself or reporting her own true responses, then ask leading questions in which the "correct" answer is strongly implied in the question: "You'd do whatever we asked you to do, right?" or "We like people here at Decco Corporation who think for themselves. You think for yourself, don't you?" Such questions, of course, usually are not particularly useful; in fact, most questioners who use them are unaware of how much they are leading their interviewees. Our advice? Be aware of this technique and consciously avoid it.

Follow-up questions. Anytime you feel that the interviewee's answers are too short, too quick, or too superficial, ask follow-up questions. Probe beneath the surface of a response by restating the part that concerns you and directing a more incisive question: "You stated that you weren't happy with Decco Corporation's approach when you were laid off last month. Exactly what was it in their approach that displeased you?"

In a less obtrusive and directive way, you might follow up with a short open-ended probe ("Really?" or "And?" or "You did?"), or even a questioning glance, a raised eyebrow, or a nod. These probes will encourage the interviewee to continue his response into areas you want to examine further.

These, then, are the major kinds of interviewing questions. And rarely will you use only one type of question in an interview. Instead, you'll find opportunities to plan a variety of question types, and sometimes you'll react to an opportunity in an unplanned but advantageous way. Knowing the range of question types will help you elicit the information you need to accomplish your objectives.

Organizing Questions. Before beginning the interview, organize the various areas or topics you want to cover. Decide what those topics are and in which order you'll introduce them. For example, you may organize by chronology, covering events that happened last year, last month, and this week before ending with a look at the next few months. Or you may organize by functional areas, cause-and-effect relationships, or a list of employee responsibilities. Whichever method you choose, however, avoid jumping back and forth from one point to another. Your interviewee is likely to become confused — and ultimately so are you.

Once you order the major areas to be covered in the interview, decide the order in which you'll ask useful questions within each area. Depending upon the effect or response you hope to elicit in a given situation, you'll have several orders to choose from, including funnel, inverted funnel, and mixed.

Funnel order. In the world of physical labor, funnels are especially useful for capturing a huge amount of splash and narrowing it down through a small opening. Likewise, in the world of interviewing, you can begin questioning with large, open-ended questions, and gradually change over to precise, closed questions — especially if your interviewee knows much or feels strongly about the subject. If you're talking to an employee about a prospective promotion, for example, then you might use the following funnel sequence of questions.

- *Open:* How do you feel about working here at Decco Corporation now that you've been here two years?
- *Less open:* What would you say were the best and worst things about working in the sparkle department of the polishing division?
- *Narrowing:* You mentioned last month that you're interested in taking on new responsibilities here. What one thing would you do to improve productivity in sparkle if we put you in charge up there?
- *Closed:* Considering the increase in both responsibility and pay, will you accept a promotion to department head?

The funnel sequence is most useful for four reasons:

1. It relaxes the interviewee and thus leads to more useful initial responses.
2. It shows the interviewee the context of the interview.
3. It allows the interviewer time to discover general information before committing to a specific line of questioning.
4. It ensures that the interviewer accomplishes a precise objective.

Inverted funnel order. The inverted funnel sequence begins with precise questions and proceeds to more general inquiries. This order is most useful when you are after general information or impressions and you know that the interviewee does not respond well to open-ended questions. Or you may find it productive when you are unable to ask general questions without first obtaining specific answers, such as in the following interview.

- *Closed:* Jim, you've had a chance to read my recommendations. Which one do you prefer?
- *Less closed:* Is that a clear-cut choice, or do I sense some reservations?
- *Widening:* Tell me why you prefer the second choice?
- *Open:* Can you point out some possibilities I haven't thought of, or some factors I haven't considered?
- *Open:* So what would you suggest we do, Jim?

The inverted funnel sequence may lead you to territory that you've not yet considered, territory that is potentially productive or possibly uncomfortable, threatening, or downright debilitating. Use the technique only when you're genuinely open to what you might hear.

Mixed order. As with most opposites, mixed orders — that is, combinations of funnel and inverted funnel questions — are not only possible but also useful. Counseling sessions often begin well with a funnel sequence and end best with an inverted funnel sequence. In that case, you may begin by focusing on open questions about human relations, move to questions of acceptable behavior, focus on a specific problem, and then end with open-ended questions to elicit the interviewee's suggestions for positive change.

You also may wish to begin with details, move to generalities, and end with specifics — a shift from inverted funnel to funnel sequences. Or you may decide that your purpose is best accomplished with one type of question all the way through the interview, either all open-ended and general or all closed and specific. But as you ponder these variations, let your objective and your knowledge of your interviewee be your guides.

....

Ending the Interview

When you've reached the end of your interview time or accomplished your purpose, then bring the interview to a close. In doing so, however, don't glance at your watch, stand, and mutter, "Well, I guess that about does it. See you later." Instead, plan your ending carefully to satisfactorily summarize, project, and close the interview.

Summarize by reviewing the interview's major points or significant accomplishments. Use the summarizing process to ensure that you've completed your agenda and that no misunderstandings remain. Be alert to signs of either disagreement or lack of understanding from your partner. If these are present and you have no time to reconsider them, then make a note to resolve these difficulties in a subsequent interview.

Project into the future by scheduling the next interview or telling the interviewee what comes next. Be explicit about times, places, and responsibilities, asking the interviewee if this information is clear or if she has any questions. If you plan to meet again but haven't decided on when and where, then be clear about who is responsible for scheduling the meeting and by what time it must be scheduled. Once again, be sensitive to possible misunderstandings and clarify when necessary.

Close with emotionally satisfying gestures — rise from your seat, offer a warm handshake, smile, and thank the interviewee for her contributions. A hasty or insincere closure may undo much of the rapport that you deliberately built early in the interview and worked so hard to maintain. So plan ahead to close with grace. Of course, if your best-laid plans break down and your interview is forced to end too abruptly, then rely on expressions of respect for your interviewee (perhaps buttressed by a touch of gentle humor) to reassure her of your appreciation and your expectations.

SPECIFIC INTERVIEW SITUATIONS

All of these variables come together differently in different interview situations, and no one set of formulas is guaranteed to produce perfect interviews. But here are our views on doing your best in several specific interview situations. We concentrate on techniques for the interviewer, because understanding them will also help you perform more successfully in the interviewee's role. But because the employment interview is so crucial for that initial position, we'll first examine your dual role as job applicant and employment interviewee.

The Employment Interview

When you're looking for a job, the employment interview is the big one, the first, the most crucial — and the most anxiety-producing. "How should I act? What should I wear? What should I know? What should I say?" These are the questions that will race through your mind as you approach the employment interview. Because this situation generates so much concern, we'll cover it thoroughly and answer these common questions in ways that will help you present your best self.

We'll also look at the employment interview from the other side. What's it like to *conduct* the interview? How can the interviewer ensure that the best person is hired?

You as Interviewee

Getting an interview. When organizations look for new employees, the application process usually is clear. The applicant applies and gains an interview by following directions and filling out the proper forms.

But when *you* are the one initiating the job search, then you must be more creative. Search through classified newspaper advertisements, contact an employment agency, use your college's or university's place-ment service, or, better yet, ask your friends and family—your *network*. Research is clear on this point: A large percentage of jobs are obtained through people you already know.[4]

Writing application letters. Many fruitful contacts are made through letters, resumés, or telephone calls—singly or in combination. An appli-cation letter should follow the general advice given in Chapter 2, "Writ-ing Effectively in Organizations" (see also the sample letter in Figure 8.1). Write as if you were speaking to the reader, but keep the tone comfortably formal. Address a specific person at the organization by name and title (a telephone call may yield this information). Your letter must tell:

- what you want
- how you know about the position
- why the reader should be interested in you
- how and when you can be reached (both your address and phone number should be included) and
- what you expect or will do to follow up the letter.

Preparing resumés. Should you put together a resumé? Yes, although don't rely on it to obtain an interview. More often than not, resumés work best as reminders to follow up an interview.[5] In constructing your resumé, you should seriously think about what you have to offer—in general, and for specific jobs and organizations. We recommend tailor-ing a resumé for each position you seek, even if it means extra typing or printing from your word processor.

Every resumé should include the following information.

- *Personal data:* At a minimum, include your name, address, and phone number(s). You may include date of birth and marital status, but only if you think it will not harm your chances.
- *Career objective:* Your career objective is the position or kind of job you're after.
- *Experience:* Organize your work experience either by previous employment or by functional areas. If by previous employment, then begin with your most recent (or current) position and work backward. Start with dates, positions held, names of orga-nizations, and then brief summaries of duties and accomplish-ments. If by functional area, then start with the most pertinent work accomplished (such as budgeting, teaching, administra-tion, or clerical) and describe briefly what you've done in that

```
            9123 Neptune Drive
            Cellophana Beach, CA  98652
            1 April 1993


            Ms. B. D. Yize, Personnel Director
            Wunderbar Advertising Associates
            667 Madison Avenue
            Los Angeles, CA  98649


            Dear Ms. Yize:


            Your colleague, Mr. James dePhurst, informed me yesterday
            that you are searching for a sales representative in your
            public-relations division. Two years as a successful sales
            representative for Esko Artichoke Farms has done much to
            prepare me for this position. I would like to talk with
            you about joining your firm.

            At Esko, I have devised new sales techniques and promo-
            tional literature that resulted in a remarkable increase
            in sales in my territory. Last year I was named the top
            sales representative in my eight-person territory and was
            recognized as Esko's Outstanding Salesperson for 1991. I
            enjoy all aspects of the work, from nurturing productive
            relationships with clients to creating computer-graphics
            packages on my personal computer.

            Could we meet this next week to discuss my qualifications?
            My schedule is flexible enough that we can meet at your
            convenience. You may reach me at work at (801) 469-1986
            or (801) 444-2325 after 6 P.M.

            Thank you for considering me. I look forward to meeting
            you soon.

            Sincerely,



            Shannon Stanley
```

Figure 8.1 Sample Application Letter

```
                          RESUMÉ
                       Shannon Stanley

9123 Neptune Drive
Cellophana Beach, California 98652
Telephone: (801) 444-2325

CAREER            Responsible career position in public
OBJECTIVE:        relations.

EXPERIENCE:
  1992—           Sales Representative, Esko Artichoke Farms,
  Present         Manurva, California. Devised sales techniques
                  and promotional literature, called on pro-
                  spective customers, processed and delivered
                  orders. Top sales rep for eight-person terri-
                  tory; named Outstanding Salesperson for 1991.

  Summers and     Waiter, Le Bistro, Newport, Rhode Island. As-
  Christmases,    sisted customers, ensured satisfaction, pro-
  1990—1992       moted special menu items, performed crucial
                  maintenance, assisted in planning menu and
                  event calendar. Named Employee of the Quarter,
                  Summer 1990.

EDUCATION:
  1992            Bachelor of Arts, University of California,
                  Major in Philosophy, Minor in Communication.
                  GPA of 3.7 on 4-point scale.
  1988            Graduated from Palmer H.S., Coralano Springs,
                  California, in top 5% of class. GPA of 4.6 on
                  5-point scale.

ACTIVITIES:       • Volunteers for Literacy in America, 1990—
                    present.
                  • Staff Writer, The Campus Conundrum, 1990–1992.
                  • Cross-country ski team, lettered two years,
                    1989–92.

COMPUTER          Graphics, word processing, data processing.
SKILLS:

REFERENCES:       Mr. John W. Flank        Dr. Randolph Hearst
                  Business Manager         Department of Psychology
                  Esko Artichokes          University of California
                  Manurva, CA 92356        Berkeley, CA 97645
                  (837) 345-8574           (746) 947-9854

                  Ms. Wilma Root           Rev. Burton C. Andrus
                  Le Bistro                First Baptist Church
                  1325 Nexus Dr.           45 Main St.
                  Newport, RI 02840        Berkeley, CA 97645
                  (401) 845-2465           (746) 941-6834
```

Figure 8.2 Sample Resumé

area. Follow with several more areas in which you think you can contribute to the organization.

- *Education:* At a minimum, list college degrees, schools, and major area of study. You also might add brief comments on grades, awards, and extracurricular activities if they add to your desirability.
- *Additional information:* Add anything that will prove your value to a prospective employer, and nothing that won't. You might include special skills (pilot, computer programming), languages, memberships, publications, patents, or honors.
- *References:* Include the names, titles, and addresses of at least three people who are willing and able to describe your effectiveness in the area at hand. But be sure they've agreed to this ahead of time.[6]

Finally, keep your resumé short and clear (see Figure 8.2). Use plenty of white space to frame your key points. And, if possible, keep it on one page: That's about all the time a busy personnel manager has.

Preparing for the interview. It's 2:30 on a Tuesday afternoon. You're sitting at the kitchen table, poring over the classified ads, listing job possibilities and checking off those you've already tried. Suddenly the phone rings, and you find yourself talking to the secretary to the personnel director for Decco Corporation. Your application was impressive, you're told, and you're being granted an employment interview at 10:30 A.M. the following Tuesday. Can you make it?

"Yes," you hear yourself say. "Tuesday at 10:30 will be fine. Thanks very much. See you Tuesday!"

If you're a bit nervous about going into this interview, the first thing we should say is welcome to the club. But there are many more things we can say — things which we think you'll find helpful as you prepare for and finally experience an employment interview.

The first bit of advice: *Plan ahead.* If Decco Corporation is your objective, then know something about the company: its product, purpose, service, history, organizational philosophy, and even its "bottom line" — its financial well-being over the past few years.

Your library is one source of up-to-date information. Another source will be printed material distributed by the organization itself, such as a public-relations booklet describing its mission and organization or an end-of-year financial report. A third source of information will be any acquaintances you have who already work for or do business with Decco Corporation. Ask what it's like to work there: What are the problems, the successes, the oddities, the major personalities, the unusual policies, the things you ought to know before going to an employment interview?

You'll also want to know something about the people who are most likely to interview you. What are their jobs, their interests, their tendencies? If you can talk with someone who already has been through an interview with these people, then ask what kinds of questions they ask, especially those that seemed difficult or would require careful thought before answering.

What else might you need to know? One embarrassingly obvious piece of information that is sometimes neglected is exactly how to get to the precise location of the interview. You may know approximately where Decco Corporation is, but unless you've asked for and been given precise directions to the room, you may end up lost with just four minutes to go. To avoid such a self-defeating prospect, know where you're going. You might even scout out the route and locate the right building (perhaps even the room) days ahead of the event, just to be sure.

In addition to knowing the company, you'll want to know as much as you can about the job you're seeking. What will you be expected to do? Have you done it before? Have you experienced similar work or done things that might prepare you for this job? Has anyone shown you a job description? If not, it's appropriate to ask for one well before your interview. One study found that although students applying for a job expect interviewers to describe the job in detail, less than half of the recruiters do so. "Conversely, recruiters expected the students to know the job description, as well as have a thorough understanding of skills and abilities routinely used on the job."[7] So investigate the job you're applying for *before* the interview.

You'll also want to know *your* objectives in seeking this job. Why do you want it? What are your short- and long-term goals? Where would you like to be a year from now? Ten years from now? What makes you particularly suited to this job? How can you contribute to the company? What puts you ahead of your competitors? What are your strengths and weaknesses? How can you best communicate these personal views so that they are both honest and positive?

Preparation is one of the most important keys to success in an employment interview. And that preparation should include not only pre-thinking but also writing and practicing. Write out some of the questions you think you might be asked, and compose answers on paper. For example, you might write the question, "Why do you want to work at Decco Corporation?" Next write your answer, or several versions of it, until you get one that feels right. Then give your answers out loud, as if you were talking with an interviewer. Better yet, practice with someone who will play the interviewer. Or you might record and listen to your answers. Throughout the preparation process, however, don't try to memorize and repeat, word for word, the "correct" answers to these questions. Instead, get used to certain words and ideas that you want to use during the interview. Feel comfortable and conversant with them, and feel confident that you know your own mind, your abilities, and your goals.

Be ready, too, for the ultimate open-ended question we mentioned earlier. The interviewer may well ask, "Do you have any questions for me?" You're better off thinking this one through well before the interview. The opportunity to respond may not come up, but if it does, a well-prepared question will communicate volumes about your attitude and abilities: "I've heard rumors that you're building a new wing on the main building. Is the company expanding?" When she hears this, the interviewer hears interest and alertness, positive qualities in any potential employee.

The morning of the interview comes all too soon, but you're mentally prepared. Now comes the more physical part of your preparation: dressing appropriately. Should you dress casually "so as not to put on airs"? Or should you wear a three-piece black suit with wingtip shoes and red tie? What's the rule?

The rule is this: Discover *beforehand* the degree of formality observed by those who work at the level for which you're applying. Observe first-hand if you can, and question others if possible. Then for the interview wear the style of clothing that your potential co-workers wear. If your potential peers at Decco Corporation wear conservative suits, then wear a conservative suit to the interview. And if you have a range of styles to choose from, then you're better off dressing just a little up than a little down. If these employees wear slacks and short-sleeve dress shirts, some with ties and some without, then wear slacks, a short-sleeve dress shirt, and a tie. After all, you're communicating your attitude toward the job just as surely by what you wear as by what you say.

Be certain to be well groomed, too. Your hair and nails ought to project an image of someone who's competent and who has a positive self-image. And yes, check your shoes. If they're not freshly shined, shine them. In every way possible you should look healthy and conscientious.

Next, be on time. Better yet—be early! Don't be obvious about it, arriving in the outer office at 7:15 for your 10:30 appointment. But if you're not sure how long it will take you to get to the appointed place or exactly how you'll find the right office, then leave home early. If you're fortunate enough to arrive an hour early, then perhaps you'll be able to spend the extra time strolling the grounds, walking the hallways, or even reading a magazine in some unobtrusive niche. But one of the worst mistakes you can make is to show up late for this first appointment. Go out of your way to anticipate any little thing that might go wrong, and prevent it by beginning your trip to the interview early.

When you arrive at the appointed place, introduce yourself and state your purpose to someone, usually a secretary or receptionist. Be sure that person has a record of your appointment and can assure you that you're in the right place. More than one applicant has been sitting in the wrong outer office well past his interview appointment time only to discover too late that he should have been on the floor above.

When you're finally shown into the room, take a deep breath, tell yourself things will go well, and walk in confidently. Follow the lead of your interviewer, but be ready to shake hands with a firm grasp, look your interviewer directly in the eye, smile, and greet her: "Good morning, Ms. Wellington. I'm glad to meet you." Remember, you've done your best to get here; now that you're here, you're genuinely *glad* to be here.

So begins the interview. You're prepared. You've thought about the organization and the role you might be able to play in it, so you're ready for the questions that might come your way.

Conduct in the interview. What about mannerisms? Posture? Eye contact? These things count, at least at the unconscious level, and often at the level of conscious observation as well.[8] Indeed, numerous studies have found a positive correlation "between nonverbal skills and assessments of confidence, assertiveness, motivation, and enthusiasm" in the employment interview.[9] So avoid irritating mannerisms such as nervously clicking a ballpoint pen over and over. Sit up attentively in your chair and occasionally lean toward your interviewer as you answer. Demonstrate your concern and your enthusiasm by your body language as well as by your oral answers. Let your face and hands speak with some degree of animation. And maintain eye contact as you answer.

Answer questions directly and honestly. Don't try to sense your questioner's lead and run with it against your better judgment. Instead, give your answers, your reactions, and your observations as truthfully and directly as you can. Why? For several reasons. First, this is the ethically correct thing to do. Second, truthfulness will lead to a better match if you're eventually hired. Finally, a skillful employment interviewer will be able to sense insincerity and opportunism fairly consistently. When sensed, they're powerful marks against you.

What should you do if you are asked illegal questions — that is, inquiries about race, sex, national origin, religion, age, or marital status? You have the right to avoid answering, but do your best to be polite when declining. For example, if asked "Are you married?" you might parry, "Is that a requirement for the job?" If you have reason to think that you were denied a job because of your answers to such questions, then you should consider seeking legal assistance.

Remember, not all questions require long answers. A few may even require only a simple *yes* or *no*, although if you sense that your questioner seeks an explanation of your initial response, give it. If you *only* answer yes or no throughout the interview, you'll be remembered as an

"Any qualifications other than being very comfortable with yourself?"

Drawing by Bernard Schoenbaum; © 1990 The New Yorker Magazine, Inc.

unimaginative and unenthusiastic prospect. So remember that yes or no generally will require some follow-up explanation.

If a question isn't clear to you, then ask the interviewer to repeat or clarify it. And don't be afraid to pause before answering complex, open-ended questions. Give yourself time to think. Studies indicate that interviewers appreciate a thoughtful answer over a quick one, even if the thoughtful one takes a bit more time.[10] Finally, when you don't know the answer to a question, say so.

If a given question leads you to respond in the direction of one of your strengths, however, and if the questions have been relatively open-ended, then move from weakness to strength. For example, your interviewer might ask you, "Have you had much experience writing reports or business letters?" This is where your preparation pays off. You know your weaknesses, and you're alert for a chance to answer by stressing your strengths. If you've had valuable experience editing and producing a newsletter in a previous job, but you haven't written extensively yourself, then you might answer, "No, although I've had extensive experience editing and producing our corporate newsletter." This answer tells the truth while giving the interviewer a lead to follow during more open-ended questioning—a lead that will allow you to elaborate one of your strengths.

Remember, in asking open-ended questions, your interviewer isn't looking merely for correct answers. Instead, there's a sense in which *you* yourself are the answer he's looking for. So look for opportunities to answer open-ended questions with your views, and answer out of your own enthusiasm, knowledge, and experience. Project your enthusiasm for this job in particular and the challenges of life in general. Yes, be yourself — but be yourself at your best. All of us project slightly different selves in different situations and to different audiences, so don't feel you're wrong to project your best self in this crucial circumstance. Project the self that's confident, caring, curious, and competent.

In Chapter 5 we discussed how to use your voice well during presentations. Many of those points are equally valid in the employment interview. For example, avoid speaking in a monotone. Instead, use natural shifts in inflection to indicate interest. Speak clearly, don't run words together, and keep your volume at a useful conversational level.

One warning: Your interviewer will evaluate you not only by *what* you say but also by *how* you say it. Most corporate employment interviewers know that intelligence, competence, composure, and fluency of speech correlate positively with favorable hiring decisions.[11] Your grammar and diction thus are seen as clues to your capabilities. So avoid such fractured speech as "Yeah, man, so the boss comes in and I'm like, 'What's yer problem, man?' and he's, y'know, like really steamed or somethin'. I mean, like I'm, like I don't get it — know what I mean?" Even though the person who can generate such creative and penetrating dialog could turn out to be a tremendous addition to the payroll at Decco Corporation, he's more likely to end up low on the list of prospective employees when the interview results are in. So avoid using slang and phatic fillers, such as "like," "man," "y'know," "um," "uh," "I dunno," and "stuff like that."

Occasionally, an employment interview occurs over lunch. If you find yourself in this situation, remember that your manners speak loudly. Posture, timing, and etiquette will prove as important as your ability to answer questions. If you find yourself in an unusual situation, go slowly and observe how others proceed before digging in yourself. One of our students found himself in a luncheon interview where artichokes were served. Artichokes were unknown in his family, and unfortunately he made a point of asking early on, "How do you eat these things? Do you cut 'em up with your knife and fork or what?" Patience would have proven a virtue, and observation would have shown him how to proceed. So go easy during dining interviews: Relax, be your best self, follow the interviewer's lead, order medium-priced and manageable items, take small bites, rest your fork on your plate between bites, and generally give priority to the interview over the eating.

Whether over a meal or in an office, when your interviewer indicates that the interview is nearing an end, ask yourself if you've left any important questions unanswered. When will you hear from the organization? Are you supposed to follow up in any way? Often you'll be given the opportunity to ask such final questions, so take advantage of that opportunity.

End much as you began: Follow the lead of your interviewer, shake hands with a firm grip, smile, and maintain eye contact. Don't merely mumble whatever comes to mind in response to the interviewer's last words ("Okay, you bet, me too. . . ."). Instead, say something thoughtful and positive during this last moment with the interviewer, and use her name as an indicator of your interest: "Thanks for this chance to talk, Ms. Wellington. I've enjoyed it, and look forward to hearing from you."

After leaving, take a few moments to review the interview. You might even jot down some of the more memorable segments while they're still fresh in your mind. Because each interview is a valuable experience, the smart job applicant learns from each one.[12] And if during the interview you promised to do something afterward, such as send the interviewer a resumé, a clipping, or an address, then make a note to do it — and by all means do it that very day.

As both a courtesy and a reminder, always send a thank you letter to the interviewer within two or three days. The letter should be short, polite, and personable.

If you don't hear from the organization in a reasonable time, or by the time mentioned, call. You're not making a pest of yourself. Instead, persistence may be seen as a virtue and, within reasonable bounds, indicates interest and commitment. Mention your interview, and courteously ask if there's any word on the results.

We've now taken you from the beginning to the end of the employment interview as if you were the interviewee. These tips will prove useful if you plan ahead and present your best self to the interviewer.

You as Interviewer. From the organization's point of view, your role as an employment interviewer is crucial. One survey of 450 managers revealed that the cost to a corporation of hiring the wrong $30,000 employee is $75,000 in wasted salary and benefits, relocation and training costs, poor service to customers, reduced morale, wasted recruitment time and money, and missed opportunities.[13]

When you conduct an employment interview, you generally have two objectives: To observe and evaluate the applicant and to introduce the organization and the job to the applicant.

Observation and evaluation. The first objective of the employment interview, observation and evaluation, extends from the personal and subjective to the professional and objective levels. At its simplest level, it calls for at least one company representative (often more than one) getting to know the applicant in person. This introduction includes observing and evaluating such subjective factors as the applicant's appearance, behavior, personality, character, and integrity. At this stage, the applicant is a potential team member. As such, one of the most important considerations is her ability to fit in, to work with the other team members as well as with the team's leadership.

The introduction also requires more objective information on the applicant's knowledge, abilities, education, experience, and attitudes. This information is difficult to obtain in the oral interview. In fact, one study has found that "in many cases interviewers take less than five minutes to determine an applicant's suitability for the job. . . . Rarely in that limited time can an interviewer determine other such vital elements of a good employee as work attitudes, motivation, skills and knowledge."[14] This vital information may be better gained through a combination of written and oral answers.

Often the applicant will answer an extensive questionnaire, sometimes computer-coded, and the answers will be correlated with organizational norms and supplied to you, the interviewer, before the actual interview. Some companies claim to cut turnover in half through the use of scored responses on such questionnaires.[15] In addition, you can ask original and open-ended questions in person, as well as follow up on uncertainties or opportunities raised in the questionnaire. At this stage you may collect personal and professional information, check the applicant's suitability for the job in terms of knowledge and temperament, and check such intangibles as motivation and perseverance. Your ultimate goal is to gain the information necessary to help you decide whether the applicant is capable of doing the job and of working well within the organization.

In a recent study of firms that have successful hiring programs — such as Hewitt Associates, which claims a 98 percent success rate — Bradford Smart identified the following nine common attributes or techniques that the best interviewers consistently use.[16]

1. *Use of better "person specifications."* Typical person specifications include little more than experience and education. More extensive (and more productive) person specifications tell what's actually required to do the job well and are based on such important variables as work habits, integrity, and interpersonal relations.
2. *Expanded use of the application form.* Job candidates can reveal much about themselves in writing. The best application forms request full salary data, require the applicant to account for every month and year since entering grammar school, demand

names and titles of all immediate supervisors, and lead the applicant to believe that the hiring organization will check out these claims thoroughly.

3. *In-depth interviews of finalists.* To clarify questions or confirm suspicions by testing beliefs about each candidate, they are interviewed in-depth. Productive interviews go far beyond a mumbled "So, tell me about yourself" and fifteen minutes of banter. In fact, three to four hours of well-planned probing may well be required to find precisely the right person for the job.

4. *Use of a matrix interview format.* A matrix format combines questions about chronological history with specifically focused questions about all person specifications such as work habits, management style, interests, and goals. Only such a conscientiously designed format can reveal the sorts of breakdowns and inadequacies in an applicant's past that ordinarily will evade discovery.

5. *Use of an interview guide.* An interview guide uses precisely worded questions and enough space in which the interviewer can write responses and impressions. You will be able to keep a record of each interview, and different interviews will be easier to compare over time.

6. *Improved record checking.* Follow-up record checking includes telephone calls to previous supervisors. Based on the results of your guided interview, ask for both general comments on and specific examples of the applicant's strengths and weaknesses.

7. *Use of the threat-of-records-check (TORC) technique.* According to Bradford Smart, the TORC technique is "a powerful method for motivating selection candidates to tell the whole truth." If you ask for permission to contact each past supervisor and ask the candidate to set up the calls, then you've created the impression that you'll be checking things carefully. You then can expect more honest answers to the basic TORC question: "What is your best guess as to what your supervisor truly felt were your strengths, overall performance, and shortcomings?"

8. *Thorough training of interviewers.* By thoroughly training its interviewers, an organization can ensure that it avoids the following:
   • showing bias or prejudice, or relying on stereotypes;
   • giving too much weight to first impressions;
   • hiring in one's own image;
   • biasing responses;

- succumbing to halo effects ("He's from IBM? Say, he really looks good!") or order effects ("Last is best");
- projecting change;
- failing to quantify;
- losing control of the interview; and
- asking illegal questions (where race, sex, national origin, religion, age, or marital status is probed).

Such training might take the form of two-day workshops with instruction, practice, and feedback on what does and does not work.

9. *Organizational reinforcement of professionalism in selection.* By systematically supporting selection interview training and rewarding those personnel who interview correctly and productively, an organization reinforces a high level of professionalism.

These techniques reinforce the first of the two objectives of employment interviews: to observe and evaluate the applicant.

Introducing the organization. The second objective of the employment interview is to introduce the organization and the position to the applicant. The employment interview often is accompanied by a tour of the facilities and a chance for the applicant to see potential teammates in action. As the interviewer, you ensure that the applicant has the opportunity to ask you any questions he may have about the organization — its history, plans, policies, problems, and benefits. By answering such questions honestly and thoroughly, you will ensure a happy match if the applicant does join the organization.

The Performance-Appraisal Interview

The performance-appraisal interview is another common event in any organization that values effective communication. Unfortunately, it's often neglected. Either it's not being done properly or, worse yet, it's not being done at all. Yet this interview can cement positive employee–supervisor relations, enable more effective day-to-day communications, and lead to a more productive communication climate throughout the entire organization — all of this in addition to clarifying and adjusting your working arrangements.

One of the most important fundamentals of successful management is ensuring that you communicate your views to your subordinates, and that they have a channel to let you know their views, including their reactions to your views. In the performance-appraisal interview, you evaluate a subordinate's job performance and discuss that evaluation with her. This interview is prepared and conducted more formally than the more frequent and perhaps daily exchanges of information that occur. In many organizations, this interview is scheduled once or twice a year, but sometimes can be as often as every three months.

Although the format that you'll use will vary according to your organization's needs and its corporate culture, certain constants emerge. In fact, this is your opportunity to:

- let your subordinates know what you think of their performance,
- discover your subordinates' views of their performance,
- praise and encourage positive trends,
- point out desired changes,
- strengthen organizational commitment,
- point out opportunities for advancement, and
- keep a record of progress over time.

Positive rapport is vital to the performance-appraisal interview. Seek to establish an open and affirming climate in the rapport-building stage and keep that climate constant throughout the interview.

Structure, as well as good will, should be apparent. In the orientation stage, let the interviewee know what's coming. Begin with strengths, move to areas that need improvement, and end with positive expectations. A day or two before the interview, you may do well to give your interviewee a list of areas you plan to cover. And often the performance-appraisal interview is based on a written performance report that becomes part of the employee's permanent record. Thus, it may be constructive to give your subordinate a copy of the written report well before the interview and to use it as a foundation for what follows.

Choosing what you say will be important, but just as crucial is encouraging the interviewee to contribute. Avoid the following sorts of mistakes that discourage a subordinate's participation.

Mistake. Some interviewers talk too much, rarely soliciting input from the subordinate. Such an event is less an interview than a pep talk; it may inform, direct, and evaluate, but it does not inquire.

Fix. Give the interviewee plenty of opportunities to talk. Ask questions. Get her opinions on the job, her performance, her future. Encourage depth in her answers. Don't jump in whenever you sense a second of silence: Let your interviewee think and respond at her own rate.

Mistake. Some interviewers ask only direct, closed questions to draw out specific answers: "Did you meet your production quota last month?" Closed questions fail to solicit the interviewee's opinions, and they pass up opportunities to uncover valuable truths.

Fix. Ask open-ended questions to underscore your observations but base them on the interviewee's perceptions: "What were some of the bright spots for you over this past six months?"

Mistake. Some interviewers fail to ask follow-up questions that probe beneath superficial or sensitive answers.

Fix. Listen carefully for opportunities to move into areas on your agenda. If your interviewee mentions in passing the name of someone with whom you know he's been in job-related conflict recently, then follow up with a probe: "Jill—she's working with you on the Anchovy project, isn't she? I understand the two of you have had a few problems. . . ."

Mistake. Some interviewers are intimidating and rely overtly on authority, while others are cold and unresponsive in what they say as well as by how they act.

Fix. Get out from behind your desk. Smile—and mean it. Value your subordinate not only for his contribution to your organization but also for his own intrinsic worth. Use some of the facial animation and active gestures that you rely on in less formal conversations.

Mistake. Perhaps the worst interviewers are those who treat the interview as a waste of time, a duty to be accomplished as quickly and painlessly as possible: "Okay, Staley, sit down. It's that time of the year again. Let's get it over with."

Fix. Realize how truly important this interview is for the organization, for the interviewee, and ultimately for you. Without these exchanges, you lack an important avenue for motivating and directing your subordinates based on mutual observations and interaction. And you don't know how they're reacting to the challenges of their jobs or the adequacy of your leadership. Because performance-appraisal interviews are opportunities for direction, recognition, and growth, treat them with respect and even anticipation—and talk that way: "Come on in, Staley. I've been looking forward to this meeting for quite awhile now, because it will give us both a chance to. . . ."

What sorts of problems will you run into on the part of the interviewee?

- Some interviewees may be shy, quiet, and overly respectful. Your challenge is to help them open up by giving them time to answer nonthreatening open-ended questions.
- Some interviewees may be happy, self-confident, and overly talkative. These you'll want to encourage without losing control of the interview. Let such a person know when it's time to move on to a new subject, but do so tactfully.
- Some interviewees may be bluntly honest, concerned, and assertive. Don't be put off by this strength, and don't mistake it for insubordination. Listen, evaluate, and watch for your own potentially defensive reactions.
- Some interviewees may be truly insubordinate, or have an ax to grind. With these sorts (and they're few and far between in our experience), be firm and honest. Let them know directly and honestly what sorts of responses are counterproductive and direct them to more positive behavior. If unacceptable behavior continues, it's time to document it — write about what you've observed and place it in their file — and counsel them on the alternatives.

Throughout the performance-appraisal interview, remember that people learn something best when they discover it for themselves. Try to guide your interviewees into realizations rather than simply tell them what you think.

The Grievance Interview

The employee in a grievance interview has an opportunity to express a complaint or a grievance to someone higher in the organization. If you're the employee, this is your chance to formalize what might previously have been unspoken, or at least unheard, dissatisfaction. If, on the other hand, you're the supervisor, then look upon the grievance interview as a chance to gather healthy information that is useful to both the organization and you as a manager. You also can see this event as a healthy release of what might otherwise grow into pent-up resentment, or even anger, over some event or policy not previously acknowledged by the organization. Such a release is important, because repressed or unexpressed dissatisfaction is unlikely to go away on its own; instead, it probably will show itself in substandard work, poor morale, and an increasing number of similar problems.

The grievance interview is an opportunity for positive change, but both sides must be careful not to personalize the grievance — sometimes a difficult challenge. Both the employee and the supervisor should keep to the central issue and avoid name calling, defensive arguing, and recriminations. And even though both sides want the problem solved in the end, an immediate solution isn't mandatory. Indeed, unless the grievance involves an obvious and easily corrected misunderstanding, the best policy may be mutual agreement that the interview will air the grievance rather than correct it immediately. If both sides are given a chance to state their positions, if both sides hear the other's point of view, then the interview has provided the first opportunity for the release of pent-up anger and the search for corrective action.

The Counseling Interview

Sometimes employees come to the supervisor not to complain but to ask for help. Family problems, personal disappointments, career uncertainties, romantic reversals — these are among the reasons why an employee may seek you out as a surrogate parent. In such spontaneous counseling interviews, be careful not to take on more than you are capable of handling. For example, if you are not a trained marriage counselor but act like one, then you may create problems for your employee, yourself, and your organization. Often the best course in such cases is to listen carefully and sympathetically and then propose that the subordinate seek professional help from a minister, psychologist, or other professional.

Often, however, the counseling interview is a grievance interview in reverse. Here the supervisor, in the role of "counselor," tells the employee of long-term personal practices or attitudes that the employee needs to change for the good of both the organization and the employee. Drug abuse, alcoholism, health or family problems, absenteeism, tardiness, and chronic errors are all frequent subjects of counseling interviews. But no matter what the problem, the objective of the counseling interview is twofold: to help the employee solve his problem and help the organization avoid the negative consequences of the employee's problem.

To counsel employees effectively, the supervisor (and as a foundation, the leadership of the organization itself) must believe these basic tenets:

1. People can change for the better.
2. Counseling is an investment.
3. Counseling involves learning.

4. Counseling involves confrontation.
5. The counselee has inherent self-worth.
6. Counseling takes time.
7. Counseling varies in effectiveness.[17]

Maurice Brown has identified four basic tenets that are necessary for counseling to be effective:

1. Individuals learn those things that they discover for themselves.
2. As adults, individuals must be responsible for their own behavior.
3. When facing a problem, the person must be committed to solving it.
4. Commitment to solving the problem increases when the person is involved in the problem solving.[18]

Given these four tenets, Brown has identified the following four stages in the counseling process:

1. Identify the problem
2. Check commitment
3. Solve the problem
4. Follow up the solution

Stage 1: Identify the Problem. Identifying the problem involves helping the employee identify and articulate not merely the problem but also its *causes*. To put these causes into words, use the following techniques.

1. *Empathetic response:* The counselor reflects the employee's words and emotions.
2. *Paraphrase:* The counselor restates or paraphrases the employee's words.
3. *Open-ended statement or question:* The counselor solicits more information.
4. *Pauses:* The counselor allows the employee time to reflect.
5. *Nonverbal acknowledgment:* The counselor encourages the employee to talk by sympathetic looks or gestures.

Stage 2: Check Commitment. If the employee demonstrates little or no commitment to solving the problem, then the counselor should ask questions that reveal the negative consequences of continuing business as usual. For example, if the employee has not taken steps previously suggested or has stated that the problem doesn't really seem worth worrying about, then the counselor might ask, "What will happen to you if this problem persists?" and "How will you feel if we're forced to take these steps?" These questions don't demand immediate answers, and the counselor wisely gives the employee time to reflect before counseling continues in a later session. But when the answers do come out, the level of employee commitment should be more apparent.

If the employee shows insufficient commitment after these checks, it's time to consider removing the employee from the organization. If, however, the employee shows some commitment to solving the problem, then the counselor should move on to the next stage.

Stage 3: Solve the Problem. Conceivably, the counselor could dictate a solution to the employee. According to the tenets stated earlier, however, the problem will be resolved more effectively if the employee is involved in generating, evaluating, and selecting alternative corrections. Thus the counselor might take the following steps:

1. Ask questions that will prompt the employee to suggest possible solutions and finally choose one that might work.
2. Be sure that both parties understand the alternative that is finally selected.
3. Be sure that the selection is accepted as an action plan — something that can be accomplished and observed.

Stage 4: Follow Up the Solution. The counselor must let the employee know that they will meet again at a specified time to review the results of their action plan. If the situation has improved, then praise or some other observable reward is in order. If the situation has not changed or has deteriorated further, then the next meeting must once again emphasize the problem and its consequences.

If the overall counseling process works, expect one of two changes: Either the supervisor sees the desired behavioral change or the employee moves to another position — or even to another organization.

The Disciplinary Interview

Generally, disciplinary interviews focus not on long-term problems but on specific violations of organizational norms. The common view is that disciplinary interviews are invariably bitter and distasteful, involving anger, harsh words, punishment, resentment, hatred, and perhaps even violence.

Despite these images, discipline is necessary for the effective operation of any organization—and it need not be the negative discipline we've just described. In his book, *Positive Discipline*, James Black describes a much more constructive and educational force at work within an organization, whether a family, school, or business:

> Discipline should be a constructive, positive force that enables people to work together harmoniously. Consider the word affirmatively and its full meaning becomes evident. Discipline to the scholar is a field of study which, if mastered, hardens or toughens the mind. The football coach refers to a championship team as "well-disciplined," meaning that it executes its plays with precision and skill. A highly trained regiment of soldiers is proud of its reputation for being disciplined; to the soldiers, discipline means that everybody knows his job and each individual works cooperatively with the group to carry out orders.[19]

Although discipline may involve punishment, it is not merely punishment. It also is an attempt to ensure order in the organization and reliability in the employee. A supervisor may discipline an employee for one or more reasons: to be just, to protect employees, to protect proper procedures, to deter future problems, and to demonstrate responsibility.[20] But for whatever reason, the supervisor should follow these guidelines when conducting a disciplinary interview:

1. Make instructions simple and understandable.
2. Know the rules.
3. Move in promptly on violations.
4. Get all the facts.
5. Discipline only in private.
6. Remain calm.
7. Permit the employee an opportunity to explain.
8. Decide what penalty suits the error.
9. Implement disciplinary action clearly and concisely.
10. Keep a record of what has happened.[21]

Disciplinary interviews may be rare, but they are important events in the life of any organization and any supervisor—as you'll discover further in Chapter 10. Prepare for them as carefully as for any of the other interview types we've discussed, and you'll find them manageable and productive.

The Exit Interview

Exit interviews assist both the person leaving and the organization. Vital financial and personnel procedures can be completed more efficiently with the employee. In addition, the organization can gain information that is potentially useful in promoting better personnel policies. In learning why some people leave, the organization may adopt hiring policies that ensure a lower turnover rate in the future. Or current procedures that promote employee dissatisfaction may be revised. Finally, careful notes on the employee's stated reasons for leaving may prove useful if a controversy arises later.

CHAPTER SUMMARY

Interviews occur regularly in organizations for many different reasons: to *hire, appraise, praise, counsel, discipline, question*, and even *fire* employees. In each case, an interview is a *prepared, structured interaction* between two or more parties in which *questions and answers are used to achieve a relatively specific and mutually understood purpose.*

You may be the *interviewer* or the *interviewee*. Each role calls for preparation. Other interviewing variables include the *purpose* of the interview, the *stages* of the interview process, and the personal interviewing *style* you choose.

Effective interviews begin with careful planning, which includes an *agenda*, a *strategy*, and an appropriate *setting*. The actual interview may be viewed as having three stages: beginning, middle, and end. The beginning includes two goals: *building rapport* and *orienting the interviewee*. The actual substance of the interview includes the use of *closed, open-ended, hypothetical, loaded, leading*, and *follow-up* questions that are organized by topic areas and follow *funnel, inverted funnel*, or *combination* sequences. End the interview by *summarizing, projecting*, and *closing*.

MEASURING SUCCESS

1. You've just been granted an appointment for an employment interview with your dream organization. The appointment is at 10:30 A.M. one week from today. Make a chronological list of all the steps you'll take to prepare for the interview.

2. Imagine that you're the personnel director of a successful corporation that manufactures and sells games and toys. You are preparing to conduct a series of employment interviews with recent college graduates for entry-level positions in marketing. Put together a list of four general questions you feel would help you select the best new employee.

3. As a recent college graduate, you recently applied for a job with the organization in Exercise 2. Write your answers to each question; when you're done, read them aloud to yourself. How do they sound? Next, give these answers out loud without reading them so they sound natural and unrehearsed.

4. As a mid-level manager in a fairly large corporation, you decide to initiate performance-appraisal interviews with your seven subordinates. The question you're considering is this: How often should you hold these interviews? Once a year? Once a week? What factors would you consider as you make this decision?

5. Label each of the following questions as *open-ended, closed, hypothetical, loaded, leading,* or *follow-up.* In an employment interview, would any of them be illegal?

a. Why were you asked to leave your last position?
b. With how many other corporations have you applied?
c. If your boss asked you to falsify your time card so that your unit would look better on the quarterly report, what would you do?
d. What's the best way to handle our current deficit?
e. What happened then?
f. We believe that our employees should contribute each year to the United Way. In fact, *all* of us contribute. Would you be willing to join us in helping this worthy cause?
g. What religious holidays do you observe?

6. You've scheduled a performance-appraisal interview with a relatively new member of your organization. She's painfully shy—so shy that last time you sat down to converse with her, she only answered questions, usually in one or two word responses. But you sense that behind her shyness is an intelligent, capable, and concerned person. How will you plan this interview to ensure that she gains as much as possible from your appraisal of her performance?

7. Which of these beliefs is most crucial in ensuring successful counseling interviews? Which is least important? Rank all seven and defend your choices.

a. People can change for the better.
b. Counseling is an investment.
c. Counseling involves learning.
d. Counseling involves confrontation.
e. The counselee has inherent self-worth.
f. Counseling takes time.
g. Counseling varies in effectiveness.

 Decco Exercise The boss has asked you to interview someone in a local organization about her interviewing practices. What kinds of interviews are conducted in this organization? What are the rules or procedures? What kinds of problems are encountered? Write a brief report that summarizes the results of your interview.

....

Notes

1. "Don't Forget Your Rug," *The Providence Journal-Bulletin*, 4 August 1989, p. D1. Reprinted by permission of Robert Half International.

2. Patricia Hayes Bradley and John E. Baird, Jr., *Communication for Business and the Professions*, 3rd ed. (Dubuque, IA: Wm. C. Brown, 1986), 157–158.

3. Douglas D. Rogers, "Computer-Aided Interviewing Overcomes First Impressions," *Personnel Journal* 66 (May 1984): 148–152.

4. Joseph McKendrick, "Your Next Job — Are You Ready?" *Career Strategies Survey* (Willow Grove, PA: Association for Management Success, 1987).

5. Richard Nelson Bolles, *What Color is Your Parachute: A Practical Manual for Job Hunters and Career Changers* (Berkeley, CA: Ten Speed Press, 1989), 150–159. Annual editions of this book are

among the most imaginative and useful guides to job hunting that we've run across.

6. Adapted from Cal W. Downs, G. Paul Smeyak, and Ernest Martin, *Professional Interviewing* (New York: Harper & Row, 1980), 148–152; Richard P. Shemetulskis, "Selling You," *Career Strategies Survey* (Willow Grove, PA: Association for Management Success, 1987); Richard C. Huseman et al., *Business Communication: Strategies and Skills*, 2nd ed. (Chicago: Dryden, 1985), 555–567; Artie Adams Thrash et al., *Communication in Business and the Professions: Speaking Up Successfully* (New York: Holt, Rinehart & Winston, 1984), 80–82.

7. Donna Bogar Goodall and H. Lloyd Goodall, Jr., "The Employment Interview: A Selective Review of the Literature with Implications for Communications Research," *Communication Quarterly* 30 (September 1982): 116–122.

8. Keith G. Rasmussen, Jr., "Nonverbal Behavior, Verbal Behavior, Resume Credentials, and Selection Interview Outcomes," *Journal of Applied Psychology* 69 (4) (1984): 551–556.

9. Goodall and Goodall, "The Employment Interview," 119.

10. J. G. Hollandsworth, R. C. Glazeski, and M. E. Dressel, "Use of Social Skills Training in the Treatment of Extreme Anxiety and Deficient Verbal Skills in the Job Interview Setting," *Journal of Applied Behavior Analysis* 11 (1978): 259–269.

11. Goodall and Goodall, "The Employment Interview," 119.

12. H. D. Tschirgi, "What Do Recruiters Look For?" *Journal of College Placement* 33 (December 1972–January 1973).

13. Bradford D. Smart, "Progressive Approaches for Hiring the Best People," *Training and Development Journal* 41 (September 1987): 46.

14. Rogers, "Computer-Aided Interviewing," 148.

15. Michael W. Mercer and John J. Seres, "Using Scorable Interview 'Tests' in Hiring," *Personnel* 64 (June 1987): 57–60.

16. Smart, "Progressive Approaches," 46–53.

17. Adapted from Downs et al., *Professional Interviewing*, 190–193.

18. Maurice Brown, "Counseling Skills," *SAM Advanced Management Journal* 5 (Winter 1986): 32–35.

19. James Black, *Positive Discipline* (New York: American Management Association, 1970), 27.

20. Downs et al., *Professional Interviewing*, 217–218.

21. Adapted from Jane Whitney Gibson and Richard M. Hodgetts, *Organizational Communication: A Managerial Perspective* (Orlando, FL: Academic Press, 1986), 347.

Chapter 9 ✐⊷ **Communicating**

and Leading in Small Groups

✍ *One either meets or one works. One cannot*

do both at the same time. — Peter Drucker ✍

Meetings! Meetings! Meetings! To say that

communicating in groups is likely to con-

sume large amounts of your time as an organi-

zational communicator is an understatement.

Organizations abound with committees, conferences, quality circles, action teams, task forces, staff meetings, department meetings, function meetings — you name it. Every day, 11 million meetings are held in the United States alone. Worldwide, conservative estimates stand at 50 million meetings.[1]

Just how much time can you expect to devote to this pervasive, necessary, and yet potentially productive activity? Consider the following statistics. If you make it to the top, as a typical corporate executive you will spend approximately twenty-one 40-hour work weeks each year in meetings, or seventeen hours of each work week, for a total of 852 hours per year! Or moving down the ranks, many nonexecutives — entry-level, mid-level, and upper-level managers, for example — easily devote 50 percent to 80 percent of their time to meetings.[2]

With all of this frenetic activity, you might think that meetings must be an efficient way to do business. Wrong! Meetings are the most costly communication activity occurring in organizations — more so than the millions of long-distance telephone calls made, the countless letters, reports, and memos sent out, or the thousands of expensive computer systems installed. A dozen well-paid people sitting around a conference table for two hours can easily total $1,000 or more. Now multiply that figure by the statistics we just gave you: If a company of 6,000 employees holds only 1,000 meetings per year, then costs can climb well beyond the $1 million mark![3]

If meetings aren't necessarily efficient, their widespread use must be attributed to the fact that meetings are the most effective means of communicating in organizations. Right? Wrong again! In one of the studies we noted above, executives pronounced 29 percent of the meetings that fill those twenty-one work weeks per year to be wasteful or unnecessary.[4] The average meeting in the United States is a staff meeting that takes place in a company conference room, begins at 11 A.M. with only two hours' notice, has no written agenda distributed in advance, uses handouts, involves nine people, and lasts approximately two hours.[5] If you've ever been a member of a student government task force, served on a sorority or fraternity committee, or participated in a class work group, then chances are that you can identify with the sentiments expressed in the quotation that opened this chapter.

But what about group communication at its best? Although executives rated 29 percent of their meetings as unnecessary and wasteful, the remaining 71 percent must have been productive. Our job here is to increase that percentage for you by expanding your knowledge, improving your skills, and thereby heightening your productivity as a group communicator throughout your career. In this chapter, we'll focus on the

> "People can be motivated to be good not by telling them that hell is a place where they will burn, but by telling them it is an unending committee meeting. On judgment day, the Lord will divide people by telling those on His right hand to enter His Kingdom and those on His left to break into small groups."
> — The Reverend Robert Kennedy

problem-solving process that should take place in groups, the group roles you'll assume in committees and meetings, and the responsibilities of group leadership.

PROS AND CONS OF GROUP COMMUNICATION IN ORGANIZATIONS

Just why is group communication so pervasive in business and the professions? Let's analyze the situation in more detail.

Advantages of Communicating in Groups

Groups Generate More and Better Solutions. One definite advantage of group communication is that groups are more likely to find solutions than are individuals, all other things being equal. If a problem-solving group within your organization is working to find a more cost-effective way to produce toothbrushes, then hearing others' ideas may trigger your own, possibly snowballing everyone toward a workable solution. Of course, if you alone are the company's toothbrush production expert, then you may come to a better solution entirely on your own and in less time. However, many studies demonstrate that two (or more) heads are often better than one, not only for generating ideas but also for critically evaluating alternatives.

Groups Have Built-In Buy-In Power. Another advantage groups have over individual contributions is the "buy-in" power of collaboration. Research (and our own experience) demonstrates that all of us are more likely to accept a solution that we have helped generate. Think back to your high school days, for example. You probably were more likely to abide by a curfew or adhere to an allowance if you helped establish these guidelines than if they were imposed on you by your parents, right? The same principle holds true in organizational settings. If a company's leadership wants its employees to abide by new safety guidelines, then a task force of representatives should be convened to propose them.

Groups Provide Opportunities to Display Skills. Group communication has many other distinct advantages. The group is an opportune way for you to display your competence and commitment to the organization. In his classic book, *The Organization Man*, William H. Whyte, Jr., makes the following bold assertion:

> For a young man [or woman] . . . on the [move], there is no better vehicle than the conference way. Where fifty years before he might have had to labour unseen by all but his immediate superior, now via the conference he can expose himself to all sorts of superiors across the line of command. Given minimum committeemanship skills, by an adroit question here and modest suggestion there, he can call attention to himself and still play the game.[6]

With more than "minimum committeemanship skills" (we hope), the contributions you make in meetings display your communication competence and your job expertise to superiors, peers, and subordinates. For this reason, learning about group communication now may give you an important edge when you arrive on the job.

Groups Help Meet Social Needs. Because most of us are social animals, group communication is enjoyable; it helps meet our "high-touch" needs. While sitting around a conference table, coffee cups in hand, you and other group members have the opportunity to offer support to one another. When you affirm someone else's ideas, offer public praise for a job well done, or provide thanks for contributed time and talent on a particular task, you not only solidify interpersonal relationships but also, in the real world of negotiation and bargaining, build up "credits" for such displays of support and encouragement from others when you need them to reciprocate.[7]

Groups Are a Good Way to Test the Waters. One of the primary functions of groups is allowing for the flow of information among individuals. This basic function, however, is more complex than it may seem. You might say that groups provide two types of information, one relating to ideas and the other to people and personalities. For example, you might present to the group an idea that is just beginning to jell in your mind and determine others' reactions before you commit yourself in a formal, written proposal. You can observe their actions, assess their communication styles, and watch for positive and negative signals. The context is rich with interpersonal cues, as well as useful facts and figures.[8]

Groups Are Adaptable Problem-Solving Tools. Today's best-run organizations are characterized as "adhocracies" in which small groups serve as the "chunking devices" that break up the work load and move the organization toward action. Just what is an "adhocracy"? The best way to understand the term may be to contrast it to our traditional understanding of a "bureaucracy."

A bureaucracy is a formal organizational structure that has been established to deal with day-to-day business. It's the paperwork, the red tape, the hierarchical levels you wade through when you're trying to apply for a permit or resolve a mistakenly received parking ticket. By comparison, an "adhocracy"—coming from the Latin term *ad hoc* ("toward this" or "for this special purpose")—is characterized by adaptability.

> You can't wander around long in the [Hewlett Packard] Palo Alto facilities without seeing lots of people sitting together in rooms with blackboards, working casually on problems. Any one of those ad hoc meetings is likely to include people from R&D [research and development], manufacturing, engineering, marketing, and sales.[9]

An ad hoc group is a temporary one formed in response to a short-term problem. At its worst, an adhocracy is pure pandemonium if no one knows who's responsible for what. At its best, however, an adhocracy deals efficiently with new issues or ambiguous issues that fall between the cracks. Evidently, today's best-run companies have mastered the use of small groups, particularly ad hoc task forces, as problem-solving tools.[10]

Disadvantages of Group Communication

Groups Are Prolific Time-Eaters. On the negative side, group communication is sometimes boring, always time-consuming, and generally overused as a problem-solving device. Some tasks require the collaborative input of many participants; others, however, are better accomplished by the swift action of a single person. But many companies pay little attention to the most appropriate communication medium to solve a particular problem. Every issue goes to a committee or task force.

Groups Sometimes Bring Out the Worst in People. Even skillful communicators sometimes fall into ineffective patterns in group settings. Such patterns include the roles played in groups, the effects of groupthink, the results of distributed responsibilities, and the negative effects of conflict.

Communication Styles and Group Roles. Some potential problems in groups emerge from the personalities and communication styles of the people involved. Members may not speak up because they are legitimately shy or easily intimidated by other more powerful and verbally aggressive people. Some members have fragile egos that don't respond well to perceived negative signals from those who may disagree with them. And noncommunicators aren't the only problem; overcontributers are equally troublesome. Nervous chatterers, domineering personality types, and group members with inflated egos may make participation in the group a less-than-satisfying experience for others.

Groupthink. A second threat to productive communication is *groupthink*, a phenomenon that occurs when a group is composed of people who think the same way and avoid controversy. Groupthink can seriously damage the quality of a group's decisions. Watch out for the following characteristics of groupthink:

- *believing the group is invulnerable.* "Decco Corporation is miles ahead of its competitors. We can raise our rates on windsurfing equipment and still remain number one in the marketplace because of who we are."
- *discounting negative information.* "The sales projections are probably inaccurate just like they were once back in 1988. Let's move full steam ahead on the new Model III Windsurfer."
- *ignoring ethical considerations.* "Let's not worry about possible lawsuits if buyers have problems assembling the new model. The production teams are ready to roll. Let's face it—we can waste a lot of valuable time worrying about every possible problem."
- *creating negative stereotypes of competitors.* "Those duds at Sportscrafters Corporation could never come up with a design this elegant and sophisticated."
- *pressuring dissenters.* "You may have a point, Bob, but the rest of us have already thought that one through, and we're convinced that advertising our new line of windsurfing equipment on cable TV will work. You don't want to be the odd man out, do you? How about it?"
- *remaining silent rather than voicing opposition.* Thinking "I probably shouldn't bring up a similar situation at Sportscrafters Cor-

poration in which they were forced to pay out $650,000 to a customer who crashed on the rocks. Their equipment probably had a number of flaws other than the jammed compass that showed up on our test model."

- *believing that unanimity exists within the group.* Thinking "I must be the only one with doubts. Everyone else seems convinced that we've got nothing to lose."
- *acting as mindguards to protect the group from negative information.* Taking Fred aside: "Listen, Fred, you may have some good ideas about caution on this project, but the last thing the group needs now is a wet blanket. We've been working on these plans for eight months, and the chairman needs everyone's support."[11]

The path of history is paved with the perilous results of groupthink, including such disasters as Pearl Harbor, the Bay of Pigs, and Vietnam. Presidential cabinets or groups of military leaders who think in similar ways without challenging one anothers' ideas sometimes have made monumental mistakes that have affected the lives of thousands of people.

One way to avoid the threat of groupthink is to appoint one member as "devil's advocate" to continually challenge the group's thinking. Or invite an outsider who is likely to have a more objective view. Another alternative is to assign a problem to two or more decision-making groups simultaneously and compare notes after they have reached a conclusion. As part of your overall strategy to avoid groupthink, take it upon yourself as either group leader or group member to encourage objections and a realistic point of view.[12]

Distributed Responsibility. Responsibility for the group's actions may fall on no one individual. Such distributed responsibility may result in several problems. It may generate risky decisions, or it may simply lead to apathy and inaction.

The *risky shift* effect in groups is well documented.[13] Individuals in group settings sometimes will opt for more extreme points of view than would each individual on her own. Because the decision belongs to the group collectively, no one person risks her personal reputation when and if things go wrong. In an organization, a risky decision may well mean a costly mistake that translates into big financial losses — proceeding with a risky new product based on overly optimistic sales projections, for example.

On the other hand, distributed responsibility throughout the group may lead to a *sense of apathy* when volunteers for a group task are solicited: "Let someone else do it; I'm already busy enough." If everyone develops this attitude, then the group will stagnate into oblivion, and the organization will end up wasting valuable time and brain power. Or the few people who care about the group's success will shoulder all the responsibility and eventually experience burnout.

Conflict. Finally, groups sometimes factionalize, form coalitions, and accomplish little because of excessive internal conflict. At a cost of $1,000 or more per meeting, organizations can suffer large losses of time and money when groups stagnate or deadlock over disagreements about the proper course of action.

Despite these weaknesses, organizations do solve many of their problems through meetings, primarily because of the advantages we've identified. For example, a marketing department's decision on whether to introduce a new product six months ahead of schedule inevitably will involve representatives from engineering, manufacturing, and sales. The complex problems that face organizations often call for more expertise than any one person has.

STEPS IN THE PROBLEM-SOLVING PROCESS

> *When we've got a big problem here, we grab ten senior guys and stick them in a room for a week. They come up with an answer and implement it.* — Senior executive at Digital Equipment Corporation[14]

To help groups solve problems efficiently, a variety of schemes have been prescribed. Many of these are based on John Dewey's approach to rational thinking, which was published early this century.

Dewey's Reflective-Thinking Model

According to Dewey, six specified steps will lead to the best possible solution. Although it's important to remember that no one prescription will work for every situation, Dewey's model of reflective thinking appears to work reasonably well in cases having a limited number of solutions.[15] Of the several variations around, here's the one we prefer:

Step 1. A problem is felt or expressed.
Step 2. The problem is clearly defined.
Step 3. The problem is analyzed.

Step 4. Possible solutions are put forth.

Step 5. Solutions are compared by testing each one against established criteria, and the best solution then is selected.

Step 6. The best solution is implemented.[16]

Let's examine Dewey's model in a case based on one of our consulting experiences.

Jack Clemson, general manager at Roanoke Electronics, assumed his new position six months ago after a long and distinguished career in a smaller organization on the West Coast. Production levels at Roanoke continue to rise, new contracts pour in at almost alarming rates, and morale is generally high. In fact, now with 3,500 employees, Roanoke has outgrown its facility, and plans are underway to start building a new, multimillion dollar complex within the next three months.

Despite these favorable conditions, Jack has been nagged by one problem that continues to sap his time and energy. The marketing department and the sales department have been embroiled in a major battle, one that began long before Jack joined the company. After news of a recent flare-up reaches him, Jack decides it's time to take action. He calls a meeting of his executive staff to find a solution to this problem **(Step 1)**.

Jack explains why he called the meeting, and committee members start to define the problem in detail. They begin with a general statement of the problem: "The marketing and sales departments at Roanoke do not get along." But they decide this definition is much too general to be of much help. Their second try is more specific: "Poor communication between the marketing and sales departments at Roanoke is sapping energy and hurting sales." They now have a definition statement that is useful for the remainder of their discussion **(Step 2)**.

The executive committee's next task is to analyze the problem it has defined **(Step 3)**. After a great deal of discussion, the committee members decide that both interpersonal and organizational issues are involved. For example, because of its location on the East Coast, its reputation, and its standing within the industry, Roanoke has succeeded in hiring the best and brightest graduates from highly competitive, top-flight Eastern schools. The marketing department is populated with Ivy League MBAs, and the psychological profile of the average member of the sales force shows an extremely aggressive, dynamic, and ambitious person.

These people compete against other firms in order to make Roanoke successful. Unfortunately, they also compete fiercely with one another. The result is an interpersonal climate of defensiveness, hostility, and sparse communication. Although a team spirit may exist between the engineering and manufacturing departments at Roanoke, it's strikingly absent between the marketing and sales departments.

From an organizational point of view, the current structure requires remarkably little cooperation between the two departments. Because each unit is housed in a different building within the complex, it's possible for each autonomous unit to complete its own marketing or sales tasks with meetings between the two occurring only quarterly.

Following the analysis meeting, the executive committee begins to propose alternative solutions to this dilemma **(Step 4)**. One member proposes that both departments be brought together for a disciplinary meeting during which the general manager tells them to "shape up or ship out." Another member proposes a mandatory communication training program for both departments. A third member proposes redesigning a wing in one building of the new complex to house both departments. He suggests that the two departments might soon work out their problems if they are forced to share facilities, secretaries, and rest rooms.

Following several sessions of lively debate, the executive committee begins to narrow the possibilities by testing each solution against a list of criteria **(Step 5)**. The committee decides that the final solution must be cost-effective, realistic, and acceptable to both departments.

Although communication training is perceived as a useful option, the committee recognizes that the training budget for the current year does not allow for a new program of this scope. They also recognize that a disciplinary meeting would most likely make matters worse. However, the committee is intrigued by the third option, which would involve relatively inexpensive changes to the physical layout of the new building. After consulting with the architect and with the chairperson of the environmental design department of a nearby university, the committee selects this third option. In the meantime, Jack agrees to meet with the heads of both the marketing and the sales department and solicit their advice on what could be done until the new facility is ready.

Months later, as the executive committee members walked through the redesigned wing, they concluded that they had reached a productive decision **(Step 6)**. Tension between the two departments had eased, effective communication had increased, and the prospects for increased sales clearly were improved.

Differences Between Problem Solving and Decision Making. Our hypothetical situation describes a *problem-solving* group with *decision-making* authority. The distinction is an important one. Often in organizations, *problem-solving* groups are asked to study a problem and recommend a solution. The actual decision, however, rests with a senior member of the organization who holds the power and controls the purse strings. Other groups, such as Jack Clemson and his executive staff, are *decision-making* groups with the authority to implement their own decisions.

According to some experts, groups are only as good as the quality of the decisions they make and the likelihood of their implementation. Researcher Randy Hirokawa and others have identified particular factors that lead to effective versus ineffective group decision making.[17] For example, accepting opinions and assumptions without question — an easy trap to fall into in a group situation — rather than adequately evaluating such contributions leads to poor decisions. Beginning a discussion without first analyzing the problem and then proposing possible solutions also represents a major stumbling block.

Consensus, Compromise, and Voting. When it comes to actually reaching a decision, *consensus*, or unanimous agreement, is the ideal. But when consensus isn't possible, the group may be able to *compromise* if each person is willing to give a little. A compromise is the median position between winning (having all the requirements of your preferred decision met) and losing (having none of the those requirements met). And, of course, if neither consensus nor compromise are viable alternatives, then the group may have to resort to *voting*. The problem with voting, particularly if it becomes the group's usual decision-making strategy, is that losers may harbor resentment toward winners.[18]

Dewey's original work has served as the basic formula for group success; however, it's probably safe to say that most groups in organizations don't follow Dewey's prescription. As we reported earlier, the average American meeting occurs on short notice without a prepublished agenda. Unprepared groups can take a number of detours around Dewey's ideal problem-solving steps. Studies indicate that most groups change topics as often as once every minute.[19] Because of time constraints, groups sometimes limit the number of ideas generated and inadvertently omit proposing the best solution. Often groups fail to identify criteria by which to measure alternative solutions. And at an even more basic level, groups incorrectly define the nature of the problem. Allow us to show you what we mean.

Causality-Based Versus Meaning-Based Problems. Consider the case of Sam McAllister, who took over as director of product design six weeks ago. This promotion made him the head of one of Atco Productions' most motivated and creative departments. To help him get the lay of the land, Sam decided to bring in an outside consulting team to help him assess the department's efficiency. After a week of interviews and observation, the team alerted Sam to one problem worth remedying.

Two of his employees, Ken and Marlene, appeared to have overlapping duties. Sam was surprised that his predecessor, a friend of his at Atco, would allow such redundancy. But at the team's recommendation, Sam called Ken and Marlene into his office, told them they were both valuable employees, and separated their duties. Within one week, department morale had plummeted, errors were rampant, and the department had fallen behind schedule on a major project for the first time ever. Sam was baffled until one of his engineers asked him privately why he had decided to pull Marlene off the promotion track. Evidently, Sam's predecessor had promised Marlene a shot at a management position if she performed well at the duties Sam had just taken away from her. The department was upset that Sam had made a snap judgment about Marlene. Everyone respected her work and thought she deserved a promotion. By taking the advice of a consulting group who incorrectly defined the problem, or solved the wrong problem, Sam had earned himself the reputation of someone who "shoots from the hip" and an impulsive leader with sexist tendencies.[20]

"Right" problems, on the other hand, are those that are compatible with the norms of the organization. Moving into a new company or a new position requires learning a new culture. If you decide to change a training program that has been in place for the last five years because you think it lacks value, avoid stepping on anyone's toes. Make sure the program isn't the brainchild of someone higher up in the organization. "Right" problems also are recognized as problems to stakeholders in the situation. Sam could have saved himself a good deal of professional embarrassment if he had taken the time to ask Ken and Marlene their perceptions of the "problem" of overlapping duties. And finally, "right" problems lead to solutions that usually have positive or at least neutral results.[21]

According to experts, it's important for problem solvers to recognize the difference between *causality-based* problems with cause–effect links and well-defined boundaries, and *meaning-based* problems with ambiguous boundaries and multiple causes. For example, if a computer link-up fails, we can trace from one connection back to another and discover the point where the problem originates. If a training program fails, on the other hand, the problem could originate with the trainer, the trainees, the facilities, the relevance of the content, or any combination of these factors. Sam's group of consultants in the hypothetical example above wrongly identified a meaning-based problem as a causality-based one.[22]

Even though groups sometimes miss the mark when it comes to following Dewey's formula or solving the right problem, individual group members still can have significant influence in moving the group in the right direction. If you understand Dewey's model of reflective thinking, then you may be able to encourage its use even if the model is not formally and consciously adopted by the group. Research identifies the benefits of using a systematic approach to problem solving.[23]

FOSTERING CREATIVITY IN GROUPS

Although Dewey's model represents the primary prescriptive approach to problem solving in organizations, many variations exist.

Creative Problem-Solving Approach

Consider the following scheme, which concentrates not only on a rational, left-brain problem-solving process but also on right-brain creativity and analogical thinking:

Step 1: *Defreeze.* Relax, slow down, disengage the left side of the brain. Stimulate the right side of the brain by generating drawings, analogies, or stories about the problem.
Step 2: *Accumulate.* Gather criteria for judging possible solutions.
Step 3: *Deliberate.* Analyze criteria for their usefulness and then prioritize them.
Step 4: *Incubate.* Try to achieve distance from the problem. Let some time lapse and allow group members to remove themselves from the problem so that their subconscious minds can go to work.
Step 5: *Illuminate.* Propose solutions, evaluate them, and select the best option.

Step 6: *Accommodate.* Ask how well the solution fits the real constraints of the situation. Resolve any remaining differences and doubts. Compare costs and benefits.

Step 7: *Finalize.* Clarify the final solution and steps for implementing it. Get approval at the appropriate levels in the organization after the group reaches consensus.

Step 8: *Reinforce.* Confirm the support of all group members before implementing the solution. Resolve any last-minute doubts and lingering uncertainties.[24]

As we said earlier, this approach emphasizes creativity. Because many organizational problems are meaning-based rather than causality-based, groups need both structure *and* freedom in coming to the best solutions. Let's take a closer look at ways to foster creativity in problem-solving groups.

"Creativity," "innovation," and "*intra*-preneurship" have become buzz-words in today's organization. Recently, Hallmark Cards opened a $20 million technology and innovation center. Eastman Kodak has an in-house office of innovation. At Young & Rubicam, an international advertising and corporate communications company, creativity training is a major, ongoing effort. Many companies now hire consultants to develop an environment in which creativity flourishes and to teach people how to think more creatively. The creativity business is booming.[25]

....

Creative Thinking: Five Techniques

How can we teach people to think more creatively? In this next section we will examine specific creative techniques that are used in many organizations: *brainstorming, nominal group technique, brainwriting, morphological analysis,* and *synectics.*

Brainstorming. This process deliberately encourages output quantity rather than output quality. The object of this technique is for a group to generate as many ideas as possible. No idea is too bizarre, no criticism is allowed, and combining or improving on others' ideas is welcomed. The more ideas the group comes up with, the better. You probably have been in situations in which a teacher has asked you to brainstorm for a speech topic, a class project idea, or the focus of a research paper. Did the process encourage you to come up with creative ideas?

The primary objective during a brainstorming session is for the group to temporarily suspend orderliness and structure and to free itself from inhibitions that may restrict creativity. In theory, if the overall number of ideas proposed is increased, the number of *good* ideas should increase proportionately. Evaluation and analysis should come at a later time. When the group reconvenes, for example, ideas can be explored, clarified, expanded, and combined. Although brainstorming has its benefits, it is not a foolproof path to creativity. Sometimes reticent group members hold back ideas with great potential because they fear sounding foolish. Or domineering members will monopolize the process and as a result control a brainstorming session's outcome.

Nominal Group Technique. A useful alternative to brainstorming for generating ideas is Nominal Group Technique (NGT). Initially, NGT minimizes discussion by allowing group members to turn inward and clarify their thoughts in writing. Working independently on paper, all group members begin on equal footing, and no one is able to dominate the process.

The leader begins by asking participants to write down their ideas or solutions to the problem at hand. Proceeding one by one around the table, participants read what they have written, and the leader records ideas on a flipchart. After each person's input has been recorded, ideas may be discussed one at a time to clarify them or provide a rationale for including them. Redundant ideas are eliminated and similar ideas may be collapsed. Finally, the leader asks participants to select the top three to five ideas and rank order them according to their importance, urgency, or practicality. NGT may be used in the decision-making process to identify criteria, generate solutions, and prioritize problems, among other possibilities.

Brainwriting. Another alternative to brainstorming or NGT is brainwriting. Here, too, group members are asked to write rather than discuss. Specifically, each participant is asked to list four ideas on a sheet of paper, place the paper in the center of the table, and exchange it for someone else's paper. Participants then add in writing to the four ideas already listed by combining or improving on those ideas or by coming up with additional new ideas. For the next thirty minutes or so, group members focus on one paper at a time, adding their own ideas until the leader instructs them to stop. This technique, which originated at the Battelle Institute in Frankfurt, emphasizes both quantity and quality.[26] Theoretically, well-developed ideas should emerge from groups who use the brainwriting technique.

Morphological Analysis. Developed by mathematician Frank Zwicky and later refined by Myron Allen, morphological analysis is a way of solving problems by breaking them down into their components. You begin by specifying the characteristics of a problem and making a grid or matrix to fill in. For example, if you are trying to develop a new water-recreation product, you might label the horizontal axis "energy" and label the columns "wind," "solar," "gasoline," and so on. You might label the vertical axis "number of users" with columns "individual," "two-person," and "group." Where "wind" and "individual" intersect, you would think of windsurfing; where "gasoline" and "group" intersect, you'd think of power boating. But where "solar" and "individual" intersect, for example, you might hit upon the idea of developing a new solar-powered innertube for children.[27]

Synectics. Our final example is synectics, a creativity technique that focuses on "making the familiar strange and the strange familiar." The word comes from the Greek *synektikos*, which means "the joining together of apparently irrelevant elements." A fairly complicated procedure, synectics consists of (1) defining the problem, (2) briefly analyzing the problem, (3) clarifying and simplifying the problem, (4) reinterpreting the problem through an analogy or metaphor, (5) leaving the problem to "play" with analogies, (6) force-fitting a metaphor onto the original problem, and (7) redefining the problem in this "new light."[28]

Let's say, for example, that a recent study has shown that 30 percent of your company's employees are leaving the building before the 5 P.M. quitting time. This problem represents a significant amount of lost time and money, and you decide that it must be solved. Using synectics, you would do the following:

1. State the problem.
2. Analyze the problem: "Perhaps employees are trying to beat the traffic; long exit lines sometimes mean sitting in the parking lot for twenty to thirty minutes. Employees also may have children to pick up from school or day care. Managers are unable to stay on top of the problem because of poor management skills. Other employees also may begin to wonder whether they can get away with leaving early too, and so on."
3. Simplify the problem: "Nearly one-third of company employees are leaving work early each day."
4. Reinterpret the problem through an analogy: "It's as if employees are drawn by large magnets outside the building."
5. Leave the problem to "play" with analogies: "Magnets pull things; magnets can have strong power; the end of a day is like a tug of war with forces pulling from inside and outside."

6. Force-fit a metaphor onto the original problem: "Demagnetize either the forces drawing employees away from their work early, or the forces attempting to keep them at work until 5 o'clock."
7. Redefine the problem in this "new light": "One of the magnetic forces pulling on employees is the need to pick up children early. The other is our internal rule on quitting time. We can't demagnetize the outside force. But we can demagnetize the internal force by staggering leaving times so children can be picked up when necessary. Thus the traffic problem is eased."

A Creative Climate

Techniques such as these are important in fostering creativity in groups, but perhaps a broader question should be explored: How can we establish a *climate of creativity* in work groups? Some experts would say that it's up to management to create conditions that are conducive to creative teamwork.[29] In other words, managers should take personal responsibility for developing a creative climate in which their people can work.[30] What are the conditions that will encourage subordinates to come up with creative ideas? Creativity cannot be mandated ("Now I want you people to tackle this problem *creatively!*"), so how do you nurture a free and open climate that is characterized by creativity and innovation?

According to Arthur VanGundy, an expert on creativity in the work group, three factors determine a work group's creative climate: the *external environment*, the *internal creative climate* of individuals within the group, and the *quality of interpersonal relationships* among its members.[31] The survey in Table 9.1 can be used to assess a group's creative climate based on these three factors. Let's focus our attention on the first of VanGundy's factors: positively influencing a work group's external environment.

A group's external environment includes variables that can affect either the group's task or its members; for example, the degree of control by management, rewards that are offered for creative solutions, feedback about how the group is doing, and resources the group needs to be creative or to implement a creative solution. As a leader or manager, how can you develop the external factors that foster creativity? Consider the following suggestions on page 337.[32]

Table 9.1 *Assessing a Group's Creative Climate*

●●

This questionnaire was designed as a tool to help group leaders and other members of organizational units assess their group climates for creativity. External, individual, and interpersonal factors—key to the establishment of a strong creative environment—have been incorporated into the questionnaire as the basis for reaching a quantitative rating.

The questionnaire is not intended to tell you how creative your group is. Rather, it was devised to help provide a better understanding of the specific factors that contribute to the development and maintenance of a creative group climate; how your organization scores, on the basis of your own ratings, should provide some idea of its creative potential while working on creative problem-solving tasks.

If your group climate is relatively open, you might consider completing the questionnaire as a group assignment, with all members, including the group leader, participating on an equal basis. Try to achieve a consensus in your ratings; use voting or averaging only as a last resort. However, if you consider the group climate to be somewhat closed or characterized by defensiveness, the questionnaire should be completed individually and the results averaged.

Instructions: For each of the following items, circle the one number that describes best the extent to which you agree or disagree with the item. Even though you may have trouble deciding among responses for a statement, circle only one number. Work as fast as you can, and do not spend too much time on any one statement. Your first reaction is likely to be your most accurate one.

---

1 = Disagree	4 = Slightly
2 = Slightly disagree	agree
3 = Neutral or	5 = Agree
undecided	

THE EXTERNAL GROUP ENVIRONMENT

Overall, this organization:
1. Makes it easy to try new ways of performing tasks.   1 2 3 4 5
2. Maintains a moderate amount of pressure to get the job done.   1 2 3 4 5
3. Provides challenging yet realistic work goals.   1 2 3 4 5
4. Emphasizes a low level of supervision in performing tasks.   1 2 3 4 5
5. Encourages leaders to delegate responsibilities.   1 2 3 4 5
6. Encourages participation in decision making and goal setting.   1 2 3 4 5
7. Encourages use of the creative problem-solving process to solve unstructured problems.   1 2 3 4 5
8. Provides immediate and timely feedback in regard to task performance.   1 2 3 4 5
9. Provides the resources and support needed to get the job done.   1 2 3 4 5

Total task score: _____

10. Encourages open expression of ideas.   1 2 3 4 5

11. Accepts divergent ideas and points of view.   1 2 3 4 5

12. Encourages risk taking and buffers resisting forces.   1 2 3 4 5

13. Provides time for individual creative thinking.   1 2 3 4 5

14. Provides opportunities for professional growth and development.   1 2 3 4 5

15. Encourages people to interact with others outside their primary work group.   1 2 3 4 5

16. Promotes constructive intragroup and intergroup competition.   1 2 3 4 5

17. Recognizes worthy ideas.   1 2 3 4 5

18. Demonstrates confidence in people.   1 2 3 4 5

Total people score: _____

Total environmental (task plus people) score: _____

INDIVIDUAL CREATIVE CLIMATES OF GROUP MEMBERS

In general, the members of this group can be described as:

1. Curious.   1 2 3 4 5
2. Independent.   1 2 3 4 5
3. Able to defer judgment.   1 2 3 4 5
4. Able to test assumptions.   1 2 3 4 5
5. Optimistic.   1 2 3 4 5
6. Humorous.   1 2 3 4 5
7. Self-confident.   1 2 3 4 5
8. Open to new ideas.   1 2 3 4 5

9. Persistent when problem solving.   1 2 3 4 5
10. Able to concentrate.   1 2 3 4 5
11. Tolerant of ambiguity.   1 2 3 4 5
12. Self-aware.   1 2 3 4 5
13. Committed.   1 2 3 4 5
14. Flexible.   1 2 3 4 5
15. Willing to take risks.   1 2 3 4 5
16. Disciplined.   1 2 3 4 5
17. Uses imagery to help solve problems.   1 2 3 4 5
18. Able to toy with ideas.   1 2 3 4 5
19. Impulsive.   1 2 3 4 5

Total individual climates score: _____

QUALITY OF GROUP MEMBER INTERPERSONAL RELATIONSHIPS

When interacting with one another, the members of this group usually exhibit:

1. A high degree of interpersonal trust.   1 2 3 4 5
2. Acceptance of deviant behaviors.   1 2 3 4 5
3. A willingness to listen for understanding.   1 2 3 4 5
4. Friendliness toward one another.   1 2 3 4 5
5. A spirit of cooperation.   1 2 3 4 5
6. Open confrontation of conflicts.   1 2 3 4 5
7. Respect for each other's feelings.   1 2 3 4 5
8. A lack of defensiveness.   1 2 3 4 5
9. Very definite attempts at including all members in group discusions.   1 2 3 4 5

Total interpersonal relationships score: _____

(continued)

Table 9.1 *Assessing a Group's Creative Climate (continued)*

Scoring and Interpretation: Add the numbers circled for each of the three major categories and obtain a total score for each. (Note: Subtotal scores for the task and people factors of the external environment category are provided for supplemental interpretation purposes only. Use the total environmental score to compute the group's overall creative climate score.) Next, compute an average score for each category. Then multiply the three average category scores together to obtain your group's overall creative climate score (CCS). (See the formula for computing CCS at the bottom of the table.)

Because the three category scores are multiplied together, a low score on any one of the categories will result in an overall low CCS for the group. This procedure reflects the synergistic aspects of a creative climate that could not be evidenced by summing the three scores. All three categories must interact at a relatively high level to produce a creative group climate — it can be produced only if a group is fulfilling its synergistic potential.

Possible average scores for all three categories range from a low of 1 to a high of 5. For the overall CCS score, possible average scores range from 1 to 125. In general, the higher the score, the more conducive a group's climate is to creative problem solving.

Use the following table as a rough guide to interpreting your group's actual scores.

Category	Average Score	Interpretation
External environment	1–2	Low
	3	Moderate
	4–5	High
Individual climates	1–2	Low
	3	Moderate
	4–5	High
Interpersonal relationships	1–2	Low
	3	Moderate
	4–5	High
Overall creative climate score (CCS)	1–41	Low
	42–84	Moderate
	85–125	High

These scoring guides are only approximate, and you will have to use your own best judgment in interpreting the scores for your group. However, a low score in any area indicates that the group could benefit from special training in creative thinking before engaging in many creative problem-solving activities. Of course, a low score on the external environment probably could be increased only by actions that may be outside the control of an individual group. If this is the case, you will have to decide to what extent a nonconducive external environment would affect your group's ability to exercise its creative potential (assuming it has moderate to high scores on the other two category scores).

$$CCS = \left[\frac{External}{environment} \div 18\right] \times \left[\frac{Individual}{climates} \div 19\right] \times \left[\frac{Interpersonal}{relationships} \div 9\right]$$

From Arthur G. VanGundy, "How to Establish a Creative Climate in the Work Group," *Management Review* 73 (August 1984): 26–27. © 1984 Arthur G. VanGundy. Reprinted by permission of AMACOM, a division of American Management Association, New York.

1. Provide freedom so that the group can try new ways of doing things.
2. Maintain a moderate amount of work pressure; too much pressure may repress the group, yet too little may fail to motivate it.
3. Establish challenging but realistic work goals.
4. Provide work that is rewarding both for the group and for individuals.
5. Emphasize a low level of supervision; allow groups and individuals some measure of self-direction.
6. Delegate responsibilities to others.
7. Encourage the group to engage in participative decision making and creative problem solving.
8. Provide group members with immediate feedback so that they can make needed adjustments during the creative process.
9. Provide the support and resources the group needs to get the job done. Be a "basher-in-chief of small barriers and facilitator-in-chief of trivial aids to action," as Tom Peters puts it.[33]
10. Maintain open channels of communication.

Now what about encouraging creativity from individuals within the work group? The following suggestions can be taken to accomplish that goal.[34]

1. Act as a role model by expressing ideas openly. As a manager, you set the tone for your subordinates.
2. Accept different points of view from your subordinates. Encouraging homogeneity or a "party line" tends to suppress individual creativity.
3. Continue to develop subordinates' creative ideas if they get stuck along the way. You may need to make suggestions that will help your subordinates overcome seemingly insurmountable obstacles.
4. Encourage subordinates to take risks while supporting them in the face of possible resistance from those above you in the chain of command.
5. Discover individuals' creative specialties and the areas in which they would most like to contribute creative ideas.
6. Provide time for individual creativity apart from the group effort. Ideas sometimes need time to jell in isolation, and group members need time to think creatively without worrying about how others will react to their ideas.
7. Allow subordinates opportunities for training and develop-

ment. Stimulation in the form of classes or conferences may help employees keep creative ideas flowing.

8. Reward valuable creativity. Tangible and intangible incentives help to foster a spirit of creativity.

9. Encourage people to interact with those outside the group as a way to introduce new ideas into the group.

10. Allow limited competition among group members. Excessive competition will destroy the team spirit needed in a creative group, but some competition can keep the group's entrepreneurial spark alive.

11. Regard mistakes as opportunities for learning.

12. Expect creativity and demonstrate your confidence in the group's ability. Setting up expectations within the group and communicating your own expectations to its members can do a great deal to spur them on.

As a future leader or manager, one of the most important decisions you can make is to play a role in fostering creativity within the organization. According to management expert Tom Peters,

> No skill is more important than the corporate capacity to change per se. The company's most urgent task, then, is to learn to welcome — beg for, demand — innovation from everyone. . . . Following and administering rules might have been dandy in the placid environments of yesteryear. Not today. Managers must create new worlds. And then destroy them; and then create anew. Such brave acts of creation must begin with a vision that not only inspires, ennobles, empowers, and challenges, but at the same time provides confidence enough, in the midst of a perpetual competitive hurricane, to encourage people to take the day-to-day risks involved in testing and adapting and extending the [organization's] vision.[35]

Even if your organization's culture is traditional, structured, and cautious, you still can do your part to continually revitalize the organization. How? By communicating to your employees the view that problem solving is a team effort and that creative solutions are a valuable commodity.

ROLES GROUP MEMBERS ASSUME

As this chapter and Chapter 7 have stressed, people are what make organizations tick. And, as Chapter 7's opening epigram asserted, "People have one thing in common: they are all different." We now explore how those differences show up in group settings. Throughout our discussion of group roles, think about your own tendencies and how you might work to expand your repertoire of roles.

To accomplish a job single-handedly, you must put on many hats or play many roles. For example, to write an important paper for a college course, you might become a *philosopher* (thinking up a topic important enough to write about), *researcher* (gleaning information from countless books and journals in the library), *writer* (penning words of wisdom on a legal tablet), *employer* (hiring a professional typist to put the finished product on paper for you), and *proofreader* (carefully scanning for typographical, grammatical, and factual errors).

When you communicate in groups, things get even more complicated. Each group member is required to play many kinds of roles to get the job done. Although you may change hats repeatedly during the course of one meeting, others may peg you as one sort of role player because you do it well, because you do it better than others in the group, or because there's no one else to do it: "John, can't you make these two people see eye to eye? You're the harmonizer in this group." John may well be the group's harmonizer, but he most likely fills a variety of roles, perhaps as the group's *recorder*, keeping careful notes; *energizer*, giving people the boost they need to keep working; or *initiator*, getting the discussion off the ground.

In other words, we can look at group roles from two perspectives. First, we can examine the communication behavior that group members display moment to moment — when they ask for information or smooth over conflict among members, for example. Second, we can consider the relatively permanent attitudes and behaviors that group members display over time and the challenges you'll face in your role as a leader-manager working with the diverse styles of group communicators.

Regardless of the group's objective or how it is accomplished, groups expend energy in two basic ways. Some energy will be directed at getting the job done; these *task functions* are the kinds of steps we've just been discussing, such as generating alternatives, examining criteria, and proposing solutions. Equally important, however, are the *maintenance functions* that promote harmony, good will, and an interpersonal climate conducive to accomplishing the task at hand. Of the total energy available, each group divides it differently. Some groups are able to focus most of their attention on the task itself because the interpersonal fits are good ones. Some groups fail to expend any energy on maintenance functions and do not generate a unified effort toward the task. And some groups never get to the task because all of their time is spent trying to maintain themselves as a group rather than fragmenting or dispersing. The roles assumed by group members were first identified in 1948; that list remains a good delineation of group roles.[36]

Group Task Roles

1. The *initiator* proposes new ideas, procedures, goals, and solutions to get the group started. For example, "Why don't we all state our positions, then we'll discuss all the issues we've brought to the table."

2. The *information giver* supplies evidence and relates experiences that pertain to the group's task. "I've seen the production figures for last month and they're up .5 percent over the previous month."

3. The *information seeker* asks for information and clarification from other participants. "Does anyone remember last month's exact sales figures?"

4. The *opinion giver* states his or her own beliefs, thoughts, and perspectives. "My sense is that the department will go along with whatever we decide."

5. The *opinion seeker* asks others to relate their opinions and feelings and asks for clarification of their positions. "Deb, what issues do you think will surface at Friday's board meeting?"

6. The *elaborator* builds on the ideas of others by giving examples or providing explanations. "Pam's point is well taken. We *have* faced serious budget cutbacks before — in 1989, for example."

7. The *energizer* stimulates the group to work actively to complete the task. "Come on, folks, let's try to move on to point three on the agenda. We're making good progress."

8. The *reviewer* summarizes the group's progress throughout the discussion. "We've talked about several good reasons to proceed with production, including an encouraging projected completion date, favorable consumer trends, and a willingness on everyone's part to take the risk."

9. The *recorder* writes down ideas and solutions that are proposed by the group. "I'll type up a summary of our discussion and distribute it to everyone by Friday afternoon."

Group Maintenance Roles

1. The *encourager* provides positive reinforcement for contributors and helps to create a supportive climate. For example, "I think Tom's right on target. Good point!"

2. The *harmonizer* attempts to reconcile differences and, if necessary, introduces compromises and mediates conflicts that arise. "Despite their differences, I think Kim and Linda agree on what our decision has to be."

3. The **tension reliever** keeps the atmosphere relaxed by reducing formality and interjecting humor at the right moments and also helps the group keep emotions in check. "Never say never — that's what I'm beginning to learn about this group!"

4. The **gatekeeper** controls the flow of communication by encouraging participation from undercontributors and tactfully reducing participation from overcontributors and other negative role members. The gatekeeper also ensures that all members get an equal chance to take part. "Nina's got a good idea here, but we haven't heard anything from Don or Mike. What do you two think we should do next?"

Nonfunctional Roles

In addition to task and maintenance roles, several nonfunctional or negative roles often appear in groups, especially during emotionally charged discussions.

1. The **blocker** constantly objects to others' ideas and opinions and often plays "district attorney" by cross-examining others in an attempt to impede the acceptance of an idea. For example, "We've tried that idea before; it won't work. So what makes you think things are any different now?"

2. The **aggressor** insults and criticizes other group members in order to promote him or herself. "What a ridiculous idea! Why not reconsider my earlier proposal?"

3. The **storyteller** often tells interesting but irrelevant stories that lead the group astray. "You'll never believe what happened on the way to this meeting!"

4. The **recognition seeker** calls attention to his or her own accomplishments. "When I chaired this committee last year, I got the group to come up with twice as many ideas."

5. The **dominator** monopolizes group interaction for selfish reasons or because of high interest and good preparation. "My earlier idea leads me to suggest another alternative. . . . I also suggest we consider. . . . Furthermore, I'd like to propose. . . ."

6. The **confessor** uses the group as a substitute for group therapy to share personal problems. "I've always felt inferior because I didn't finish college. It's a wonder I've made it this far in the company."

7. The **special-interest pleader** represents another group or a special cause and argues this point of view relentlessly. "The training department folks aren't going to like us infringing on their

territory. They have needs and special requirements, too. I worked in that department for three years, and I think we should look at things from their perspective."

8. The **comedian** distracts the group with jokes and "off-the-wall" comments. He or she often is well liked and thus difficult to handle. "Hey, hey, what do you say we run down to Bumstead's office and raid his candy jar!"

9. The **mute** participates little or not at all, possibly because of lack of preparation or nervousness. (Silence. . . .)

When You Are In Charge

When you're in charge of a committee, quality circle, task force, or other organizational group that meets regularly, you'll want to help group members expand their repertoires of task and maintenance roles. You'll also want to diminish the effect of nonfunctional roles. Handling nonfunctional role members requires tact, courage, and sensitivity. The mute may be quiet because she is unprepared for the meeting, intimidated by more senior participants, or apprehensive about communicating in group settings. When you're in charge of a meeting, consider the following suggestions: set a positive tone, monitor seating arrangements, give negative role members specific tasks or maintenance roles, encourage undercontributors, and use formats and rules when needed.[37]

1. *Set a positive tone.* As a group leader, you can do a great deal to set the tone of the meeting. Greet participants as they enter the room. Engage each person in casual conversation before beginning business. Carefully construct your opening remarks and begin by noting how much time is available for discussion. Announce that you'll be limiting remarks and steering the discussion to keep it focused. Setting operating procedures *before* the discussion is easier than after everyone plunges in. And most group members will try to conform once they understand how and why you are structuring their time together.

2. *Monitor seating arrangements.* If you can control seating arrangements by using placecards or by putting personalized work materials at each spot, then you can enhance the group process. Seat a dominator between two extremely quiet people so that the two styles are contrasted. The dominator may realize his contributions are somewhat excessive, and the quiet people may realize they need to contribute more. If this strategy doesn't work or is impossible, then break in when an over-

contributor pauses to take a breath, summarize her position, and quickly ask someone else to take over. Whatever you do, don't give a dominator a new entree by making the mistake of asking whether you've represented her view accurately. You may try saying something like, "Ellen has a number of good ideas, but several of you haven't expressed your views yet. What does someone else think about this topic?" Seat an aggressor next to you so that you can avoid eye contact, which is an invitation to communicate in our society. Look only at those members whom you want to speak. Seat a mute in one of the "power" seats at the ends of a rectangular table; the expectations associated with the position may encourage him to contribute more.

3. *Give negative role members specific tasks or maintenance roles.* For example, before a meeting mention to the dominator that the upcoming meeting is likely to be an important one. Ask him to assume the role of gatekeeper so that everyone has a chance to express a view. Or ask him to record the minutes for the group. Concentrating on his changed role actually may transform his behavior during the meeting.

4. *Encourage undercontributors.* Give undercontributors positive feedback only. Ask mutes direct questions only when you're sure they are experts on the subject. Even then, give them a choice in responding: "Jane, I know your department had a similar experience recently. Would you care to share your thoughts with us now or perhaps in a few minutes?"

5. *Use formats and rules when necessary.* When you expect that circumstances will bring out the worst in group members, then you may want to invoke formality and rules. Begin by announcing that the meeting's format will be for members to present their comments in order, with three minutes allotted to each. Obviously, this strategy eliminates many of the advantages of group communication and should be used only when absolutely necessary.

Behavioral and Attitudinal Profiles

Another way to view group roles is by examining profiles of behaviors and attitudes. As we have discussed, roles relate to temporary styles of communication. During a particular meeting, you may serve as the group's initiator, elaborator, opinion giver, opinion seeker, and comedian.

Behavioral and attitudinal profiles, on the other hand, reflect permanent psychological tendencies and their communication effects. The following discussion is based on ideas of H. Lloyd Goodall, Jr., in *Small Group Communication in Organizations*.[38] Use the information to increase your awareness and develop better strategies for effective communication.

1. The *Good Soldier* is the stable, reliable, solid citizen who is found in every organization. Generally a conservative company man or woman, this person is a passive but dependable team player. Good Soldiers are content with rules and regulations; they prefer to "go with the flow" rather than "make waves." Leadership and power don't really interest them. Although they rarely have creative tendencies, Good Soldiers are technically competent people and thus are valued highly within organizational groups.

2. The *Altruist* is a person who has high ethical standards and sacrifices personal career aspirations for some higher cause. The Altruist may tell some unpleasant truth about the company or confront an individual about unethical behavior and lose her job because of it. Perhaps you've heard the term "whistleblower" or the phrase "shooting the messenger," which refers to the unfortunate fate of the bearer of bad tidings. Altruists are rare in group situations and present a true enigma for organizations.

3. The *Prince* is a highly Machiavellian, highly manipulative, and highly political person — the opposite of the Altruist in organizational groups. As Goodall puts it, the Altruist often does the right things for the right reasons, whereas the Prince does the right things for the wrong reasons. The ends justify the means for the Prince, who is motivated by a thirst for power. Selfish goals override group goals. Often attractive, seductive, and well-spoken, beneath the surface the Prince is a cold, calculating, and fickle person. Beware!

4. The *Courtier* (a term taken from a sixteenth-century book on gaining favor at Court) is the classic sycophant (or "brown-noser") who attempts to influence others with ingratiating behavior. Motivated by a desire to please, the Courtier strategizes about how to "get in good" with those in power — Princes, for example. Blessed by intelligence and agility, the Courtier usually performs well, knows how to adapt, and quickly learns how to please. Although a Courtier can bolster the confidence of leaders, an alliance with one may produce resentment and jealousy from other group members.

5. The *Power Broker* usually is a senior member of an organizational group (it takes time to amass the knowledge needed to wield power) and a skilled communicator. In meetings, he tends to downplay his power by doodling and saying little; he knows the score, however, and plays to win. Power Brokers may, in fact, be ruthless and vengeful. A single Power Broker can be a useful resource in a group because of her experience and expertise, but more than one may bring conflict and dysfunctional group communication.

6. The *Facilitator* is a reminder of the popular therapy groups or sensitivity groups of the 1960s and 1970s. Facilitators often make statements to the group such as, "It seems there's some hostility on this issue, am I right?" or "Let's be completely honest about our views on this subject" or "What feelings are we expressing here today?" The ostensible goal of the Facilitator is to achieve open and honest communication; this person, however, often is distrusted by Princes, Power Brokers, and Courtiers because his verbal techniques are not always sincere or may not seem so. Facilitators usually are more concerned with group maintenance functions than with group task functions.

7. The *Narcissist* is a disproportionately self-centered person who uses the group and its members as vehicles to achieve her own goals while rejecting the validity and importance of the group's task. Narcissists refuse any group assignment that won't bring them glory and recognition and usually represent a counterproductive force in an organizational group.

8. The *Yea-sayer* and the *Naysayer* are organizational group members who are either agreeable, usually to a fault, or disagreeable, casting a negative shadow on the group's efforts. As weak and ineffective group members, Yea-sayers tend to agree with everyone, particularly the leader. They are precisely the type of communicators who contribute most to groupthink. Naysayers, on the other hand, agree only with people whose perspectives are similar to theirs. Perhaps best described as domineering bullies, they tend to commandeer the group while denying that they seek power. For obvious reasons, they usually are not well received in organizational groups.

9. The *Angry Young Rebel* has a personality profile that combines the strategy of the Prince or Courtier with the self-centeredness of the Narcissist. The result is an impatient and highly emotional person. Rebels are likely to resent rules, bureaucracy, and the "uselessness" of mundane tasks. They sometimes

have inflated impressions of their own worth to the group and often try to gather forces for an issue-oriented battle. Although they can jolt a group out of its complacency and into productive conflict, Rebels also can create destructive factions and occupy more than their share of group time.

These are a few of the attitudinal and behavioral profiles that you'll run across throughout your career. We present them in this chapter not as a device to help you "pigeonhole" people, but to allow you to begin thinking about productive communication strategies with various types of group members. For example, Princes require very careful verification with outside sources about their true positions on important issues; do not take their communication at face value. Yea-sayers are comforting group members, particularly if you are the leader; however, they can lure you and the group into groupthink. And you should remember to capitalize on the expertise and experience of the group's Power Broker, who can serve as an excellent resource for information about the organization's past, present, and future. As we've said before, people are what make organizations tick, and the one thing people have in common is that they are all different.

HOW TO LEAD A PRODUCTIVE MEETING

Defining Leadership

No discussion of group communication in organizations would be complete without discussing the concept of leadership. We all realize the effect a good leader can have on a group; for example, the manager who can motivate her group to set records in new sales or the president who can persuade a board of directors to triple last year's budget. Literally speaking, leadership is being out in front of others and directing the way. As one expert puts it, however, we seem to have a "love–hate ambivalence about power wielders. And we especially dislike anyone who tries to boss us around. Yes, we admire the Washingtons and Churchills, but Hitler and Al Capone were leaders too." For most of us, leadership is a rather hazy abstraction.[39]

Leadership Versus Management. What about leadership in organizational settings? Are leaders and managers the same thing? Not necessarily. Some managers are effective leaders; some leaders are excellent managers. Both sets of skills are needed in organizations. Managers who cannot lead may emphasize details, time frames, and rules while holding little regard for inspiration, risk taking, and long-term strategies. Leaders who cannot manage may empower others and inspire them while paying little attention to structure, short-term planning, and immediate problem solving.

According to leadership experts, the single most important distinguishing characteristic of leaders is their sense of vision. Management is about coping with complexity; leadership is about coping with change. Managers are concerned with doing things right, while leaders focus on doing the right thing for themselves and their organizations.[40] Managers focus on planning and budgeting, organizing and staffing, controlling and problem solving. They produce predictability and order. Leaders, on the other hand, establish direction, align people, motivate and inspire, and produce change (see Table 9.2). As one expert notes, "there is an enormous difference between the person who is content to squirt oil on the existing machinery of an organization and one who envisions and builds new machinery."[41] Managers are responsible for the present, while leaders have a keen sense of the organization's future. The research of Harvard University's John Kotter has led him to the following assertion: "Most U.S. corporations are overmanaged and underled" (see Table 9.3).[42]

The Trait Approach. Years ago, experts believed that leaders were born, not made. Indeed, the *trait approach* has taught that some people simply have what it takes to become leaders, such as physical attractiveness and stature, intelligence, sociability, verbal skills, and a desire for leadership.[43] Researchers in the first half of this century noted that leaders seemed to have certain traits in common, and many studies sought to identify the specific traits that enabled a person to rise to a position of leadership. In 1940, however, one researcher reviewed all of the trait studies to that time and found that only some 5 percent of the traits identified in previous studies were common to four or more studies. In other words, "all we know about leadership traits. . . is that some leaders differ from some followers on some traits, sometimes."[44]

The Behavioral Approach. More recently, researchers have concentrated their efforts on the *behaviors* displayed by emerging leaders. They note, for example, that leaders take an active role in the discussion instead of laying back, and they communicate in an informed, intelligent, and skilled manner. From an organizational point of view, a range

Table 9.2 *A Comparison of Management and Leadership*

	MANAGEMENT	LEADERSHIP
Creating an agenda	*Planning and Budgeting* • establishing detailed steps and timetables for achieving results • allocating necessary resources to make that happen	*Establishing Direction* • developing a vision of the future and strategies for producing the changes needed to achieve it
Building a human network	*Organizing and Staffing* • establishing a structure • staffing it with people • delegating responsibility and authority to carry out the plan • providing policies and procedures to guide people • developing systems to monitor implementation	*Aligning People* • communicating the direction with words and deeds to everyone whose cooperation and commitment are needed to create teams and coalitions who understand the vision and believe in it
Execution	*Controlling and Problem Solving* • monitoring results • identifying deviations • planning and organizing to solve these problems	*Motivating and Inspiring* • energizing people to overcome major political, resource, and bureaucratic barriers to change by satisfying unfilled human needs
Outcomes	*Produces some degree of predictability and order, and has the potential of consistently producing key expected results*	*Produces change, often to a dramatic degree, and has the potential of producing extremely useful change*

Source: John Kotter, *A Force for Change* (New York: Free Press, 1990), 139. Copyright © 1990 John P. Kotter, Inc. Reprinted with permission of The Free Press, a Division of Macmillan, Inc.

of behaviors characterize effective leadership. Beyond the ability to focus others' attention on the future, effective leaders do the following[45]:

1. *Emphasize simple values*, which they continually stress in speeches, written materials, and meetings.
2. *Stay in touch with people* by listening to and communicating with employees inside the company and contacts outside the organization. They know how to "squint with their ears."

Table 9.3 *How Executives in a Dozen Successful U.S. Firms Rate Their Managers*

••

MANAGEMENT

		Weak	*Strong*
LEADERSHIP	*Strong*	Nearly half say they have "too few" people like this	Virtually all report "too few" people in this quadrant
	Weak	Half say they have "too many" people like this	Nearly two-thirds report "too many" people here

Respondents were given three general response categories: (1) too few, (2) too many, and (3) about right.
Source: John Kotter, *A Force for Change* (New York: Free Press, 1990), 143. Copyright © 1990 John P. Kotter, Inc. Reprinted with permission of The Free Press, a Division of Macmillan, Inc.

3. *Manage change* by building organizational support for new ideas, dealing with risk, sequencing decisions appropriately, and having a well-developed sense of timing.
4. *Select the best and brightest employees* by recruiting talented subordinates from other organizations or promoting them from within the company—and they know how to keep them once they're on board.
5. *Avoid do-it-all-ism* by realizing that no one is omniscient—that is, everyone's abilities are finite—and by incorporating the help they need to successfully "run" the entire organization or a part of it.
6. *Face up to failure* by learning from mistakes and moving on. In Chapter 2, we told the story of Lee Iacocca, who some would call one of the great industrial leaders of our day. In a scandal a few years ago, Iacocca admitted that some Chrysler dealers were guilty of tampering with odometers on test cars. His response: "Did we screw up? You bet we did!" The motto of the poor leader, on the other hand, is: "It's not whether you win or lose, it's how you place the blame."[46]

Training guru John Zenger puts it another way: Leaders create values through communication, develop committed followers, inspire lofty accomplishments, model appropriate behavior, focus attention on important issues, and connect their groups to the outside world.[47]

Leadership Styles. As researchers have focused on the behaviors associated with leadership, much emphasis has been placed on leadership *styles*. Examinations of style have focused on three factors:

1. power, or how a leader exerts influence;
2. social emphasis versus task emphasis, or whether the leader is more concerned with the task facing the group or the group itself and its members; and
3. participation, or how much the leader allows the group to take part in the decision-making process.

The oldest of the styles theories developed in the late 1930s and early 1940s when researchers identified autocratic, democratic, and laissez-faire leadership styles.[48]

The *autocratic* leader uses the blind communication style that was described in Chapter 7. Somewhat aloof and impersonal, autocratic leaders allow little participation from group members, which evokes rampant hostility and discontent. If the group comprises highly skilled and motivated members, then the autocratic approach will backfire. However, if the leader is capable, or if the group is large and unwieldy, autocratic leadership can be highly effective. Autocratically led groups often reach decisions quickly and make fewer errors than do other groups.

Democratic leaders are open communicators and involve other group members in the decision-making process. Although it takes time and considerable skill to be an effective democratic leader, the resulting levels of group satisfaction, commitment, motivation, and creativity are higher than are those in autocratically led groups.

Laissez-faire or "hands-off" leaders act as resource persons, available if needed, but generally uninvolved in the group's activities. Unless the group is composed of highly motivated people who need little direction, dissatisfaction and low productivity usually result in groups that are headed by laissez-faire leaders. And if the leader abdicates or a new leader is not appointed, then the entire group must assume leadership responsibilities.

Probably the best known of all the styles approaches is Robert Blake and Jane Mouton's Managerial Grid® (republished as the Leadership Grid by Robert R. Blake and Anne Adams McCanse — see Table 9.4). It examines the task versus social dimensions of group leadership. The horizontal axis measures to what extent the leader is involved with the task at hand, and the vertical axis measures the importance the leader places on people, feelings, and relationships within the group. According to Blake and Mouton, one dimension need not be sacrificed for the sake of the other. Pushing hard to complete a task doesn't mean that

Table 9.4 *The Leadership Grid®*

● ●

High
9

1,9

Country Club Management

Thoughtful attention to needs of people for satisfying relationships leads to a comfortable, friendly organization atmosphere and work tempo.

9,9

Team Management

Work accomplishment is from committed people; interdependence through a "common stake" in organization purpose leads to relationships of trust and respect.

Middle of the Road Management
5,5

Adequate organization performance is possible through balancing the necessity to get out work with maintaining morale of people at a satisfactory level.

CONCERN FOR PEOPLE

Impoverished Management

Exertion of minimum effort to get required work done is appropriate to sustain organization membership.

Authority-Compliance

Efficiency in operations results from arranging conditions of work in such a way that human elements interfere to a minimum degree.

1,1

1
Low

9,1

1
Low

CONCERN FOR PRODUCTION

9
High

®

From Robert R. Blake and Anne Adams McCanse, *Leadership Dilemmas—Grid Solutions* (Houston, TX: Gulf Publishing Company, 1991), 29. Copyright © 1991, Scientific Methods, Inc. Reproduced by permission of the owners.

people's needs must be ignored. The best leaders, they contend, show equally high concern for both task and people, realizing that task and people are critical to the group's success.

Table 9.5 Leadership Style Inventory

The inventory is designed to assess your method of leading. As you fill out the inventory, give a high rank to those words that best characterize the way you lead and a low rank to the words that are least characteristic of your leadership style. You may find it hard to choose the words that best describe your leadership style because there are no right or wrong answers. Different characteristics described in the inventory are equally good. The aim of the inventory is to describe how you lead, not to evaluate your leadership ability.

Instructions

There are nine sets of four words listed below. _Rank order_ each set of four words, assigning a 4 to the word which best characterizes your leadership style, a 3 to the word which next best characterizes your leadership style, a 2 to the next most characteristic word, and a 1 to the word which is least characteristic of you as a leader. *Be sure to assign a different rank number to each of the four words in each set.* Do not make ties. Now, total the *columns*, using only the set numbered below in the scoring section.

1. 4 Forceful	6 Negotiating	4 Testing	4 Sharing
2. 5 Decisive	6 Teaching	2 Probing	3 Unifying
3. 4 Expert	3 Convincing	1 Inquiring	5 Cooperative
4. 4 Resolute	4 Inspirational	4 Questioning	2 Giving
5. 3 Authoritative	1 Compelling	3 Participative	2 Approving
6. 5 Commanding /	1 Influential	2 Searching	1 Collaborating
7. 1 Direct	4 Persuasive	2 Verifying	4 Impartial
8. 4 Showing	8 Manuevering	3 Analytical	3 Supportive
9. 2 Prescriptive	9 Strategical	4 Exploring	2 Compromising

SCORING

T		S		C		J	
1 5 2		1 4		14		1 2	
2 3 4 5 7 8 10		1 3 6 7 8 9		2 3 4 5 8 9		1 3 6 7 8 9

Developed by J. F. Veiga, University of Connecticut. From Natasha Josefowitz, *Paths to Power* (Reading, MA: Addison-Wesley, 1980), 205. © 1990 Natasha Josefowitz. Reprinted by permission of the publisher.

Let's pause in our discussion of leadership styles to discover your own personal style. Complete the Leadership Style Inventory in Tables 9.5 and 9.6. Although you may have limited organizational experience, undoubtedly you have participated in class work groups, on committees, or in church or club activities. Base your responses on any group experiences you have had until now.

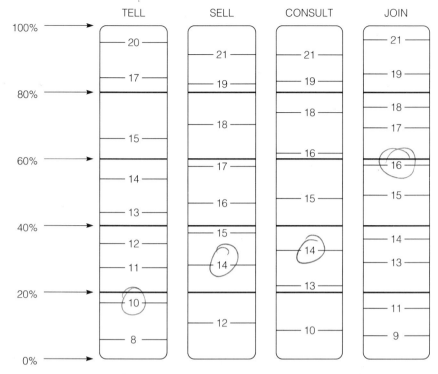

Table 9.6
*Leadership
Style Profile
(Normative Data)*

From Natasha Josefowitz, *Paths
to Power* (Reading, MA: Addison-
Wesley, 1980), 206. © 1990
Natasha Josefowitz. Reprinted by
permission of the publisher.

The above chart can be developed into a profile of your leadership style. Shade in the area which corresponds to your score on each dimension. For example, if you scored 15 on the TELL scale, then shade the area up to the 15 under TELL on the above chart. The ruled-in percentile provides you a way of comparing yourself to others who have taken the inventory. The percentiles are keyed to style scores to indicate the number of people who scored below a particular score. For example, a score of 15 on the TELL style means you scored higher than almost 65 percent of the people tested.

The completed inventory assesses your view of the way in which you lead in group situations based on your own preferences, and eventually, the reactions of your subordinates. (For a more objective view, compare your responses with feedback from people who have worked with you.) Identifying your tendencies now will help you reflect on your style and perhaps make necessary adjustments when you face challenging leadership roles later in your career. Using group participation as the foremost variable, the instrument divides behaviors into four leadership styles: TELL, SELL, CONSULT, and JOIN.[49]

TELL describes the style of a leader who identifies a problem, weighs possible solutions, makes a decision, and then announces it to subordinates. Whether or not the leader considers the input of others, he provides no real opportunity for subordinates to participate in the decision-making process.

SELL describes the style of a leader who also identifies problems and arrives at a decision single-handedly; in this case, however, the leader anticipates possible resistance and tries to persuade subordinates to accept the decision.

CONSULT differs from the first two styles because the leader identifies a problem and then consults subordinates for possible solutions before making a final decision. This leader realizes that participating in the decision-making process gives subordinates a sense of ownership in the decision and that soliciting their input provides alternatives that she may have overlooked.

JOIN is the style used by a leader who defines a problem and then passes the right to make a decision to the group (including the leader as a member). The JOINing leader believes that subordinates have a right to an equal voice and that their ideas are equal to or better than those of the leader.

Of course, an important factor to consider in thinking about leadership styles is the kind of subordinates with whom a leader works. If the group is mature, responsible, and fairly senior in the organization, JOINing makes good sense. If, on the other hand, you work with junior people who have little experience or who lack maturity and responsibility, then TELLing may be your only alternative. *Your style may, and should, vary from group to group based on three important factors: (1) leader-member relations, (2) task structure, and (3) leader's power.*

What we're describing is known as the *contingency* or *situational approach* to leadership; it comes from the extensive research of psychologist Fred Fiedler (see Chapter 1).[50] When conditions are very good or very poor, successful leaders focus more on task than on relationship dimensions. In other words, when a leader is fully vested with power, the task is well defined, and relationships between the leader and the group are positive, then a leader can afford to emphasize the task. When the leader's power is limited, the task is undefined, and relationships are rocky, then the leader must focus on the task itself to get the job done. But when conditions are somewhere in between, a relationship-oriented approach may be the leader's most effective strategy. According to Fielder's theory, leaders and situations should be well matched if groups are to be as effective as possible.

Preparing for Leadership

Now that we share a basic understanding of the leadership process, let's get down to the practical realities of leading organizational groups.

We've compiled suggestions from our organizational experience as both insiders and outside consultants.

Leadership Requires Planning. Although you may notice that leadership comes more easily to some people than to others, effective leadership doesn't just happen. Heading a successful task force, quality circle, or departmental committee — now or in your future career — requires a great deal of *planning and preparation* on your part. When we work as organizational consultants teaching group communication skills, the complaint we most often hear is that participants and leaders frequently attend meetings unprepared, expecting the "magic" of the moment to produce results. Everyone in an organization is busy, time is at a premium, and there is much to be done. Planning and preparation are sacrificed for more concrete tasks.

Instead of falling into the same traps, when *you* are in charge, use the following checklist.

Leadership Checklist

1. Notify people of an upcoming meeting in plenty of time to clear their calendars. Invite the right people and make certain that all participants know why they are invited.
2. Circulate a preliminary agenda that notifies members of the specifics to be covered. In fact, ask participants for additions to the preliminary agenda and incorporate them into the final agenda. The agenda should indicate the who, what, when, where, and why of the meeting. Attach any materials that you want members to preview before the meeting.
3. Assign individuals specific tasks before the meeting so that they can come prepared to discuss or report on particular topics. Jot messages to these people on their copies of the meeting announcement or prearrange their meeting roles in person.
4. Reserve a meeting room and verify your reservation at least once. Check the room immediately before the meeting begins to make sure it's empty and to arrange the table and chairs as you want them. Stock the room with writing pads and pencils, water pitchers, coffee, or whatever is needed to make participants comfortable.
5. Anticipate issues that may arise during the discussion and try to predict the positions of particular participants. The more you prepare, the less you will have to deal with surprises that may catch you off guard.

6. Analyze your "audience" in the same way that you would analyze an audience before a presentation. Think about the communication styles of attendees and the task and maintenance roles they tend to play in group discussions. Consider their attitudinal and behavioral profiles — the power brokers, angry young rebels, and good soldiers, for example. You even may want to invite another individual, if doing so is justified by the task, to "round out" the array of players.
7. Formulate your opening remarks, strategize about ways to keep the discussion on track, prepare a list of questions to encourage participation, and think about ways to include everyone in the discussion.
8. Analyze the group itself, not just individual participants, particularly if the committee or task force will continue to meet for some time to come.

Phases of Group Discussion. Communication scholar B. Aubrey Fisher identified four phases of "decision emergence," or how groups arrive at their decisions. When group members first begin their work, they spend most of their time getting to know one another, making ambiguous comments to avoid offending others, clarifying others' ideas, and agreeing with one another (*orientation*). During this initial phase, group members are busy forming impressions of one another and opinions about the task ahead. After the orientation stage, conflict is likely to arise as members disagree with one another, try to change others' opinions, become polarized by taking sides, or vie for leadership (*conflict*). In the third phase, participants make ambiguous statements as they soften their positions, and polarization dissipates (*emergence*). Finally, members arrive at a decision and reassure themselves that their choice is a good one (*reinforcement*).[51]

Another way to look at group life cycles is by thinking of these stages as equivalent to the developmental stages humans move through from infancy to childhood, adolescence, and adulthood. A group starts out as children, dependent on the leader, deciding who the most valuable members will be (experts call this the *forming* stage). From here, a group moves into adolescence or counterdependence, with members vying for control and challenging the leader (*storming*). The group next moves toward independence by establishing norms for members to work together (*norming*). Finally, a group reaches interdependence, with members working as a unit to reach their task-oriented and people-oriented goals (*performing*).[52]

All groups appear to work their way through these four stages, although not necessarily in this particular order. (Remember vacillating between childhood and adulthood when you were an adolescent?) A leader's plans should take these developmental stages into account, gauge where the group is, and time her own contributions accordingly. If the group has finally reached its *performing* stage, and you attempt to establish new *norms* for operating, then your efforts will be counterproductive.[53]

Although stages and life cycles are real phenomena in groups, the results of more recent research argue that group decision making is too complex to be described by a single, overarching pattern. Poole, for example, describes three types of *activity tracks* that groups may follow: *task process activities* (which relate to managing the task), *relational activities* (which relate to managing intragroup relationships), and *topical focus* (general themes or major arguments that are unrelated to task or relationships). Groups switch tracks at what Poole calls *breakpoints* by shifting topics, by cycling back to an earlier point, or by adjourning, for example. Breakpoints can signal periods of extreme difficulty or high creativity for a group.[54] Whether you watch and listen for breakpoints or for the stages we described earlier, as leader you are responsible to know the course of the discussion at any given moment.

Leadership Requires Understanding. Besides arranging for all the tangible and intangible details of effective leadership, leaders also must focus direct attention inward toward *understanding* themselves and their own communication strengths and weaknesses. Leadership is a privilege, some might say, but it also bears considerable responsibility at times. And in organizational settings, the leader will be held responsible for the group's success or failure in getting the job done.

When you face a challenging leadership task, we recommend that you take the following two steps.

1. Analyze your stylistic tendencies during past leadership positions. Have you tended to overcontrol or undercontrol? Are you most comfortable with an autocratic approach, a democratic approach, or a laissez-faire approach? Do you prefer to TELL, SELL, CONSULT, or JOIN?
2. Decide which kind of leadership is needed, based on the situational factors at hand. Consider the contingency variables discussed in this chapter: (1) the quality of your relationships with individuals in the group (leader-member relations), (2) the clarity and complexity of the task ahead (task structure), and (3) the amount of power you have, through either your position or your expertise (leader's power). Based on these factors, you may sense whether you should modify your natural tendencies or capitalize on them.

Throughout this chapter, you have read about various ways to improve group communication. Group communication at its worst may earn the reputation expressed by the quotations at the beginning of this chapter, but group communication at its best is a productive use of organizational time and an effective way to accomplish organizational goals.

CHAPTER SUMMARY

Communicating in groups may be one of the most time-consuming activities in which you will engage during your career. Although meetings can be highly productive vehicles of communication in organizations, they tend to be overused and often poorly run. The opening quotation described the negative attitudes toward group communication that organizational communicators sometimes share.

Group communication has its advantages and disadvantages. Groups generate more and better solutions, have built-in buy-in power, provide opportunities to display our skills, help meet our social needs, and act as a way to test ideas before committing to them. On the other hand, groups are prolific time eaters, sometimes bring out the worst in people, suffer from the hazards of groupthink and distributed responsibility, and act as the stage for intense conflict.

Many experts have prescribed problem-solving formats for groups. John Dewey's rational thinking model describes six traditional steps. The Creative Problem-Solving Approach focuses on unleashing the creative power on the right side of the brain. Brainstorming, nominal group technique, brainwriting, morphological analysis, and synectics all help groups to generate ideas. Fostering a creative climate is an important part of a manager's or group leader's role. The chapter provided suggestions for doing so.

The diversity of group members presents one of the most challenging aspects of group communication. Participants assume task, maintenance, and nonfunctional roles. They also display relatively permanent attitudinal and behavioral profiles. This chapter has explored some typical roles and profiles and provided suggestions on how to deal with both.

The final section of the chapter focused on leadership by defining the trait, behavioral, styles, and situational approaches. We concluded with the practical realities that are involved in preparing you to lead organizational groups.

MEASURING SUCCESS

Cameron Jones

A. *Description.* Imagine that you are the senior vice-president of Decco Corporation. You've been in this position for only three months (the CEO is in Europe) when several members of the executive staff approach you with a serious problem.

Cameron Jones, Decco's compensation manager, reportedly has been misappropriating funds and falsifying trip reports for some time. Several members of his staff indeed have suspected him of these charges, but they feel vulnerable because Jones writes their performance reports. Finally, however, they've come forward, the evidence is clear, and you're convinced that Cameron Jones must be removed from the staff. Morale is low in his department, and you fear adverse effects spreading throughout the organization and to Decco's reputation in the community if you fail to act. However, you also know that Jones is well liked by some senior managers. Over the past five years, he has formed many alliances with these administrators.

This afternoon you are told that these senior manager allies of Jones have voiced angry opposition to your plans for removing him, and you sense some of them are afraid they may be next to go. They have called an urgent meeting for tomorrow afternoon—a meeting to which you and Cameron Jones have been invited.

In response, you call a meeting of selected members of the executive staff—a meeting which will convene in just a few minutes. You want this meeting to result in an overall *strategy* for handling tomorrow's confrontation, and a detailed *plan* for communicating these events and your responses to the CEO and the board of directors. Colleagues who represent several of the behavioral profiles described in this chapter also will be attending your meeting.

B. *Role-Play.* Form groups of five or six persons to role-play the executive staff meeting called to prepare for tomorrow's confrontation. But first, spend a few minutes as *yourselves*. Discuss how you would prepare for and execute this challenging group leadership task; use the principles discussed in this chapter, as well as the benefits of your various experiences working in groups.

When you get the signal from your instructor, assume the role you've been assigned: senior vice-president, good soldier, courtier, angry young rebel, narcissist, or power broker. Senior vice-presidents, convene your meetings and begin working with your group to develop a strategy for handling tomorrow's confrontation and a plan for communicating these events and your responses to your CEO and the board of directors. Role-players, reread the descriptions of your roles in the chapter and display the attitudinal and behavioral profiles you have been assigned as faithfully as possible.

C. *Writing Assignment.* After you have concluded your meeting, individually or as a group, write a memo to your CEO, describing the situation the organization finds itself in and detailing the action you plan to take.

....

Notes

1. Winston Fletcher, *Meetings, Meetings* (New York: William Morrow & Co. 1983), 20.

2. Joseph W. Leonard, "Gather 'Round!: Putting a Method in Your Meetings," *Management World* 15 (February 1986): 32–33.

3. Norman B. Sigband, "Meetings with Success," *Personnel Journal* 64 (May 1985): 48.

4. Leonard, "Gather 'Round!", 33.

5. "Take a Meeting . . . Please," *Training & Development Journal* 44 (May 1990): 11–12.

6. Fletcher, *Meetings*, 25.

7. Fletcher, *Meetings*, 26.

8. Fletcher, *Meetings*, 26.

9. Thomas J. Peters and Robert H. Waterman, Jr., *In Search of Excellence: Lessons from America's Best-Run Companies* (New York: Harper & Row, 1981), 122–123.

10. Peters and Waterman, *In Search*, 121–134.

11. Irving L. Janis, "Groupthink." In Bobby R. Patton and Kim Giffin, Eds. *Decision-Making Group Interaction*, 2nd ed. (New York: Harper & Row, 1978), 243–255.

12. Robert W. Goddard, "The Healthy Side of Conflict," *Management World* 15 (June 1986): 12.

13. Actually, the group environment often produces a *polarized* decision, one that is either more risky or more conservative than a similar decision made by individuals. For example, see Rebecca J. Cline and Timothy R. Cline, "A Structural Analysis of a Risky-Shift and Cautious-Shift Discussions: The Diffusion-of-Responsibility Theory," *Communication Quarterly* 28 (1980): 26–36; Timothy R. Cline and Rebecca J. Cline, "Risky and Cautious Decision Shifts in Small Groups," *Southern Speech Communication Journal* 44 (1979): 252–263; Rolf O. Kroger and Irene Briedis, "Effects of Risk and Caution Norms on Group Decision Making," *Human Relations* 23 (1970): 181-190; Michael E. Mayer, "Explaining Choice Shift: An Effects Coded Model," *Communication Monographs* 52 (1985): 92-101.

14. Peters and Waterman, *In Search*, 13–14.

15. John K. Brilhart and Gloria J. Galanis, *Effective Group Discussion*, 6th ed. (Dubuque, IA: Wm. C. Brown, 1989), 280.

16. John Dewey, *How We Think* (Boston: Heath, 1910); B. Aubrey Fisher, *Small Group Decision Making* (New York: McGraw-Hill, 1974), 131.

17. Randy Hirokawa and Roger Pace, "A Descriptive Investigation of the Possible Communication-Based Reasons for Effective and Ineffective Group Decision Making," *Communication Monographs* 50 (December 1983): 363-379; Randy Hirokawa, "Group Communication and Problem-Solving Effectiveness: An Investigation of Group Phases," *Human Communication Research* 9 (Summer 1983): 291-305; also see Randy Hirokawa et al., "Understanding the Sources of Faulty Group Decision Making: A Lesson from the Challenger Disaster," *Small Group Behavior* 19 (November 1988): 411–433; Randy Hirokawa, "Discussion Procedures and Decision-Making Performance: A Test of a Functional Perspective," *Human Communication Research* 12 (Winter 1985): 203–224; Randy Hirokawa, "Group Communication and Problem-Solving Effectiveness II: An Exploratory Investigation of Procedural Functions," *Western Journal of Speech Communication* 47 (Winter 1983): 59–74.

18. Julia T. Wood, "Alternative Methods of Group Decision Making: A Comparative Examination of Consensus, Negotiation and Voting." In Gerald M. Phillips and Julia T. Wood, Eds., *Emergent Issues in Human Decision Making* (Carbondale, IL: Southern Illinois University Press, 1984), 3–18.

19. David M. Berg, "A Descriptive Analysis of the Distribution and Duration of Themes Discussed by Task-Oriented Small Groups," *Speech Monographs* 34 (1967): 172–175; and Ernest G. Bormann

and Nancy C. Bormann, *Effective Small Group Communication*, 2nd ed. (Minneapolis, MN: Burgess, 1976), 132. For evidence of the assertion that groups do not necessarily solve problems using a step-by-step, linear process, also see Robert F. Bales and Fred L. Strodbeck, "Phases in Group Problem Solving," *Journal of Abnormal and Social Psychology* 46 (1951): 485–495; Thomas M. Schiedel and Laura Crowell, "Idea Development in Small Groups," *Quarterly Journal of Speech* 50 (1964): 140–145.

20. Jane Elizabeth Allen, "How to Solve the Right Problem," *Training* 24 (February 1987): 39.

21. Allen, "How to Solve," 39–41, 45.

22. Allen, "How to Solve," 40–41.

23. Dennis S. Gouran, Candace Brown, and David R. Henry, "Behavioral Correlates of Perceptions of Quality in Decision-Making Discussions," *Communication Monographs* 45 (1978): 51–63; Linda L. Putnam, "Preference for Procedural Order in Task-Oriented Small Groups," *Communication Monographs* 46 (1979): 193–218; Randy Hirokawa, "Consensus Group Decision-Making, Quality of Decision, and Group Satisfaction: An Attempt to Sort Fact from Fiction," *Central States Speech Journal* 33 (1982): 407–415; Randy Hirokawa, "Why Informed Groups Make Faulty Decisions: An Investigation of Possible Interaction-Based Explanations," *Small Group Behavior* 18 (1987): 3–29.

24. Ichak Adizes and Efraim Turban, "An Innovative Approach to Group Decision Making," *Personnel* 62 (April 1985): 48.

25. Jack Gordon and Ron Zemke, "Making Them More Creative," *Training* 23 (May 1986): 30–34, 39–45.

26. Arthur G. VanGundy, *Managing Group Creativity: A Modular Approach to Problem Solving* (New York: American Management Association, 1984) and *108 Ways to Get a Bright Idea* (Englewood Cliffs, NJ: Prentice-Hall, 1983).

27. Gordon and Zemke, "Making Them," 32.

28. Gordon and Zemke, "Making Them," 32; W. J. J. Gordon, *Synectics: The Development of Creative Capacity* (New York: Harper & Row, 1961).

29. Arthur G. VanGundy, "How to Establish a Creative Climate in the Work Group," *Management Review* 73 (August 1984): 24–28, 37.

30. Eugene Raudsepp, "Establishing a Creative Climate," *Training and Development Journal* 41 (April 1987): 50–53.

31. VanGundy, "How to Establish," 25.

32. VanGundy, "How to Establish," 25; Raudsepp, "Establishing," 50–53.

33. Tom Peters, *Thriving on Chaos: Handbook for a Management Revolution* (New York: Alfred A. Knopf, 1987), 265.

34. VanGundy, "How to Establish," 28; Raudsepp, "Establishing," 50–53.

35. Peters, "Thriving," 275, 400–401.

36. Kenneth D. Benne and Paul Sheats, "Functional Roles of Group Members," *Journal of Social Issues* 4 (1948): 41–49; Cheryl Hamilton with Cordell Parker, *Communicating for Results: A Guide for Business and the Professions*, 3rd ed. (Belmont, CA: Wadsworth, 1990), 292–293.

37. Adapted from Hamilton and Parker, *Communicating for Results*, 294–295.

38. H. Lloyd Goodall, Jr., *Small Group Communication in Organizations* (Dubuque, IA: Wm. C. Brown, 1985), 264–274.

39. Thomas E. Cronin, "Thinking and Learning about Leadership," *Presidential Studies Quarterly* 14 (Winter 1984): 22.

40. Warren Bennis, "Why Leaders Can't Lead," *Training and Development Journal* 43 (April 1989): 35.

41. John H. Zenger, "Leadership: Management's Better Half," *Training* 22 (December 1985): 44.

42. John P. Kotter, "What Leaders Really Do," *Harvard Business Review* 68 (May–June 1990): 104–111.

43. Marvin E. Shaw, *Group Dynamics: The Psychology of Small Group Behavior* (New York: McGraw-Hill, 1976), 275.

44. John E. Baird, Jr., and Sanford B. Weinberg, *Communication: The Essence of Group Synergy* (Dubuque, IA: Wm. C. Brown, 1977), 194.

45. Rodman L. Drake, "Leadership: It's a Rare Blend of Traits," *Management Review* 74 (August 1985): 24–26.

46. Cronin, "Thinking and Learning," 32.

47. Zenger, "Leadership," 44–46, 48, 51–53.

48. Ralph White and Ronald Lippitt, *Autocracy and Democracy: An Experimental Inquiry* (New York: Harper & Row, 1960), 26–27.

49. Natasha Josefowitz, *Paths to Power* (Reading, MA: Addison-Wesley, 1980), 204–207.

50. Fred E. Fiedler, *A Theory of Leadership Effectiveness* (New York: McGraw-Hill, 1967); Fred E. Fiedler, "Personality and Situational Determinants of Leadership Effectiveness." In D. Cartwright and A. Zander, Eds., *Group Dynamics: Research and Theory* (New York: Harper & Row, 1968); Fred E. Fiedler, M. Chemers, and L. Mahar, *Improving Leadership Effectiveness* (New York: Wiley, 1976).

51. B. Aubrey Fisher, "Decision Emergence: Phases in Group Decision Making," *Speech Monographs* 37 (1970): 53–66.

52. Josefowitz, *Paths*, 179–181.

53. Walter Kiechel III, "How to Take Part in a Meeting," *Office Hours: A Guide to the Managerial Life*, 19–23.

54. Marshall Scott Poole, "Decision Development in Small Groups, III: A Multiple Sequence Model of Group Decision Development," *Communication Monographs* 50 (December 1983): 321–341; and Marshall Scott Poole and Joel A. Doelger, "Developmental Processes in Group Decision Making." In Randy Y. Hirokawa and Marshall Scott Poole, Eds., *Communication and Group Decision Making* (Beverly Hills, CA: Sage, 1986), 35–61.

Chapter **10** ✏ **Managing In-**

terpersonal and Intergroup

Conflict in Organizations ✍

Conflict is a sign of a healthy organization—up

to a point. A good manager doesn't try to elimi-

nate conflict; he tries to keep it from wasting the

energies of his people. ✉ *—Robert Townsend*

✍ **N**ow that we have discussed basic

organizational communication skills and their application in relationships, during interviews, and within group contexts, we will examine a particular type of communication that exists in all of these settings: conflict.

Conflict is one of the most pervasive and most perplexing kinds of communication in which we engage. According to some experts, "Inability to handle conflict effectively may well be the single greatest barrier to managerial job satisfaction and success."[1] Research tells us that managers spend 18 percent to 26 percent of their time managing conflict — either their own or that of their subordinates.[2] Even though organizational conflict can be disruptive, ignoring or stifling a problem may be more damaging in the long run. We feel so strongly about the importance of your future conflict management skills in the world of business and the professions that we are devoting this entire chapter to the subject.

ATTITUDES TOWARD ORGANIZATIONAL CONFLICT

Before you read the rest of this chapter, complete the following attitude checklist. Before we tell you what *we* think about conflict in organizations, discover what *you* think. We'll use several of your reactions to begin our discussion, and we'll weave our own reactions through the rest of the chapter.

Conflict Attitude Checklist

For each statement, write the number that best expresses your level of agreement. Use the following scale:

1 = agree wholeheartedly
2 = basically agree
3 = do not know
4 = basically disagree
5 = disagree wholeheartedly.

_2_ 1. Organizational conflict can be exciting, stimulating, and helpful.

_4_ 2. Conflict usually has negative effects.

_1_ 3. If people in organizations communicated more, the amount of conflict they experience would be reduced.

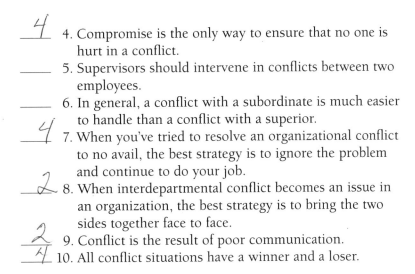

_4_   4. Compromise is the only way to ensure that no one is hurt in a conflict.

_____   5. Supervisors should intervene in conflicts between two employees.

_____   6. In general, a conflict with a subordinate is much easier to handle than a conflict with a superior.

_4_   7. When you've tried to resolve an organizational conflict to no avail, the best strategy is to ignore the problem and continue to do your job.

_2_   8. When interdepartmental conflict becomes an issue in an organization, the best strategy is to bring the two sides together face to face.

_2_   9. Conflict is the result of poor communication.

_4_   10. All conflict situations have a winner and a loser.

Now let's look at your response to the first statement. If you agreed either wholeheartedly or basically with the statement and believe that organizational conflict can be a productive experience, then good for you! Conflict is a fact of life in the world of business and the professions; it goes with the territory. As an organizational communicator, you simply cannot escape it, even if you have cultivated superb communication skills. Despite the organization's hierarchy and division of labor, policies and procedures — in other words, despite the structure and formality of organizations — conflict is unavoidable. And the larger and more complex the organization, the more the potential for conflict between and among divisions, departments, and their members.

One expert on organizational conflict has identified nine antecedent conditions; when these factors are present, conflict is likely to develop.[3]

1. *ambiguous jurisdiction:* Each party's authority in the conflict is unclear.
2. *conflict of interest:* Each party wants the same prestige, power, or resources.
3. *communication barriers:* Parties are separated by physical or psychological factors.
4. *dependence:* One party depends on another for resources.
5. *differentiation:* Differences between the two parties are maximized.
6. *association of the parties:* The parties are interrelated and must work together.
7. *need for consensus:* The need to agree exists.
8. *behavior regulations:* Rules are imposed on the parties.
9. *unresolved prior conflict:* The parties bring with them the aftermath of previous unresolved conflicts.

It's easy to see how all nine conditions would exist in many organizational settings. And although organizational conflict truly is inevitable, conflict as a form of communication is itself neutral. To a large extent, our communication choices determine whether the outcome is positive or negative. Cultivating a realistic attitude toward conflict and developing your conflict management skills now will serve you well in the future.

What about the second statement? If you agreed, then you probably share the more prevalent opinion. Conflict experts Hocker and Wilmot indicate that most people's images of conflict are negative, even volatile, as reflected in their language choices: "He *attacked* my weak point," "She *shot down* my argument," "He's about to *blow up*," or "This is a real *can of worms*."[4] Most of us find conflict to be unsettling, anxiety-provoking, threatening, and painful.

These same feelings about conflict prevail in the world of business and the professions. There will be times when your ideas are "shot down," your boss "blows up," or a problem with another employee is a real "can of worms." Above all other tasks, most managers dislike those in which conflict, or the potential for conflict, is at the heart of the situation: providing employees with productive criticism, conducting performance appraisals, or holding disciplinary interviews to solve performance problems, for example. Our goal in this chapter is to align your attitudes about conflict with organizational reality: Conflict is inevitable, manageable, and even productive if you understand the process and use all of your communication skills.

"Gentlemen! Gentlemen! May we please start the meeting?"
Drawing by Stevenson; © 1987 The New Yorker Magazine, Inc.

From an organizational point of view, "the productivity of confrontation arises from the fact that conflict leads to change, change leads to adaptation, and adaptation leads to survival."[5] In today's competitive global marketplace, conflict may be critical to an organization's success. Likewise, understanding conflict as a communication process may be critical to your success as an organizational communicator.

DEFINING ORGANIZATIONAL CONFLICT

Now that we've identified our attitudes toward conflict, let's take a closer look. Specifically, What is conflict? And even more specifically, What is the nature of *organizational* conflict?

First, organizational conflict is a multifaceted phenomenon. If you think about the conflict you have experienced in one-to-one relationships and then about the complexity of an organization of 3,000 employees, then you'll begin to see what we mean. For starters, two primary types of conflict exist in organizations. Read the following two scenarios and see if you can detect the point we're getting at.

Scenario 1

Two employees whom you supervise have decided they have a "personality clash." They do similar work and must exchange information on a continual basis. Al is an introvert who prefers to work alone, while Frank is an extravert who thrives on interaction. When Frank, an efficient worker, runs out of things to do, he helps himself to work from Al's desk, insisting that Al won't mind. Al, an accurate worker, enjoys circling Frank's typos and grammatical errors with a red pen and leaving the documents out for others to see. Both want to impress you and make the other look bad. At some point, you as supervisor may choose to intervene.

Scenario 2

Various departments in close proximity share a common storeroom for supplies. Pencils, tape, staples, typewriter ribbons, tablets, filing folders, and computer disks are all kept in the storeroom used by employees from benefits, training, safety, and compensation. Although each department manager budgets for supplies, the overall company budget is tight, and department managers are asked to pare down their projections in all budget categories. Employees begin hoarding supplies from the storeroom, and suddenly the "cupboard is bare." A full-fledged conflict erupts among departments because employees need supplies to complete their work. The hoarding has depleted supplies, but no one department is willing to use its supply budget to restock the shelves.

These two scenarios depict two types of organizational conflict: *interpersonal* conflict and *intergroup* conflict. People and their communication skills are the obvious common denominators, but there are important differences between these two types of conflict. Interpersonal conflict is more contained (although its effects can ripple through an organization) and usually is easier to manage (although not always), such as in Scenario 1. Intergroup conflict involves more people, multiple layers of authority (most likely), and widespread effects, such as in Scenario 2. Intergroup conflict has the potential to immobilize an organization; unless interpersonal conflict occurs at the top, it rarely has the same potential. We'll concentrate on intergroup conflict later in this chapter, but for now we will look at certain elements of interpersonal conflict.

INTERPERSONAL CONFLICT

Interpersonal conflict is defined as "an *expressed struggle* between at least *two interdependent parties* who *perceive incompatible goals, scarce resources, and interference* from the other party in achieving their goals" [Emphasis added].[6] Let's see how that definition applies in the case of the interpersonal conflict in Scenario 1, the "personality clash" between Al and Frank.

Is there an expressed struggle? The scenario states that the two have declared a clash; evidently both realize that a conflict exists. (Strictly speaking, a one-sided problem unknown to the other person or an individual's internal problem does not meet the criteria needed for an *interpersonal* conflict.)

Are the two parties interdependent? Al and Frank work in the same department for the same supervisor; their careers and their day-to-day work definitely are interrelated.

Do they perceive incompatible goals, scarce resources, and interference? The goals for both Al and Frank are to impress the boss and disgrace each other; in their minds, if one succeeds, the other fails. The resources they are vying for are power and self-esteem, and in their view only one of them can "win."

Because the answer to all of these questions is *yes*, Scenario 1 is an example of interpersonal conflict. Think back over all the summer jobs you've ever had—the clashes between the hostess and the waiter, the two construction workers, the cashier and the bagger—and undoubtedly you can come up with plenty of examples of your own.

The case of Al and Frank demonstrates one kind of interpersonal conflict in organizations: Indirect conflict between two subordinates whom you as a business or professional person will deal with as a third party. But you'll also be involved directly in conflicts between you and your boss or between you and a subordinate. Because we discussed communication between you and your boss in Chapter 7, "Communicating Interpersonally in Organizations," we focus our attention here on conflict between you and a subordinate. We think this topic is important, so we've included suggestions for you that range from providing employees with productive criticism to confronting problem behavior to disciplining employees. In all of these situations, you'll face the potential for interpersonal conflict, and your communication skills will be on the line.

....

Giving Productive Criticism

Let's assume that you are the Director of training and development at Decco Corporation. Below you in the hierarchy are six employees who report to you: three training specialists who design and deliver training programs, two training coordinators who schedule classes and make all the necessary arrangements, and an administrative assistant who handles correspondence, takes minutes at meetings, and keeps records. Let's also assume that your administrative assistant, Jan, is a productive worker with one major problem—carelessness. Jan prizes efficiency over accuracy; consequently everything sent out from the department contains at least one misspelled word or typographical error. Granted, the workload is heavy and you're all under pressure, but you believe that Jan's carelessness must be addressed. The question is: How do you give a subordinate productive criticism? Consider the following ten suggestions.[7]

1. *Approach the situation positively.* As you think about counseling the employee, imagine a positive exchange. A negative mind-set won't help. Use "I" messages ("*I* feel embarrassed when department documents contain errors") rather than "you" messages ("*You* are a sloppy worker").
2. *Build a bank account.* Think of your relationship with your employees in monetary terms. Every time you criticize, you make a withdrawal; every time you praise, you make a deposit.

Bosses who only approach their subordinates with bad news are in danger of being "overdrawn." Praise for positive behaviors, too.

3. *Remember the purpose of the criticism.* Some things may not be worth the energy and effort of a confrontation. If Jan wears sneakers with her business suit and no real damage is done, then you may elect to ignore the idiosyncracy. On the other hand, Jan's spelling errors may damage the department's reputation throughout the organization.

4. *Plan and rehearse.* Role-play the scenario with another colleague or someone at home. During the stress of a difficult situation, you may revert to an old style and lose control of your emotions. Rehearsing will help you reinforce productive behaviors.

5. *Identify the benefits of change.* Remind Jan that proofreading more carefully will save her time on redoing work and improve the department's image.

6. *Time your message.* Don't approach Jan after you've just been on the receiving end of criticism — productive or not — from your own boss. And don't confront her right after you've asked her to put in twenty hours of overtime work this weekend.

7. *Listen to the employee's side of the story.* Perhaps Jan has some legitimate obstacles in the way: you've overloaded her with work beyond her capabilities, for example. The exchange should be two-way, and your listening skills are key to productive communication.

8. *Offer your help.* Suggest buying a spellcheck program for Jan's PC or enrolling her in a basic grammar course at a local college or university. Do your part to help solve the problem.

9. *Check comprehension.* Ask Jan for a summary of what the two of you have discussed. Get a commitment from her on a plan of action.

10. *If there's a next time, reiterate the agreement, remove roadblocks, and be insistent.* For example, "Jan, last month we agreed to reduce the number of errors on department documents. I've seen three examples of problems this week. I'll try and slow down on the workload for awhile, but you're going to have to make good use of your dictionary until the new spellcheck program comes in."

Before we leave the topic of criticism, we should consider one other question: What if the tables are turned and your employee criticizes you? Two simple suggestions can keep this kind of communication exchange productive as well.[8]

First, *ask for more information.* This strategy helps you understand the specific complaint and decide whether it is valid or whether you should justify your original position.

EMPLOYEE: "You don't give me enough support."

BOSS: "What kind of support do you need?"
"Are you referring to the travel request I couldn't approve because of the budget freeze?"
"You're feeling out on a limb on this project?"

Second, *agree and qualify.* Agree with the accurate portion of the message, although you don't have to accept the accompanying judgment.

EMPLOYEE: "You sure overreacted and blew your cool at that meeting."

BOSS: "You're right, I *was* upset with the way Mary was trying to control the situation."
"I can see how you'd think I overreacted, but Greg and I have locked horns on this issue for a long time."

Confronting Performance Problems

Let's continue our example. Assume that in the last month, you also have noticed that Ron, one of your training coordinators, has developed a tardiness problem. He's been late for work at least three times a week. When employees come in at 8 A.M. to check room assignments for training classes, Ron is nowhere to be found. And when he finally does show up, his attitude leaves a great deal to be desired. You want to give Ron the benefit of the doubt and ignore the problem, particularly because you don't want to be the "bad guy." But you fear others in the department may begin to follow his example and morale may suffer. Now we move beyond the realm of productive criticism to the difficult area of confronting performance problems.

Most superiors admit that confrontation is their most dreaded task. They fear social repercussions, physical repercussions, and a loss of control (see Table 10.1). In their worst nightmares, they anticipate employee reactions such as:

"You can expect to hear from my attorney!"
"You've never liked me!"
"Our last boss never expected me to work this hard!"

Table 10.1 Why Do We Avoid Confrontation?

• •

Managers have stated three main reasons for avoiding confrontations with problem employees. Consider the antidotes listed below to help alleviate the stress you may feel when a confrontation is needed. In each case, focus on the objective aspects of the situation — on the infraction or problem, the consequences of it, and the organization's systems for dealing with the infraction — rather than on the employee's personality.

WHY MANAGERS DON'T CONFRONT	ANTIDOTE
1. Social Repercussions I won't be liked or perceived as a nice person if I confront an employee.	The occasional "bad guy" image does crop up in a manager's turf; ironically, however, the manager who thus avoids dealing with a problem employee hurts his or her own image as an effective manager. A problem employee causes problems for the entire department in the long run, so concentrate on the fact that it's worth incurring the displeasure of one person to preserve the well-being of the department as a whole. Also, by keeping the confrontation focused on objective issues, you can make the employee aware that performance, not personality, is being discussed.
2. Physical Repercussions I'm afraid the confrontation may be dangerous. The employee may become upset with me and retaliate in some way.	Bark is worse than bite 9 out of 10 times. There may be times when a violent employee retaliates, but the chances of this are unlikely. Plus, it's better to confront the individual early in the situation to avoid an escalation of bad feelings. Moreover, the longer a problem continues, the greater the aggravation becomes. This in itself is a physical (stress) repercussion. Remember that personnel and security departments are resources to help deal with a potentially violent employee.
3. Loss of Control Because I don't know how the confrontation will end, I'm afraid of losing control as the manager.	When you *plan* for a confrontation using these strategies, your control over the outcome is much greater than a hit-or-miss approach. Use the confrontation worksheet at the end of the chapter to help you anticipate the employee's reactions and prepare appropriate responses to maintain control. Learning to gain and maintain control is essential to managerial success.

Adapted from M. Michael Markowich and JoAnna Farber, "Managing Your Achilles' Heel," *Personnel Administrator* 32 (no. 6) (June 1987), 137–149. Used with permission of the authors.

"I'm sorry I've disappointed you." (Tears)
"Why pick on me? Everyone else did the same thing."
"You never told us about the new policy."
"You were a nice person until you became a boss."[9]

Many superiors have the tendency to wait it out and hope the problem goes away on its own. But think about the implications of doing nothing: Some employees lose respect for a superior who ignores problems, others may assume the negative behavior is acceptable and try it, and departmental productivity and morale may suffer. And when the superior finally decides to confront the employee, she must defend her earlier decision *not* to confront and her current decision *to* confront ("You've never mentioned this problem to me before. Why are you bringing it up now?"). In truth, a problem with an employee is like a toothache: "The sooner it's managed, the quicker relief will come."[10] Table 10.2 contains suggestions for dealing with various employee confrontation styles; a confrontation worksheet also can be found in the Measuring Success section at the end of this chapter. Save it for later use, or adapt it to a challenging interpersonal confrontation that you now face.

Performance problems rarely are solved in one problem-solving session with an employee. But superiors who focus on the problem and not the person and protect the employee's self-esteem have more favorable outcomes. Concrete behaviors should always be the focus of problem-solving discussions, rather than personality issues or attitudes. "You really have a rotten attitude" is a vague description of the problem. On the other hand, "Last week you hung up on a customer and told three people in the department to 'shut up'" is both quantifiable and specific.

....

Disciplining Employees

What if your problem-solving session with Ron produces no results or only temporary results? Or what if Ron's behavior continues to deteriorate: He develops an absence pattern driven by substance abuse, he's caught stealing a piece of company equipment, or he threatens you physically? What if disciplinary action is necessary? What do you do?

In Chapter 8, we discussed guidelines for conducting disciplinary interviews. Undoubtedly, the organization for which you work will have policies and procedures or at least unwritten guidelines for handling problems of this kind. Many organizations practice what is called

Table 10.2 *Confrontation Styles: Is One of Them Your Achilles' Heel?*

• •

You can take some of the sting out of confrontation by preparing well for the session. Learn to identify and positively control those confrontation styles that are your Achilles' Heels. Here are five major styles managers say consistently trip them up and helpful antidotes.

CONFRONTATION STYLE	ANTIDOTE
1. Intimidating	
Is combative in a confrontation. Demands "Who, me?" then heads for a fight. May raise voice during the discussion, may take each statement as an insult or an affront. Feathers are ruffled easily.	Prepare for hostility and accusations by going over your agenda well in advance. Don't get baited. Keep your tone even. Keep eye contact firm. Refer to specifics as objectively as possible.
2. Bellyaching	
Complains about nearly everything as a means of defending his or her actions. Is overworked, abused, misled, or anything else that may excuse his or her actions.	Avoid going on a guilt trip. If complaints appear worthy of further investigation, then follow up. Ask for specifics. Then get back to the issue at hand and stay there.
3. Playing Dumb	
Readily agrees to whatever you say, although more as manipulation than as sincere accord. Will placate you with "I'll try harder" or plays dumb with "I didn't know that was. . . ."	Play show and tell. If there are documents supporting your statements, bring them out. Jog the employee's memory. Be sure to specify expectations so that future "playing dumb" tactics won't work.
4. Playing Dodgeball	
Also readily agrees to what you say, but lays the blame elsewhere: "The policy is not clear" or "My predecessor did it this way" or "You never told me what you wanted."	Dodging issues is as wily as playing dumb about them; so use the same probing, prompting, and clarifying approach. Don't get sidetracked by peripheral issues the employee raises. Investigate them later; stick to the agenda now.

Table 10.2 *(Continued)*

CONFRONTATION STYLE	ANTIDOTE
5. Putty in Your Hands	
This is such a nice person that you feel rotten about confronting performance problems. Always agreeable, always trying to do the right thing, this person is like putty during a meeting. You feel bad about confronting him or her.	Remember that when you take corrective action, you're not trying to hurt the employee, you're trying to help.

Adapted from M. Michael Markowich and JoAnna Farber, "Managing Your Achilles' Heel," *Personnel Administrator* 32 (no. 6) (June 1987), 137–149. Used with permission of the authors.

progressive discipline, a four-step process that is interrupted if the employee's behavior improves:

Oral Warning

↓

Written Warning

↓

Suspension

↓

Discharge

Progressive discipline works like this. During a private interview, an employee is told that a particular behavior is unacceptable. She then is warned of future disciplinary actions that will be taken if she fails to correct the problem. If she corrects the problem, then the case is closed. If she does not, she is again counseled during a private interview and presented with a written warning, which is placed in her personnel file. If the problem still is not corrected, then she is suspended without pay for one or more days and finally discharged if the problem still exists when she returns. Of course, even though this is the normal progression, the severity of the offense is taken into account. Needless to say, an employee caught loading a company VCR into his car probably would be discharged immediately.

We advise that you seek counsel from company experts early, keep your own boss informed of the situation, and communicate as directly, clearly, and supportively with your subordinates as you can. Although conflict over employee discipline probably will consume only a small percentage of your overall time on the job, when problems do occur, they may consume a great deal of your attention and energy. They present the ultimate test case for using all of your conflict management skills.

The ability to manage superior–subordinate conflict productively is a key skill set to take with you into the organization. Of course, handling conflict after its onset is only part of the picture; doing everything in your power to prevent conflict by communicating responsibly is an important deterrent. The differences between two approaches that a superior might take, consciously or unconsciously, are given below for seven factors: consistency, autonomy, fairness, reasonableness, clarity, sensitivity, and long-range vision. Imagine the results in each case.[11]

Consistency

"I'm consistent. What I say today applies tomorrow, too."   *versus*   "What's in today may well be out tomorrow. You'll have to wait and see."

Autonomy

"I'm liberating. Do the job the best way you know how and come to me with problems."   *versus*   "Check with me before doing anything, including breathing."

Fairness

"I'm fair. The rules are there for everyone, and that's the way I apply them."   *versus*   "The people I like can bend the rules from time to time, but the people I don't had better not try it."

Reasonableness

"I'm reasonable. If you've got a better way of doing something that makes sense, go ahead and do it."   *versus*   "I don't care if it *is* a good idea; we've never done it that way before."

Clarity

"I'm clear. You'll know my thinking, whether you agree or not, all the way along."

versus

"You may not know what I think until it's too late. Why can't you read my mind?"

Sensitivity

"I'm sensitive. I think I understand the obstacles you face, and I'm willing to help you with them."

versus

"Can't you figure this out? There's a simple solution you should have thought of."

Long-Range Vision

"I anticipate. I see where you may stumble and warn you beforehand."

versus

"How in the world did you screw up this badly?"

Communicating with supportiveness, empathy, and openness may not prevent every potential conflict from erupting, but these characteristics of quality communication certainly contribute to positive relationships both on and off the job.

INTERPERSONAL CONFLICT MANAGEMENT STYLES

Every human benefit and enjoyment, every virtue and every prudent act is founded on compromise and barter. — Edmund Burke, 1775

One of the biggest challenges in interpersonal conflict is reconciling what appear to be two mutually exclusive sets of needs. On one hand, we have *me* needs: "I want to win," "I need power," "I must be successful." On the other hand, we have *we* needs: "I need to be part of a satisfying relationship," "I enjoy being part of a productive work team." How can we meet both *me* needs and *we* needs in conflict situations?

Let's personalize our discussion of interpersonal communication by looking at how these two sets of needs intersect and by examining our own communication tendencies in conflict. Do you tend to focus on your own needs exclusively, your partner's needs exclusively, both sets

Figure 10.1
Conflict Styles
Adapted from Kilmann and
Thomas, 1975.

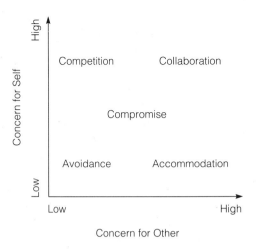

These descriptive statements are based on the assumption that most of us get "stuck" in a particular conflict style.[12] We make the same communication choices in conflict after conflict until our responses become comfortable and predictable. The statements are derived from the work of Kilmann and Thomas, who created a widely used instrument for determining conflict style, which is summarized in the explanatory diagram in Figure 10.1. The vertical axis measures your concern for your own goals and the horizontal axis measures your concern for your partner's goals.[13]

of needs, or neither set of needs and thus avoid the whole problem? Which of the following descriptions characterizes you?

- A conflict *avoider* who would rather suffer in silence than risk a potentially ugly confrontation.
- An *accommodator* who always lets the other person win rather than pushing for your own way.
- A *competitor* who feels a need to win over your partner.
- A *compromiser* who prefers to give up a little to gain a little.
- A *collaborator* who is willing to do whatever it takes to explore mutually satisfying solutions.

Let's look at each of the five conflict management styles: *avoidance, accommodation, competition, compromise*, and *collaboration*. Think about your tendencies and the implications of your preferred style in an organizational setting. Note that each style can be productive or destructive, depending on the situation.[14]

- *Avoidance* is a passive, uninvolved, and nonassertive conflict style. Avoiders don't pursue their own goals or their partner's goals. They simply refuse to "engage." They may sidestep an is-sue, pretend to be otherwise involved, or simply leave. Some-times an issue is so volatile that two people avoid discussing it. Avoiding a conflict neither prevents nor corrects the problem, however; avoidance is simply the strategy used to "manage" the conflict. Avoidance is positive and productive when the issues are trivial or when time is needed for "cooling off." On the nega-tive side, avoidance can allow conflicts to "smolder" and later explode or give others the impression that you don't care. Needless to say, working for a boss who is a conflict avoider is a frustrating experience.

- *Accommodation* is the style used when you subordinate your needs to your partner's needs. It can be an effective conflict-management choice when someone else's goals are more impor-tant to him or her than your goals are to you. It also is wisely chosen when you probably will lose anyway or when you find out you are wrong. As a boss, accommodating the needs of subordinates can be a way of developing employees by letting them make their own decisions and learn from their own mis-takes. From the employee's perspective, many situations call for accommodation. If you follow directives when you don't agree with them, for example, then you are using an accom-modating style.

- *Competition* is the style used when you are uncooperative, ag-gressive, and seeking to win at the expense of someone else. There may be times in the organization when you must make a quick decision or when the immediate goal is more important than your relationship with another person. In these cases, a competitive style may be appropriate. However, competition tends to reduce conflicts to black-and-white issues: *yes* or *no*, *right* or *wrong*, *for* or *against*. The competitive style usually characterizes a clear winner and a definite loser, a *win–lose* con-frontation. When ongoing work relationships are at stake, a competitive style usually is counterproductive.

- *Compromise* occurs when each party is willing to give up some-thing to reach a solution. If I want to eat lunch at a downtown hotel and you want to eat at the local fast-food restaurant, then we may compromise and eat in the company cafeteria. Compro-mise is a positive conflict management style in that it equalizes power and serves as a good backup style when other styles fail. However, compromise becomes a problem when it is held up as an ideal when in fact no one actually "wins." In truth, compro-mise represents a *lose–lose* conflict-management strategy. Over the long haul, if it is used repeatedly, compromise begins to lose its appeal.

- *Collaboration* is a conflict management style that requires commitment, energy, and time from both parties. It means moving beyond compromise to explore creative new options in which everyone "wins." Collaboration is a conflict style that helps meet both *me* and *we* needs, a true *win–win* approach. But because of the time and commitment needed for collaboration, it should only be used when investment in the professional relationship or the issue at hand is large.

Here's an example of collaboration in action. Two software engineers in the same department each want to be project leader on a new government contract. A conflict erupts. Don wants to learn a new programming language that is required for the project and also gain visibility in the organization; Susan worked on the first phase of the project three years ago and wants to continue that work. The boss could split the work or give it to a third person (both courses are examples of compromise) or she could work with the employees to reach a solution in which both parties win. Solution: Both employees are assigned to the project team. Don is named chief programmer on the project and takes a course at a local university at company expense to master the new programming language. Susan is designated project leader because she knows its history. Both employees achieve their real goals.

Understanding conflict styles is valuable in helping you recognize both your own and others' patterns. In important professional relationships, understanding conflict styles may lead to "metacommunication," or communicating about the way you communicate in order to find a better fit. If your boss's style is competitive and yours is accommodating, then you may work well together. If you both operate from competitive postures, however, you may end up in conflict over the way you both "do" conflict. Remember: All five styles have their advantages and disadvantages. As an organizational communicator, you'll need to develop a repertoire of conflict styles for the many kinds of situations you will face and the varied styles used by your colleagues.

....

Characteristics of Productive and Destructive Conflict

How do you know when you've taken part in productive interpersonal conflict? Think back over your experiences working in organizations. Are these the kinds of answers you probably would give?

The conflict was productive when:

I learned something about myself.
I learned something about my boss or co-worker.
I learned something about the organization.
I listened and was listened to.
I developed more appreciation for my relationship with my boss
    or co-workers.
We were able to reach an appropriate solution.
We were satisfied with the outcome of the conflict.
We became a more cohesive team.
We were able to generate superior ideas.
We stuck to the issues.
The discussion was open.
The discussion was realistic.
Both task and relational issues were resolved.
Management's issues and employees' issues were resolved.

Now consider the opposite case: How do you know when organizational conflicts are destructive? Does your experience tend to validate these responses?

The issues expanded beyond the problem at hand.
The conflict sidestepped the real issues.
The conflict escalated out of control.
The conflict was characterized by manipulation, coercion,
    threats, or deception on one or both sides.
Work relationships were irreparably damaged.
Management's solution ignored employees' concerns.
The conflict was never actually managed.
Everyone was dissatisfied with the outcome.

This negative list is a good place to start in helping you understand some of the characteristics of destructive conflict. In addition we direct your attention to specific destructive behaviors that are used in interpersonal conflict in organizations. Our discussion originates in the work of Dr. George Bach, psychotherapist and coauthor of *The Intimate Enemy* and *Creative Aggression*.[15] Bach teaches clients the difference between clean and dirty fighting, or "crazymaking." Instead of facing conflict head on, crazymakers use indirect aggression and sneak attacks to vent their resentments. Because they can't or won't express their thoughts and feelings openly and constructively, they trick their partners into capitulating or withdrawing, and they usually destroy the potential for quality communication in the process. Ten specific crazymaking roles are described below.[16]

The **pseudoaccommodator** refuses to engage in conflict either by giving in immediately or by pretending that nothing is wrong. For example:

> BOSS: Jean, I have some work for you, OK? Here's a memo to the personnel manager that I need you to type by 1 P.M., a report I need to have in Mr. Clark's hands by 1:45, and an announcement on next week's training session that has to be stuffed in all the engineers' mailboxes by 3:30.

> JEAN: Ellen, I'm sorry but I'm still working on that policy change you gave me late yesterday afternoon and the transparencies for Mr. Reilly's seminar.

> BOSS: Look, I understand you're busy. We're all overworked and underpaid around here. If you just manage your time, I'm sure you can get all of this done. Now, I've got to grab some lunch. See you later.

The **mind reader** takes over the confrontation and cuts off a partner by insisting he knows what his partner *really* means or what *really* is going on. For example:

> DAVE: Jim, I'm really discouraged about our working relationship. You're supposed to be training me, but every time I walk into your office to ask you a question, you're away at a meeting or talking with someone else.

> JIM: You know what your real problem is, Dave? I'll tell you what your real problem is. It's not me, and it's not our relationship. It's you. You have no confidence. I've already taught you a lot about this job. You're just afraid to trust your instincts. That's the *real* problem here.

The **trapper** asks for a particular response from his partner and then attacks her when she responds. For example:

> BOSS: Well, Joan, you've been with us here in the department for six months now. We're pleased to have you. How are things going?

> JOAN: Pretty well, I guess.

BOSS: Because this is your first performance review, let me ask you, are there any ways in which you think you could improve?

JOAN: I don't know.

BOSS: Come on, Joan, let's be completely open and honest with each other. How do you think you could be an even better employee?

JOAN: Well, I guess I could proofread my work more carefully.

BOSS: OK. Anything else?

JOAN: Yeah, I really should take a computer class to learn how to run that new software.

BOSS: You know, Joan, now that you've brought those things up, I've been meaning to talk with you about both your carelessness and your lack of computer skills. Let's take the carelessness issue first. Last week I was completely embarrassed when I found out that my memo to Mr. Steinberg had four typos in it. That just won't do. And as for your computer deficiencies, well, frankly I'm surprised that you've had that new package for two months now and have done nothing with it. When we spend company money on software, we expect it to be put to good use. But I'm glad we can have this kind of honest, straightforward discussion. Any other ways you could improve?

JOAN: No.

BOSS: Not at all?

JOAN: Not at all!

The **gunnysacker** saves up grudges and resentments and then dumps several weeks' or months' worth on an unsuspecting partner. For example:

ANN: Ed, you forgot to write that article for the company newspaper. Yesterday was the deadline.

ED: Wait a minute. You're not perfect either, you know. I remember last week when I asked you for a company correspondence handbook and you said you'd get me one. I'm still waiting.

And then there was the time I covered for you when you couldn't attend that meeting. Never a word of thanks. And when I first came here as a new employee, you ignored me for the first two weeks. You know, if you'd spend more time working and less time drinking coffee, a lot more would get done around here.

The **joker** trivializes an issue by kidding around when his partner has a serious conflict to discuss. For example:

PAUL: Hey, Pete, how come everyone else in the department prefers Hastings for the new communications specialist position and you prefer Kowalski?

PETE: I guess I just like good Irish names like Kowalski.

PAUL: Come on, Pete. How come you're the only person who won't vote for Hastings?

PETE: Because Hastings has a better moustache than I do, and I'm jealous.

PAUL: She does not! Come on, Pete, how come you're holding out on us?

PETE: Lighten up, Paul, will you?

The **beltliner** hits below the belt by pinpointing a partner's weak point and going after it. He may focus on a physical trait, a past behavior, intelligence, personality issues, or any other sensitive item to get even or hurt his partner. We won't provide an example because this technique is personal and individual, but you're probably familiar with what we mean.

The **hit-and-run fighter** brings up a volatile accusation, unleashes her wrath, and then walks away, leaving her partner at a loss for words. For example:

BOSS: Bill, I was completely embarrassed by the way you handled yourself at this morning's meeting! You blew your cool and made me and the rest of the department look bad. It'll take me months to repair the damage. I'm so upset I don't even want to discuss it.

The **blamer** is more interested in finding out who to blame for a problem than in solving it. For example:

BOSS: Well, it's 8:45, and I'm off to my 9 A.M. meeting with Mr. O'Neil.

SECRETARY: I've scheduled you for a 9 A.M. meeting with Mrs. Tipton.

BOSS: Are you kidding?! You expect me to be in two places at once? Didn't you check my appointment book?

SECRETARY: Perhaps I could call Mr. O'Neil to see if he could squeeze you in this afternoon.

BOSS: I can't believe it. You've done this to me before. You never think of checking my personal schedule before making a commitment.

SECRETARY: I know Mr. O'Neil is usually free on Thursdays right before the staff meeting. I'm sure he could see you then.

BOSS: You've ruined my entire day.

The **withholder** punishes her partner by holding back something crucial to the relationship such as conversation, interaction, or feedback. Bach describes an example similar to the following. Chris, a new employee, habitually comes in late each day and spends the first half-hour drinking coffee and the second half-hour making personal phone calls. Chris's boss is displeased with these habits but fails to confront the problem, not wishing to be the "bad guy." Instead, the boss expresses resentment passively by withdrawing and avoiding feedback. In the meantime, without feedback to the contrary, Chris assumes things are going well. When the boss finally decides to take action, Chris's transfer to a new department comes as a complete shock.[17]

The **Benedict Arnold** uses sabotage, often going behind his partner's back to encourage displeasure from others. The following two scenes involve three secretaries—Jane, Meg, and Marie.

Scene 1: Jane and Meg are in Meg's office.

JANE: Meg, what did you think of Marie's memo to the assistant general manager about secretaries refusing to make coffee?

MEG: To tell you the truth, I thought it was a tactical error on her part. She probably shouldn't have gone over her boss's head.

JANE: I know exactly what you mean!

Scene 2: Jane and Marie are in Marie's office.

JANE: Hey, Marie, I need to tell you that Meg's *really* upset about that memo you sent the assistant general manager. She's absolutely boiling.

MARIE: I wish she wouldn't fly off the handle like that.

JANE: I know exactly what you mean!

Crazymakers do exactly what the term implies: They make their victims crazy. Whether the crazymaker is a boss, peer, or subordinate, he or she is a destructive force in an organization. If the crazymaking boss, peer, or subordinate is yours, then what are your options? You can avoid the problem person, particularly if the association is one of choice rather than of necessity. If the relationship is important, however, then you can metacommunicate with the crazymaker about your perceptions openly, honestly, and supportively. If neither of these suggestions works, then you may want to consider transferring to a new department or leaving the organization, depending on the severity of the problem and its effects on you. Recognizing these destructive patterns helps us understand our communication choices and their implications.

POWER AND INTERPERSONAL CONFLICT

Before we leave the subject of interpersonal conflict and move on to intergroup conflict in organizations, we want to discuss an important topic: power. As we're sure you realize, power and conflict often are related variables in organizations. Indeed, *power struggles* make compelling newspaper copy and rumor-mill topics.

When a manager or leader exercises power, she can trigger *commitment, compliance,* or *resistance* from her employees. Table 10.3 differentiates these responses by source of influence — that is, the type of power. Power in organizations comes from a variety of sources. If you rule with an iron fist, then you have *coercive power*, or power based on fear of reprimand or dismissal. If you are the company CEO, then you operate from a base of *legitimate power* that relies on your position. If you have a particular type of expertise, knowledge, or skill, then you may influence

Table 10.3 *Power and Influence*

SOURCE OF INFLUENCE	TYPE OF OUTCOME		
	COMMITMENT	COMPLIANCE	RESISTANCE
Referent Power	• *Likely* if request is believed to be important to boss	• *Possible* if request is perceived to be unimportant to boss	• *Possible* if request is for something that will bring harm to boss
Expert Power	• *Likely* if request is persuasive and subordinates share boss's goals	• *Possible* if request is persuasive but subordinates are apathetic about task goals	• *Possible* if boss is arrogant and insulting, or subordinates oppose task goals
Legitimate Power	• *Possible* if request is polite and appropriate	• *Likely* if request or order is seen as legitimate	• *Possible* if arrogant demands are made or request does not appear proper
Reward Power	• *Possible* if used in a subtle, very personal way	• *Likely* if used in a mechanical, impersonal way	• *Possible* if used in a manipulative, arrogant way
Coercive Power	• *Very unlikely*	• *Possible* if used in helpful, nonpunitive way	• *Likely* if used in a hostile or manipulative way

Adapted from Gary A. Yukl, *Leadership in Organizations*, 2e, (Englewood Cliffs, NJ: Prentice-Hall, 1989), 44, © 1989. Adapted by permission of the publisher.

others because of your *expert power*. If you have the ability to promote people, make salary and budget decisions, or provide recognition, then you have *reward power*. If you have influence because others like and admire you, then you demonstrate *referent power*. If you have access to valuable information that others do not, then you have *information power*. Finally, if you have well-developed connections to people in high places, then you operate from a base of *connection power*.[18]

Is there a best power base from which to operate? Some studies indicate that employees comply with superiors most often because of legitimate and expert power. However, satisfaction and productivity are highest in organizations in which expert and referent power are used.[19] A word of caution, though. The point we've made throughout this text still holds: As an organizational communicator, your goal should be to develop a repertoire of skills and styles to meet particular needs of particular situations.

The following considerations about power are important to keep in mind, especially as power relates to interpersonal conflict in organizations:[20]

1. As an organizational leader, you may have several power bases in operation at once: legitimate power based on your position, expert power based on your special knowledge, and referent power based on your popularity. Indeed, one person can operate from several bases at once.

2. Power is seldom, if ever, distributed equally in organizations. Some people are more powerful than others, and people in powerful positions resist any redistribution of power. New employees with legitimate, expert, or referent power, for example, may be held at a distance until others are comfortable with their impact on the existing power structure.

3. Power is related to the degree of dependency we perceive we have relative to someone else. If someone controls your work assignments, salary, and future with the organization, then that person probably has a great deal of power in your eyes. You may see someone else's boss as less powerful. Power is in the eye of the beholder.

4. No one person holds all the power available in an organization. Even the CEO answers to a board of directors, which in turn answers to stockholders. Everyone has a boss.

5. Power is an important variable in organizational conflict. The traditionally structured organization with a clearly defined chain of command fosters the use of competitive conflict styles by managers and accommodating styles by employees. Although we typically think of managers as having more power than their subordinates, remember that subordinates have power, too. When subordinates have skills that are difficult to replace easily, specialized knowledge that others in the organization lack, an impact on meeting organizational or departmental goals, and the support of friends on the job, then it's impractical and unwise to try to "pull rank" as a means of getting the job done.[21] Using your authority to impose a conflict solution simply because you're the boss will erode your interpersonal effectiveness over time.

6. Organizations that deemphasize hierarchy and include employees in decision making are more likely to encourage compromise and collaboration as approaches to resolving conflicts.

INTERGROUP CONFLICT

In Chapter 1, "Communicating in Organizations," and Chapter 9, "Communicating and Leading in Small Groups," we made the case that most large organizations consist of many smaller groups: divisions, departments, functions, standing committees, ad hoc groups, task forces, and so on. Let's look at a real example.

One of us worked for a Fortune 100 company in a training and development function within a human resources department. Aside from actually designing and conducting training sessions, a key part of the job consisted of coordinating the following committees:

• a *scholarship committee* to send select employees for graduate degrees at the company's expense,
• an *external education committee* to approve company-sponsored undergraduate and graduate degrees for employees,
• an *internal education committee* to develop in-house noncredit courses, and
• a *colloquia committee* to put together lunchtime brown-bag informative talks.

Although small groups such as these within a single organization should cooperate to achieve the company's mission, they often fight among themselves for status, power, and resources, just as do individuals.[22] Because each person represented a different part of the organization, committee members often disagreed on what needed to be done, who should do it, and how it should get done. Indeed, according to experts:

> Conflicts arise because today's complex organizations with their high degree of occupational specialization, variety of employees with diverse backgrounds, and constantly changing environments not only put incredible pressure on the organization to adapt, but also present a difficult challenge to those who must work with one another.[23]

To be more specific, intergroup conflict in organizations stems from three major causes: communication differences, structural differences, and personal differences.[24]

Communication Differences

Communication differences result when different groups within organizations perform different tasks that require specialized languages and from which unique perceptions form. For example, if Susan is a design engineer drawing the initial plans for a project and Bob is a mechanical engineer working on final production, then they and their respective groups may talk different languages. Susan's design may look feasible on paper, but Bob knows more about the costs of production. It's not hard to see how intergroup conflict between these two groups of professionals could develop.

Structural Differences

Structural differences are the product of specialization and division of labor. Many organizations differentiate among monthly employees (professionals such as managers), weekly employees (nonprofessionals such as secretaries), and hourly employees (union members in a factory). Monthly employees have certain privileges that come with rank such as longer vacations and extra sick days. Hourly employees, on the other hand, may have benefits and protection negotiated by their union that seem like "good deals" to employees in the other two groups.

Personal Differences

Personal differences result from the values, norms, beliefs, and loyalties that develop within organizational groups. Departments, for example, tend to develop their own personalities based on those of their members. In a high-tech firm, engineers may see the human resources department as a "country club" and engineering as the organization's lifeblood. The human resources employees, on the other hand, may see themselves as gregarious, service-oriented people and engineers as introverts who are happy to spend each day in front of a computer terminal.

The underlying cause of intergroup conflict, however, is the same as for interpersonal conflict: When one or both groups begin to feel frustrated because it cannot reach its goals, conflict results. Communication failures occur, work flow is impeded, and delays and mistakes lead to negative feelings.

INTERGROUP CONFLICT MANAGEMENT STRATEGIES

What can be done about intergroup conflict? For example, if you as a manager face this problem, how should you proceed? What if Scenario 2 — conflict over scarce supplies (page 369) — describes you and your employees? Here are five suggestions for reducing intergroup conflict.[25]

1. Make sure that both groups have equal access to the information they need to solve problems. Consider having representatives from both groups regularly meet to work on problem areas and develop joint recommendations.
2. If possible, rotate group members. This technique may not work if the conflict is between a technical group and a non-technical group or between two different technical groups, but it may work well for groups within a single department or division, for example. This technique may help each side see the other's perspective.
3. Increase an outside threat so that the two groups must join forces to fight a common enemy — a competing company or audit team, for example.
4. Bring the two groups face to face to meet; or place their offices within close proximity of each other. Knowing they must face each other or work side by side may help to dissipate conflict.
5. Help the two groups identify a set of common goals or a single shared goal that supersedes their everyday work.

Another way to look at reducing intergroup conflict is by a formal model, such as the Two-Dimensional Matrix Model for Conflict Reduction (see Figure 10.2).[26] The vertical axis represents the degree of task interdependence (or how interrelated the jobs in the two groups are), and the horizontal axis represents the degree of value similarity between the two groups. As a possible future manager, think about the model's possibilities and contrast it with the Kilmann and Thomas conflict styles diagram presented earlier (page 380 and Figure 10.1).

The two-dimensional matrix model is based on the following management principles:

1. Time is a scarce management resource.
2. Some conflicts are more important to resolve than others.
3. Different groups respond differently to different conflict resolution techniques.

Figure 10.2

*Two-Dimensional
Matrix Model
for Conflict
Reduction*

From Ferraro and Adams, 1984,
p. 19. Used by permission.

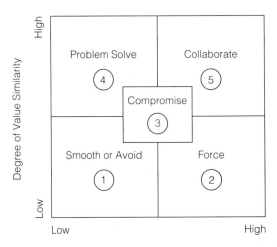

4. Conflict resolution techniques should be suited to the situation and the people involved.
5. The more similar the groups, the more a manager may appeal to some common frame of reference or identity.
6. The more interrelated the jobs of the two groups, the more necessary it may be for management to become involved in resolving the conflict for the good of the organization.

Let's look at how the model might work in various situations.[26]

1. *Low similarity, low interdependence.* In this situation, the groups have neither similar values nor interrelated jobs. Because the groups are very different and need not work together, your best option as a manager may be to play down or smooth over the conflict rather than invest large amounts of valuable management time in resolving it.
2. *Low similarity, high interdependence.* In this situation, groups do not share common values, but their work is highly interrelated. Because coordination between the two groups may be critical to the organization's success, a manager may have to impose or force a solution. If this strategy is used, you must be fair, follow up to make sure the forced solution actually is implemented, and provide feedback after it has been.
3. *Moderate similarity, moderate interdependence.* This situation calls for a middle-of-the-road response. Compromise may be the best management path because the groups share common

ground and job relatedness. They may be able to bargain to reach a solution.

4. *High similarity, low interdependence.* Here the two groups have a great deal in common, but their work is unrelated. Because of their similarity in terms of shared goals and attitudes, problem solving may be the best approach. These two groups may be able to sit down at a table together and find common points of agreement.

5. *High similarity, high interdependence.* Both shared values and interrelated work may produce a situation in which collaboration is possible. Research indicates that shared values make collaboration an easier task, and the necessity for task interdependence also may act as an incentive. In this scheme, collaboration goes beyond problem solving to working with a third-party manager to create new options or superordinate goals.

The stakes are often high when entire groups are involved in organizational conflict, but we hope the information we've provided helps you deal with intergroup conflict successfully.

NEGOTIATION, MEDIATION, AND ARBITRATION

Negotiation

A lean compromise is better than a fat lawsuit.
—George Herbert, 1640

Everyone negotiates. When you were in high school, you probably negotiated with your parents about curfew times, car privileges, and permission for special activities. As an organizational communicator, you will negotiate for salary increases, special job assignments, a bigger office with a view—you name it.

What is *negotiation?* In organizations, negotiation is what takes place between management and labor; among the engineering, manufacturing, and marketing departments; or between a manager and her employees. Negotiation is a "discussion between two or more people with a goal of reaching agreement on issues separating the parties when neither side has the power—or the desire to use its power—to get its own way."[27] A boss has the power to simply mandate compliance, but the costs of such a power tactic may outweigh the resulting benefits. Instead, managers spend about 20 percent of their time resolving real and potential conflicts, and much of that time is best characterized as time spent negotiating. As one expert puts it, "The structure of power today means you can't just tell people what to do, even within an organization. The art of negotiation becomes almost the key skill you have."[28]

What are the ins and outs of negotiation? What practical communication strategies work best? The following ten guidelines may help you prepare to negotiate with superiors, subordinates, and peers in business or the professions.[29]

1. *Prepare to negotiate.* Ask yourself, "What do I want to achieve and why?" Be specific in your answers. Ask the same questions about the other side, either beforehand, if possible, or at the first meeting. Never begin bargaining without adequate preparation; ask for a delay, if necessary. "Common beliefs to the contrary, negotiation is usually a contest of preparation, not a macho battle where contestants are willing to lose rather than admit they are not ready to fight."[30]

2. *Be organized.* Prepare an agenda and take notes. Leaving note taking to your opposition is a tactical error. Set deadlines to keep the discussions moving.

3. *Recognize that both sides will have very different perceptions.* For a recent study, executives were asked to describe both their own and their opponents' behaviors during conflict. Both sides described their own behavior as cooperative and informative and their opponents' as hostile, hard-nosed, and demanding. In negotiations, it's best to keep a positive attitude. Escalating emotions bog down the process, and the party who remains calm and collected usually controls the climate. One suggestion is to apologize as a way of defusing negative feelings: "I'm sorry we're having trouble with this issue. We both have good reasons for our positions. Why don't you explain your point of view one more time, and I'll listen as carefully as I can."

4. *Don't paint yourself or your opposition into a corner.* Giving an ultimatum or making a proclamation from which you cannot back down has a way of tipping the scales from rational discussion to bloody battle. Winning, rather than solving the problem, becomes the goal. Rather than trying to get your opposition to change its stated position, figure out the issues behind the position and bring those into the discussion.

5. *Be professional and aboveboard.* Never provide inaccurate infor-

mation or use tricks to win. If tricks are used against you—putting you in a chair that makes you look four feet tall, for example—make it clear that you recognize the trick ("I assume we'll be switching chairs tomorrow"), but don't validate the effectiveness of the trick with an emotional reaction.

6. *Be creative.* Brainstorm for imaginative solutions. When negotiation really works, both sides win. Several years ago, for example, Borden brought a $200 million lawsuit against Texaco for antitrust claims and breach of contract. Attorneys had put in thousands of hours of work on the case, which could have taken years of courtroom litigation. Instead, the two companies agreed to try a new negotiation strategy. The executive vice-presidents for both companies gathered in a room with their two attorneys, who were each allotted only one hour to present their side of the case. After that, the negotiation process began. The process took weeks, but the companies finally reached a satisfactory and totally unexpected agreement. Instead of Texaco paying Borden cash, the two sides rewrote a gas-supply contract that profited both parties.[31]

7. *Use silence as a tool.* As one professional negotiator put it, "You never give anything away by keeping your mouth shut." As a rule of thumb, limit your speaking to 50 percent or less of the time. Most of us are uncomfortable with silence and feel the need to fill it. Instead, get your opponents to fill it by asking questions and exploring their issues.

8. *Make trade-offs.* "The essence of excellent bargaining is to trade what is cheap to you, but valuable to another, for what is valuable to you, but cheap to another."[32] If two hungry people find an orange and start to fight over it, they should stop and take stock. It may be that one wants to grate the peel for a cake and throw away the fruit, and the other wishes to eat the fruit and throw away the peel. Dividing the orange in half is not always the best solution.[33]

9. *Help the other party reach an agreement.* Many negotiators assume that they must look out only for themselves and their interests. However, it *is* in your best interest to help the other side by realizing that its problems are your problems, too.

10. *Line up fallback positions.* Not all negotiations lead to workable agreements. However, the strength of your negotiating position will depend to some extent on the attractiveness of the alternatives available to you. Being able to walk away from the negotiation empty-handed because you have lined up other alternatives is a strong bargaining tactic.

Mediation

Litigation is a machine in which you go in as a pig and come out a sausage. — Ambrose Bierce

Mediation is another method for managing organizational conflict. A neutral third party helps two parties change their positions in order to reach a negotiated solution. The mediator has no power to force agreement or make decisions; however, she actively controls the negotiation process and helps the two parties reach a fair agreement. The aim of mediation "is not to suppress argument but to give it meaningful form and coherent process."[34] Mediation is an intermediate step between negotiation and adjudication before a judge or jury.

Successful mediation consists of eight steps within three major phases as shown in the following outline.[35]

Phase I: Forum

Step 1. *Exploration:* The mediator talks with both sides to discover whether mediation is an appropriate conflict management technique in the situation at hand.

Step 2. *Entry:* The mediator explains the process to be used and gets each party to agree to her participation.

Step 3. *Information gathering:* The mediator listens to each party and learns as much as possible about the conflict.

Phase II: Strategic Planning

Step 4. *Analysis:* The mediator studies the issues, history, information gathered, positions, and interests involved in the conflict.

Step 5. *Design:* The mediator develops an action plan to resolve the conflict and gets both sides to concur with the plan.

Phase III: Problem Solving

Step 6. *Implementation:* Using a variety of techniques such as joint meetings, shuttle diplomacy, or caucusing, the mediator identifies possible solutions for the two parties.

Step 7. *Joint decision making:* Using creative problem-solving methods and negotiating techniques, the mediator helps the two parties articulate their arguments through their own creative problem solving.

Step 8. *Closure:* The agreement reached is recorded and the process ends.

Arbitration

Arbitration also involves a third party but goes one step further. Arbitration is what takes place when the third party has special training in the issues at stake and is given the power to decide the outcome of the conflict by both parties. Within organizational contexts, negotiation, mediation, and arbitration are used in a variety of situations, from labor–management disputes to disciplinary problems to takeovers and buyouts.

Conflict affects every aspect of organizational life. Society may tell you that the best ways to manage conflict are to "Never give an inch," "Stick to your guns," and "Give 'em heck." Instead, whether the conflict is interpersonal or intergroup, whether you are directly involved or intervene as a third party, keep an open mind and learn as much as you can about conflict as a communication process. You will find that understanding the process affects the quality of the outcomes.

CHAPTER SUMMARY

Conflict is not only inevitable, but also a constant reality in organizations. Although most of us have negative attitudes toward conflict, learning to manage interpersonal and intergroup conflict productively is an essential communication skill to have as you enter business or a profession.

Interpersonal conflict in organizations is defined as "an expressed struggle between at least two interdependent parties who perceive incompatible goals, scarce resources, and interference from the other party in achieving their goals." As examples, we discussed the kinds of confrontational situations often experienced by superiors on the job: giving productive criticism, addressing performance problems, and disciplining employees. Recognizing conflict style tendencies (avoidance, accommodation, competition, compromise, and collaboration) and the characteristics of productive and destructive conflict also help us to manage interpersonal conflict productively in organizations. Crazy-making techniques are highly risky and potentially volatile when used as indirect conflict management alternatives. Power was addressed as the final variable to consider under the topic of interpersonal conflict in organizations.

Intergroup conflict arises from communication differences, structural differences, and personal differences in business and the professions. The chapter presents suggestions for reducing intergroup conflict and a model based on the variables of similarity and interdependence.

The closing section of this chapter dealt with negotiation, mediation, and arbitration. Negotiation often occurs between two individuals or groups directly, while mediation and arbitration both involve a third party. The difference between the two rests in the degree of power the third party has to enforce outcomes. We presented ten guidelines for effective negotiation and the necessary steps for effective mediation.

Understanding the process of organizational conflict affects the quality of its outcomes. Gaining that understanding now will prepare you to face the conflicts ahead.

MEASURING SUCCESS

1. Write descriptions of the following scenarios: a boss gives a subordinate productive criticism; a subordinate criticizes a boss; and a boss confronts an employee's performance problem. Prepare and perform three role-plays with a partner to demonstrate both positive and negative communication techniques. Discuss them in class.

2. As either an individual or a group project, rewrite the crazymaking scripts included in this chapter. If possible, videotape the scenes with classmates role-playing superiors, subordinates, and peers. Show the tape to other class members to see if they can identify the crazymaking techniques that you have depicted.

3. Imagine the following scenario. A conflict over smoking erupts between two employees in your department. Employee A chain smokes three packs a day; Employee B is allergic to cigarette smoke. Your boss asks you to intercede and resolve the situation. Describe the steps you would follow to investigate the problem, the conflict-management strategy you might select, and possible reactions to your intervention.

4. As mentioned earlier in this chapter, you may save this confrontation worksheet for later use or adapt it to a challenging interpersonal conflict you're facing now. It will take some thought to complete but is invaluable in identifying issues and possible responses that may arise in a confrontation. This systematic approach controls your limitations and helps you overcome any fear of confrontation. The worksheet also pinpoints the consequences of *not* confronting an employee. When these risks are put in writing, you can more readily see the potential problems from not facing them.

1. What do you risk by not confronting the employee and letting the problem continue?

   a. Impact on other employees _____

   _____

   b. Impact on my ability to manage _____

   _____

   c. Impact on attaining general department goals _____

   _____

2. a. What are the specific problems I want to discuss with the employee? (Focus on work-related consequences of any "personality characteristics.")

   _____

   _____

   b. What specific examples will I use during the discussion to illustrate the problem?

   _____

   _____

3. What suggestions for changing the problem will I make to the employee?

   _____

   _____

4. What do I anticipate as the employee's reaction? How will I respond?

   Employee's Possible Reaction   *My Response*

   _____   _____

   _____   _____

   _____   _____

Adapted from M. Michael Markowich and JoAnna Farber, "Managing Your Achilles' Heel," *Personnel Administrator* 32 (no. 6) (June 1987), 137–149. Used with permission of the authors.

Decco Exercise Think about a real interpersonal or intergroup organizational conflict you have observed on or off campus. Now translate the incident into an organizational one. (For example, if the incident occurred between you and a friend, imagine instead that it is occurring between you and a co-worker.) Write a memo to your boss at Decco, analyzing the conflict and detailing the productive steps you must take to resolve it.

....

Notes

1. James R. Wilcox, Ethel M. Wilcox, and Karen M. Cowan, "Communicating Creatively in Conflict Situations," *Management Solutions* 31 (October 1986): 18.

2. Kenneth W. Thomas and Warren H. Schmidt, "A Survey of Managerial Interests with Respect to Conflict," *Academy of Management Journal* 19 (1976): 315–318.

3. Alan C. Filley, *Interpersonal Conflict Resolution* (Chicago: Scott, Foresman, 1975), 9–12; Rosemary S. Caffarella, "Managing Conflict: An Analytical Tool," *Training and Development* 38 (February 1984): 34–38.

4. Joyce L. Hocker and William W. Wilmot, *Interpersonal Conflict*, 3rd ed. (Dubuque, IA: Wm. C. Brown, 1985), 25–30.

5. Richard Walton, *Interpersonal Peacemaking*. Cited in Robert W. Goddard, "The Healthy Side of Conflict," *Management World* 15 (June 1986): 8–10, 12.

6. Hocker and Wilmot, *Interpersonal Conflict*, 12.

7. Adapted from Robert McGarvey, "Winning Criticism," *U.S. Air* 11 (October 1989): 20–28.

8. Ron Adler and Neil Towne, *Looking Out/Looking In*, 5th ed. (New York: Holt, Rinehart & Winston, 1987), 325–332.

9. M. Michael Markowich and JoAnna Farber, "Managing Your Achilles' Heel," *Personnel Administrator* 32 (June 1987): 137–149.

10. Markowich and Farber, "Managing," 144.

11. Michael E. Cavanagh, "Employee Problems: Prevention and Intervention," *Personnel Journal* 66 (September 1987): 35–36, 38, 40.

12. Hocker and Wilmot, *Interpersonal Conflict*, 138–140.

13. Ralph Kilmann and Kenneth Thomas, "Interpersonal Conflict-Handling Behavior As Reflections of Jungian Personality Dimensions," *Psychological Reports* 37 (1975): 971–980. Although recent research identifies limitations of the Kilmann and Thomas scheme (see Hocker and Wilmot, *Interpersonal Conflict*, 3rd ed., p. 119), the "Thomas-Kilmann Conflict Mode Instrument" is widely used in corporate training.

14. Hocker and Wilmot, *Interpersonal Conflict*, 2nd ed. (Dubuque, IA: Wm. C. Brown, 1985), 40–48; H. Kent Baker and Philip I. Morgan, "Building a Professional Image: Handling Conflict," *Supervisory Management* 31 (February 1986): 24–29.

15. George R. Bach and Herb Goldberg, *Creative Aggression* (New York: Doubleday, 1974); George R. Bach and Peter Wyden, *The Intimate Enemy: How to Fight Fair in Love and Marriage* (New York: Avon, 1976); Adler and Towne, *Looking Out*, 345–346.

16. These scenarios are based on scripts written by Don Morley for a staff workshop held at the University of Colorado, Colorado Springs, in 1983.

17. Bach and Goldberg, *Creative Aggression*, 302.

18. J. R. P. French, Jr., and B. Raven, "The Bases of Social Power," in D. Cartwright and A. Zander, eds., *Group Dynamics: Research and Theory* (New York: Harper & Row, 1968), 259–269; Paul Hersey and Kenneth H. Blanchard, *Management of Organizational Behavior: Utilizing Human Resources* (Englewood Cliffs, NJ: Prentice-Hall, 1982), 178–179.

19. Hersey and Blanchard, *Management*, 179–180; M. Afzalur Rahium, "Relationships of Leader Power to Compliance and Satisfaction with Supervision: Evidence from a National Sample of Managers," *Journal of Management* 15 (4), 545–556.

20. Adapted from Michele Tolela Myers and Gail E. Myers, *Managing by Communication* (New York: McGraw-Hill, 1982), 198–202.

21. John Kotter, *Power and Influence* (New York: Free Press, 1985), 82.

22. R. Wayne Pace and Don F. Faules, *Organizational Communication*, 2nd ed. (Englewood Cliffs, NJ: Prentice-Hall, 1989), 221.

23. Vincent L. Ferraro and Sheila A. Adams, "Interdepartmental Conflict: Practical Ways to Prevent and Reduce It," *Personnel* 61 (July–August 1984): 12.

24. Ferraro and Adams, "Interdepartmental Conflict," 13–14.

25. Edgar F. Huse and James L. Bowditch, *Behavior in Organizations:*

A *Systems Approach to Managing* (Reading, MA: Addison-Wesley, 1973), 129–131; Pace and Faules, *Organizational Communication,* 222–223.

26. Ferraro and Adams, "Interdepartmental Conflict," 21–22.

27. Joseph F. Byrnes, "Ten Guidelines for Effective Negotiating," *Business Horizons* 30 (May–June 1987): 7.

28. Jeremy Main, "How to Be a Better Negotiator," *Fortune,* 19 September 1983, 141.

29. Byrnes, "Ten Guidelines," 7–12; Main, "How to Be," 141–142, 144, 146; Paul Kirvan, "Negotiating — The Art of Getting What You Want while Also Making Others Feel Good about It," *Communications News* 24 (May 1987): 97–99.

30. Byrnes, "Ten Guidelines," 8.

31. Main, "How to Be," 146.

32. Byrnes, "Ten Guidelines," 11.

33. Roger Fisher and William Ury, *Getting to Yes* (Boston: Houghton Mifflin, 1981), 59.

34. Peter S. Adler, "The Balancing Act of Mediation Training," *Training and Development Journal* 38 (July 1984): 55–58.

35. Adler, "The Balancing Act," 58.

Part IV  The Unspoken Word

Chapter 11  Communicating Nonverbally in Organizations

Man is a multi-sensory being; occasionally he verbalizes. — *Ray Birdwhistell*

It's Monday morning, the first day of your new job at Decco Corporation. You roll over at 5:45 A.M., remember what day it is, and leap out of bed, eager to begin your new adventure. You shower, spray or pat yourself with a variety of scents, polish your shoes until you can see your reflection, and "glue" each hair into place. As you open the closet door, you survey the choices: the navy suit, the tan jacket, or the plaid blazer? After downing coffee and a roll, you load your car with an armload of books (*The One Minute Manager, Communicating in Business and the Professions, Webster's Dictionary*, and so on); the leaded glass paperweight your grandmother gave you for graduation; your diploma, framed in black; a reproduction of *Place de l'Europe on a Rainy Day* by French painter Gustave Caillebotte; and a small *Ficus* tree. You strap yourself in for the commute ahead. You know you only have one chance to make a first impression, and from your very first day on the job, you want to create the right image.

The preceding description may sound routine to most of us, the kind of morning we'd expect to have in similar circumstances, give or take a few particulars. What most of us don't realize, however, is the extent to which nonverbal communication enters the picture. The truth is that nonverbal communication plays an important role not only in our personal lives but also in our professional lives. In fact, researchers report that from 60 percent to 93 percent of the meaning transferred between two or more people is communicated by the nonverbal channel.[1]

Our opening example of a first day on the job uses the word *image* as the new hiree works to create an impression through dress, grooming, and office decor. Whether we use *image* or another currently popular label, experts tell us that the nonverbal channel is more pervasive, more salient, and often more informative than the verbal channel. Believe it or not, the average person talks for a total of only some twenty-five minutes per day.[2] The nonverbal channel, on the other hand, cannot be turned off.

In other words, our posture, facial expressions, eye contact, clothing, touch, tone of voice, and distance between ourselves and others — these things often communicate more than the words we sometimes craft so carefully. While verbal communication usually is deliberate and often planned, nonverbal behaviors often are unintentional and difficult to self-monitor.

In recent years, the business and professional world has zeroed in on the importance of nonverbal communication. Our word *image*, for example, has become a byword in today's corporation. Many companies hire image consultants to teach their executives how to dress and present themselves. Jack Hilton, chairman and CEO of Jack Hilton, Inc., a media-image consulting company, reported being retained by 320 of the Fortune 500 companies as well as by scores of other companies in 1985.[3] Both large and small companies hire interior designers to make the most effective use of color and space. Some companies even hire consultants who use movement theory (the shape and flow of physical movement) to analyze employees' decision-making styles. From their analyses, these consultants claim that they can strengthen employee's sales skills, put together better teams, and help organizations make better hiring decisions.[4] As one professional image consultant puts it:

> How important is image? Look at two types of cars — the Toyota and the Mercedes. Both have four wheels, a steering wheel, and an instrument panel. The Toyota gets you from point A to point B and does a fabulous job. However, given a choice, most of us would rather go from point A to point B in a Mercedes. Why? Because of image. People will pay an extra 20 to 25 thousand dollars for the image of that automobile. That's the way it works — in business and with you. Many times, you're not just selling yourself — you're selling the *image* you have created, the image that surrounds you.[5]

Even an entire corporation has an image, one that it projects to the general public to affect its credibility, profitability, and overall success. "Institutional body language," as it has been called, is "the often inadvertent, often unintended communication that calls into question the accuracy and sincerity of previous statements."[6] Several years ago, for example, CEOs of U.S. automakers asserted that "either a three-year wage freeze or a renewal of government supported quotas on Japanese auto imports or both were necessary to enable the industry to survive competition with the Japanese."[7] That same year, while the average raise for rank-and-file workers at General Motors was set at approximately 1.9 percent, 5,801 company executives received bonuses of $181.7 million, an average of $31,000 apiece. Chrysler's Lee Iacocca received a $115,000 raise, 150,000 shares of common stock (worth almost $4 million), and a bonus of nearly $1 million. Ford chairman Phillip Caldwell, then listed in *Business Week* as the second highest-paid person in the United States, was given a $900,000 bonus. What was not publicized widely was that during Chrysler's three worst years, Iacocca received an annual salary of only $1; or that during the years Ford did not grant bonuses to top executives, it lost five of its best people to Subaru, seven to Toyota, and twenty-eight to Nissan. Nevertheless, "the public reaction was decidedly negative and the public perception, even at government level, surprisingly damning."[8]

The "inside word" has been our theme throughout *Communicating in Business and the Professions*. Now that we've discussed "The Word" (principles of communication in organizations), "The Written Word" (the power of effective writing), and "The Spoken Word" (the role of spoken language in organizational contexts), we want to focus your attention on "The Unspoken Word." In this chapter, we'll explore two questions. First, what is the role of nonverbal messages in organizations? Second, how can you become a better nonverbal communicator? We'll cover such particulars as body movement or kinesics, interpersonal space, physical characteristics, dress, artifacts, paralanguage, touch, and environmental cues, especially office arrangement. Our goal is to increase your sensitivity to nonverbal messages and to help you improve your own nonverbal skills as a future businessperson or professional.

THE ROLE OF NONVERBAL MESSAGES

Principles of Nonverbal Communication

Before we discuss specific areas of nonverbal communication in organizations, let's set the stage with some general principles. What generalizations can be made about nonverbal communication? We offer the following five statements for you to think about.[9]

1. *Whenever people are together, nonverbal communication occurs.* If you've taken a basic course in interpersonal communication, you learned this principle as the following axiom: You cannot *not* communicate. Even though the verbal channel can be turned on and off at will, the nonverbal channel is continuous. Consider the absurdity of saying to your colleagues at the office, "Don't bother looking at me today to figure out how I feel about things because I will not use any facial expressions" or "Forget it, folks. Today I refuse to have posture!" Although you may be able to "flip a switch" to turn your voice on and off, your body sends nonstop signals. Whenever people are together, nonverbal communication is a given.

2. *Nonverbal messages are contextual.* Think of all the ways your boss could express the phrase, "Nice job!" One version may sound sincere, one obligatory, and one sarcastic. Correctly interpreting subtle changes in tone of voice (which is considered to be nonverbal information) depends on how the message is related to the context; being congratulated by "Nice job!" immediately after a successful presentation is praise, but being chided with "Nice job!" after forgetting to submit your monthly report on time is sarcasm. Even smiles, nods, and winks can carry different meanings depending on the circumstances at hand.

3. *Nonverbal messages are packaged rather than isolated.* If you zero in on only one type of nonverbal message, you may inaccurately read the nonverbal communication of others. Facial expressions or one area of the body—arms, for example—don't tell all. Contrary to popular opinion, crossed arms do not always mean that a person feels defiant or argumentative. Sometimes we cross our arms because we're cold, we feel more comfortable that way, or we don't know what else to do with them. In other words, crossed arms as a potential nonverbal cue does not occur in isolation. Instead, it occurs in a given context, with an accompanying facial expression, posture, level of eye contact, and so forth. Experts put it this way: You'd learn little about the game of baseball if you elected to watch only one player. You must watch the interaction between players to understand the game. The same is true of nonverbal messages.

4. *Nonverbal messages communicate affect.* In business and professional interactions, you will be able to tell how others are responding to you and your ideas by the nonverbal messages they send. You will use the nonverbal channel to ascertain the power structure in the organization. You also will communicate to others your awareness of them and their importance to you. Nonverbal messages serve as the vehicle for transmitting three kinds of affective information: *immediacy* (liking versus disliking), *dominance* (controlling versus submissiveness), and *responsiveness* (awareness of and reaction to others).[10]

   Immediacy refers to the evaluative dimension of nonverbal messages. As nonverbal communication expert Albert Mehrabian asserts, "People are drawn toward persons and things they like, evaluate highly, and prefer; and they avoid or move away from things they dislike, evaluate negatively, or do not prefer."[11] Salespersons, for example, soon learn to distinguish between the item a client prefers and other products he is merely considering.

   Dominance or power is also communicated nonverbally in organizations. Typically, the size and location of a person's office, how accessible she is, how accessible you are to her, the number of status symbols she surrounds herself with or is privy to (a private secretary, a company car, access to the executive dining room, and so forth) are directly proportional to the amount of influence and decision-making power this individual has. Some companies have opted to deliberately flatten their organizational structures and reduce the number and types of status symbols. However, many traditional organizations still use them to differentiate between hierarchical levels and to motivate employees to work hard enough to move up the organizational ladder.

Responsiveness, the third affective dimension of nonverbal messages, reflects our awareness of other people and their importance to us. An employee who walks down the corridor with her eyes focused straight ahead, unaware of others who smile or otherwise greet her, demonstrates low responsiveness to others. An employee who readily expresses his anger, joy, and hurt feelings to those around him demonstrates high responsiveness in his emotional reaction to others.

5. *Nonverbal messages are highly believable.* Perhaps because nonverbal messages often are affective in nature, they are highly credible. When we are presented with conflicting verbal and nonverbal messages, the nonverbal message usually is the more convincing. If a colleague begins a presentation with knees and hands shaking, voice trembling, and feet pacing but verbally denying a bad case of nerves, the audience knows beyond the shadow of a doubt which message to believe. Sigmund Freud once said, "He that has eyes to see and ears to hear may convince himself that no mortal can keep a secret. If his lips are silent, he chatters with his fingertips; betrayal oozes out of him at every pore."[12]

The Relationship Between Verbal and Nonverbal Cues

Now that we've examined five basic principles of nonverbal communication, let's look at a related question: What is the relationship between verbal messages and nonverbal messages? According to Ray Birdwhistell, a pioneer in the study of nonverbal communication, the two are inextricably related. In fact, he asserts that studying nonverbal communication in isolation is akin to studying "noncardiac" physiology.[13] In truth, it can't be done. Therefore, let's explore the question: Just how do verbal and nonverbal messages coordinate? Consider the following six ideas.[14]

1. *Nonverbal messages repeat verbal messages.* To ensure being understood, we sometimes double up on messages. This is what happens when your secretary yells in from the hallway, "How many copies of the quarterly report did you want?" and you hold up two fingers and at the same time yell back, "Two."

Better to be redundant than to risk losing the message because of noise, confusion, or distance.

2. *Nonverbal messages contradict verbal messages.* Although contradiction between verbal and nonverbal communication forms the basis for sarcasm, we often are unaware that we send conflicting messages. For example, consider a supervisor who *tells* you during your first week on the job that she believes in an "open door" policy; that is, if you have any questions or concerns, then you may feel free to bring them to her. The first time you try this approach, however, it backfires. When you knock on her door, she heaves a sigh, rolls her eyes in disgust, and gives you a curt "Yes?" As we discussed earlier, we usually choose to rely on nonverbal information instead of conflicting verbal information. Mixed messages are confusing, and if they persist, we become defensive and distrustful.

3. *Nonverbal messages substitute for verbal messages.* Sometimes words alone don't do the job. When your best friend, who has three children at home, a fourth in college, and another one on the way, gets a pink slip telling him he's just been laid off, you may be at a loss for words. Instead of saying anything at all, you may simply give him a reassuring squeeze on the arm to communicate your support. When you come home from an unusually stressful day at the office — a major presentation for senior management in the morning, a conference over lunch, nonstop meetings in the afternoon — your roommate or spouse may be able to "read" your nonverbal cues accurately before you say a word.

4. *Nonverbal messages complement verbal messages.* We often use nonverbal messages to bring our words to life. When you're sitting in the corporate lunchroom and telling colleagues about watching *Halloween XII* last night on cable television and you say, "And then, she chopped off his head and blood gushed all over the floor" while wincing your face in disgust, you're embellishing your verbal message to make it more vivid. If you're giving a new employee directions to the marketing department and you draw a map in the air with your hands by pointing this way and that, you are complementing your verbal message with a nonverbal one to increase the likelihood that your listener will understand.

5. *Nonverbal messages accent verbal messages.* Nonverbal messages often are used to stress a point or to sharpen or punctuate a message. When your boss pounds his fist on the table

and yells "Time out!" to get everyone's attention during a heated meeting, he's undoubtedly accenting his verbal message nonverbally. In another instance, just as you would underline a word in writing, you may provide a nonverbal accent by emphasizing or stressing a particular part of your message: "You *said* you'd have the report by last Wednesday. It's now Monday morning. . . ."

6. *Nonverbal messages regulate the back-and-forth flow of verbal messages.* Although most of us don't realize it, human conversation is an art form. When two people interact, each one sends subtle nonverbal signals to indicate, for example, "It's my turn to talk," "I'm about finished; it's your turn," "Wait a minute, I'm not quite through," or "I really have to be leaving now." We do all this by making eye contact, taking a breath, raising a hand to gesture, and leaning forward when we want to talk, or by looking away, leaning back, and lowering a gesture when we don't. The stream of such turn-taking signals during the give and take of meetings is continuous. Leave-taking signals work in a similar fashion. When an employee is taking more time than you have available to fill you in on a departmental squabble, you probably will glance at your watch, orient your body toward the door, break eye contact, and possibly even stand up to signal your desire to end the interaction.

PERSONAL CUES

Stand tall. The difference between towering and cowering is totally a matter of inner posture. It's got nothing to do with height, it costs nothing, and it's more fun. — Malcolm Forbes

Now that we've looked broadly at the role of nonverbal messages in communication, let's personalize the discussion. What areas of nonverbal communication are important to your future role in business or the professions? We'll next examine five types of nonverbal messages that occur in organizational contexts: kinesics; proxemics; physical characteristics, dress, and artifacts; paralanguage; and touch.

Kinesics

Kinesics, or body movements such as gestures, posture, facial expressions, and eye movements, play an important role in organizational communication. Your handshake with a new hiree, your air-sketched directions to the training and development department, your well-rehearsed gestures during an important presentation — all of these are examples of kinesic behavior. According to researchers Ekman and Friesen, kinesic behaviors fall into five categories: emblems, illustrators, affect displays, regulators, and adaptors.[15] Let's look at examples of each within an organizational context.

Emblems are nonverbal signals that have direct verbal translations. If you're talking on the telephone in your office and a colleague comes to the door, you are likely to give a wave of greeting, perhaps hold up your palm to communicate "wait," then make a beckoning motion to tell him to enter, and finally point to the empty chair to invite him to sit. You need not say a word; your signals are interpreted easily. Likewise, if you make an imaginary pistol with your hand and pretend to shoot yourself in the temple upon hearing that next week's deadline has been moved up to tomorrow or you pinch your nose with your thumb and index finger to communicate that the latest company policy change "stinks," then you are communicating with emblems.

Be aware, however, that emblems translate differently from one culture to another. Although the handshake may be a universal or near-universal emblem to communicate goodwill, most emblems are culturally specific. Years ago, then Vice-President Richard Nixon nearly created an international incident when he stepped off a plane in Latin America and flashed the OK sign to a booing crowd. In that culture, the verbal translation of our OK sign was "Screw you!" If international business is your intended career field, then beware!

Illustrators are the appropriately named nonverbal "sketches" that accompany language. If you are asked how thick last year's report was, and you measure off three inches with your thumb and index finger, or if you define an angular intersection on the new product with your hands during a sales demonstration, then you are using nonverbal signals to *illustrate* your verbal message. Strictly speaking, almost all of the normal gestures we use during speech are classified as illustrators. As you know, some of us use them sparingly, while some of us would be almost speechless with our hands tied behind our backs!

Affect displays are facial expressions of emotion. According to researchers, all cultures use and recognize at least six universal affect displays: anger, happiness, sadness, fear, disgust, and surprise.[16] However, it's estimated that the face is capable of producing more than 20,000 expressions.[17] Blends of emotions—anger plus fear, for example—and micromomentary flashes of emotion make matters more complicated. Unlike emblems and illustrators, which are fairly conscious acts, affect displays can be difficult to self-monitor. When you invoke a "stiff upper lip" after leaving a difficult session with your boss and your secretary says, "Gee, you look stressed out today!", your affect display has just given you away. Your face is the primary vehicle for communicating affect, although your entire body also can droop with sadness or tense with anger.

Regulators are the subtle signals we use to control the give and take of conversation. In meetings, for example, you probably will lean forward, raise your index finger in midair, draw in a breath, and look directly at the speaker to signal that you want to speak next. If the speaker is willing to relinquish the floor, she will look at you, drop her own midair gesture, and lean back in her chair. If she is unwilling to relinquish the floor, she will probably raise her voice, accelerate her speech, and perhaps touch your arm to "squelch" you if you're close enough or give you a "wait a minute" hand gesture. All of these signals are sent subtly and quickly, usually without premeditation. Although we rarely perceive regulators at a conscious level, they usually are an effective means of controlling interaction.

Adaptors are nonverbal movements designed to meet a physical or emotional need. They include many self-touching acts: scratching an itch, rubbing your eyes, or biting your fingernails, for example. Watch a novice speaker in your organization during his first high-stakes presentation, and you probably will see a range of adaptors, from jingling the change in his pockets to rubbing his nose repeatedly or wringing his hands.

Posture and eye behavior also are considered to be part of our kinesic repertoires. Posture appears to communicate three primary messages: our emotional states, our status, and our general attitudes.[18] In organizations, you'll notice that those with higher status tend to use more relaxed postures than do employees of lesser status. Although the types of possible positions fall into three basic categories—standing, bent-knee positions, and lying down—1,000 possible postures have been recorded.[19]

Eye behavior, which also is considered to be in the realm of kinesic cues, communicates control, involvement, and credibility in organizations.[20] For example, those with more status and *credibility* usually receive more eye gaze than those with lower status. In meetings, leaders often *control* communication flow by making eye contact with individuals to grant permission to take the floor. And paying dutiful attention as a listener communicates *involvement* in the interaction.

Proxemics

Think of all the things that space communicates in an organization: power, status, position, ownership, and territoriality, to name a few. Space is a factor in the interpersonal dynamics between you and others in the organization, whether you're involved in a one-to-one discussion in your office, participating in small group meetings in a conference room, or lunching with other employees in the company cafeteria. The spatial configuration of furniture and offices also plays a major role in the way organizational communicators interact. We now direct your attention to the interpersonal dimensions of space in organizations, while leaving environmental factors for a later discussion.

Individuals appear to interact within four proxemic zones based on several factors, such as how well we know our conversational partners and the nature of the interaction between us.[21] Are all four evident in organizations? See what you think.

The *intimate distance* ranges from actual touching to a distance of 1½ feet. Obviously, it is the distance reserved for those with whom we are intimate or for those who must interact with us at close range; a physician, tailor, or barber, for example. In organizations, interactions of this nature are limited. You may lean over and whisper something to a colleague or give someone a congratulatory pat on the back, but most of us are uncomfortable conducting business within the intimate distance zone.

The *personal distance*, which ranges from 1½ to 4 feet, describes colleagues sitting side by side or across the table at lunch or conversing around the coffee pot while on break. The farther range of this zone is most common when we conduct business. You probably would stand 4 feet from your secretary while giving instructions about the room arrangement for tomorrow's training session, for example.

Social distance, on the other hand, ranges from 4 to 12 feet, the distance at which we most likely conduct more formal, impersonal business either with colleagues we don't know well or with people from other organizations. We also can take steps to manipulate the environment to create a *sense* of additional space, moving from personal to social distance when we feel the need. For example, when space is at a premium but social distance is required for psychological reasons, we create barriers or structure the environment in particular ways. If you were forced to share an office with another employee, you might face your desks toward opposite walls or separate the room with a bookcase or credenza to put more "distance" between you.

Finally, a *public distance* of from 12 to 25 or more feet is reserved for both strangers and people we fear or hold in awe. If you are summoned to the CEO's plush, ocean-view office for unknown reasons, you might enter the room and stop abruptly. Without realizing it, you may not wish to penetrate the public zone of this person whom you've never met and whose position you respect greatly.

In organizations, space signals status, power, and territoriality. In both subtle and obvious ways, space communicates who you are and how much the organization values your contribution. It's important to be sensitive to the information carried by proxemic cues and to carry on your business at ranges that are comfortable to others.

Physical Characteristics, Dress, and Artifacts

You never get a second chance to make a good, *first impression.*
—John Molloy

Physical appearance plays an important role in business and professional communication. Your body shape, height, grooming, dress, and artifacts are among the factors that act as cues for the judgments others make about you. Some aspects of physical appearance—sex, height, and race, for example—are permanent. Other characteristics such as your hairstyle and grooming habits are determined by you.

In organizations as much as most other social situations, tall, trim, attractive people seem to have an advantage. If you do not fit the company's image because your hair is bushy or because your dress is too "far out," you probably will be told so either directly or indirectly—or you won't be hired in the first place. If you have a large, round, soft body rather than a tall and thin or muscular and athletic body, then you may have difficulty breaking through societal stereotypes. If others judge you to be unattractive, you may have to work harder to impress them. Fair or not, packaging counts. And, of course, one of the primary ways we package ourselves is through our choice of clothing.

If you went to your local bookstore to find advice on professional dress, you probably would come across two books written by "America's first wardrobe engineer," John T. Molloy. For many years, two Molloy books, *Dress for Success* and *The Woman's Dress for Success Book*, were regarded as the Bibles of corporate dress.[22] Molloy told the corporate American to adopt a conservative business image by dressing in a dark blue or gray suit, a white or pastel shirt or blouse, a conservatively patterned tie or scarf darker than the shirt, and plain, laced shoes for men and pumps for women. More than 1.5 million copies of *Dress for Success* are in print, along with 775,000 copies of Molloy's sequel for women,

Drawing by Shanahan; © 1990 The New Yorker Magazine, Inc.

and Molloy has served as an image consultant to 380 of the United States' Fortune 500 companies.[23]

Today many of Molloy's basic principles have more liberal interpretations. Although most companies still require conservative dress codes for their employees, those with relaxed cultures allow for more individuality and, in some cases, more casual attire. The key to business dress remains understatement, but today's executive has more latitude in terms of color, style, and accessories.[24] Men now can express themselves with patterned socks, suspenders, and pastel shirts; women also have moved away from the dark suit, white blouse, and silk bow tie — the replica of the male "uniform":

> Silk foulards, a dark navy male-type suit, and a hard-sided briefcase for a woman. A dark vested pin-stripe suit, white shirt, and striped tie for a man. Those were the corporate uniforms when women had to prove they were serious about their jobs and careers and when men were too insecure and companies too intolerant to allow for broader individual choice. In the 80's, both corporations and individuals [turned] away from the carbon-copy look.[25]

Although most experts agree that trends have changed since Molloy's books of the 1970s, your dress choices on the job still depend on several factors. One is the type of job you hold. For a man who works in production as a manufacturing engineer on the floor of a factory, casual slacks and shirt sleeves may be the norm, but if he interviews potential new employees in the personnel department, wearing a suit or sport coat may be a requirement of the job.

The same advice holds true for women. According to experts, three different career profiles for women require three different images: Corporate, Communicator, and Creative.[26] The Corporate woman works as a banker, attorney, or manager; the Communicator may be a professor, politician, or television reporter; and the Creative woman is an artist, musician, writer, or fashion designer. All three types wish to appear competent and professional, but the Corporate woman should project an image of efficiency and objectivity, the Communicator must appear credible and personable, and the Creative woman should emphasize her innovativeness and imagination. Frills, ruffles, and plunging necklines remain off limits, but today's organizational woman wears bolder prints, more jacketed dresses, and softer lines, in addition to the standard business suit.

If the style and comfort of your dress are important to you, then consider this aspect of an organization's culture as you interview with various organizations. Your own personal style and taste must be in tune with the culture of the organization in which you will work. Informal cultures allow relaxed dress; conservative cultures require more formal attire. Even though more liberal dress codes exist in some companies, don't assume they exist in all organizations.

In the beginning, of course, err on the side of conservatism. The farther down the organizational ladder your position, the more conservative your dress should be. Pay particular attention to the idiosyncrasies of the organization you join. According to one recent survey, many organizations still have strict but subtle and unspoken guidelines. At Goldman Sachs, an investment firm, three-button jackets for men are unacceptable; two-button jackets are the rule. Nearly all men at IBM wear white shirts and black wing-tip shoes; on Wall Street, brown suits are out. Slacks for women are forbidden at major New York law firms, and women who work at *Glamour* and *Vogue* magazines wear black tights exclusively instead of flesh-toned stockings.[27]

In business and the professions, dress rules are communicated by "osmosis" and generated by the nature of your job, the image of your company, the audience you are addressing, and your own personality: "Good fashion is not a ticket to the top. But it's a secure means whereby you won't be criticized."[28] In short, your dress sends a powerful nonverbal message:

The difference between a product that has been packaged well and one that hasn't may be the difference between success and failure. No one will know if the cookies taste good if they never buy the box. And one package won't work for everything. . . . Each package should say something special about the contents and each product must be packaged appropriately for its audience. The same applies to people. You may have more talent than anyone else in your field, but unless you present the right kind of package, no one will bother to find out about you.[29]

Artifacts, the personal items we wear or keep close to us, are another important aspect of physical appearance. Women, for example, should use makeup tastefully and keep jewelry to a minimum. Jingling bracelets and dangling earrings detract from an image of credibility. Men should avoid earrings altogether in conservative companies.

Paralanguage

As mentioned earlier, a single thought can be expressed in many ways. "Nice job!", for example, may be said with sincerity, jealousy, or sarcasm. *How* you say what you say is considered the nonverbal component of spoken language. You may vary a message by changing the pitch of certain words from low to high, the rhythm from smooth to halting, the rate from fast to slow, the articulation from forced to relaxed, and so forth. In fact, much of the meaning we interpret during everyday conversation comes from the affective components, or *paralanguage*, rather than from the actual words themselves. Consider the words, "I'm going to the meeting," and the various messages made possible by varying the paralinguistic features:

I'm going to the meeting. (I'm not sending you.)
I'm *going* to the meeting. (I'm not going to stay here at my desk twiddling my thumbs.)
I'm going *to* the meeting. (I'm on my way there; I'm not on my way back.)
I'm going to *the* meeting. (The one we've all been waiting for.)
I'm going to the *meeting*. (I'm not going to lunch.)

Paralanguage communicates important information. A revealing example of the power of paralanguage occurred in 1974 when the House

Judiciary Committee, which was investigating impeachment charges against President Richard Nixon, refused to accept written transcripts of White House tapes. Committee members complained that inflection, stress, and other nuances would be missing from written transcripts and so demanded that the White House provide the actual voice tapes. Obviously, vocal cues provide listeners with information about your personality, your emotional state, and your identity, including your age, sex, race, and possibly even regional origin and economic status.[30]

....

Touch

In the organizational setting, touch plays a predictable, although limited, communication role. The following five functions of touch, however, can be observed in most organizations.[31]

functional-professional: impersonal touch with a clear professional purpose (a doctor examining a patient)
social-polite: recognized touch traditions in social interaction (two professionals shaking hands to close a deal)
affectionate-intimate: touch that invades personal space (patting a colleague on the back)
relational-dominant: touch that reinforces roles in superior–subordinate relationships (a male boss who feels free to put his arm around a female employee)
relational-manipulative: touch that helps a person achieve a particular outcome (a politician who shakes hands with hundreds of voters).

Aside from an occasional handshake or pat on the back, touching is mostly *verboten* in most organizations. Laws against sexual harassment have heightened our awareness of the dangers of unsolicited touch in the workplace. An innocent squeeze on the arm may be misinterpreted as an indication of romantic attraction. Even though we get to know our co-workers well, the task orientation of the work environment tends to focus our attention away from intimate social interaction. At work, touch takes prescribed and predictable forms, although the colleagues you work with every day may behave somewhat differently at a social gathering. The unspoken rules for comfortable interaction distance and touch may be suspended or at least relaxed a bit.

ENVIRONMENTAL CUES

....

How the Environment Affects Organizational Communicators

We shape our buildings, thereafter they shape us. — Winston Churchill

Return to the beginning of this chapter for a moment and picture yourself on the job that first day, walking into your new office for the first time. Look around. What do you see: a spacious, plush, penthouse suite with a 360-degree view? the corner office overlooking the harbor? the generic third office on the left? or the cramped, unadorned cubicle at the end of a dark hallway?

The first view probably is too much to hope for, and the last isn't particularly motivating, but you should be aware of several factors when it comes to office environments. Research indicates that office design has a substantial effect on employee reactions toward the workplace. In one study, for example, dense, accessible, and dark offices were associated with low satisfaction and a tendency to spend coffee breaks outside the office.[32] Besides influencing your reactions, features such as space, decor, and furnishings and their arrangement probably will play a role in communicating to others in the organization your position, status, and power as well as something about the kind of person you are.

Unfortunately, many office buildings are built to enhance the company image rather than the productivity and comfort of workers. Some would say that the high-technology appeal of the design, which sometimes attempts to create a mental connection to the product or service represented, has become overly important. Offices are drab white, tan, or gray and offer little inspiration to employees. Architects and designers should realize that during an average five-day work week, workers spend one-half of their waking hours on the job. Satisfaction with the work environment is related to job performance.[33]

....

The Office Environment

In some ways, your office is an extension of your personality. According to psychologists and architects, extroverts are likely to place their desks facing the door so that they can keep in touch with the people walking by. They also tend to position the visitor's chair in a side-by-side or corner-by-corner arrangement and have papers strewn all over their desks so that they can work on several projects at once. Introverts, however, prefer to face a wall, sometimes even the wall opposite the door so that their backs are toward the door (which sometimes is seen by others as a hostile act). If they are detail-oriented people, then their offices will be orderly and impersonal. Even gender differences in preferences for office arrangement can be important. Women are more likely to choose side-by-side seating arrangements than are men.[34]

Your office thus communicates information about your personality. In many organizations, however, office features such as *accessibility*, *floor space and layout*, and *decor* are also recognized symbols of status.

Accessibility. A well-known axiom of organizational communication holds that the higher up in the hierarchy your position, the more inaccessible you will become. You will spend more of your time secluded in your office or away from it in meetings, and its physical location will be separated more from your subordinates. Ironically, the rule of thumb seems to be that the higher your position and the more subordinates you manage, the less physically accessible you become. At the top of the hierarchical ladder, you probably will be in a private office, not a cubicle, hidden away on the top floor, with several secretarial buffers between you and the outside organizational world. (No, it doesn't make much sense.) In one study, 68 percent of management-level employees but only 38 percent of nonmanagement employees reported having private offices.[35]

Proximity to the boss or to a desirable window or corner location also indicate status.[36] According to Michael Korda, a noted expert on organizational power, maximum power usually is found in the four corner offices, with power lines running in an **X** pattern. Korda asserts that "to the person for whom work is the exercise of power, the place where it is done becomes the board on which power games are played, the central source from which power is derived."[37]

By contrast, a lower-rank office is characterized by an "open" arrangement, a practice that has received mixed reviews. According to its proponents, movable panels (rather than floor to ceiling walls) encourage communication, promote cooperation, and stimulate friendships among employees. Critics, however, charge that the plan actually offers a means of surveillance by superiors.[38] Employees resent minimal privacy, feel crowded, and report lower motivation and satisfaction. Because of the increase in noise and distractions, they contend, efficiency suffers.[39]

Floor Space and Layout. The size of your office is a second indicator of organizational status. The American aphorism "bigger is better" holds true in most organizations. In fact, a Fortune 500 CEO making a six- or seven-digit salary but working in a postage stamp–sized office probably would seem bizarre. Think about it: the company president in his $1,000 Italian suit sitting behind a desk in a room slightly larger than a closet. Contrast that image with the more usual one in which the same president is dwarfed behind a huge desk in an office so large that voices echo.

Office Decor. Both the square footage of your office and its furnishings are other indicators of status. Research indicates that professionally related objects (diplomas, awards, and so on) and aesthetic objects (such as paintings and plants) appear to have a positive impact on the occupant's perceived trustworthiness and authoritativeness.[40] The amount, quality, and type of furniture in your office also sends a message about you and your hierarchical rank. A large desk; the presence and thickness of carpet; multiple work surfaces; wooden furniture as opposed to metal furniture; fine woods such as cherry, rosewood, or walnut over less expensive woods such as teak or mahogany — all of these elements communicate status.[41]

The single most important office status symbol may be the executive's desk. FBI Director J. Edgar Hoover communicated his position by sitting at a large, elevated desk with visitors below him at a small table to the side. Nelson Rockefeller's desk was unique: "I couldn't believe how simple his New York office was. But the big thing was his trick desk. It had a large pull-out drawer with steps on it. Rockefeller would strut up and step onto the top of his desk in order to address any assembled group."[42] Desks can operate as status symbols, as "platforms," or as barricades. Power expert Michael Korda advises businesspeople to lure colleagues from behind their desks to a more egalitarian sitting area if they wish to be truly persuasive: "Note that people with old-fashioned desks that serve as barriers almost always leave them to say 'yes,' and sit behind them to say 'no.' Once they have taken refuge behind five-hundredweight of mahogany, you can't argue with them."[43]

Such status symbols as private offices, plush carpeting, nameplates, and large desks serve three basic functions: They act as rewards for superior service, serve as incentives for future performance, and aid communication by clarifying rank within the organization.[44] In some organizations, status symbols are serious business. The story is told of one lower-level manager who was moved to a small office during a corporate expansion. The new office happened to have carpeting. Because the manager was not entitled to carpeting at his rank in the organization, his boss had the carpet torn up and removed, despite the expense of doing so.[45] Unfortunately, status symbols often consume a disproportionate amount of the emotions and energy of employees in organizations.[46]

"While you were on vacation, Zooker, a motion was made and seconded to saw five and a half inches off your chair legs."

The Conference-Room Environment

If you work in a large corporation, much of your communication will take place in conference rooms. Staff meetings, committee work, and private interviews with your employees often must be conducted on neutral territory. Let's examine two important variables that influence communication in a conference-room environment: seating arrangements and table configurations.

Seating arrangements around a conference table often are a matter of habit or rank: The department head *always* sits at the head of the table. If you've always sat to his immediate left at Monday morning staff meetings, then you'll probably continue to do so. After all, human beings are territorial animals. To you, your position at the table belongs to you just as if your name were written on the chair; if a new department member unknowingly takes your normal seat, then you may resent the intrusion.

What if a new group meets in a conference room for the first time and all members have relatively equal status in the organization? In this case, there are particular communication factors to consider. For example, whoever occupies the position at the end of the table is most likely to be perceived as the leader. In fact, this perception is so strong that normally reticent people placed at the head of a table actually communicate more.

The reason for this perception and the resulting behavior is pragmatic. The vantage point at the end of a long table provides maximum eye contact with people in every other position. This advantage allows you to exert the most control over the interaction. In our society, eye contact is an invitation to communicate; catching someone else's eye is a "go-ahead" signal. Conversely, others' participation in a group tends to increase relative to their visual access to the leader.[47]

Table configuration also plays a role in conference-room communication. If the above assertions hold, then it stands to reason that leadership is easier at a rectangular table with its perceived power position at the end. A round table tends to equalize status among group members and provide them with common visual access, which facilitates communication. In one study, L-shaped seating arrangements, in contrast with circular arrangements, provoked negative reactions and made group members fidgety, uncomfortable, and unwilling to involve themselves in the discussion.[48]

Computer Workstations

By the mid-1980s, more than seven million workers in North America were using visual display terminals (VDTs), and the numbers of desktop, portable, and lap-top computers continue to increase every day. Although we all realize the advantages of automation, VDT operators have reported more health complaints than any other group to the National Institute of Occupational Safety and Health because of eyestrain; back, neck, and shoulder pain; headaches; burning eyes; irritability; and fatigue. Some experts believe VDTs themselves are not the problem; instead, the real culprits are poorly designed work spaces that have glare, poor lighting, and poor layout.[49] However, some states and municipalities such as San Francisco are requiring organizations to consider the adverse affects of VDTs and provide safeguards such as frequent breaks to reduce strain.

When you work on a flat plane such as a desk, you need overhead lighting. When you work at a terminal, your line of sight is raised, and the same overhead lighting can produce a glare on a screen or cause reflections from your clothing, walls, or objects around the room to appear on the screen. Lights are typically too bright for the terminal screen as well, causing the characters to be difficult to read. When workstations are designed with these factors in mind, productivity increases by almost 25 percent. If you work at a VDT workstation, you should follow these guidelines:[50]

1. Reduce the light level to below that in a normal office; 20–24 footcandles was preferred in one study.
2. Occasionally look off into the distance 15 feet or more to relax your eye muscles.
3. Design or change existing lighting to reduce on-screen glare. Block out excessive daylight and paint walls with a flat finish.
4. Place the terminal below eye level and allow approximately 14–20 inches from eye to screen.
5. Take frequent breaks — 15 minutes every 2 hours for moderate use and 15 minutes every 1 hour for heavy use.

Creating a Productive Work Space

Although many features of your office will be controlled by your superiors rather than by you, you still can take steps to create a comfortable and productive work space. In fact, you should tailor your office to the type of work you do, to company standards, and to your own personal preferences because you will spend eight of every sixteen waking hours during the work week on the job. And research tells us that satisfaction with the environment is a definite factor in how well a person performs her job.[51]

You may not have much control over the size of your office, the color and thickness of the carpeting, or the dimness or brightness of the lighting, but you can control the arrangement of furniture (see Figures 11.1 and 11.2). You also can control the personal objects you choose to display. At the beginning of this chapter, for example, our hypothetical new hiree elected to decorate his office with his diploma framed in black, a reproduction of an art masterpiece, a leaded glass paperweight, several impressive books, and a small *Ficus* tree — all items that would contribute to the image of a well-educated, competent, and cultured employee.

On the other hand, if you *can* control the color of the walls and carpeting, how would you decide? As color specialists tell us, colors can produce many moods:

- red conveys excitement and dominance
- blue is calm and secure
- yellow produces inspiration and cheerfulness
- purple is dignified and stately
- green is tranquil and refreshing
- black provokes anxiety and fear
- brown is sad and despondent
- white creates a sense of joy and light.[52]

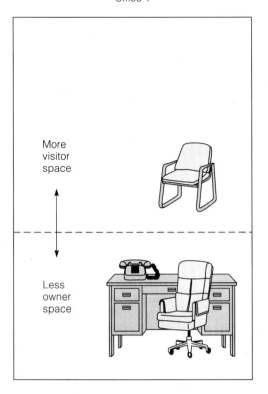

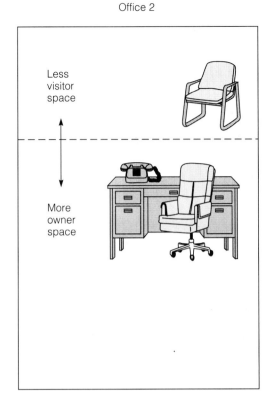

Figure 11.1 *Which office offers the greatest power advantage to its owner? Office 2 minimizes the space available for the visitor, giving the owner more territory and power.*[53]

Taking that information into account, you might decide you want an office environment that uses white walls, blue carpet, and red, yellow, green, or purple accents around the room.

Time as a Nonverbal Message

Think about the fact that an employee who earns $40,000 a year makes roughly $20 an hour. Everytime someone in the organization keeps that employee waiting ten minutes for an appointment or meeting,

••••••••••••••••••
Figure 11.2
*Where would you
sit to control an
interaction?*[54]

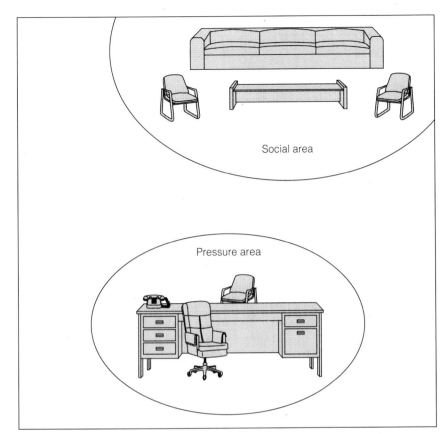

Social area

Pressure area

the organization loses $3.33. Multiply that figure by the number of times such instances occur each day times the number of employees in the company, and you have an astronomical figure. In organizations, time is money in a very literal sense.

Time also is related to status in organizations. Those with status can keep others waiting. They can talk longer than those with less power. They have more control over their own work schedules than do others. Waiting time, talk time, and work time all are affected by one's power and position in an organization.[55]

Aside from status determinations, our use of organizational time influences superior–subordinate relations, affects others' perceptions of our competence, and determines the control of outcomes.[56] Being late with a report, for example, can damage your relationship with your boss, influence her perception of your competence, and delay an important action until it is too late. Punctuality and time management thus are critical organizational skills.

IMPROVING NONVERBAL SKILLS

Throughout this chapter, we have discussed many aspects of nonverbal communication in business and the professions. Allow us to close the chapter with the following summarized principles for you to think about.

1. *Recognize the impact of nonverbal messages.* Your physical appearance, dress, posture, and a host of other factors will influence others' willingness to communicate with you and ultimately your advancement toward success in the organization. Nonverbal skills are an important component of your repertoire of overall communication skills.

2. *Cultivate your nonverbal sensitivity.* Learn to be a people watcher; observe others' nonverbal communication and the responses they receive. The ability to read nonverbal cues is an invaluable organizational skill. Much of what is important in organizational success entails persuading others — your boss, subordinates, and peers — to consider your point of view. Nonverbal sensitivity will allow you to track your degree of success in each situation. If you are proposing a controversial change in the organization, you must pick up paralinguistic cues and read facial expressions to determine the level of support you have from others, in addition to listening to what people have to say.

3. *Work for congruency between your verbal and nonverbal messages.* If your subordinates repeatedly are forced to choose between your words and your body language, then they will become confused, frustrated, and resentful. Some bosses give lip service to sound management practices, but when they are approached for assistance, even though their verbal messages are supportive, their nonverbal messages betray their irritation. Subordinates usually respond to this communication style by steering clear of the boss and finding answers to important questions elsewhere. The superior–subordinate relationship that is so important to both parties never has a chance to develop into the meaningful dialogue it should become. Even though you may be busy with a dozen simultaneous projects, don't fall into this communication trap.

4. *Attempt to fit in with the nonverbal aspects of your organization's culture.* As we've discussed throughout this chapter, much of an organization's culture is reflected in the nonverbal messages it sends. Spoken and unspoken dress codes, the number and

types of status symbols used, and the formality and privacy of office environments are clues about how the organization sees itself and its employees. Look for a good match between your own values and those of the organization as reflected in its nonverbal messages.

5. *Use the nonverbal channel to communicate your competence.* Not all of the impressive work you do in the organization will take place on paper or even through the spoken word. "Competence," as we reported earlier, "like truth, beauty and a contact lens, is in the eye of the beholder." We're not suggesting that image is everything, but we are suggesting that your nonverbal messages will play an important role in your overall success as an organizational communicator. Dress as professionally as possible in keeping with your organization's standards and reflect that professionalism in the appearance of your office. Work to create an image of competence through your nonverbal behavior.

6. *Use the nonverbal channel to achieve organizational goals.* Study situations, people, and communication styles in order to make decisions about structuring environments that help you achieve important organizational goals. If you must move a committee toward a deadline, for example, arrange the meeting room to help you do so. You could use name cards or individual folders with names on the fronts to control the seating arrangement. Or you could meet in neutral territory so that no group member has a "home-field" advantage.

Nonverbal communication affects each of us in business and the professions. Understanding the power of the unspoken word is key to becoming a successful organizational communicator. As one expert puts it:

While words are important, nonverbal messages frame the meaning we attach to those verbal symbols. Neglecting to "read" as many nonverbal signals as possible can result in a lost deal or promotion; paying attention to these signals can make the difference in organizational survival and success.[57]

CHAPTER SUMMARY

Chapter 11 answers two basic questions about nonverbal communication. First, What is the role of nonverbal communication in organizations? Second, How can you become a better nonverbal communicator?

The chapter began by describing the basic principles of nonverbal communication, examined both personal and environmental cues, and concluded with suggestions for you to consider as an organizational communicator.

The basic principles of nonverbal communication discussed are:

1. Whenever people are together, nonverbal communication exists.
2. Nonverbal messages are contextual.
3. Nonverbal messages are packaged rather than isolated.
4. Nonverbal messages communicate affect.
5. Nonverbal messages are highly believable.

Nonverbal messages are a powerful means of communication, no matter the type of business or profession you enter or the particular organization you join.

Because verbal and nonverbal communication are inextricably related, this chapter also looked at the relationship between the two: Nonverbal messages *repeat*, *contradict*, *substitute for*, *complement*, *accent*, and *regulate* verbal messages.

We then explored *personal cues* in nonverbal communication. *Kinesics*, or body movement, includes emblems, illustrators, affect displays, regulators, and adaptors.

Proxemics, or the way people use space, is an important type of nonverbal message in organizations. We allow few if any colleagues to interact with us at the intimate distance of from zero to 1½ feet, more people to approach us at the personal distance range of 1½ feet to 4 feet, and even more to interact at the social distance of 4 to 12 feet, which is where most business takes place. Limited interaction takes place within the public distance range of 12 to 25 or more feet, simply because organizations are composed of many people within a limited amount of space.

Physical characteristics, *dress*, and *artifacts* also play a role in organizational communication. Dress in particular has received considerable attention in the last fifteen years, with many popular self-help books available. We offered practical advice for dress in today's organization. The truth is that packaging counts in organizations.

Paralanguage, or *how* you say what you say, also is a powerful communication tool. Finally, the chapter discussed the role of interpersonal *touch* as a type of personal cue in business and the professions.

The importance of *environmental cues* in organizations cannot be understated. The office environment, including accessibility, floor space, layout, and decor, communicates both your power and position in the organization and your personality. The conference-room environment, including table arrangement and table configurations, influences the communication patterns and flow that take place. Computer workstations, a new environmental consideration resulting from the electronic age, require particular care in use to avoid physical strain. This section of the chapter concluded with suggestions on how to create a productive work space and then examined time as a nonverbal message.

Finally, Chapter 11 closed with the following summarized principles on improving nonverbal skills:

1. Recognize the impact of nonverbal messages.
2. Cultivate your nonverbal sensitivity.
3. Work for congruency between your verbal and nonverbal messages.
4. Attempt to fit in with the nonverbal aspects of your organization's culture.
5. Use the nonverbal channel to communicate your competence.
6. Use the nonverbal channel to achieve organizational goals.

MEASURING SUCCESS

1. Imagine that you are researching various organizations to work in after you graduate from your college or university. Select two organizations, local or national, that you suspect are characterized by fairly different cultures, one relaxed and informal and one conservative and formal. Through personal or telephone interviews, letters of inquiry, annual reports, or other research methods, determine the dress codes of the two organizations. Write a short report about each, including a detailed account of what you would wear on your first day of employment.

2. Watch a movie about life in the corporation: for example, *Working Girl*, *Nine to Five*, *Network*, *Big Business*, or *Wall Street*. Pay particular attention to the nonverbal messages sent between superiors and subordinates, and write a brief report that details your findings.

3. You are president of a large New York–based advertising firm, Enhanced Images, Inc. Because of recent economic trends, your firm has recently hired a financial analyst. Mr. Darryl Likt, a consultant from Bleak Outlook Ltd. in Los Angeles, is to review the corporation's present status and make recommendations for the future. Now you must advise your executive staff against accepting Likt's recommendation to sell your

company to a larger and more successful advertising firm, Creative Hype, Inc. You strongly disagree with his recommendation; however, you anticipate a mixed reaction from others within the firm. In your opinion, selling out to another company would create more problems than it would solve.

According to company policy, no action can be taken until a decision is reached by executive officers. It is up to you to schedule a meeting to vote on Likt's recommendation in approximately one month. Present at that meeting will be the company's vice-presidents:[58]

- Mr. Ray Beeze, Marketing
- Ms. Leda Doggslife, Communication
- Mr. X. O. Verrisi, Finance
- Ms. Dewanna Dantz, Public Relations
- Mr. Juan Annatoo, Artistic Design
- Ms. Bertha D. Blues, Personnel
- Mr. Dan Druff, Facilities

You happen to know that Ms. Blues and Mr. Annatoo currently are "enemies" because of a recent personnel matter; the two have not spoken for weeks. Ms. Doggslife is a strong feminist, while Mr. Verrisi and Mr. Druff are older and extremely conservative, having been with the firm since its inception. Mr. Druff has an abrasive personality and generally is disliked, while Ms. Dantz has come up quickly in the organization because of her efficiency and her ability to work well with people. The only opinion you now know is that of Mr. Beeze, who agrees with you. In fact, you long have considered him to be your "right-hand man."

The east wing of Enhanced Images, Inc., currently is being remodeled. The main conference room is almost completed; however, you have time to put on the "finishing touches" with furnishings, color, and so on. The room is large, approximately twenty feet by thirty feet.

In light of this meeting's importance, what can you do to structure the environment, seating arrangements, and so on to influence communication and achieve your purpose? Draw a floor plan and include as much detail as possible. Your assignment not only is to be creative but also to support your plans with information from this chapter.

 Decco Exercise Work with a classmate to develop a dress code for Decco Corporation employees. Jointly draft a proposal to your boss for inclusion in the Decco Employee Handbook.

Notes

1. Sandra M. Ketrow, "Nonverbal Communication in the Organization." In Sherry Devereaux Ferguson and Stewart Ferguson, Eds., *Organizational Communication* (New Brunswick, NJ: Transaction Books, 1988), 201–222.

2. Walter D. St. John, "You Are What You Communicate," *Personnel Journal* 44 (October 1985): 40–43.

3. Jenny Burman, "Lights, Camera, Action," *Madison Avenue* 27 (February 1985): 8.

4. Sharon Nelton, "Beyond Body Language," *Nation's Business* 74 (June 1986): 73–74.

5. Bobbie Gee, "The 'I' in IBM," *Management World* 1 (June 1986): 1.

6. David Alan Safer, "Institutional Body Language," *Public Relations Journal* 41 (March 1985): 26, 28, 30.

7. Safer, "Institutional," 26.

8. Safer "Institutional," 26, 28, 30.

9. Joseph A. DeVito, *The Interpersonal Communication Book*, 5th ed. (New York: Harper & Row, 1989), 215–225.

10. Albert Mehrabian, *Silent Messages* (Belmont, CA: Wadsworth, 1971), iii–v.

11. Mehrabian, *Silent Messages*, 1.

12. Sigmund Freud, "Fragment of an Analysis of a Case of Hysteria (1905)," *Collected Papers*, Vol. 3 (New York: Basic Books, 1959).

13. Mark L. Knapp, *Nonverbal Communication in Human Interaction*, 2nd ed. (New York: Holt, Rinehart & Winston, 1978), 3.

14. Judee K. Burgoon and Thomas Saine, *The Unspoken Dialogue: An Introduction to Nonverbal Communication* (Boston: Houghton Mifflin, 1978), 10, 12–13; Paul Ekman, "Communication Through Nonverbal Behavior: A Source of Information About an Interpersonal Relationship." In S. S. Tomkins and C. E. Izard, Eds., *Affect, Cognition, and Personality* (New York: Springer, 1965), 390–442; and Knapp, *Nonverbal Communication*, 21–26.

15. Knapp, *Nonverbal Communication*, 13.

16. Knapp, *Nonverbal Communication*, 270.

17. Burgoon and Saine, *Unspoken Dialogue*, 54.

18. Loretta A. Malandro, Larry Barker, and Deborah Ann Barker, *Nonverbal Communication* (New York: Random House), 107.

19. Malandro et al., *Nonverbal Communication*, 107.

20. Ketrow, "Nonverbal Communication," 213

21. Edward T. Hall, *The Hidden Dimension* (New York: Doubleday, 1966), 116–125.

22. John T. Molloy, *Dress for Success* (New York: Wyden, 1975) and *The Woman's Dress for Success Book* (New York: Warner, 1977).

23. Walter Kiechel III, *Office Hours: A Guide to the Managerial Life* (New York: Harper & Row, 1988), 204–205.

24. Aimee Stern, "The Ins and Outs of Executive Dress," *Dun's Business Month* 128 (November 1986): 58–60.

25. Brian S. Moskal, "Corporate Uniforms Yield to New Images," *Industry Week* 222 (9 July 1984): 33, 35.

26. Janet Wallach, *Looks That Work* (New York: Viking Penguin, 1986), 16.

27. "Dress Codes at Work," *Providence Journal-Bulletin*, 5 July 1990, p. E-1.

28. Michael Gross, "Admit It or Not, Work Dress Codes Are a Fact of Life." In Joseph A. DeVito and Michael L. Hecht, Eds., *The Nonverbal Communication Reader* (Prospect Heights, IL: Waveland Press, 1990), 152.

29. Wallach, *Looks*, 22

30. Ketrow "Nonverbal Communication," 208.

31. Ketrow, "Nonverbal Communication," 216.

32. Greg R. Oldham and Nancy L. Rotchford, "Relationships Between Office Characteristics and Employee Reactions: A Study of the Physical Environment," *Administrative Science Quarterly* 28 (1983): 542–556.

33. Frank H. Mahnke and Rudolf H. Mahnke, *Color and Light in Man-Made Environments* (New York: Van Nostrand Reinhold, 1987), 71.

34. Laura M. Luckert, "Creating a Welcome Workspace," *Women in Business* 37 (January–February 1985): 14–15.

35. L. Harris and Associates, Inc., "The Steelcase National Study of Office Environments: Do They Work?" In Ellen Konar, Eric Sund-

strom, Christine Brady, David Mandel, and Robert W. Rice, "Status Demarcation in the Office," *Environment and Behavior* 14 (September 1982): 561–580.

36. F. C. Duffy, "Role and Status in the Office," *Architectural Association Quarterly* 1 (1969): 4–13; Jack Halloran, *Applied Human Relations: An Organizational Approach* (Englewood Cliffs, NJ: Prentice-Hall, 1978).

37. Michael Korda, "Office Power — You Are Where You Sit," *New York*, 13 January 1975, 36–44; *Power: How to Get It, How to Use It* (New York: Random House, 1975).

38. Nancy Henley, *Body Politics: Power, Sex, and Nonverbal Communication* (Englewood Cliffs, NJ: Prentice-Hall, 1977), 58; Dale G. Leathers, *Successful Nonverbal Communication: Principles and Applications* (New York: Macmillan, 1986), 277.

39. F. D. Becker, *Workspace: Creating Environments in Organizations* (New York: Praeger, 1981), 104–111.

40. E. W. Miles and Dale G. Leathers, "The Impact of Aesthetic and Professional Related Objects on Credibility in the Office Setting," *The Southern Speech Communication Journal* 49 (1984): 361–379.

41. Konar et al., "Status Demarcation," 562–564.

42. Felecia Roosevelt, quoted by Marian Christy, "Famous Doors, Doers Open Up to a Roosevelt," *Boston Globe*, 4 May 1975, p. D4.

43. Korda, *Power*, 177.

44. Konar et al., "Status Demarcation," 565.

45. F.I. Steele, *Physical Settings and Organizational Development* (Reading, MA: Addison-Wesley, 1973); in Konar et al., "Status Demarcation," 565.

46. Steele in Konar, 564.

47. C. S. Green, "The Ecology of Committees," *Environment and Behavior* 7 (1975): 411–425; Leathers, *Successful*, 274–275.

48. Leathers, *Successful*, 275.

49. Mahnke and Mahnke, *Color and Light*, 73.

50. Mahnke and Mahnke, *Color and Light*, 74, 78–81.

51. Mahnke and Mahnke, *Color and Light*, 71.

52. Judee Burgoon and Thomas Saine, *Unspoken Dialogue*, 110; Mahnke and Mahnke, *Color and Light*, 11–16.

53. For a full discussion, see Korda, *Power*, 194–202.

54. Korda, *Power*, 194–202.

55. Peter A. Andersen and Linda L. Bowman, "Positions of Power: Nonverbal Influence in Organizational Communication." In DeVito and Hecht, *The Nonverbal*, 402–403.

56. Ketrow, "Nonverbal Communication," 218–219.

57. Ketrow, "Nonverbal Communication," 219.

58. Hypothetical names are drawn from John E. Baird, Jr., and Sanford B. Weinberg, *Communication: The Essence of Group Synergy* (Dubuque, IA: Wm. C. Brown, 1977).

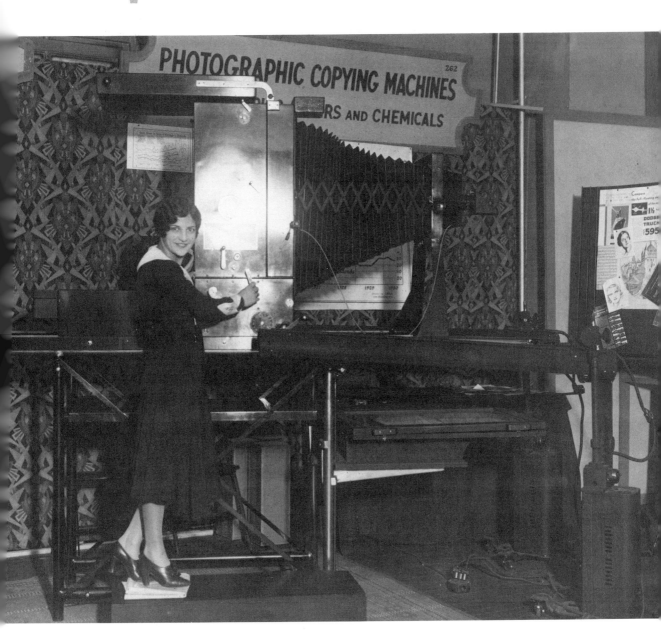

PHOTOGRAPHIC COPYING MACHINES
262
...RS AND CHEMICALS

Chapter 12 ✑ Communicating Technologically in Organizations

✍ *The new electronic independence re-creates the world in the image of a global village.* ✉ *—Marshall McLuhan* ✍ You've just finished lunch, and your boss at Decco Corporation calls you into her office. She sounds excited and a bit worried.

"Fuller has called a sudden meeting. We need all the information we can get on the Porcaro project by 2:15 this afternoon," she exclaims. "The plans are over in the engineering division, the restrictions are up at the Federal Housing Authority office, and the financial projections are at the Manhattan International Bank. See what you can get for me — fast!"

So what do you do? Send out neatly typed business letters? Start making phone calls? No, you don't have time for any of these old-fashioned communication techniques.

Instead, you walk calmly and confidently into your office workstation, sit down at your computer terminal, and call up everything you need on your monitor — building plans, FHA restrictions, MIB projections — in minutes flat. In fact, you even print out the plans, statistics, charts, and color graphs *your* boss will need to impress *her* boss at this afternoon's meeting. And your updated computer calendar even reminds you of your new meeting ten minutes before it's to begin.

Amazing? Yes, by yesterday's standards. But the automated office just described is increasingly common in today's organizational world.

CHANGE IS HERE TO STAY

Throughout this book, we've talked about communicating effectively within your organization. For the most part, we've discussed your interactions with other human beings through your ability to speak, write, listen, and read. And at times, we've discussed the office environment in which you'll work. In this chapter, we provide a useful look at the rapidly changing office technology you'll use throughout your career.

Rapidly changing? Yes. And the rate of change is increasing year by year. The pen and pencil have been around in one form or another for many hundreds of years, and in most organizations they represented the primary technology for recording and communicating vital information. Picture Herman Melville's "Bartleby the Scrivener," poor man, scrivening away day after day, month after month, on the same stool behind the same table, copying figures account after account. No wonder he "preferred not to."

But as the twentieth century progressed, the typewriter became an indispensable communication tool, augmented by the miracle of the carbon-copying technique. (We still say, "She's a carbon copy of her mother" rather than "She's a xerox. . . .") The mimeograph helped with larger duplication chores, but intra- and interorganizational distribution of information was largely by hand — whether personally, by messenger, or by mail.

The explosion in the information-processing industry over the past decade has accelerated this change tremendously. Not only is the average modern office automated and computerized, but the average life cycle of an electronics product is just three to five years. As a result, your mastery of any given information technology will be useful for only several years.[1] As a result, no one can expect you to enter the business world fully competent to handle every system in use: There's just too much change and too much variety out there.

But no matter how rapid the change or how variable the technology, the automated office is the environment in which you will most likely be working. And experts estimate that computer-based technology has changed the job requirements of 40–50 million people, almost half the U.S. work force.[2] The more familiar you become with that technology, the more comfortable you'll be in it, the more confidence you'll have, and the more productive and successful you'll be. Or, in more straightforward terms, you *must* learn basic computer skills if you are to succeed in today's organizations.

Although the term "office automation" often conjures images of machines or even robots, the main objective of the new electronic microtechnology is to support and enhance human performance.[3] But even with that objective, other changes also may be occurring, changes that call into question the utility of our current organizational structures and patterns.

In her seminal examination of these changes, *In the Age of the Smart Machine*, Shoshana Zubroff notes that the new smart machines not only accomplish physical tasks but also produce information about those tasks. In her terminology, the new machines "informate" — produce information about and add it back into — their accomplishments, and indeed their overall work environments. This new tendency to produce and manage information within and between machines, without specific human intervention, may be radically (and increasingly rapidly) changing both the nature of work and the organizations that have traditionally controlled that work.[4] This means that the organizational environment in which you will work may differ markedly from yesterday's more predictable, rigid, and hierarchical structures.[5]

....

Where Did All of This Come From?

The 1960s: Decade of the Mainframe. By today's standards, mainframe computers were big, heavy, and slow. These early computers required large amounts of space and a carefully controlled environment to keep their vacuum tubes and other circuitry from overheating. They also consumed relatively large amounts of electricity. The now common term "bug"—an unexpected computer problem—comes from an incident in which an early mainframe computer "crashed" because a moth was caught in its circuitry.[6] Because of the special environment in which these dinosaurs were kept, they were not a part of most office surroundings. In fact, they were operated by data-processing specialists who seemed to most office personnel like the high priesthood of some secret cult. Mainframes were used primarily for accounting and personnel tasks that called for hard data and lots of "number-crunching."[7]

The 1970s: Decade of the Word Processor. The word processor can be called the Trojan Horse of office automation. Although these machines looked like advanced electronic typewriters, they truly were computers. Each had its own central processing unit, main memory, keyboard, monitor, and printer, although each was dedicated to one function only. Clerical productivity increased by some 20 percent after these machines were introduced into offices. However, management was not affected immediately by these advances. Only data-processing specialists and clerical personnel were involved in the shift.[8]

The 1980s: Decade of the Personal Computer. During the latter years of the 1970s, new technology allowed word processors to do more with what looked like less. The microchip, or integrated circuit, took the place of bulky transistors, diodes, and vacuum tubes. These microchips, about the size of a single letter on this page, can hold roughly the amount of information in the phone book of a large city. Using these marvels, computers became smaller, cheaper, and less picky about their environment. Software, too, became cheaper and more versatile.[9] In the early 1980s, the personal computer (or desktop computer), often called the PC, worked its way into the business scene. Data processing became information processing and everyone in the office, from secretary to CEO, was doing it. By the end of the 1980s, experts estimated that more than 100 million PCs were in use worldwide (see Figure 12.1).[10]

In the early 1980s, one expert calculated that if the automobile industry had developed at the same rate as the computer industry had during the preceding 20 years, you could buy a Jaguar for $1.50, use it once, and throw it away. Or you could buy a Rolls Royce for about the same price, get 1 million miles to a gallon of gas, and have enough horsepower to tow the Queen Elizabeth II.[11] Considering the developments since then, think of the startling comparisons you might make now. At present, more information is stored in digital form and transmitted electronically than is contained in print in all of the world's libraries.

Figure 12.1
*Estimated Growth
in Personal
Computer Use
Worldwide*

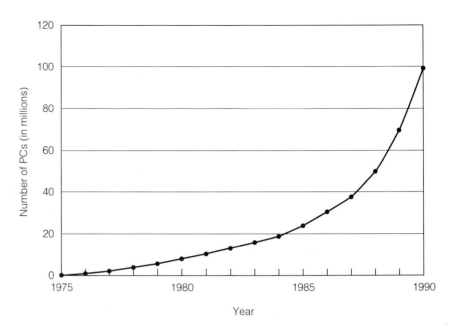

The 1990s: Decade of Integration and Extension. Although the changes have been rapid and vast, you still can discern a basic structure to the automated office that you inherit. The integration and extension of office functions are the primary themes. In fact, what we call "office automation" is the result of integrating and extending the three main kinds of office functions: information processing, communications, and office machines (see Figure 12.2).

INTEGRATION THROUGH LOCAL AREA NETWORKS (LANs)

How are all of these functions integrated? The most common way is through *local area networks*, or *LANs*.[12] A LAN operates on the same principle as a domestic electricity supply: A cable is installed with sockets at various points into which equipment can be plugged (see Figure 12.3). Coaxial cable such as that used in cable television has been the most common, but fiber-optic cable is rapidly replacing it.[13] You also might find a wireless version that consists of an adapter board, a radio-frequency transceiver for each workstation, and a software package.[14]

Figure 12.2
*Integration and
Extension of Office
Functions*

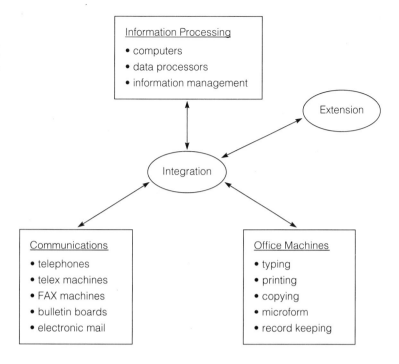

LAN Functions

A LAN allows a personal or desktop computer or a terminal to gain access to:

- a bigger computer, such as a mainframe or a minicomputer (although the distinction between these machines continues to diminish as desktop computers become more powerful)
- another personal computer
- a printer
- telephone and data lines — which means access to other networks
- FAX transmitters.

Increasingly, each office worker will have a desktop computer or terminal hooked into a LAN for use with a wide variety of tasks. New technological developments change the list almost daily, but the following seven functions are some of the basic ones you can expect to manipulate with your computer.

Star

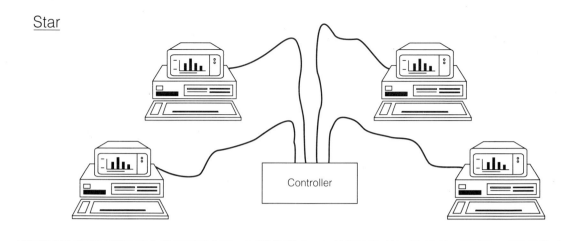

Controller

Ring

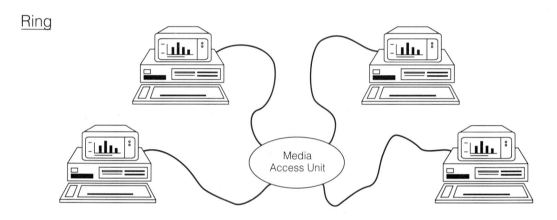

Media
Access Unit

Distributed Bus

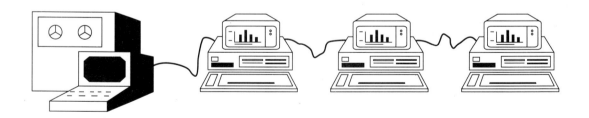

Figure 12.3 *Common LAN Connections*[15]

1. *Use the computer as a word processor to draft memos, letters, and reports.* Much work of this kind initially was done with pencil and paper or was dictated and then given to a secretary for typing. Remember: One of the most remarkable changes in this decade is that computing no longer is confined to clerical and data-processing specialists. Older and more senior staff members have taken longer to adjust to this change, because they traditionally looked upon working at a keyboard as a clerical function. But because many of the younger executives who join the work force each year have used computers since they were in elementary school, this picture is changing.

2. *Make your own paperless files in which to keep notes about projects and correspondence.*

3. *Keep an appointment calendar; many have a tickler file to remind them of important dates and deadlines.* The first thing many people do when they come to work is check their electronic calendar for the day. It also is possible to check others' calendars through the LAN to identify open blocks of time. This can greatly speed the process of getting a group or team together for a meeting.[16]

4. *Send messages to others in the office using electronic messaging.* This convenience puts an end to "telephone tag" and allows you to review messages at your leisure. You also can print a hard copy to take home and examine in greater depth, and you can keep records (both hard and soft) of messages you send and receive. Charles Steinfield has reported many innovative uses of electronic messaging, such as workers using distribution lists to send requests for information to large numbers of employees on the system. They also asked for opinions and conducted surveys, with results received within the day. Steinfield also reported socioemotional uses, such as maintenance of informal social networks and distribution lists that reflect hobbies or common interests.[17]

5. *Access company files.* More and more companies are converting their files from filing cabinets (holding reams of paper) to electronic records. Not everyone in every company can or should have access to everything in an internal data base, but increasing numbers of management-level personnel are making use of the information in company files.

6. *Exploit decision-support systems and executive-support systems, or "smart systems."* These software systems present executives with problem-solving steps that allow them (by inserting

actual company data) to make long-term forecasts, develop financial models, and assess the impact of possible changes in key variables.[18] Using an analytical investigation package, executives can pose unstructured questions and pursue answers from different directions, playing "What if," following hunches, and uncovering hidden relationships.[19]

7. *Access shared peripheral equipment* such as:

- the FAX transmitter — documents can be transmitted to facsimile stations for delivery to parties not on the LAN.
- printers — some LANs have several printers strategically stationed throughout the organization, which allows printing on the closest and most convenient machine.
- the graphics plotter — graphics development can be done at each individual desk, with printing done at a central location.

Altogether, these capabilities indicate a movement among organizations toward more timely and flexible communication, with the entire organization more closely resembling a single organism. In this "living" being, the LAN becomes its nervous system, and each person at a workstation acts the part of a brain cell (see Figures 12.4 and 12.5).

The first two words of LAN — "Local Area" — indicate only that the LAN is relatively contained. In theory and increasingly in practice, however, the principles of integration and extension are pushing these connections toward satellite-based global networks (see Figures 12.6 and 12.7).

LAN Advantages

Weidlein and Cross point out the following advantages of networks over stand-alone computers.

- Information is more easily shared, which makes it more comprehensive and more useful to other departments and the overall organization.
- Flow of information is more structured and consistent.
- Managers have more control over information resources, which improves work flow, work quality, and productivity.
- Regular and distributed communications are encouraged among individuals, work groups, and departments.

Figure 12.4
*An Office Local
Area Network*[20]

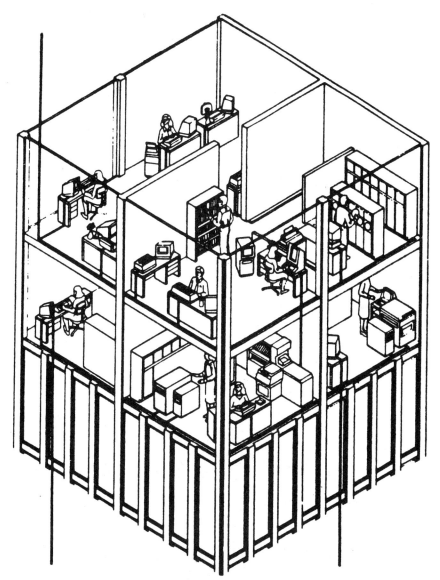

- Distributed communications and work flow are more consistent with current management concepts.
- Multiuser access to centrally stored software often eliminates the need for redundant software on individual PCs. Text and data files can be transferred, and memos and letters can be sent to several users simultaneously (electronic mail).
- The expenses of peripheral equipment, such as printers, plotters, and hard disks, can be shared.
- Centralized data bases may be shared more easily.
- The security of information is ensured more easily.[21]

Figure 12.5
The "Intelligent
Building"
Network[22]

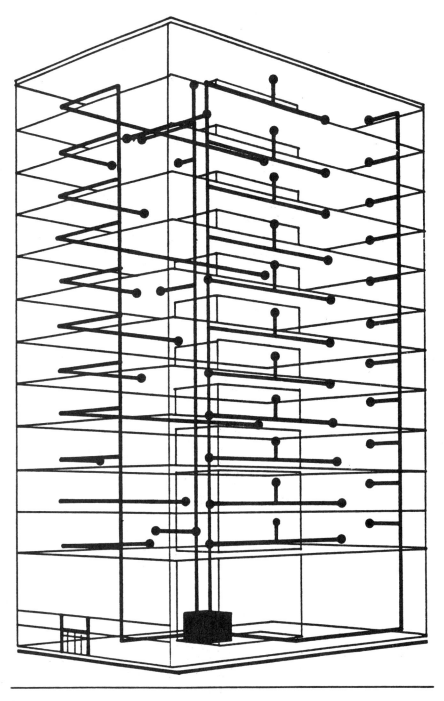

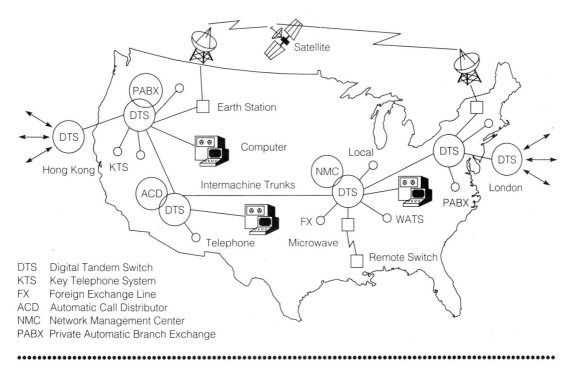

Figure 12.6 *National and International Communications Networks*[23]

DTS   Digital Tandem Switch
KTS   Key Telephone System
FX   Foreign Exchange Line
ACD   Automatic Call Distributor
NMC   Network Management Center
PABX Private Automatic Branch Exchange

Figure 12.7
*From Local
Area to Global
Networks*[24]

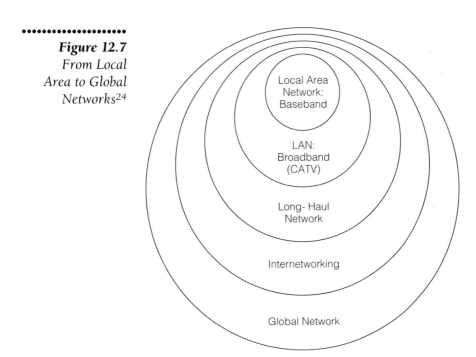

Figure 12.8 Peripheral Sharers.[25] *Peripheral-sharing devices are designed for small groups that need to share printers, plotters, and modems. They offer between three and ten input–output connections for PCs and peripherals.*

You also may find your organization taking advantage of less expensive "sub-LAN" systems that provide only some of the benefits of a fully developed LAN. See Figures 12.8 through 12.11 for illustrations of these alternatives.

Figure 12.9 *Data Switches. Like peripheral sharers, data switches allow several PCs to share peripherals. But data switches also allow the transfer of files between PCs and also exchange electronic mail.*

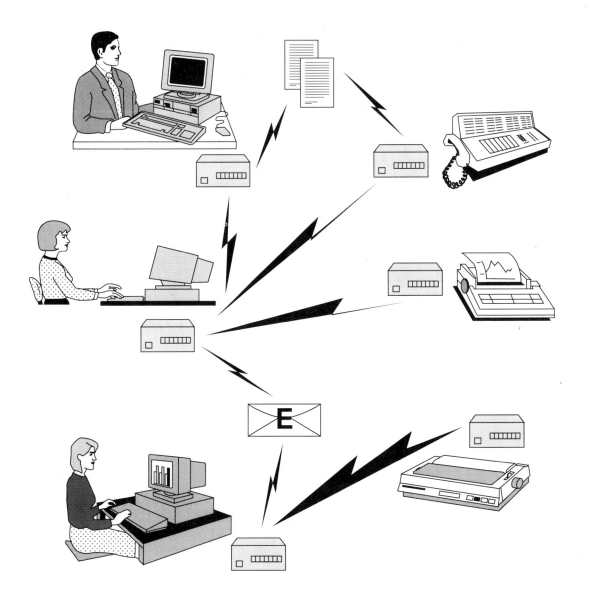

Figure 12.10 *Cableless Connections. Wireless LANs handle peripheral sharing, file transfers, and electronic mail without the physical links such as wires or cables that are common to other options. Instead, each PC on the wireless network uses a transmitter–receiver to send and receive data.*

Figure 12.11 Bulletin Boards. *When you need to share files and electronic mail but not peripherals, a bulletin-board system (BBS) may be the answer. A BBS requires a dedicated PC that you can contact for messages or files. You also can configure a BBS to handle multiple phone lines.*

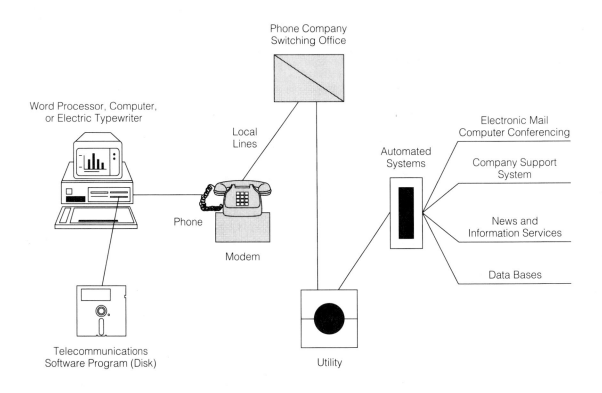

Phone Company
Switching Office

Word Processor, Computer,
or Electric Typewriter

Local
Lines

Automated
Systems

Electronic Mail
Computer Conferencing

Company Support
System

Phone

News and
Information Services

Modem

Data Bases

Telecommunications
Software Program (Disk)

Utility

Figure 12.12 *Modem Connections to Online Services*[26]

INTEGRATION THROUGH MODEMS

Even if your PC is not connected to a LAN, you still can contact the outside world through a *modem* (short for *modulator–demodulator*). This device converts your computer's electronic signals into sound patterns that are capable of traveling through a telephone system. A computer modem at the other end of the phone line converts the sounds back into electronic signals (see Figure 12.12). Don Johnson, editor of *Administrative Management*, says, "Today the average person with a computer and a modem has access to the accumulated knowledge of the world.... Some of the things you can do with the new databases bring new meaning to the term 'mind boggling.'"[27] You'll find the following kinds of "accumulated knowledge" available.

1. *Bulletin board services.* An electronic BBS serves the same function as any bulletin board: publicizing information, needs, services, and opportunities. They often are organized by special-

interest groups or clubs. These BBSs serve a social function similar to that provided by the citizens' band (CB) radio networks that became so popular in the 1970s. BBS subscribers usually use pseudonyms and freely air gripes and opinions to anyone who will "listen." Typically, someone "hosts" the bulletin board, keeping track of what goes on it and periodically weeding it.[28]

2. *Subscriber data bases.* In 1990, more than 4,000 external data bases were in existence, offering the latest news and stock-market information, anwers to legal questions, shopping services, and travel information. In addition, special data bases provide research information to scientists, physicians, and businesspeople. Users pay subscription fees and rates for "connect time."

3. *Other computers.* You also can communicate with another person or even your office or home computer without the aid of a special service. In fact, a modem at home allows you access to your company LAN and all of its advantages.

4. *Electronic mail (E mail) services.* No more trips to the post office! The simplest form of E mail is computer to computer: Senders originate documents on their computers and dispatch them to a mail service via the telephone network, where they are stored in a central computer. When an addressee logs onto her computer and checks her "mailbox," a note indicates she has incoming mail. Mail then can be "downloaded" into her computer and read and then stored, printed, or erased. Many mail services offer the option of printing a letter and then mailing or delivering it. These services operate worldwide, are less expensive than Western Union or telephone (the average computer-to-computer message costs 86 cents), and are faster than the postal system.[29]

INTEGRATION THROUGH RADIO CONNECTION

Recently, IBM and Motorola announced programs that allowed roving employees such as sales and repair personnel to communicate with their headquarters' computers by radio. This service will permit high-speed data communications in more than 8,000 U.S. cities over a network of radio towers that IBM has built to connect telephone lines. The system permits the use of desktop or portable computers or special handheld computers that can send and receive messages or data at high speed.

Some experts speculate that this development could compete successfully with modems connected to advanced cellular telephone systems.[30]

EXTENSION OF OFFICE FUNCTIONS

Extending Information Transfer: The Facts About FAX

Using facsimile-transmission, or FAX, machines, copies of documents are sent (or "faxed") over telephone data lines from one machine to another. Add-on boards for microcomputers with modems have been developed that allow them to act as FAX transmitters. Documents then are printed on the receiver's printer. The ability to send hard copies of documents instantly, without relying on the postal system, greatly speeds the process of doing business.

The number of FAX machines is increasing steadily. The first directory of FAX numbers was published in 1986 and contained 27,000 listings; the 1987 edition jumped to 85,000! And these are only the publicly available listings. During this same period, the number of FAX machines installed rose from 330,000 to 540,000. We estimate that far more than 2 million are in use in the early 1990s.[32] One can now install a FAX machine in the family car or add an expansion board that allows FAX operations from your PC (see Figure 12.13).

Figure 12.13
FAX Boards Allow Computer Operation[31]

Extending Information Transfer: Teleconferencing

Several types of conferences can be conducted by telephone line. Such forms of *teleconferencing* include the following.

Audioconferencing (voice only). Once upon a time, your organization would have to put people in the same room if it wanted to hold a conference. That cost time and money, especially if those people worked on different coasts. But not many years back, telephone technology developed a method of connecting people in several locations on one conference call. It can link as many parties as you wish, but with more than fifteen it can get out of hand. You can all talk together—but you miss out on the nonverbal stimuli so necessary in many conversational situations.

Videoconferencing (full-motion video). Now, using one- or two-way video and audio, you can sit alone in a room and at the same time engage in a sight and sound conference with any number of participants located anywhere else in the world. This allows you to pick up visual nonverbal cues. But some participants complain that using this format is like being in a boardroom with a sheet of glass down the middle. Because this operation still is extremely expensive, only the largest corporations currently use this technology.

Freeze frame video (slow-scan video). Regular telephone signals transmit constant audio and a still picture every thirty seconds or so or whenever the subject moves significantly. This format is much less realistic than full-motion videoconferencing, but it also is less costly.

Audiographic. This method uses telephone conferencing combined with some type of visual-information exchange, such as a computer or FAX machine. This format works well for informative sessions, with the visual exchange used for graphics.

Computer conferences. In this variant of computer talking to computer, the "conversation" is not restricted to just two computers. Nor must conferees be together in place or time. Approximately 80 percent of computer conferences are asynchronous.[33] The technical requirements are simpler and less costly than for videoconferences.

Advantages and Disadvantages of Teleconferencing. Besides eliminating the expense and time of travel, teleconferencing can result in more thoughtful communication, greater community of feeling, and (in the case of computer conferences) a written record of proceedings. Computer-mediated conferences have been shown to be more efficient, and the decisions generally are of higher quality.[34] In addition, some studies have shown a greater equality of participation in computer conferences, where all participants are reduced to a screenful of writing. Other studies show that conferees sometimes are reluctant to commit certain things to writing.[35] In a purely informational setting, however, teleconferences can be more efficient than face-to-face meetings because participants find less opportunity for small talk and digressions.[36]

But teleconferencing is considered less effective for bargaining or negotiating sessions than it is for informational meetings. When you can't shake hands with someone, sense nonverbal cues, and feel an actual physical presence with you, it may be harder to establish trust and understanding; and perhaps you won't receive the warning cues you need in order to know when you *shouldn't* trust someone. Because of such difficulties in building rapport, *teleconferences usually are more successful when the participants already know one another*. If such a conference is to be among strangers, then they should spend time becoming acquainted first.

Presentation Graphics: Hardware and Software

It is no secret that superb graphic displays are powerful presentation tools. Reports can be clearer, more interesting, and more effective. We say *can be* because advanced technology also is poorly used, overused, and even abused. If you were to use all of the capabilities of your organization's computerized graphics software to fill each slide with nineteen colors, bar graphs, pie charts, numbers, ideograms, keys, cartoon figures, and text, you would end up with the sort of graphics one critic calls "SBB — Slick But Bad!"[37]

But at the bottom line, an organization saves time (which is, of course, money) when its decision makers can see *simple and effective graphic illustrations of complex data*.[38] Such professional-looking graphics used to be just that: *professional*. And it took time and money to get them. Now software packages can produce eye-catching colorful charts, graphs, and drawings quickly and inexpensively.

Some of these innovations are basic business graphics packages that allow anyone using a desktop computer to make bar graphs, pie charts, and line graphs. These are so easy to produce that they can be included in a letter, report, or even a memo. They often can be created in less time than it would take to explain the information verbally. For important presentations, more sophisticated results might be desired, which requires graphics packages that use a mainframe computer and a special graphics plotter. Still other packages generate such sophisticated products that they remain strictly in the domain of graphic artists. But no matter how they are created, any computer graphic can be turned into paper handouts or film slides or simply stored in the computer memory for later use. It also is possible to project a graphic image directly from a computer onto an overhead screen. As participants in a meeting review various situations, they can see the effects of changing data even as they are discussed.

For the standard kinds of graphs and charts, you'll normally use a keyboard to input your data. The computer asks what kind of graph and what figures you want to use. You type in the information and the computer produces a graph. For artwork, however, light pen and digitized tablet systems are the preferred input devices. The pen simulates the artist's traditional freehand drawing tools, while the digitized tablet can be used for tracing. A *mouse* (a small handheld device for moving the cursor around the screen) generally is used for computer-assisted design (CAD) and drafting-related tasks.[39]

Desktop Publishing

Communication professionals often are responsible for producing company newsletters. Whether the requirements are large or small, software and hardware are available that allow company publications to be produced faster, cheaper, and more efficiently. In the past, you might have had to use the services of a typesetter for the finished product. Now, even one person can do the entire job—and in one day.[40] Articles and information can be transmitted electronically from anywhere in the company to the "publisher," who can edit without retyping the whole document. And desktop-publishing software allows fast and simple integration of text and graphics.

In today's large decentralized companies, internal communications play a vital role. Automation cuts production time to one-fourth of what it was. In-house communications and publications departments now can handle more and bigger jobs, although there is a drawback: Desktop publishing is so easy that anyone can do it—even those who have nothing worthwhile to say. Thus you may notice a proliferation of what some observers disdainfully call "lasercrud."[41]

Telecommuting or Teleworking

Some experts guesstimate that in 10 to 15 years, 10 million workers in the United States will be involved in *teleworking*—that is, staying at home while working with their corporations or clients through their modems and FAX machines.[42] This work arrangement is especially helpful for convalescing employees, handicapped workers, and parents of small or otherwise home-bound children. But despite teleworking's clear advantages, some homeworkers miss the stimulation of co-workers; for this reason, some companies require homeworkers to spend a designated amount of time in the office. Other homeworkers are afraid that they may be forgotten come promotion time. Conditions under which teleworking seems to be most successful are when the worker is self-motivated, has definite reasons for preferring to work at home, and has a specific task to do, or when the situation is temporary.[43]

PERSONAL EFFECTS OF OFFICE AUTOMATION

Office automation will continue to have ten major personal effects on communication in business and the professions.

1. Much of our modern electronic communication technology eliminates our ability to experience such nonverbal stimuli as inflection, body language, and paralinguistics. This change means that clear, concise writing is more important than ever. For instance, face-to-face interaction allows you to know immediately by facial expression whether your conversational partner understands you. A puzzled look allows you to restate and clarify until you see the light of comprehension dawn. And even over the telephone, inflections and "tone of voice" transmit meaning. But with most electronic communication, you've lost these cues. Knowing that nonverbal signals thus cannot be relied on may give us the incentive to communicate more accurately.
2. Electronic communication is so easy to use that individuals may be indiscreet and later regret the messages they have sent. Be careful what you "broadcast" electronically, and be careful who has access to your files. It is unwise to put everything in writing, even if access is limited.

3. Communication interaction often is asynchronous. People are able to work odd hours at home, in hotel rooms, and from other remote locations. For example, a workstation that includes a computer with a modem, a telephone, and a FAX machine has been installed at the top of Colorado's Aspen Mountain for the use of busy executives who like to climb both mountains and organizational ladders. However, their less-mobile colleagues may not be working at the same time. This technological advance can be a great time-saver, but its use must be effective and appropriate so that work flow can be maximized.

4. The new technology means written communication is more interactive than it ever has been.[44] Letters used to take days to arrive, and responses took just as long. Now the written word can generate the sort of quick response you could get previously only with a phone call.

5. The ease and speed of electronic writing now is being termed a "secondary orality."[45] People seem to write more the way they speak, especially in informal communication such as electronic mail and computer conferencing. Written documents are generated more quickly, and some studies have shown that they are of higher quality.[46] This change has both positive and negative aspects. It can speed the demise of "legalese" and enhance the flow of creativity. But it also can allow so much freedom of expression that people "run off at the fingers" and clog a network. As one person puts it, "too little editing, too much trash."

6. More people have access to more information from more people, more easily. Information overload is a real danger. The smart information manager learns to use filtering mechanisms, and sets up regular procedures for filing and deleting information.

7. Too much reliance on electronic communication can contribute to feelings of isolation. However, the anonymity of keyboarding a message allows some people to express themselves more freely than they would in face-to-face or telephone interaction.[47] In addition, Rice and Love have found that "computer-mediated communication systems *can* support socioemotional communication," depending on the user's expectations.[48]

8. Electronically mediated communication is neither inherently bad nor good; it has its own characteristics, just as does any other channel. Professionals must learn how to use it effec-

tively, which may mean that the organization must teach its people *how*. Once the technical problems are mastered, electronic communication is so quick and easy that organizational communicators should remember (or be taught) the following tips:

- Think before you write and know exactly what you want to say.
- Consider who your readers are, what they want, and what they need.
- Write what needs to be said — no more and no less.
- State the message in as few words as possible without sacrificing clarity.
- Keep sentences under control — short, simple, and direct.
- Use words common to all readers — avoid jargon and puzzling acronyms.
- Think twice about using emotionally loaded phrasings.
- If a message is important or complicated, show it to someone else before sending it.
- Reread your writing with an eye not only for typos and poor grammar but also for the impression it will make and the reaction it will elicit.
- After all of these steps, and when you're satisfied with what you've written, hit the "send" key.[49]

9. Some observers hope that the new technologies will allow office work to be done so efficiently that more time will be available for meaningful informal chats and thus an improved communication climate.[50]

10. In general, factors such as a rapidly changing environment and an educated and more independent work force call for an organizational structure that emphasizes decentralization and job enrichment. The companies that use electronic technologies best will encourage groups to take part in the decision-making and problem-solving processes that directly affect their members' output and working conditions.[51] The greater access to information and the freedom from routine tasks allowed by microelectronic technology tend to make for flatter, less hierarchical organizations.[52] But even though the electronic means are crucial, these organizations will need to increase training in group processes and problem-solving skills.

How to Prepare for the Future

Because each office is different and technology is changing so rapidly, you probably shouldn't try to learn how to operate specific pieces of equipment ahead of time. Experts recommend a basic familiarity with the field of office automation — such as that provided by this chapter. Many colleges and universities require students to take a microcomputer course as part of their degree program. But even if your school doesn't have such a requirement, computer literacy is essential.

After computer literacy, the ability to learn is the most helpful skill you can take with you to a new job. Research has shown that those individuals who have learned how to listen learn more easily how to use new pieces of equipment. In fact, the ability to learn new technologies increases after individuals complete listening-improvement training.[53]

Here are some suggestions to take with you into a new office environment.[54]

1. When you begin your new job, or when a new piece of equipment or software arrives, review the operations manual — and realize that this may take time. It isn't necessary to memorize it or be an expert after one reading, but a working familiarity with the capabilities of the equipment or software will be helpful. Knowing your way around the manual also will save time later.
2. Find out who in your organization has used and mastered the equipment or software. Peer support is valuable.
3. Call the help line right away. Set up rapport with your instant tutor. Knowing that a knowledgeable trainer is available can be very reassuring.
4. Tell your training department (or your boss) what you need. Tutorials, texts, computer-based training, and even seminars and workshops may be available to help you learn to use the specific equipment in your office.
5. Try to get time and money for professional seminars, classes, demonstrations, and exhibits so that you will be aware of new trends, concepts, and potential applications.
6. Join and participate in professional interest groups that exchange information on using new technologies.
7. Subscribe to and read publications that will help you understand the field of office automation.

Tomorrow and Tomorrow: Society's and Yours

Practically speaking, the new office technologies simply are machines designed to help us do our work faster and more effectively. Some scholars believe, however, that this electronic revolution has great cultural significance. Some say that just as the development of various machines brought about the Industrial Age with its attendant social changes, so our increasing advances in computer and communication technology will bring about even greater social change as we enter the Information Age.

Malcolm Richardson, for example, compares the impact of electronically mediated communication to the advent and spread of written communication in Medieval England, where such pronounced changes as widespread literacy and a standardized language eventually resulted.[55] And Marshall McLuhan reminds us that the new printing press was intended simply to save labor in producing manuscripts. No one anticipated the effects of this labor-saving device on literacy, argumentation, freedom of thought and expression, religion, politics, and art—in a word, on *history*.[56] Future generations will be left to judge whether the current revolution in information processing and communication—the advent of office automation—is an event of the same historical and cultural magnitude.

But whether or not this revolution changes history, it's changing your working environment in remarkable ways. And here's the Inside Word: By learning to master these new electronic tools, you'll open unto yourself a whole new world of opportunity using your communication skills for business and the professions.

CHAPTER SUMMARY

Office automation is a fact of life in most organizations, but the technology that brings it to us is rapidly changing. The evolution of the computer has been the driving force behind the increasing complexity and capability of this new office technology. In the 1990s, the trend is toward integrating and extending the organization's automated capabilities in three areas: information processing, communications, and office machines.

The local area network (LAN) is the chief instrument of integration and extension, allowing individual PCs access to other PCs, mainframe computers, company files, printers, plotters, FAX machines, and external networks. Modems allow individual PCs access to other computers and networks through telephone connection.

Radio connection and FAX capabilities further integrate and extend the automated office. In addition, various forms of teleconferencing — from simple telephone conference calls to full-motion videoconferencing — allow communication more extensively, more quickly, and sometimes less expensively. Computerized graphics extend our capability to visualize and present organizational information, and desktop-publishing software further extends an organization's ability to communicate internally and externally.

Even though you shouldn't try to know everything about office automation, knowing the general categories and preparing to learn specific capabilities will prove to be to your advantage.

MEASURING SUCCESS

1. Visit a variety of organizations and compare the degrees of office automation you see. Interview people in each organization whose daily routines are affected by electronic communication technologies; ask them whether their jobs are easier or harder as a result. Ask also whether these technologies extend an organization's ability to accomplish its mission.

2. Can you think of any ways in which today's young people are being prepared daily to move into the automated office of the future?

3. In what ways are the developments that were discussed in this chapter changing the patterns and skills of interpersonal communication within the organization, especially skills that may have been of greater value in the past? What new skills are supplementing them? Do you already have or are you now acquiring these skills?

4. The three areas of automation discussed in this chapter — information processing, communications, and office machines — require hardware and software of often astronomical costs. Yet organizations increasingly are willing to pay them. Why?

Decco Exercise Your boss at Decco Corporation is interested in purchasing a word-processing program for the company's personal computers. Your task is to evaluate the top candidates and recommend the best system for Decco. Depending on the boss's requirements, write a memo or prepare a presentation to support your recommendation.

··············

Notes

1. John Hoerr, Michael A. Pollock, and David E. Whiteside, "Management Discovers the Human Side of Automation," *Business Week*, September 29, 1986, 70–75.

2. Hoerr et al., "Management Discovers," 71.

3. Richard J. Long, *New Office Information Technology: Human and Managerial Implications* (New York: Croom Helm, 1987), 16.

4. Shoshana Zubroff, *In the Age of the Smart Machine: The Future of Work and Power* (New York: Basic Books, 1988), 7–12, 285–310.

5. Edgar H. Schein, "Corporate Teams and Totems," *Across the Board* 26 (May 1989): 12–17.

6. Long, *New Office*, 9.

7. Walter A. Kleinschrod, "Where is the Capital of the State of Confusion?" *Administrative Management* 48(3) (March 1987): 52–53.

8. Jack Prouty, *From Word Processors to Workstations* (New York: AMA Publications, 1983), 10.

9. Caroline Blaazer and Eric Molyneux, *Supervising the Electronic Office* (Aldershot, Hants, England: Gower Publishing, 1984), 6.

10. W. Scott Currie, *LANs Explained: A Guide to Local Area Networks* (New York: John Wiley, 1988), 14.

11. Long, *New Office*, 9.

12. For understandable explanations of the structure and uses of computer networks in organizations, see Larry E. Jordan and Bruce Churchill, *Communications and Networking for the IBM PC & Compatibles* (Englewood Cliffs, NJ: Prentice-Hall, 1987); Dimitris N. Chorafas, *Designing and Implementing Local Area Networks* (New York: McGraw-Hill, 1984); W. Scott Currie, *LANs Explained: A Guide to Local Area Networks* (New York: John Wiley, 1988); Michael Durr, *Networking IBM PCs*, 2nd ed. (Indianapolis: Que Corporation, 1987); and James R. Weidlein and Thomas B. Cross, *Networking Personal Computers in Organizations* (Homewood, IL: Dow Jones–Irwin, 1986).

13. Blaazer and Molyneux, *Supervising*, 9.

14. "A LAN With No Strings Attached," *Modern Office Technology* 33 (April 1988): 22.

15. Jordan and Churchill, *Communications*, 285.

16. Prouty, *From Word Processors*, 39.

17. Charles Steinfield, "Personal Communications Via Electronic Mail." In Frederick Williams, Ed., *Technology and Communication Behavior* (Belmont, CA: Wadsworth, 1987): 84–86.

18. Long, *New Office*, 102–117.

19. "Useful Information for the Executive," *Modern Office Technology* 33 (April 1988): 24.

20. Weidlein and Cross, *Networking*, 103. Used by permission of Thomas B. Cross.

21. Weidlein and Cross, *Networking*, 17. Used by permission of Thomas B. Cross.

22. Weidlein and Cross, *Networking*, 156. Used by permission of Thomas B. Cross.

23. Weidlein and Cross, *Networking*, 75. Used by permission of Thomas B. Cross.

24. Chorafas, *Designing*, 23.

25. Adapted from Christopher O'Malley, "Connectivity Made Simple," *Personal Computing* 14(3) (20 March 1990): 93–98.

26. Weidlein and Cross, *Networking*, 14. Used by permission of Thomas B. Cross.

27. Don Johnson, "Help Wanted — Knowledge Manager, Experience Preferred," *Administrative Management* 48(11) (November 1987): 5.

28. William Rodarmor, "The Business BBS: Better Communication Across the Board," *PC World* 7(8) (August 1989): 174–176; and Russ Lockwood, "The Corporate BBS," *Personal Computing* 14(3) (20 March 1990): 93–98. Also see Thomas B. Allen, "Bulletin Boards of the 21st Century Are Coming of Age," *Smithsonian* 19 (September 1988): 83–93 for an informative article on the BBS phenomenon.

29. Erik Mortensen, "Adapting Electronic Mail to Management's Needs," *Administrative Management* 48(8) (August 1987): 26–31.

30. *New York Times*, 31 January 1990, p. D6.

31. T. J. Byers, "Fax Boards for Fast Times," *PC World* 8(1) (January 1990): 118–130. Used by permission of Michael S. Klein.

32. "New FAX Directory Features 85,000 Listings," *Administrative Management* 48(9) (September 1987): 8.

33. Long, *New Office*, 61.

34. Starr Roxanne Hiltz, Kenneth Johnson, and Murray Turoff, "Communication Process and Outcome in Face to Face Versus Computerized Conferences," *Human Communication Research* 13(2) (Winter 1986): 225–252.

35. Walter A. Kleinshrod, "The Management Message in Electronic Messaging Media," *Administrative Management* 48(10) (October 1987): 13; and Long, *New Office*, 60–62.

36. Frederick Williams, *Technology and Communication Behavior* (Belmont, CA: Wadsworth, 1987), 91–94.

37. Robin Nelson, "Graphics: The Wretched Excess," *Personal Computing* 14(2) (February 1990): 49–58.

38. Wita Wojtkowski, "Strong Communication Impact Made With PC Graphics," *Data Management* 25 (May 1987): 27.

39. Michael Hofferber, "Digital 'Paint' Systems for Presentation Graphics," *The Office* 105(3) (March 1987): 51–52.

40. One of the best sources on desktop publishing is Roger C. Parker, *Looking Good in Print: A Guide to Basic Design for Desktop Publishing* (Chapel Hill, NC: Ventana Press, 1988).

41. Joel P. Bowman and Debbie A. Renshaw, "Desktop Publishing: Things Gutenburg Never Taught You," *Journal of Business Communication* 26(1) (Winter 1989): 57–72.

42. Carol-Ann Hamilton, "Telecommuting," *Personnel Journal* 66(4) (April 1987): 91–101.

43. Kathleen Christensen, "A Hard Day's Work in the Electronic Cottage," *Across the Board* 24(4) (April 1987): 17–23.

44. Everett M. Rogers, "Information Technologies: How Organizations Are Changing." In Gerald M. Goldhaber and George A. Barnett, Eds., *Handbook of Organizational Communication* (Norwood, NJ: Ablex, 1988), 437–452.

45. James S. Noblitt, "Writing, Technology, and Secondary Orality," *Journal of Academic Computing* 4 (August 1989): 34–35, 56.

46. Iris Varner and Patricia Marcum Grogg, "Microcomputers and the Writing Process," *Journal of Business Communication* 25(3) (Summer 1988): 69–77.

47. Ronald E. Rice and Gail Love, "Electronic Emotion: Socioemotional Content in a Computer-Mediated Communication Network," *Communication Research* 14(1) (February 1987): 85–108.

48. Rice and Love, "Electronic Emotion," 85.

49. Adapted from Chapter 2 of this book as well as from Jean Datta, "Improving Written Electronic Communications," *Administrative Management* 48(8) (August 1987): 21–23.

50. Bridget O'Connor, "Learn How to Learn," *Administrative Management* 48(3) (March 1987): 15.

51. Ralph H. Sprague and Barbara C. McNurlin, *Information Systems Management in Practice* (Englewood Cliffs, NJ: Prentice-Hall, 1986); Dale Feuer, "The Skill Gap: America's Crisis of Competence," *Training* 24(12) (December 1987): 27–32.

52. Herbert S. Dordick and Frederick Williams, *Innovative Management Using Telecommunications* (New York: John Wiley, 1987), 25.

53. Michael J. Papa and Ethel C. Glenn, "Listening Ability and Performance with New Technology: A Case Study," *Journal of Business Communication* 25(4) (Fall 1988): 5–15.

54. W. H. Weiss, "Are You Computer Literate?" *The Effective Executive*, 17 November 1986.

55. Malcom Richardson, "Business Writing and the Spread of Literacy in Late Medieval England." In G. H. Douglas and H. W. Hildebrandt, Eds., *Studies in the History of Business Writing* (Urbana, IL: Association for Business Communication, 1985), 1–3.

56. Marshall McLuhan, *The Gutenberg Galaxy: The Making of Typographic Man* (Toronto: University of Toronto Press, 1962), 176–179.

Epilogue ✍ **The Last Word . . .**

Now that you've sampled the organizational world, you're one step closer to the real thing. Whether you choose business, education, law, medicine, science, the military, the arts — no matter where you end up, you'll find yourself part of a challenging and changing organization. The assignments you completed in class may be a close fit or a distant cousin to those awaiting you, but the communication principles will be every bit as valid out there as they were in here.

The last word? Here it is: Using these principles with a mixture of integrity, enthusiasm, commitment, and common sense will go a long way toward helping you master real-world communication skills for business and the professions.

Congratulations! You've done it! Thanks for your attention, your interest, and your hard work — and best wishes for an exciting, challenging, and enriching career.

INDEX